The Legendary Soccer Quizbook

300+ Fun Trivia Questions, Bonus Sections, and Facts!

Copyright © 2025 by Playmaker Books
All rights reserved.

No part of this publication may be reproduced, shared, or distributed in any form or by any means—whether electronic, mechanical, photocopying, recording, or otherwise—without prior written permission from the publisher or author, except as permitted under applicable copyright law. To request permission, please contact **info@playmakerbooks.com**

Disclaimer:
This book is an independent publication created for educational and entertainment purposes only. It is not affiliated with, endorsed by, sponsored by, or officially connected to FIFA, UEFA, or any other international soccer governing body, competition, or tournament organizer.

Any references to international soccer tournaments, governing organizations, matches, teams, players, host nations, or related events are included solely for historical, informational, and trivia purposes. All trademarks, competition names, and references are the property of their respective owners and are used strictly for descriptive and reference purposes.

Every reasonable effort has been made to ensure the accuracy of the information presented at the time of publication; however, no guarantees or warranties, express or implied, are made regarding completeness or accuracy.

By using this book, the reader acknowledges that neither the author nor the publisher assumes any responsibility for any direct or indirect losses arising from the use of this content, including but not limited to errors, omissions, or inaccuracies.

Contents

Introduction 1

1. Greatest Matches of All Time 5
   Answers 21
2. Unforgettable Goals 25
   Answers 41
3. Legendary Coaches and Tactics 45
   Answers 61
4. The Underdogs 67
   Answers 83
5. Rivalries and Derbies 87
   Answers 103
6. Golden Boot and Records 109
   Answers 125
7. Wonders, Records, and Standout Moments .. 129
   Answers 145
8. Women's Soccer 149
   Answers 165
9. Soccer and Pop Culture 169
   Answers 186
10. Fan Culture and Traditions 191
    Answers 208

Introduction

Welcome to The Legendary Soccer Quizbook: 300+ Fun Trivia Questions, Bonus Sections, and Facts! If you're holding this book, chances are you live and breathe soccer. Whether you're a die-hard fan who never misses a match, a weekend warrior who enjoys kicking the ball around with friends, or just someone who loves testing their knowledge, this book is for you.

Soccer isn't just a game—it's a passion, a culture, and a universal language that unites millions across the globe. From the roaring stadiums of the FIFA World Cup to the dramatic last-minute goals that make history, this sport has given us unforgettable moments. Now, it's your turn to put your knowledge to the test and prove you have what it takes to be a true soccer mastermind.

This book is packed with over 300 trivia questions covering everything from legendary players, iconic goals, and historic matches to pop culture, stadiums, and even fun behind-the-scenes facts. Each question will challenge you, surprise you, and maybe even teach you something new about the beautiful game. Plus, we've included exciting Bonus Sections that go beyond the ordinary, making this quizbook a unique and immersive experience.

Are You Ready for the Ultimate Challenge?

This isn't just another quiz book—it's a journey through the world of soccer. As you progress, you'll be scoring points, ranking up, and proving your expertise. But the real reward? A chance to earn your very own Player Stats Diploma! That's right—once you complete the challenge, you can showcase your final score and claim your title as a true soccer trivia champion. Whether you earn the rank of Passionate Supporter or reach the elite level of Legendary Icon, your diploma will be proof of your knowledge, dedication, and love for the game.

How to Use This Book

- Test Your Knowledge – Answer the questions and keep track of your score.
- Challenge Your Friends – Compete with fellow soccer lovers to see who knows more.
- Learn as You Play – Even if you don't know an answer, you'll walk away with fascinating facts.
- Unlock the Bonus Sections – Special challenges await those who dare to go further!
- Earn Your Diploma – Complete the quiz, tally your score, and claim your Player Stats Diploma!

Do You Have What It Takes?

This book is your chance to step up and prove yourself. Think you can recall who scored the winning goal in a famous final? Can you recognize a stadium just by its shape? What about soccer players who crossed over into pop culture? It's all here, waiting for you to take on the challenge.

So, lace up your boots, get ready to kick off, and dive into the ultimate soccer quiz experience. Will you rise to the top and claim your legendary status? There's only one way to find out—let the games begin!

CHAPTER 1

Greatest Matches of All Time

Soccer has given us some of the most unforgettable moments in sports history. From last-minute comebacks to intense penalty shootouts, the greatest matches are filled with passion, drama, and legendary performances. In this chapter, you'll relive iconic games that stunned the world and shaped the sport. Test your knowledge and see how well you remember these thrilling clashes!

Easy Questions (1 Point Each)

1. Which match is famously known as the "Miracle of Istanbul"?

a) Liverpool vs AC Milan (2005)

b) Barcelona vs Chelsea (2009)

c) Real Madrid vs Atletico Madrid (2016)

d) Manchester United vs Bayern Munich (1999)

2. In the 2014 FIFA World Cup, which team defeated Brazil 7-1 in the semi-finals?

a) Argentina

b) France

c) Germany

d) Spain

3. What year did England win their only FIFA World Cup?

a) 1970

b) 1958

c) 1966

d) 1982

4. Which Champions League final ended with a "Zidane volley"?

a) AC Milan vs Juventus (2003)

b) Barcelona vs Manchester United (2011)

c) Liverpool vs Tottenham (2019)

d) Real Madrid vs Bayer Leverkusen (2002)

5. The "Battle of Santiago" in the 1962 World Cup was played between which teams?

a) Brazil and Argentina

b) Chile and Italy

c) Germany and England

d) Uruguay and France

Ultimate Penalty Shootout
Answer 5 questions correctly in a row to earn 5 extra points.

6. Which match ended with Diego Maradona's "Hand of God" goal?

a) Argentina vs England (1986)

b) Argentina vs Germany (1990)

c) Brazil vs Argentina (1994)

d) Italy vs Argentina (1990)

7. What's the nickname of the 1953 match where Hungary beat England 6-3 at Wembley?

a) The Match of the Century

b) The Wembley Debacle

c) The Magyars' Triumph

d) The Forgotten Final

8. In the 1999 Champions League final, Manchester United scored twice in added time to defeat which team?

a) Juventus

b) Real Madrid

c) AC Milan

d) Bayern Munich

9. Which two teams played the "Maracanazo" in 1950?

a) Uruguay and Brazil

b) Argentina and Brazil

c) Italy and Uruguay

d) Spain and Brazil

10. The "Clasico del Siglo" in 2011 was a Champions League semi-final between which teams?

a) AC Milan and Inter Milan

b) Bayern Munich and Borussia Dortmund

c) Chelsea and Liverpool

d) Barcelona and Real Madrid

> **Did you know?**
> The highest-scoring World Cup match occurred in 1954, when Austria defeated Switzerland 7-5 in a quarterfinal match!

Normal Questions (3 Points Each)

11. In which year did Spain's "Tiki-Taka" style help them dominate the FIFA World Cup final?

a) 2010

b) 2006

c) 2014

d) 2018

12. The 1982 FIFA World Cup semi-final between France and Germany is remembered for what infamous incident?

a) Platini's missed penalty

b) Germany's controversial third goal

c) Harald Schumacher's foul on Patrick Battiston

d) A 40-yard strike by Rummenigge

13. The 2006 World Cup final is best remembered for what event involving Zinedine Zidane?

a) His winning penalty

b) His red card for handball

c) His headbutt on Marco Materazzi

d) His decisive own goal

14. In 1994, which Italian player missed the decisive penalty in the World Cup final, leading to Italy's defeat?

a) Roberto Baggio

b) Bebeto

c) Romario

d) Dunga

15. Who scored the winning goal for Germany in the 2014 FIFA World Cup final?

a) Miroslav Klose

b) Thomas Müller

c) Mario Götze

d) Toni Kroos

16. The 2005 Champions League final saw Liverpool overturn a 3-goal deficit against which team?

a) Inter Milan

b) Juventus

c) AC Milan

d) Barcelona

17. In the Euro 2000 final, France defeated Italy thanks to a golden goal by which player?

a) Thierry Henry

b) Zinedine Zidane

c) David Trezeguet

d) Patrick Vieira

18. Which team broke Barcelona's 39-game unbeaten streak in 2016?

a) Real Madrid

b) Atletico Madrid

c) Sevilla

d) Valencia

19. The 2013 Champions League final was an all-German affair. Which two teams played?

a) Bayer Leverkusen and Bayern Munich

b) Bayern Munich and Schalke 04

c) Borussia Dortmund and RB Leipzig

d) Bayern Munich and Borussia Dortmund

20. In the 1998 World Cup final, which team defeated Brazil 3-0?

a) France

b) Argentina

c) Netherlands

d) Italy

Hard Questions (5 Points Each)

21. Which match is known for the "Ghost Goal" of Luis Garcia in the 2005 Champions League semi-final?

a) Liverpool vs Chelsea

b) Liverpool vs AC Milan

c) Chelsea vs Barcelona

d) Real Madrid vs Juventus

22. Which match in 1970 is referred to as the "Game of the Century"?

a) Uruguay vs Brazil

b) Brazil vs England

c) Argentina vs Netherlands

d) Italy vs West Germany

23. In the "Battle of Highbury" (1934), which two national teams faced off?

a) England vs Italy

b) England vs Germany

c) Italy vs Hungary

d) Scotland vs England

📝 **What's your all-time favorite match that left you on the edge of your seat?** Was it a dramatic comeback or an unforgettable last-minute goal? Share the match that made you a soccer fan for life.

_____
_____
_____

24. The "Final of the Century" in the 1974 World Cup featured which teams?

a) Italy and West Germany

b) Brazil and Argentina

c) West Germany and the Netherlands

d) France and Uruguay

25. Which Copa Libertadores final was controversially replayed in Madrid due to violence at the original venue?

a) River Plate vs Boca Juniors (2018)

b) Flamengo vs Gremio (2019)

c) Palmeiras vs Santos (2020)

d) River Plate vs Independiente (1986)

26. The 1954 World Cup final, known as the "Miracle of Bern," was won by which team?

a) Uruguay

b) Hungary

c) Brazil

d) West Germany

27. Which match is famously known as "The Match of Death," played during World War II?

a) Rapid Vienna vs Bayern Munich (1941)

b) Dynamo Moscow vs Spartak Moscow (1943)

c) FC Start vs Flakelf (1942)

d) Hungary vs Austria (1940)

28. The 2004 Champions League quarterfinal saw which team overturn a 4-1 first-leg deficit against AC Milan?

a) Porto

b) Liverpool

c) Deportivo La Coruña

d) Valencia

29. The 1993 UEFA Champions League final ended with which team claiming their first-ever title?

a) AC Milan

b) Marseille

c) Ajax

d) Barcelona

30. The "Fog Match" in the 1966 European Cup was played between which teams?

a) Ajax and Liverpool

b) AC Milan and Inter Milan

c) Juventus and Liverpool

d) Benfica and Real Madrid

31. Which World Cup match in 1994 is remembered for ending with Roberto Baggio's missed penalty?

a) Brazil vs Italy

b) Argentina vs Netherlands

c) Germany vs Bulgaria

d) Sweden vs Romania

32. The 1985 European Cup final between Liverpool and Juventus is infamous for what tragic event?

a) Weather-related suspension

b) Match-fixing allegations

c) Heysel Stadium disaster

d) Pitch invasion

33. Which dramatic Premier League match in 2012 ended with Sergio Agüero's stoppage-time goal to win the title?

a) Manchester City vs QPR

b) Manchester City vs Manchester United

c) Arsenal vs Tottenham Hotspur

d) Chelsea vs Liverpool

DREAM TEAM DRAFT: Pick Your Favorite Player!

Pick your favorite player from the list of three by considering their skills, achievements, and impact on the game. Think about their playing style and what makes them stand out. Choose the one you'd want on your dream team and see if your friends agree!

Goalkeeper

1. Lev Yashin (The Black Spider)	2. Gianluigi Buffon	3. Manuel Neuer

Known for his incredible reflexes and unmatched shot-stopping ability, Lev Yashin is widely considered one of the greatest goalkeepers in history. The only goalkeeper to ever win the Ballon d'Or, his commanding presence in the box and fearless style made him a legend.	A modern-day icon, Buffon is celebrated for his longevity, leadership, and calm demeanor under pressure. He was the backbone of Italy's World Cup-winning team in 2006 and is renowned for his impeccable positioning and ability to save crucial shots in high-stakes moments.	Known for revolutionizing the goalkeeper position, Neuer is a sweeper-keeper whose incredible shot-stopping abilities are matched by his skill with the ball at his feet. His role in Bayern Munich's dominance and Germany's 2014 World Cup win has cemented him as one of the greatest of his generation.

YOUR PICK: _____

Stadium Spotlight

Get ready to put your soccer knowledge to the test! You'll see a picture of a famous stadium, and your challenge is to name it. If you're unsure, don't worry, three clues at the bottom of the page will help guide you to the right answer. Take a good look and see if you can recognize these iconic soccer venues!

YOUR ANSWER: _____

- The largest stadium in Europe by capacity.
- This stadium is home to a club known for its iconic blue and red stripes.
- Located in a city famous for its Gaudí architecture.

Trophies in The Shadows

You'll see the silhouette of a famous soccer trophy. Your challenge is to guess which trophy it is just by its shape! If you need help, check the three clues at the bottom of the page. See if you can recognize them all!

YOUR ANSWER: _____

- Designed by an Italian sculptor in the 1970s.
- Made of 18-carat gold, it weighs 6.1 kilograms.
- Depicts two human figures holding up the Earth.

1. Greatest Matches of All Time - Answers

Easy Questions

1. a) Liverpool vs AC Milan (2005)
2. c) Germany
3. c) 1966
4. d) Real Madrid vs Bayer Leverkusen (2002)
5. b) Chile and Italy
6. a) Argentina vs England (1986)
7. a) The Match of the Century
8. d) Bayern Munich
9. a) Uruguay and Brazil
10. d) Barcelona and Real Madrid

Normal Questions

11. a) 2010
12. c) Harald Schumacher's foul on Patrick Battiston
13. c) His headbutt on Marco Materazzi
14. a) Roberto Baggio
15. c) Mario Götze
16. c) AC Milan
17. c) David Trezeguet
18. a) Real Madrid
19. d) Bayern Munich and Borussia Dortmund

20. a) France

Hard Questions

21. a) Liverpool vs Chelsea
22. d) Italy vs West Germany
23. a) England vs Italy
24. c) West Germany and the Netherlands
25. a) River Plate vs Boca Juniors (2018)
26. d) West Germany
27. c) FC Start vs Flakelf (1942)
28. c) Deportivo La Coruña
29. b) Marseille
30. a) Ajax and Liverpool
31. a) Brazil vs Italy
32. c) Heysel Stadium disaster
33. a) Manchester City vs QPR

Bonus Section

1. Camp Nou
2. FIFA World Cup Trophy

1. Greatest Matches of All Time – Score

Section	Multiplier	Right Answers	Total Points
Easy Questions	x1		
Normal Questions	x3		
Hard Questions	x5		
Bonus	x10		
Ultimate Penalty Shootout	5 Points		
	TOTAL POINTS		

MAX POINTS = 130

If you got 104 points or more you earned the:

Congratulations!

CHAPTER 2

Unforgettable Goals

Some goals are more than just points on the scoreboard; they become legendary moments that live on forever. From stunning long-range strikes to last-second winners, unforgettable goals have the power to define careers and change the course of history. In this chapter, you'll relive jaw-dropping goals that left fans speechless and cemented players as icons. Test your knowledge and see how well you remember these unforgettable moments!

Easy Questions (1 Point Each)

34. Who scored the famous "Hand of God" goal in the 1986 World Cup?

a) Lionel Messi
b) Pele
c) Diego Maradona
d) Johan Cruyff

35. What year did David Beckham score from the halfway line against Wimbledon?

a) 1996
b) 1994
c) 1998
d) 2000

36. Which Brazilian scored a stunning free-kick against France in 1997 that appeared to defy physics?

a) Rivaldo
b) Ronaldo
c) Roberto Carlos
d) Zico

37. Who scored the "Goal of the Century" against England in 1986?

a) Michel Platini
b) Gabriel Batistuta
c) Mario Kempes
d) Diego Maradona

38. In the 2018 FIFA World Cup, Benjamin Pavard's incredible strike was against which team?

a) Brazil
b) Croatia
c) Uruguay
d) Argentina

39. Zlatan Ibrahimovic scored a spectacular bicycle kick from 30 yards out against which team in 2012?

a) Germany
b) England
c) France
d) Netherlands

40. Lionel Messi's iconic solo goal against Getafe in 2007 drew comparisons to which legendary goal?

a) Maradona's "Goal of the Century"
b) Zidane's Champions League volley
c) Cruyff's turn
d) Pele's 1000th goal

41. Cristiano Ronaldo's stunning overhead kick for Real Madrid in 2018 was scored against which team?

a) Juventus
b) Bayern Munich
c) Barcelona
d) Atletico Madrid

42. Which player scored an iconic volley for Manchester United against Aston Villa in 1993?

a) Roy Keane
b) Ryan Giggs
c) Eric Cantona
d) Paul Scholes

> 📝 **Which goal in soccer history do you think is the most unforgettable?** Whether it's a stunning long-range strike or a cheeky dribble past defenders, tell us about the goal that still gives you chills.
>
> _____
> _____
> _____
> _____

43. In the 1970 World Cup final, Carlos Alberto scored a legendary team goal for Brazil against which country?

a) Uruguay

b) West Germany

c) Italy

d) Argentina

Normal Questions (3 Points Each)

44. What nickname was given to Geoff Hurst's controversial goal in the 1966 World Cup final?

a) The Ghost Shot

b) The Phantom Goal

c) The Wembley Goal

d) The Line Decider

45. Marco van Basten's famous volley in the Euro 1988 final was scored against which team?

a) Soviet Union
b) West Germany
c) France
d) Italy

46. In 2011, Wayne Rooney scored an iconic overhead kick in the Manchester derby against which team?

a) Manchester City
b) Chelsea
c) Arsenal
d) Liverpool

47. Dennis Bergkamp's sublime goal for Arsenal against Newcastle in 2002 involved what skill?

a) A first touch and spin
b) A long-range volley
c) A solo run from midfield
d) A chip over the goalkeeper

48. James Rodriguez's stunning volley in the 2014 World Cup was scored against which team?

a) Greece
b) Uruguay
c) Colombia
d) Japan

> ⚽ **Ultimate Penalty Shootout**
> Answer 5 questions correctly in a row to earn 10 extra points.

49. Who scored a memorable solo goal for Tottenham against Burnley in 2019, dribbling from his own half?

a) Son Heung-min
b) Harry Kane
c) Dele Alli
d) Christian Eriksen

50. Who scored a decisive goal for Manchester City in 2012 to win the Premier League in stoppage time?

a) David Silva
b) Yaya Touré
c) Edin Džeko
d) Sergio Agüero

51. In the 1998 World Cup, Michael Owen's breakthrough goal against Argentina was remarkable for what?

a) A solo dribble past multiple defenders
b) A bicycle kick finish
c) A 40-yard free-kick
d) A header from the penalty spot

52. Which team was on the receiving end of Thierry Henry's quick free-kick for Arsenal in 2004?

a) Chelsea
b) Manchester United
c) Tottenham
d) Liverpool

53. Who scored a famous long-range goal for Colombia against Cameroon in the 1990 World Cup?

a) Bernardo Redín
b) Carlos Valderrama
c) Faustino Asprilla
d) René Higuita

Hard Questions (5 Points Each)

54. In the 2009 Champions League semi-final, Andrés Iniesta scored a vital last-minute goal against which team?

a) Chelsea
b) Manchester United
c) Inter Milan
d) Bayern Munich

55. Which player scored a dramatic 93rd-minute winner for Chelsea in the 2012 UEFA Champions League final against Bayern Munich?

a) Didier Drogba
b) Frank Lampard
c) Juan Mata
d) Fernando Torres

> 💡 **Did you know?**
> In 1998, during a match in the Albanian Superliga, striker Eduard Abazi scored directly from the opening kick-off, making it one of the fastest goals ever recorded in professional soccer history.

56. George Weah's iconic solo goal for AC Milan in 1996 was scored against which team?

a) Verona

b) Juventus

c) Parma

d) Lazio

57. Which player scored the winning free-kick in the Euro 1992 semi-final for Denmark?

a) Henrik Larsen

b) Brian Laudrup

c) Michael Laudrup

d) Flemming Povlsen

58. Arjen Robben's decisive goal for Bayern Munich in the 2013 Champions League final was scored against which team?

a) Borussia Dortmund

b) Barcelona

c) Real Madrid

d) Juventus

59. Dennis Bergkamp's legendary goal in the 1998 World Cup was scored against which country?

a) Croatia

b) Brazil

c) Argentina

d) Netherlands

60. In the 2002 World Cup, which Turkish player scored a stunning 40-yard volley against South Korea?

a) Hasan Şaş

b) İlhan Mansız

c) Emre Belözoğlu

d) Hakan Şükür

61. In 1993, Al-Owairan's incredible solo goal for Saudi Arabia was scored against which team?

a) Belgium

b) Netherlands

c) Argentina

d) Spain

62. In 2016, Xherdan Shaqiri scored a breathtaking bicycle kick in the Euros against which team?

a) Poland
b) Portugal
c) France
d) Wales

63. Eric Cantona's chipped goal for Manchester United in 1996 was scored against which team?

a) Sunderland
b) Leeds United
c) Arsenal
d) Tottenham

64. Roberto Carlos' impossible goal from a tight angle in 1998 came against which team?

a) C.D.Tenerife
b) Valencia
c) Barcelona
d) Deportivo La Coruña

65. Ronald Koeman's decisive free-kick in the 1992 European Cup final was scored against which team?

a) Benfica
b) AC Milan
c) Sampdoria
d) Porto

66. The famous scorpion kick save by René Higuita happened in a friendly against which country?

a) Germany
b) Brazil
c) England
d) Argentina

DREAM TEAM DRAFT: Pick Your Favorite Player!

Pick your favorite player from the list of three by considering their skills, achievements, and impact on the game. Think about their playing style and what makes them stand out. Choose the one you'd want on your dream team and see if your friends agree!

Central Defender

1. Franz Beckenbauer	2. Virgil van Dijk	3. Bobby Moore

Often called "Der Kaiser," Beckenbauer was a master of both defense and attack, pioneering the role of the sweeper. With his elegance on the ball and ability to read the game, he led West Germany to World Cup glory in 1974 and became one of the most influential defenders in history.	A modern-day titan, Van Dijk is known for his strength, composure, and exceptional ability to lead the backline. His presence at Liverpool has been pivotal in their recent successes, including winning the Champions League and Premier League titles, and he's known for his dominance in aerial duels and tactical awareness.	As captain of England's 1966 World Cup-winning team, Bobby Moore was renowned for his cool-headedness and impeccable reading of the game. His tactical intelligence, precise tackles, and ability to start attacks from the back made him one of the most admired defenders in soccer history.

YOUR PICK: _____

Stadium Spotlight

Get ready to put your soccer knowledge to the test! You'll see a picture of a famous stadium, and your challenge is to name it. If you're unsure, don't worry, three clues at the bottom of the page will help guide you to the right answer. Take a good look and see if you can recognize these iconic soccer venues!

YOUR ANSWER: _____

- This legendary stadium is home to a club with the most UEFA Champions League titles.
- Located in Spain's capital city.
- Known for hosting "El Clásico" matches.

Trophies in The Shadows

You'll see the silhouette of a famous soccer trophy. Your challenge is to guess which trophy it is just by its shape! If you need help, check the three clues at the bottom of the page. See if you can recognize them all!

YOUR ANSWER: _____

- Sometimes nicknamed "Big Ears" because of its handle design.
- First awarded in 1956.
- A symbol of European club soccer dominance.

2. Unforgettable Goals - Answers

Easy Questions

34. c) Diego Maradona
35. a) 1996
36. c) Roberto Carlos
37. d) Diego Maradona
38. d) Argentina
39. b) England
40. a) Maradona's "Goal of the Century"
41. a) Juventus
42. c) Eric Cantona
43. c) Italy

Normal Questions

44. c) The Wembley Goal
45. a) Soviet Union
46. a) Manchester City
47. a) A first touch and spin
48. b) Uruguay
49. a) Son Heung-min
50. d) Sergio Agüero
51. a) A solo dribble past multiple defenders
52. a) Chelsea

53. a) Bernardo Redín

Hard Questions

54. a) Chelsea
55. a) Didier Drogba
56. a) Verona
57. a) Henrik Larsen
58. a) Borussia Dortmund
59. c) Argentina
60. d) Hakan Şükür
61. a) Belgium
62. a) Poland
63. a) Sunderland
64. a) C.D.Tenerife
65. c) Sampdoria
66. c) England

Bonus Section

1. Santiago Bernabéu
2. UEFA Champions League Trophy

2. Unforgettable Goals – Score

Section	Multiplier	Right Answers	Total Points
Easy Questions	x1		
Normal Questions	x3		
Hard Questions	x5		
Bonus	x10		
Ultimate Penalty Shootout	10 Points		
TOTAL POINTS			

MAX POINTS = 135

If you got 108 points or more you earned the:

CHAPTER 3

Legendary Coaches and Tactics

The greatest teams don't just rely on talent—they need vision, strategy, and leadership. This chapter explores the legendary coaches who have shaped the game and the tactical innovations that have changed how soccer is played. Get ready to test your knowledge on the masterminds behind the most iconic moments in soccer history!

Easy Questions (1 Point Each)

67. Who is known as the "Special One" in the soccer world?

a) Pep Guardiola
b) José Mourinho
c) Sir Alex Ferguson
d) Carlo Ancelotti

68. Which coach led Leicester City to their historic Premier League win in 2016?

a) Sam Allardyce
b) Brendan Rodgers
c) Nigel Pearson
d) Claudio Ranieri

69. What is the famous tactic associated with Johan Cruyff and Barcelona?

a) Gegenpressing
b) Total Football
c) Catenaccio
d) Tiki-Taka

70. Which coach managed Manchester United for over 26 years?

a) Arsène Wenger
b) Matt Busby
c) Sir Alex Ferguson
d) Jürgen Klopp

71. Which manager won three consecutive Champions League titles with Real Madrid?

a) Zinedine Zidane
b) Carlo Ancelotti
c) Vicente del Bosque
d) Rafael Benítez

72. Arsène Wenger is most associated with which club?

a) Tottenham Hotspur
b) Monaco
c) Arsenal
d) PSG

73. What defensive tactic is most associated with Italian soccer?

a) Zonal Marking

b) Gegenpressing

c) Catenaccio

d) Sweeper System

74. Which German coach is known for popularizing "Gegenpressing"?

a) Jürgen Klopp

b) Hansi Flick

c) Ralf Rangnick

d) Thomas Tuchel

75. Who was the manager of Brazil during their 1970 World Cup victory?

a) Mario Zagallo

b) Carlos Alberto Parreira

c) Luiz Felipe Scolari

d) Tele Santana

76. Pep Guardiola's managerial career started at which club?

a) Barcelona

b) Bayern Munich

c) Manchester City

d) Real Madrid

> **Did you know?**
> Sir Alex Ferguson, the legendary manager of Manchester United, won 13 Premier League titles, but he once took over a team on the brink of relegation to secure a historic comeback!

Normal Questions (3 Points Each)

77. Which coach introduced the "False Nine" role at Barcelona?

a) Johan Cruyff

b) Pep Guardiola

c) Luis Enrique

d) Tito Vilanova

78. Who led Germany to their 2014 FIFA World Cup triumph?

a) Joachim Löw

b) Jürgen Klinsmann

c) Franz Beckenbauer

d) Hansi Flick

79. Marcelo Bielsa is nicknamed what?

a) El Loco

b) El Maestro

c) El Magico

d) El Profe

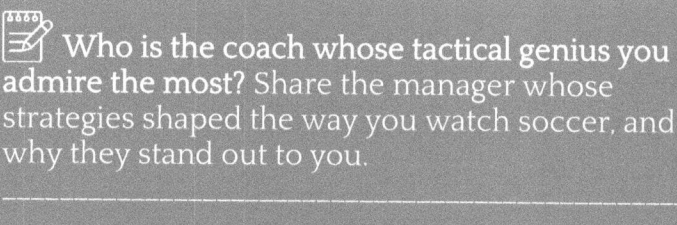

Who is the coach whose tactical genius you admire the most? Share the manager whose strategies shaped the way you watch soccer, and why they stand out to you.

_____
_____
_____
_____

80. What formation did Sir Alf Ramsey use to win the 1966 World Cup with England?

a) 4-3-3

b) 3-5-2

c) 4-4-2

d) 5-3-2

81. Helenio Herrera is credited with mastering which tactical style?

a) Total Football
b) Tiki-Taka
c) Catenaccio
d) Gegenpressing

82. Who managed AC Milan during their dominant late 1980s and early 1990s era?

a) Arrigo Sacchi
b) Fabio Capello
c) Carlo Ancelotti
d) Giovanni Trapattoni

83. Jürgen Klopp won his first Premier League title with Liverpool in which season?

a) 2019-2020
b) 2018-2019
c) 2020-2021
d) 2017-2018

84. Which manager won the treble with Inter Milan in 2010?

a) Luciano Spalletti
b) Roberto Mancini
c) Antonio Conte
d) José Mourinho

85. Who is credited with implementing the "Sweeper-Keeper" role?

a) Lev Yashin
b) Gianluigi Buffon
c) Edwin van der Sar
d) Manuel Neuer

86. Louis van Gaal is known for which tactical philosophy?

a) Long Ball Tactics
b) Gegenpressing
c) Direct Football
d) Positional Play

Hard Questions (5 Points Each)

87. Which legendary coach has not won the World Cup as both a player and a manager?

a) Franz Beckenbauer
b) Didier Deschamps
c) Mario Zagallo
d) Vicente del Bosque

88. What innovative tactic did Viktor Maslov popularize in the 1960s?

a) False Nine
b) The Libero System
c) Tiki-Taka
d) The 4-4-2 Formation

89. Who coached Ajax to their first European Cup win in 1971?

a) Guus Hiddink
b) Johan Cruyff
c) Louis van Gaal
d) Rinus Michels

90. Cesare Maldini's Milan team was known for excelling in which defensive tactic?

a) Man-to-Man Marking
b) Zonal Marking
c) Sweeper System
d) High Press

91. Which coach introduced the "WM" formation in the 1930s?

a) Alf Ramsey
b) Vittorio Pozzo
c) Herbert Chapman
d) Bela Guttmann

92. Ottmar Hitzfeld won the Champions League with which two clubs?

a) Borussia Dortmund and Schalke
b) Bayern Munich and Hamburg
c) Borussia Dortmund and Bayern Munich
d) Bayern Munich and Stuttgart

93. Vittorio Pozzo led Italy to consecutive World Cup victories in which years?

a) 1950 and 1954
b) 1930 and 1934
c) 1934 and 1938
d) 1926 and 1930

94. Which coach introduced the "Inverted Full-Back" role at Manchester City?

a) Pep Guardiola
b) Manuel Pellegrini
c) Roberto Mancini
d) Sven-Göran Eriksson

95. Who is the only coach to have won league titles in England, Spain, and Italy?

a) Pep Guardiola
b) José Mourinho
c) Carlo Ancelotti
d) Fabio Capello

> **Ultimate Penalty Shootout**
> Answer 5 questions correctly in a row to earn 15 extra points.

96. Bela Guttmann is famously associated with which club's "curse"?

a) Ajax
b) Porto
c) Benfica
d) Feyenoord

97. Which manager won five European Cups as a coach?

a) Zinedine Zidane
b) Carlo Ancelotti
c) Bob Paisley
d) Pep Guardiola

98. Who is credited with the creation of "Total Football"?

a) Ernst Happel
b) Johan Cruyff
c) Louis van Gaal
d) Rinus Michels

99. Which team did Fabio Capello lead to an unbeaten league season in Serie A?

a) Roma
b) Juventus
c) AC Milan
d) Inter Milan

100. Which coach pioneered "Zonal Marking" in Italy during the 1980s?

a) Fabio Capello
b) Giovanni Trapattoni
c) Arrigo Sacchi
d) all of the above

DREAM TEAM DRAFT: Pick Your Favorite Player!

Pick your favorite player from the list of three by considering their skills, achievements, and impact on the game. Think about their playing style and what makes them stand out. Choose the one you'd want on your dream team and see if your friends agree!

Midfielder

1. Zinedine Zidane	2. Michel Platini	3. Xavi Hernandez

A magician with the ball, Zidane was known for his elegance and vision on the field. With his unmatched ability to dictate the pace of the game, Zidane led France to two major tournament victories, the 1998 World Cup and the Euro 2000. His dribbling and playmaking were simply a joy to watch.	One of France's greatest-ever players, Platini was an attacking midfielder whose precise passing and brilliant free kicks made him a constant threat. He led France to victory in the 1984 European Championship and is remembered for his creativity and leadership on the field.	A key figure in the iconic Barcelona team of the late 2000s and early 2010s, Xavi was the ultimate playmaker. With his vision, passing accuracy, and ability to control the tempo of a match, Xavi was the heart of both Barcelona and Spain's golden era, leading Spain to victory in the 2010 World Cup and two European Championships.

YOUR PICK: _____

Stadium Spotlight

Get ready to put your soccer knowledge to the test! You'll see a picture of a famous stadium, and your challenge is to name it. If you're unsure, don't worry, three clues at the bottom of the page will help guide you to the right answer. Take a good look and see if you can recognize these iconic soccer venues!

YOUR ANSWER: _____

- Nicknamed "The Theatre of Dreams."
- Home to a club with a rich history in the Premier League and numerous English titles.
- Located in the northwest of England

Trophies in The Shadows

You'll see the silhouette of a famous soccer trophy. Your challenge is to guess which trophy it is just by its shape! If you need help, check the three clues at the bottom of the page. See if you can recognize them all!

YOUR ANSWER: _____

- Awarded annually to the best soccer club in South America.
- Its top features a soccerer standing on a globe.
- Known for its rich history of passionate rivalries.

3. Legendary Coaches and Tactics - Answers

Easy Questions

67. b) José Mourinho
68. d) Claudio Ranieri
69. b) Total Football
70. c) Sir Alex Ferguson
71. a) Zinedine Zidane
72. c) Arsenal
73. c) Catenaccio
74. a) Jürgen Klopp
75. a) Mario Zagallo
76. a) Barcelona

Normal Questions

77. b) Pep Guardiola
78. a) Joachim Löw
79. a) El Loco
80. c) 4-4-2
81. c) Catenaccio
82. a) Arrigo Sacchi
83. a) 2019-2020
84. d) José Mourinho
85. d) Manuel Neuer

86. d) Positional Play

Hard Questions

87. d) Vicente del Bosque
88. d) The 4-4-2 Formation
89. d) Rinus Michels
90. b) Zonal Marking
91. c) Herbert Chapman
92. c) Borussia Dortmund and Bayern Munich
93. c) 1934 and 1938
94. a) Pep Guardiola
95. c) Carlo Ancelotti
96. c) Benfica
97. b) Carlo Ancelotti
98. d) Rinus Michels
99. c) AC Milan
100. c) Arrigo Sacchi

Bonus Section

1. Old Trafford
2. Copa Libertadores Trophy

3. Legendary Coaches and Tactics - Score

Section	Multiplier	Right Answers	Total Points
Easy Questions	x1		
Normal Questions	x3		
Hard Questions	x5		
Bonus	x10		
Ultimate Penalty Shootout	15 Points		
TOTAL POINTS			

MAX POINTS = 145

If you got 116 points or more you earned the:

Congratulations!

We'd love to hear what you think!

If you enjoyed "The Legendary Soccer Quizbook", please take a moment to leave an honest review on Amazon. Your feedback helps us improve and helps other fans discover the fun!

https://playmakerbooks.com/leave-review

Scan the QR code or click the link to share your thoughts. Thank you!

CHAPTER 4

The Underdogs

Everyone loves a great underdog story—when the odds are stacked against a team, yet they defy expectations and achieve the impossible. Soccer has seen some of the most incredible upsets, where determination, teamwork, and belief overcame superior opposition. In this chapter, you'll dive into the most inspiring underdog triumphs in the sport's history. Get ready to test your knowledge on the teams and players who shocked the world!

Easy Questions (1 Point Each)

101. Which team famously defeated Brazil 1-0 in the 1990 FIFA World Cup to advance to the quarterfinals?

a) South Korea
b) Argentina
c) Nigeria
d) Senegal

102. Leicester City won the Premier League in 2015-16. What were their pre-season odds of winning?

a) 2500-1
b) 1000-1
c) 5000-1
d) 10-1

103. Which African nation reached the quarterfinals of the 2002 FIFA World Cup?

a) Cameroon
b) Senegal
c) Nigeria
d) South Africa

104. Which country defeated Italy in the group stage of the 1966 FIFA World Cup?

a) China
b) South Korea
c) Japan
d) North Korea

105. Greece shocked the soccer world by winning which international tournament?

a) UEFA Euro 2004
b) 1996 Olympic Games
c) 1994 FIFA World Cup
d) 2002 FIFA Confederations Cup

> **Ultimate Penalty Shootout**
> Answer 5 questions correctly in a row to earn 5 extra points.

106. What was Iceland's population during their historic run to the UEFA Euro 2016 quarterfinals?

a) 330,000
b) 1 million
c) 500,000
d) 2 million

107. Who scored the decisive penalty kick goal in Zambia's surprise victory in the 2012 Africa Cup of Nations final?

a) Stoppila Sunzu

b) Rainford Kalaba

c) Kennedy Mweene

d) Christopher Katongo

108. Which club won their first UEFA Champions League title in 1993, defeating AC Milan?

a) Marseille

b) Porto

c) Ajax

d) Borussia Dortmund

109. Which team eliminated defending champions Spain in the 2014 FIFA World Cup group stage?

a) Colombia

b) Netherlands

c) Chile

d) Mexico

110. Which nation did the United States defeat in the first FIFA Women's World Cup final in 1991?

a) Sweden

b) Germany

c) Norway

d) China

Normal Questions (3 Points Each)

111. In 1982, Algeria stunned the soccer world by defeating which European powerhouse?

a) Italy

b) France

c) West Germany

d) Spain

112. What was the final score of the famous "Miracle of Bern" where West Germany defeated Hungary in the 1954 FIFA World Cup final?

a) 4-2

b) 2-1

c) 3-2

d) 1-0

113. Which team knocked Argentina out of the 1990 FIFA World Cup?

a) Colombia
b) West Germany
c) Romania
d) Sweden

114. Which nation reached the semifinals of the 1994 FIFA World Cup as debutants?

a) Bulgaria
b) Romania
c) Sweden
d) None

115. What was the score when South Korea defeated Italy in the 2002 FIFA World Cup Round of 16?

a) 2-1 (AET)
b) 3-2
c) 1-0
d) 2-0

116. Which player scored the decisive goal in Denmark's 1992 UEFA Euro final victory over Germany?

a) Kim Vilfort
b) Brian Laudrup
c) Henrik Larsen
d) Peter Schmeichel

117. Which club eliminated Real Madrid in the UEFA Champions League semifinals in 2011?

a) Barcelona
b) Bayern Munich
c) Chelsea
d) Juventus

> 💡 **Did you know?**
> In 1992, Denmark won the UEFA European Championship despite not initially qualifying for the tournament. They were invited as a last-minute replacement for Yugoslavia and went on to defy all odds to lift the trophy.

118. Costa Rica stunned the soccer world by reaching which stage in the 2014 FIFA World Cup?

a) Quarterfinals

b) Semifinals

c) Round of 16

d) Group Stage

119. Which team defeated Manchester United in the 1995 UEFA Champions League group stage?

a) PSG

b) Ajax

c) Borussia Dortmund

d) IFK Göteborg

120. Which player scored the winning goal in the 2000 UEFA Cup final for Galatasaray against Arsenal?

a) Gheorghe Popescu

b) Hakan Şükür

c) Hasan Şaş

d) Taffarel

Hard Questions (5 Points Each)

121. Which English club shocked Rapid Wien in the 1985 UEFA Cup Winners' Cup final?

a) Aston Villa
b) Nottingham Forest
c) Everton
d) Leeds United

122. The Faroe Islands famously defeated which team in their first competitive match in 1990?

a) Austria
b) Iceland
c) Finland
d) Sweden

123. Which team won their first and only Copa Libertadores title in 2014?

a) San Lorenzo
b) Lanús
c) Atletico Mineiro
d) Nacional

124. Which team reached the 2000 UEFA Champions League final despite being underdogs?

a) Valencia

b) Deportivo La Coruña

c) Lazio

d) Monaco

> **Do you have a favorite underdog story in soccer?** Whether it's a surprise league winner or a team that pulled off the impossible in a major tournament, tell us about the moment that proved anything is possible.
> _____
> _____
> _____
> _____

125. Which goalkeeper famously scored in open play during a UEFA Cup match in 2007?

a) Jens Lehmann

b) Rogerio Ceni

c) Sinan Bolat

d) Andres Palop

126. Iceland defeated which team to reach the UEFA Euro 2016 quarterfinals?

a) England
b) Belgium
c) Portugal
d) Italy

127. Which nation ended West Germany's 43-game unbeaten streak in 1976?

a) Czechoslovakia
b) Yugoslavia
c) Hungary
d) Poland

128. Which African team reached the 1990 FIFA World Cup quarterfinals?

a) Ghana
b) Nigeria
c) Egypt
d) Cameroon

129. The "Greek Miracle" in Euro 2004 included a 1-0 win against which team in the final?

a) Spain
b) Portugal
c) Italy
d) France

130. Alaves shocked the soccer world in the 2001 UEFA Cup final, losing narrowly to which team?

a) Lazio
b) Valencia
c) Liverpool
d) Bayern Munich

131. Zambia's victory in the 2012 Africa Cup of Nations final came via which method?

a) Regular time goal
b) Extra-time winner
c) Penalty shootout
d) Golden goal

132. Who scored the winning goal in the EFL Championships play-offs semi-final between Watford and Leicester City in 2013?

a) Troy Deeney
b) Riyad Mahrez
c) Jamie Vardy
d) David Nugent

133. Which nation shocked Brazil in the 1998 CONCACAF Gold Cup Semi-finals?

a) Mexico
b) USA
c) Canada
d) Honduras

DREAM TEAM DRAFT: Pick Your Favorite Player!

Pick your favorite player from the list of three by considering their skills, achievements, and impact on the game. Think about their playing style and what makes them stand out. Choose the one you'd want on your dream team and see if your friends agree!

Striker

1. Cristiano Ronaldo

One of the best goal-scorers in soccer history, Ronaldo is known for his athleticism, powerful shots, and insatiable desire to win. His success in multiple leagues, including the Premier League, La Liga, and Serie A, along with his five Ballon d'Or titles, solidifies him as a global soccer icon.

2. Lionel Messi

Messi's dribbling, playmaking, and finishing ability have made him one of the most complete players in soccer history. With numerous La Liga titles, Champions League trophies, and six Ballon d'Or awards, Messi's magical performances on the pitch have won him legions of fans worldwide.

3. Thierry Henry

One of the Premier League's all-time greatest players, Henry combined blistering pace with exceptional finishing ability. As a key figure for both Arsenal and France, he helped lead his teams to numerous titles, including the 1998 World Cup and the 2004 Premier League title.

YOUR PICK: _____

Stadium Spotlight

Get ready to put your soccer knowledge to the test! You'll see a picture of a famous stadium, and your challenge is to name it. If you're unsure, don't worry, three clues at the bottom of the page will help guide you to the right answer. Take a good look and see if you can recognize these iconic soccer venues!

YOUR ANSWER: _____

- This stadium features an iconic arch visible from miles away.
- Hosts England's national soccer team matches.
- The site of the famous 1966 FIFA World Cup Final.

Trophies in The Shadows

You'll see the silhouette of a famous soccer trophy. Your challenge is to guess which trophy it is just by its shape! If you need help, check the three clues at the bottom of the page. See if you can recognize them all!

YOUR ANSWER: _____

- The oldest national soccer trophy in the world.
- Its design includes ornate handles and a silver body.
- First awarded in the 1870s.

4. The Underdogs - Answers

Easy Questions

101. b) Argentina
102. c) 5000-1
103. b) Senegal
104. d) North Korea
105. a) UEFA Euro 2004
106. a) 330,000
107. a) Stoppila Sunzu
108. a) Marseille
109. c) Chile
110. c) Norway

Normal Questions

111. c) West Germany
112. c) 3-2
113. b) West Germany
114. d) None
115. a) 2-1 (AET)
116. a) Kim Vilfort
117. a) Barcelona
118. a) Quarterfinals
119. d) IFK Göteborg

120. b) Hakan Şükür

Hard Questions

121. c) Everton
122. a) Austria
123. a) San Lorenzo
124. a) Valencia
125. b) Rogerio Ceni
126. a) England
127. a) Czechoslovakia
128. d) Cameroon
129. b) Portugal
130. c) Liverpool
131. c) Penalty shootout
132. a) Troy Deeney
133. b) USA

Bonus Section

1. Wembley Stadium
2. FA Cup Trophy

4. The Underdogs - Score

Section	Multiplier	Right Answers	Total Points
Easy Questions	x1		
Normal Questions	x3		
Hard Questions	x5		
Bonus	x10		
Ultimate Penalty Shootout	5 Points		
TOTAL POINTS			

MAX POINTS = 130

If you got 104 points or more you earned the:

Congratulations!

CHAPTER 5

Rivalries and Derbies

Soccer rivalries are more than just games—they're battles fueled by history, pride, and passion. Whether it's fierce local derbies or legendary international clashes, these matches bring out the best (and sometimes the worst) in teams and fans alike. In this chapter, you'll explore the most intense rivalries in soccer history. Get ready to test your knowledge on the matches that divide cities, nations, and generations!

Easy Questions (1 Point Each)

134. What is the name of the rivalry between FC Barcelona and Real Madrid?

a) El Superclásico
b) El Derbi
c) El Clásico
d) Der Klassiker

135. The Manchester Derby is contested between Manchester United and which other club?

a) Manchester City
b) Liverpool
c) Chelsea
d) Arsenal

136. Which two clubs compete in the "North London Derby"?

a) Arsenal and Tottenham Hotspur
b) Chelsea and Fulham
c) West Ham and Millwall
d) Crystal Palace and Brighton

137. The "Old Firm Derby" is between Celtic and which other club?

a) Rangers
b) Hearts
c) Aberdeen
d) Hibernian

138. The "Milan Derby" is also known as what?

a) Super Derby
b) Derby della Capitale
c) Derby d'Italia
d) Derby della Madonnina

> 📝 **What's the most thrilling soccer rivalry or derby you've watched?** From the passion to the drama, share the match that made you feel the intensity of a heated soccer rivalry.
> _____
> _____
> _____
> _____

139. Which rivalry is referred to as "Der Klassiker"?

a) Bayer Leverkusen vs. Bayern Munich

b) Schalke vs. Borussia Dortmund

c) RB Leipzig vs. Bayern Munich

d) Borussia Dortmund vs. Bayern Munich

140. The "Merseyside Derby" involves Liverpool and which other club?

a) Chelsea

b) Manchester United

c) Everton

d) Leeds United

141. Boca Juniors and River Plate contest which famous South American rivalry?

a) Superclásico

b) Clásico del Río

c) El Monumental Derby

d) Sudamericana Rivalry

142. Which two Italian clubs contest the Derby della Capitale?

a) AS Roma and Lazio
b) Napoli and Fiorentina
c) Juventus and Torino
d) Inter Milan and AC Milan

143. Which is the biggest soccer rivalry in Argentina?

a) Boca Juniors vs. River Plate
b) Independiente vs. Racing
c) San Lorenzo vs. Huracán
d) Estudiantes vs. Gimnasia

Normal Questions (3 Points Each)

144. Which two clubs are involved in the "Tyne-Wear Derby"?

a) Leeds United and Huddersfield Town
b) Newcastle United and Middlesbrough
c) Sunderland and Hull City
d) Newcastle United and Sunderland

145. What is the "Steel City Derby"?

a) Hull City vs. Barnsley
b) Nottingham Forest vs. Derby County
c) Leeds United vs. Sheffield United
d) Sheffield United vs. Sheffield Wednesday

146. The "Eternal Derby" is contested in which country?

a) Turkey
b) Greece
c) Serbia
d) Croatia

147. Which two clubs play in the "Istanbul Derby"?

a) Galatasaray and Fenerbahçe
b) Besiktas and Galatasaray
c) Trabzonspor and Fenerbahçe
d) Galatasaray and Sivasspor

148. Which Brazilian derby is called the "Paulista Derby"?

a) Corinthians vs. Palmeiras

b) Flamengo vs. Fluminense

c) Sao Paulo vs. Santos
d) Internacional vs. Gremio

Ultimate Penalty Shootout
Answer 5 questions correctly in a row to earn 10 extra points.

149. The "Battle of Britain" often refers to games between clubs from which two countries?

a) England and Scotland

b) England and Ireland

c) Scotland and Wales

d) Wales and Northern Ireland

150. The "Lisbon Derby" is contested between Sporting CP and which other club?

a) Benfica

b) Porto

c) Braga

d) Setubal

151. Which two clubs are involved in the Derby della Mole?

a) Torino and Genoa

b) Juventus and Napoli

c) Juventus and Torino

d) Napoli and Fiorentina

152. The "Clásico Tapatío" is played in which country?

a) Colombia

b) Spain

c) Chile

d) Mexico

153. The "Seville Derby" is played between Sevilla and which other club?

a) Valencia

b) Malaga

c) Real Betis

d) Getafe

Hard Questions (5 Points Each)

154. Which rivalry is referred to as "El Viejo Clásico" in Costa Rica?

a) Cartaginés vs. Saprissa
b) Herediano vs. Alajuelense
c) Saprissa vs. Herediano
d) Saprissa vs. Alajuelense

155. The "Clásico del Astillero" is played between which two Ecuadorian teams?

a) Barcelona SC and LDU Quito
b) LDU Quito and Emelec
c) Barcelona SC and Emelec
d) Independiente del Valle and Emelec

156. Which derby is called the "Revierderby" in Germany?

a) Bayern Munich vs. Borussia Dortmund
b) Schalke vs. Bayer Leverkusen
c) Borussia Dortmund vs. Schalke 04
d) Stuttgart vs. Freiburg

157. The "Casablanca Derby" is played between which two Moroccan teams?

a) Raja Casablanca and Wydad Casablanca

b) FUS Rabat and Wydad Casablanca

c) Raja Casablanca and FAR Rabat

d) Maghreb Fes and Raja Casablanca

> **Did you know?**
> The "El Clásico" between Real Madrid and Barcelona has been played over 240 times, with some matches having intense political and cultural significance in Spain.

158. What is the name of the derby between Panathinaikos and Olympiacos in Greece?

a) Derby of the Eternal Enemies

b) Greek Super Derby

c) Athens Showdown

d) Olympian Rivalry

159. Which Indian derby is called the "Kolkata Derby"?

a) Mumbai City FC vs. FC Goa

b) Bengaluru FC vs. Kerala Blasters

c) Churchill Brothers vs. Dempo SC

d) Mohun Bagan vs. East Bengal

160. What is the oldest professional soccer rivalry in the world?

a) Sheffield FC vs. Hallam FC

b) Rangers vs. Celtic

c) Aston Villa vs. Wolves

d) Wolverhampton Wanderers vs West Bromwich Albion

161. Which rivalry is referred to as the "Derby des Olympiques" in France?

a) PSG vs. Marseille

b) Lyon vs. Saint-Étienne

c) Marseille vs. Lyon

d) Bordeaux vs. Toulouse

162. The "Soweto Derby" is played between which two South African teams?

a) Kaizer Chiefs and Orlando Pirates

b) Mamelodi Sundowns and Orlando Pirates

c) Kaizer Chiefs and Cape Town City

d) Bloemfontein Celtic and Orlando Pirates

163. Which two MLS teams contest "El Tráfico"?

a) Seattle Sounders and Portland Timbers

b) LA Galaxy and LAFC

c) New York Red Bulls and NYCFC

d) Toronto FC and Montreal Impact

164. Which derby is nicknamed "The Coffee Derby" in South America?

a) Atlético Nacional vs. Independiente Medellín

b) Junior FC vs. Millonarios

c) Santa Fe vs. Deportivo Cali

d) América de Cali vs. Millonarios

165. Which rivalry is referred to as the "Battle of the South" in the USA?

a) LA Galaxy vs. LAFC

b) Atlanta United vs. Orlando City

c) Austin FC vs. FC Dallas

d) Inter Miami vs. Nashville SC

166. Which clubs compete in the "Battle of Lancashire"?

a) Burnley and Blackburn Rovers
b) Preston North End and Blackpool
c) Bolton Wanderers and Wigan Athletic
d) Burnley and Bolton Wanderers

DREAM TEAM DRAFT: Pick Your Favorite Player!

Pick your favorite player from the list of three by considering their skills, achievements, and impact on the game. Think about their playing style and what makes them stand out. Choose the one you'd want on your dream team and see if your friends agree!

Right-Back

1. Cafu	2. Gary Neville	3. Dani Carvajal

Known for his lightning pace and tireless work ethic, Cafu was a key figure in Brazil's 1994 and 2002 World Cup victories. His ability to both defend and contribute to the attack with overlapping runs made him one of the best right-backs in history.	A stalwart for Manchester United, Neville's defensive reliability and leadership made him one of the Premier League's best right-backs. Known for his no-nonsense approach, he was also capable of contributing offensively with key crosses and set-piece deliveries.	A modern-day right-back, Carvajal has been crucial to Real Madrid's successes, including multiple Champions League titles. His solid defensive capabilities and his attacking support down the flank have earned him a reputation as one of the best in the business.

YOUR PICK: _____

Stadium Spotlight

Get ready to put your soccer knowledge to the test! You'll see a picture of a famous stadium, and your challenge is to name it. If you're unsure, don't worry, three clues at the bottom of the page will help guide you to the right answer. Take a good look and see if you can recognize these iconic soccer venues!

YOUR ANSWER: _____

- Located in a city famous for Carnival and samba.
- Hosted two FIFA World Cup finals, in 1950 and 2014.
- One of the largest stadiums in South America.

Trophies in The Shadows

You'll see the silhouette of a famous soccer trophy. Your challenge is to guess which trophy it is just by its shape! If you need help, check the three clues at the bottom of the page. See if you can recognize them all!

YOUR ANSWER: _____

- A symbol of South American national team supremacy.
- Features no handles, unlike many other cups.
- First awarded in 1916, making it one of the oldest international trophies.

5. Rivalries and Derbies - Answers

Easy Questions

134. c) El Clásico
135. a) Manchester City
136. a) Arsenal and Tottenham Hotspur
137. a) Rangers
138. d) Derby della Madonnina
139. d) Borussia Dortmund vs. Bayern Munich
140. c) Everton
141. a) Superclásico
142. a) AS Roma and Lazio
143. a) Boca Juniors vs. River Plate

Normal Questions

144. d) Newcastle United and Sunderland
145. d) Sheffield United vs. Sheffield Wednesday
146. c) Serbia
147. a) Galatasaray and Fenerbahçe
148. a) Corinthians vs. Palmeiras
149. a) England and Scotland
150. a) Benfica
151. c) Juventus and Torino
152. d) Mexico

153. c) Real Betis

Hard Questions

154. d) Saprissa vs. Alajuelense
155. c) Barcelona SC and Emelec
156. c) Borussia Dortmund vs. Schalke 04
157. a) Raja Casablanca and Wydad Casablanca
158. a) Derby of the Eternal Enemies
159. d) Mohun Bagan vs. East Bengal
160. a) Sheffield FC vs. Hallam FC
161. c) Marseille vs. Lyon
162. a) Kaizer Chiefs and Orlando Pirates
163. b) LA Galaxy and LAFC
164. a) Atlético Nacional vs. Independiente Medellín
165. b) Atlanta United vs. Orlando City
166. b) Preston North End and Blackpool

Bonus Section

1. Maracanã
2. Copa América Trophy

5. Rivalries and Derbies - Score

Section	Multiplier	Right Answers	Total Points
Easy Questions	x1		
Normal Questions	x3		
Hard Questions	x5		
Bonus	x10		
Ultimate Penalty Shootout	10 Points		
TOTAL POINTS			

MAX POINTS = 135

If you got 108 points or more you earned the:

Congratulations!

Ready to Celebrate Your Skills?

Scan the QR code or click the link to download your FREE FIFA-Style Player Stats Diploma. Record your scores, show off your achievements, and proudly share your rank with friends and family. Claim your ultimate soccer bragging rights today!

https://playmakerbooks.com/player-stats-us/

CHAPTER 6

Golden Boot and Records

Scoring goals is the ultimate art in soccer, and only the greatest strikers etch their names in history. The Golden Boot is awarded to the top scorers, but behind every goal tally lies a story of skill, determination, and record-breaking moments. In this chapter, you'll dive into the players who have dominated the scoreboard and shattered records. Think you know the legends of goal-scoring? Let's put your knowledge to the test!

Easy Questions (1 Point Each)

167. Which player won the 2022 FIFA World Cup Golden Boot?

a) Lionel Messi
b) Kylian Mbappé
c) Cristiano Ronaldo
d) Neymar

168. Who was the top scorer of the 2014 FIFA World Cup?

a) James Rodríguez
b) Lionel Messi
c) Neymar
d) Thomas Müller

169. Which player holds the record for most goals in a single Premier League season (38 games)?

a) Alan Shearer
b) Erling Haaland
c) Thierry Henry
d) Andy Cole

170. Who won the Golden Boot at the 2018 FIFA World Cup?

a) Harry Kane
b) Antoine Griezmann
c) Kylian Mbappé
d) Cristiano Ronaldo

171. Which player is the all-time top scorer of the UEFA Champions League?

a) Lionel Messi
b) Cristiano Ronaldo
c) Raúl González
d) Robert Lewandowski

> 💡 **Did you know?**
> Oleg Salenko of Russia holds the record for the most goals scored by a single player in one World Cup match, netting five goals against Cameroon in 1994.

172. Which country has won the most FIFA World Cup Golden Boots?

a) Germany
b) Brazil
c) Argentina
d) France

173. Who holds the record for the most goals scored in a calendar year in soccer?

a) Cristiano Ronaldo

b) Lionel Messi

c) Neymar

d) Robert Lewandowski

174. Who is the all-time top scorer of the Serie A league?

a) Francesco Totti

b) Cristiano Ronaldo

c) Alessandro Del Piero

d) Silvio Piola

175. Which player won the Golden Boot at the 2010 FIFA World Cup?

a) David Villa

b) Thomas Müller

c) Wesley Sneijder

d) Landon Donovan

176. Which club did Lionel Messi play for when he won the most goals in a La Liga season?

a) Barcelona
b) Paris Saint-Germain
c) Manchester City
d) Real Madrid

Normal Questions (3 Points Each)

177. Which player scored the most goals in a single World Cup tournament (13 goals)?

a) Ronaldo Nazário
b) Miroslav Klose
c) Gerd Müller
d) Just Fontaine

178. Who was the top scorer of the 2022 UEFA Champions League season?

a) Robert Lewandowski
b) Karim Benzema
c) Erling Haaland
d) Lionel Messi

179. Which player holds the record for most goals scored in the history of the Copa América?

a) Lionel Messi

b) Pelé

c) Norberto Méndez

d) Gabriel Batistuta

> **Who is your favorite top scorer in soccer history?** Share the player you think deserves to hold the record for most goals, and why their goal-scoring ability stands above the rest.
> _____
> _____
> _____
> _____

180. Who is the all-time top scorer of the Bundesliga?

a) Gerd Müller

b) Robert Lewandowski

c) Claudio Pizarro

d) Miroslav Klose

181. Which player scored the most goals in a single Copa del Rey competition?

a) Lionel Messi
b) Cristiano Ronaldo
c) Raúl González
d) Josep Samitier

182. Who is the youngest player to win the European Golden Boot?

a) Kylian Mbappé
b) Wayne Rooney
c) Erling Haaland
d) Cristiano Ronaldo

183. Who scored the most goals in the 2010/11 Premier League season?

a) Didier Drogba
b) Dimitar Berbatov
c) Robin van Persie
d) Javier Hernández

184. Which player scored the most goals in the history of The African Cup of Nations tournament?

a) Samuel Eto'o
b) Ahmed Hegazi
c) Roger Milla
d) Ndaye Mulamba

185. Which country scored the most goals in the Women's FIFA World Cup?

a) United States
b) Germany
c) Brazil
d) Norway

186. Which player won the most European Golden Shoes?

a) Lionel Messi
b) Cristiano Ronaldo
c) Thierry Henry
d) David Villa

Hard Questions (5 Points Each)

187. Which player scored the most goals in a single season of the Copa Libertadores?

a) Alberto Spencer
b) Gabriel Batistuta
c) Fernando Morena
d) Lionel Messi

188. Who scored the fastest goal in World Cup history, at 11 seconds?

a) Hakan Şükür
b) Clint Dempsey
c) Giovanni van Bronckhorst
d) Tim Cahill

189. Who holds the record for the most goals scored in the history of the UEFA European Championship (Euros)?

a) Michel Platini
b) Alan Shearer
c) Cristiano Ronaldo
d) Antoine Griezmann

190. Who scored the most goals for the Italian national team?

a) Roberto Baggio
b) Francesco Totti
c) Gigi Riva
d) Giuseppe Meazza

191. Which player is the top scorer in the history of the World Cup Qualifiers?

a) Carlos Ruiz
b) Gabriel Batistuta
c) Lionel Messi
d) Cristiano Ronaldo

192. Which player holds the record for the most goals scored in a single UEFA European Championship (Euros) tournament?

a) Cristiano Ronaldo
b) Michel Platini
c) Alan Shearer
d) Antoine Griezmann

193. Which club did Ronaldo Nazário set the record for the most goals in a single season in La Liga?

a) Barcelona

b) Real Madrid

c) AC Milan

d) PSV Eindhoven

194. Which country has scored the most goals in a World Cup tournament?

a) Brazil

b) Hungary

c) Argentina

d) Italy

> ⚽ **Ultimate Penalty Shootout**
> Answer 5 questions correctly in a row to earn 15 extra points.

195. Who holds the record for most goals in a single FIFA Confederations Cup tournament?

a) Romario

b) Thierry Henry

c) Franck Ribéry

d) Edson Arantes do Nascimento (Pelé)

196. Which soccer team has won the most cups in the history of the African Nations Championship (AFCON)?

a) South Africa
b) Nigeria
c) Egypt
d) Cameroon

197. Who scored the most goals in a single World Cup qualifying campaign?

a) Ali Daei
b) Zlatan Ibrahimović
c) Lionel Messi
d) Harry Kane

198. Who is the all-time top scorer of the Copa América for Brazil?

a) Ronaldo Nazário
b) Zizinho
c) Romário
d) Pelé

199. Who holds the record for most goals in a single Africa Cup of Nations?

a) Samuel Eto'o
b) Youssef Msakni
c) Laurent Pokou
d) Didier Drogba

DREAM TEAM DRAFT: Pick Your Favorite Player!

Pick your favorite player from the list of three by considering their skills, achievements, and impact on the game. Think about their playing style and what makes them stand out. Choose the one you'd want on your dream team and see if your friends agree!

Left-Back

1. Roberto Carlos	2. Ashley Cole	3. Marcelo

Famous for his incredible free kicks, Roberto Carlos was also an explosive left-back with pace and power. His attacking runs and ability to deliver dangerous crosses made him a key part of Brazil's World Cup-winning teams in 1994 and 2002, as well as a legend at Real Madrid.	One of the most consistent and accomplished left-backs in Premier League history, Ashley Cole was known for his exceptional defensive positioning, speed, and ability to stop some of the best wingers in the world. He also contributed to attack with precise crosses.	With his flair and creativity, Marcelo revolutionized the role of left-back, blending attacking and defensive skills seamlessly. He was a crucial player in Real Madrid's dominance during the 2010s, helping them win numerous Champions League titles with his marauding runs down the wing.

YOUR PICK: _____

Stadium Spotlight

Get ready to put your soccer knowledge to the test! You'll see a picture of a famous stadium, and your challenge is to name it. If you're unsure, don't worry, three clues at the bottom of the page will help guide you to the right answer. Take a good look and see if you can recognize these iconic soccer venues!

YOUR ANSWER: _____

- This stadium's exterior changes colors depending on the team playing.
- Home to a German club that has won numerous Bundesliga titles.
- Located in Munich.

Trophies in The Shadows

You'll see the silhouette of a famous soccer trophy. Your challenge is to guess which trophy it is just by its shape! If you need help, check the three clues at the bottom of the page. See if you can recognize them all!

YOUR ANSWER: _____

- A unique golden trophy with a circular base and a crown-like top.
- Introduced in the early 2000s to replace older designs.
- Recognized as the pinnacle of African international soccer.

6. Golden Boot and Records - Answers

Easy Questions

167. b) Kylian Mbappé
168. a) James Rodríguez
169. b) Erling Haaland
170. a) Harry Kane
171. b) Cristiano Ronaldo
172. b) Brazil
173. b) Lionel Messi
174. d) Silvio Piola
175. b) Thomas Müller
176. a) Barcelona

Normal Questions

177. d) Just Fontaine
178. c) Erling Haaland
179. c) Norberto Méndez
180. a) Gerd Müller
181. d) Josep Samitier
182. c) Erling Haaland
183. b) Dimitar Berbatov
184. a) Samuel Eto'o
185. a) United States

186. a) Lionel Messi

Hard Questions

187. a) Alberto Spencer
188. a) Hakan Şükür
189. c) Cristiano Ronaldo
190. c) Gigi Riva
191. a) Carlos Ruiz
192. b) Michel Platini
193. a) Barcelona
194. b) Hungary
195. a) Romario
196. c) Egypt
197. a) Ali Daei
198. b) Zizinho
199. c) Laurent Pokou

Bonus Section

1. Allianz Arena
2. African Cup of Nations Trophy

6. Golden Boot and Records - Score

Section	Multiplier	Right Answers	Total Points
Easy Questions	x1		
Normal Questions	x3		
Hard Questions	x5		
Bonus	x10		
Ultimate Penalty Shootout	15 Points		
TOTAL POINTS			

MAX POINTS = 140

If you got 112 points or more you earned the:

Congratulations!

CHAPTER 7

Wonders, Records, and Standout Moments

Soccer is a sport full of magic—unbelievable records, jaw-dropping moments, and feats that defy logic. From stunning comebacks to incredible streaks, these wonders have captivated fans and written history. In this chapter, you'll explore the most remarkable achievements and unforgettable highlights the game has ever seen. Are you ready to test your knowledge of soccer's most extraordinary moments?

Easy Questions (1 Point Each)

200. Which country won the first-ever FIFA World Cup in 1930?

a) Argentina
b) Germany
c) Brazil
d) Uruguay

201. Who scored the winning goal in the 2014 FIFA World Cup final?

a) Lionel Messi
b) Mario Götze
c) Neymar
d) Thomas Müller

202. Which country hosted the 1998 FIFA World Cup?

a) Italy
b) Brazil
c) France
d) South Korea

203. Which team won the most World Cup titles in the 20th century?

a) Brazil
b) Germany
c) Argentina
d) Italy

204. Who was the top scorer of the 1994 FIFA World Cup?

a) Roberto Baggio
b) Hristo Stoichkov, Oleg Salenko
c) Romário
d) Gabriel Batistuta

Ultimate Penalty Shootout
Answer 5 questions correctly in a row to earn 5 extra points.

205. Which player holds the record for the most goals in World Cup history?

a) Ronaldo Nazário
b) Miroslav Klose
c) Lionel Messi
d) Pelé

206. Which country won the 2010 FIFA World Cup?

a) Argentina

b) Spain

c) Brazil

d) Netherlands

207. In which year was the first FIFA World Cup held in Africa?

a) 2006

b) 2010

c) 1998

d) 1982

208. Which player scored the famous 'Hand of God' goal in the 1986 World Cup?

a) Diego Maradona

b) Pelé

c) Lionel Messi

d) Zinedine Zidane

209. Which country has hosted the most FIFA World Cups?

a) France
b) Germany
c) Mexico
d) Italy

Normal Questions (3 Points Each)

210. Which team was defeated in the 2006 FIFA World Cup final by Italy?

a) Germany
b) France
c) Brazil
d) Argentina

211. Who won the Golden Boot at the 1982 FIFA World Cup?

a) Paolo Rossi
b) Michel Platini
c) Gary Lineker
d) Diego Maradona

212. Who was the first-ever player to score a hat-trick in a World Cup final match?

a) Geoff Hurst
b) Ronaldo Nazário
c) Just Fontaine
d) Pelé

213. Which country won the 2002 FIFA World Cup?

a) Brazil
b) Germany
c) France
d) South Korea

214. Which team reached the World Cup final three times but never won it?

a) Netherlands
b) Argentina
c) England
d) Portugal

> **Did you know?**
> The 1966 World Cup ball, nicknamed the "Challenge 4-Star," was the first official tournament ball to feature a fully synthetic coating, a revolutionary design for its time.

215. Who was the first non-European player to win the World Cup Golden Ball?

a) Zinedine Zidane

b) Diego Maradona

c) Pelé

d) Ronaldo Nazário

216. Which country became the first to win the World Cup twice in a row?

a) Germany

b) Brazil

c) Italy

d) Argentina

217. Which country is the only one to win the World Cup on four continents?

a) Argentina

b) Brazil

c) France

d) Italy

218. Which player holds the record for most goals in a World Cup match?

a) Miroslav Klose
b) Ronaldo Nazário
c) Oleg Salenko
d) Gerd Müller

219. Who won the 2018 FIFA World Cup Golden Ball for best player?

a) Luka Modrić
b) Kylian Mbappé
c) Harry Kane
d) Cristiano Ronaldo

Hard Questions (5 Points Each)

220. Which World Cup final had the most goals scored in a single match?

a) 1970
b) 1982
c) 1958
d) 1954

221. Which country has finished in 4th place at the World Cup the most times?

a) Brazil
b) Uruguay
c) Netherlands
d) France

223. Which team holds the record for most goals scored in a single World Cup tournament?

a) Brazil
b) Germany
c) Hungary
d) France

224. Which player scored the winning goal in the 1998 World Cup final?

a) Zinedine Zidane
b) Thierry Henry
c) Emmanuel Petit
d) David Trezeguet

225. Who is the youngest player ever to play in a World Cup match?

a) Pelé
b) Norman Whiteside
c) Michael Owen
d) Samuel Eto'o

226. Which country was the first to win the World Cup without losing a match?

a) Brazil
b) Italy
c) Argentina
d) Uruguay

227. Who is the only player to have scored in five different World Cups?

a) Pelé
b) Miroslav Klose
c) Cristiano Ronaldo
d) Lionel Messi

228. Which World Cup is known for the "Miracle of Bern," where West Germany defeated Hungary in the final?

a) 1954

b) 1966

c) 1974

d) 1982

> 📝 **What is your most memorable World Cup moment?** Whether it's a stunning goal, an unforgettable celebration, or a game-changing play, tell us about the moment that made the World Cup unforgettable for you.
> _____
> _____
> _____
> _____

229. Which team holds the record for the most goals conceded in a single World Cup tournament?

a) South Korea

b) Brazil

c) El Salvador

d) Spain

230. Which team became the first to win the World Cup after losing its opening match?

a) Germany
b) Argentina
c) Spain
d) Brazil

231. Which country scored the most goals in a single World Cup tournament, with 27 goals?

a) Brazil
b) Germany
c) Hungary
d) France

232. Which World Cup tournament featured the infamous "Battle of Santiago" between Chile and Italy?

a) 1962
b) 1954
c) 1970
d) 1982

233. Who was the first goalkeeper to win the Golden Glove award as the best keeper at the World Cup?

a) Manuel Neuer
b) Gianluigi Buffon
c) Lev Yashin
d) Michel Preud'homme

DREAM TEAM DRAFT: Pick Your Favorite Player!

Pick your favorite player from the list of three by considering their skills, achievements, and impact on the game. Think about their playing style and what makes them stand out. Choose the one you'd want on your dream team and see if your friends agree!

Central Midfielder

1. Diego Maradona	2. Andrea Pirlo	3. Frank Lampard

Maradona's genius on the ball was unrivaled, with his creativity and dribbling skills earning him the nickname "The Hand of God." His leadership and brilliance were key to Argentina's 1986 World Cup victory, where his solo goal against England became an iconic moment in soccer history.	A true maestro in the midfield, Pirlo was known for his precise passing, vision, and ability to dictate play. His influence was felt across Italy's 2006 World Cup win and Juventus' multiple Serie A triumphs, making him one of the best midfielders of his era.	One of the greatest goal-scoring midfielders in Premier League history, Lampard was known for his late runs into the box, brilliant passing, and leadership. His numerous domestic titles and Champions League victory with Chelsea cemented his place as a Chelsea legend.

YOUR PICK: _____

Stadium Spotlight

Get ready to put your soccer knowledge to the test! You'll see a picture of a famous stadium, and your challenge is to name it. If you're unsure, don't worry, three clues at the bottom of the page will help guide you to the right answer. Take a good look and see if you can recognize these iconic soccer venues!

YOUR ANSWER: _____

- This iconic stadium is shared by two rival Italian clubs.
- Known for its unique cylindrical towers and steep stands.
- Located in Milan.

Trophies in The Shadows

You'll see the silhouette of a famous soccer trophy. Your challenge is to guess which trophy it is just by its shape! If you need help, check the three clues at the bottom of the page. See if you can recognize them all!

YOUR ANSWER: _____

- Features a crown on top, symbolizing supremacy.
- Two lions are part of its design—one on top and one in the league's logo.
- Clubs with the most wins receive a special gold version.

7. Wonders, Records, and Standout Moments - Answers

Easy Questions

200. d) Uruguay
201. b) Mario Götze
202. c) France
203. a) Brazil
204. b) Hristo Stoichkov, Oleg Salenko
205. b) Miroslav Klose
206. b) Spain
207. b) 2010
208. a) Diego Maradona
209. c) Mexico

Normal Questions

210. b) France
211. a) Paolo Rossi
212. a) Geoff Hurst
213. a) Brazil
214. a) Netherlands
215. b) Diego Maradona
216. c) Italy

217. b) Brazil
218. c) Oleg Salenko
219. a) Luka Modrić

Hard Questions

220. c) 1958
221. b) Uruguay
223. c) Hungary
224. c) Emmanuel Petit
225. b) Norman Whiteside
226. d) Uruguay
227. c) Cristiano Ronaldo
228. a) 1954
229. a) South Korea
230. c) Spain
231. c) Hungary
232. a) 1962
233. d) Michel Preud'homme

Bonus Section

1. San Siro
2. The Premier League Trophy

7. Wonders, Records, and Standout Moments – Score

Section	Multiplier	Right Answers	Total Points
Easy Questions	x1		
Normal Questions	x3		
Hard Questions	x5		
Bonus	x10		
Ultimate Penalty Shootout	5 Points		
TOTAL POINTS			

MAX POINTS = 130

If you got 104 points or more you earned the:

Congratulations!

CHAPTER 8

Women's Soccer

Women's soccer has come a long way, breaking barriers and shattering expectations. From historic victories to inspiring role models, the women's game has grown into a global phenomenon. With incredible talent and passion, female players have proven time and again that they can hold their own on the world's biggest stages. In this chapter, you'll dive into the milestones and unforgettable moments that have defined women's soccer. Are you ready to test your knowledge of this inspiring and thrilling side of the game?

Easy Questions (1 Point Each)

234. Who won the Golden Boot in the 2019 FIFA Women's World Cup?

a) Ellen White
b) Megan Rapinoe
c) Alex Morgan
d) Marta

235. Which country won the 2015 FIFA Women's World Cup?

a) United States
b) Germany
c) Brazil
d) Japan

236. Which player is considered the all-time top scorer in FIFA Women's World Cup history?

a) Abby Wambach
b) Marta
c) Birgit Prinz
d) Christine Sinclair

237. Which country hosted the 2019 FIFA Women's World Cup?

a) United States
b) Canada
c) France
d) Germany

238. Which team won the most titles in the UEFA Women's Champions League?

a) Lyon
b) Barcelona
c) Wolfsburg
d) Arsenal

239. Who was the captain of the U.S. Women's National Team when they won the 1999 Women's World Cup?

a) Alex Morgan
b) Abby Wambach
c) Carla Overbeck
d) Carla Werden

240. Which nation has won the most FIFA Women's World Cup titles?

a) United States
b) Germany
c) Brazil
d) Japan

241. Which country won the first-ever Women's World Cup in 1991?

a) United States
b) Norway
c) China
d) Germany

242. Who won the Ballon d'Or Féminin in 2020?

a) Megan Rapinoe
b) Ada Hegerberg
c) None
d) Sam Kerr

243. Which player holds the record for the most goals scored in a single Women's World Cup tournament?

a) Alex Morgan
b) Abby Wambach
c) Marta
d) Michelle Akers

> **Which woman soccer player has inspired you the most?** Share your favorite female player and what makes her stand out in the history of the game.
> _____
> _____
> _____
> _____

Normal Questions (3 Points Each)

244. Which team did the U.S. Women's National Team defeat in the 2019 Women's World Cup final?

a) Brazil
b) Netherlands
c) France
d) Japan

245. Who was the first woman to score 100 goals for the U.S. Women's National Team?

a) Tiffeny Milbrett
b) Mia Hamm
c) Alex Morgan
d) Christine Sinclair

246. Which country won the 2017 UEFA Women's Euro?

a) Germany
b) Norway
c) Netherlands
d) Sweden

247. Which player became the first woman to score a World Cup goal in the 1991 Women's World Cup?

a) Carin Jennings
b) Mia Hamm
c) Linda Medalen
d) Ma Li

248. Which country won the 2017 FIFA U-20 Women's World Cup?

a) United States

b) Japan

c) France

d) England

> ⚽ **Ultimate Penalty Shootout**
> Answer 5 questions correctly in a row to earn 10 extra points.

249. Which player scored the fastest goal in Women's World Cup history, in just 30 seconds?

a) Birgit Prinz

b) Ellen White

c) Lena Videkull

d) Christine Sinclair

250. Who is the all-time top scorer in the history of the UEFA Women's Champions League?

a) Ada Hegerberg

b) Lotta Schelin

c) Inka Grings

d) Helen Ward

251. Which country was the host of the 2011 FIFA Women's World Cup?

a) Japan
b) Germany
c) China
d) United States

252. Who was the first woman to play in a professional men's match in England?

a) Alice Cooke
b) Emma Hayes
c) Stephanie Houghton
d) Stephania Leigh Roche

253. Which club did the legendary U.S. player Abby Wambach retire from in 2015?

a) Chicago Red Stars
b) Washington Spirit
c) Western New York Flash
d) Seattle Reign

Hard Questions (5 Points Each)

254. Which team has won the most titles in the history of the FA Women's Super League?

a) Arsenal
b) Manchester City
c) Chelsea
d) Liverpool

255. Which team did Brazil defeat to win their first Copa América Femenina title in 1991?

a) Argentina
b) Colombia
c) Chile
d) Paraguay

256. Which country won the 2022 FIFA U-20 Women's World Cup?

a) Japan
b) Spain
c) United States
d) France

257. Who was the first African woman to win the BBC Women's Footballer of the Year award?

a) Asisat Oshoala

b) Perpetua Nkwocha

c) Ngozi Okobi

d) Evelyn Nsiah-Asare

> **Did you know?**
> The first-ever goal in a FIFA Women's World Cup was scored by China's Ma Li during the opening match of the inaugural tournament in 1991.

258. Which country was the host of the 2023 FIFA Women's World Cup?

a) Canada

b) United States

c) Australia and New Zealand

d) France

259. Which team won the 2007 FIFA Women's World Cup?

a) Germany

b) United States

c) Norway

d) Brazil

260. Which player scored the first-ever goal in a Women's Olympic soccer final?

a) Cristiane
b) Heather O'Reilly
c) Abby Wambach
d) Shannon MacMillan

261. Which country was the first to win the Women's Olympic soccer tournament in 1996?

a) United States
b) Germany
c) Brazil
d) Norway

262. Who is the all-time top scorer for Canada's women's national soccer team?

a) Christine Sinclair
b) Diana Matheson
c) Kara Lang
d) Sophie Schmidt

263. Which country won the first-ever FIFA Women's U-17 Soccer World Cup in 2008?

a) United States
b) Brazil
c) France
d) North Korea

264. Who scored the decisive penalty that secured Japan's victory in the 2011 FIFA Women's World Cup Final?

a) Nadine Angerer
b) Birgit Prinz
c) Simone Laudehr
d) Saki Kumaga

265. Who was the first woman to score 500 goals for a soccer club?

a) Marta
b) Abby Wambach
c) Christine Sinclair
d) Carli Lloyd

266. Which country was the first to host the Women's FIFA World Cup twice?

a) United States
b) Germany
c) France
d) Japan

DREAM TEAM DRAFT: Pick Your Favorite Player!

Pick your favorite player from the list of three by considering their skills, achievements, and impact on the game. Think about their playing style and what makes them stand out. Choose the one you'd want on your dream team and see if your friends agree!

Attacking Midfielder

1. Ronaldinho	2. Johan Cruyff	3. Kevin De Bruyne

A magician with the ball at his feet, Ronaldinho's flair, creativity, and skill made him one of the most entertaining players to ever play the game. With his dazzling dribbles, no-look passes, and audacious tricks, he led Brazil to a World Cup in 2002 and won numerous titles with Barcelona.	One of the pioneers of Total Football, Cruyff was a visionary and a genius. His intelligence on the field and his ability to score and assist with ease made him a legend at both Ajax and Barcelona, and his influence still shapes modern soccer today.	De Bruyne is a modern maestro in the midfield, known for his incredible passing range, vision, and ability to create scoring opportunities for his teammates. His contributions have been key to Manchester City's dominance in English soccer over the past decade.

YOUR PICK: _____

Stadium Spotlight

Get ready to put your soccer knowledge to the test! You'll see a picture of a famous stadium, and your challenge is to name it. If you're unsure, don't worry, three clues at the bottom of the page will help guide you to the right answer. Take a good look and see if you can recognize these iconic soccer venues!

YOUR ANSWER: _____

- Famous for its "Yellow Wall," a massive single-tier stand.
- Located in a German city known for its passionate fans and black-and-yellow colors.
- Home to Borussia Dortmund.

Trophies in The Shadows

You'll see the silhouette of a famous soccer trophy. Your challenge is to guess which trophy it is just by its shape! If you need help, check the three clues at the bottom of the page. See if you can recognize them all!

YOUR ANSWER: _____

- Redesigned in 2019 with a sleek and modern look.
- Its intricate design features petal-like elements.
- Awarded to the best national team in Asia.

8. Women's Soccer - Answers

Easy Questions

234. b) Megan Rapinoe
235. a) United States
236. b) Marta
237. c) France
238. a) Lyon
239. c) Carla Overbeck
240. a) United States
241. a) United States
242. c) None
243. d) Michelle Akers

Normal Questions

244. b) Netherlands
245. a) Tiffeny Milbrett
246. c) Netherlands
247. d) Ma Li
248. d) England
249. c) Lena Videkull
250. a) Ada Hegerberg
251. b) Germany
252. d) Stephania Leigh Roche

253. c) Western New York Flash

Hard Questions

254. c) Chelsea
255. c) Chile
256. b) Spain
257. a) Asisat Oshoala
258. c) Australia and New Zealand
259. a) Germany
260. d) Shannon MacMillan
261. a) United States
262. a) Christine Sinclair
263. d) North Korea
264. d) Saki Kumaga
265. a) Marta
266. a) United States

Bonus Section

1. Signal Iduna Park
2. AFC Asian Cup Trophy

8. Women's Soccer – Score

Section	Multiplier	Right Answers	Total Points
Easy Questions	x1		
Normal Questions	x3		
Hard Questions	x5		
Bonus	x10		
Ultimate Penalty Shootout	10 Points		
TOTAL POINTS			

MAX POINTS = 135

If you got 108 points or more you earned the:

CHAPTER 9

Soccer and Pop Culture

Soccer's influence extends far beyond the field, leaving a lasting mark on pop culture around the world. From movies and music to fashion and advertising, the beautiful game has inspired creativity and captivated millions. Whether through iconic players, unforgettable commercials, or memorable moments in entertainment, soccer has become an integral part of global culture. In this chapter, you'll explore the fascinating ways soccer has intersected with pop culture. Ready to test your knowledge of the game's impact on the world outside the pitch?

Easy Questions (1 Point Each)

267. Which famous pop star did not perform at the opening ceremony of the 2014 FIFA World Cup in Brazil?

a) Claudia Leitte
b) Shakira
c) Pitbull
d) Jennifer Lopez

268. Which soccer player appeared in the 2006 movie Goal!?

a) Lionel Messi
b) Cristiano Ronaldo
c) Zinedine Zidane
d) Wayne Rooney

269. Which soccer legend appeared in the 1981 movie Escape to Victory alongside Sylvester Stallone?

a) Diego Maradona
b) Pelé
c) Johan Cruyff
d) Michel Platini

270. Which soccer player has a famous friendship with rapper Drake?

a) Lionel Messi

b) Cristiano Ronaldo

c) Daniel Sturridge

d) Zlatan Ibrahimović

271. Which singer released the 1998 World Cup anthem, "La Copa de la Vida"?

a) Ricky Martin

b) Enrique Iglesias

c) Shakira

d) Pitbull

> **Did you know?**
> In 1998, British pop group "The Spice Girls" teamed up with soccer stars to create a global cultural phenomenon known as "The Spice Boys," combining soccer and music in a way never seen before.

272. Which Hollywood actor played the role of a soccer player in the 2005 film Goal!?

a) Tom Cruise

b) Kuno Becker

c) Matthew McConaughey

d) Brad Pitt

273. Which team was the subject of the 2009 documentary The Beckham Experiment?

a) Manchester United
b) LA Galaxy
c) Paris Saint-Germain
d) Real Madrid

274. Which soccer player was famously featured in the 2005 video game FIFA Street?

a) Ronaldinho
b) Thierry Henry
c) Pelé
d) David Beckham

275. Which famous singer performed the opening act of the 2010 FIFA World Cup in South Africa?

a) Shakira
b) Beyoncé
c) Alicia Keys
d) Black Eyed Peas

276. In the 2000 movie Love Actually, which soccer player is seen on a wedding cake decoration?

a) David Beckham
b) John Terry
c) Ryan Giggs
d) Frank Lampard

Normal Questions (3 Points Each)

277. Which soccer legend starred in the 2014 film The Class of '92, a documentary about his rise at Manchester United?

a) Wayne Rooney
b) Eric Cantona
c) David Beckham
d) Ryan Giggs

278. Which famous soccer player made a cameo appearance in the 2004 movie EuroTrip?

a) Vinnie Jones
b) Zinedine Zidane
c) Ronaldo Nazário
d) Frank Lampard

279. Which rapper wrote and performed the song "Wavin' Flag," which became an anthem for the 2010 FIFA World Cup?

a) Jay-Z
b) K'naan
c) Drake
d) Pitbull

280. Which soccer player had his own clothing brand named after him, called "CR7"?

a) Neymar
b) Lionel Messi
c) Cristiano Ronaldo
d) Wayne Rooney

281. Which team did actor Will Ferrell famously support during the 2014 FIFA World Cup?

a) United States
b) Germany
c) Brazil
d) Spain

282. Which soccer star owns a chain of hotels?

a) Neymar Jr.
b) Lionel Messi
c) Cristiano Ronaldo
d) Zlatan Ibrahimović

283. Which famous soccer player made a cameo appearance in the TV show The Simpsons but was not included in the original U.S. broadcast?

a) David Beckham
b) Pelé
c) Cristiano Ronaldo
d) Thierry Henry

> **What's your favorite instance of soccer crossing over into pop culture?** Whether it's a commercial, a music video, or a movie cameo, tell us about the moment when soccer and pop culture collided in a memorable way.
> _____
> _____
> _____

284. Which famous pop icon had a famous feud with soccer legend David Beckham in the early 2000s, before they became friends?

a) Justin Bieber

b) Britney Spears

c) Paris Hilton

d) P. Diddy

285. In the 2009 movie The Ugly Truth, which soccer player does Katherine Heigl's character mention as being her "dream man"?

a) Lionel Messi

b) Cristiano Ronaldo

c) David Beckham

d) John Terry

286. Which famous soccer player appeared in the music video for the song "Miss Sarajevo" by U2?

a) Pelé

b) Cristiano Ronaldo

c) Diego Maradona

d) Lionel Messi

Hard Questions (5 Points Each)

287. Which singer collaborated with Shakira on the song "La La La (Brazil 2014)", the official anthem for the 2014 FIFA World Cup?

a) Carlinhos Brown
b) Rihanna
c) Beyoncé
d) Usher

288. Which famous soccer player had a recurring role on the television show The Simpsons?

a) David Beckham
b) Pele
c) Thierry Henry
d) Cristiano Ronaldo

289. Which soccer player appeared on the cover of the U.S. version of FIFA 98: Road to World Cup?

a) David Beckham
b) Roy Lassiter
c) Paolo Maldini
d) Raúl González

290. Which famous rapper gifted Neymar Jr. a custom-made diamond chain featuring his initials?

a) Drake
b) Travis Scott
c) Snoop Dogg
d) Jay-Z

291. Which soccer star voiced a character in the animated film Metegol (also known as Underdogs)?

a) Lionel Messi
b) Cristiano Ronaldo
c) Neymar Jr.
d) None

292. Which famous German soccer goalkeeper made a cameo appearance in the 2003 film The Miracle of Bern, which tells the story of the 1954 World Cup?

a) Oliver Kahn
b) Manuel Neuer
c) Jens Lehmann
d) Uli Stein

293. Which famous pop artist featured in a World Cup commercial for Coca-Cola in 2010?

a) Shakira
b) Beyoncé
c) Lady Gaga
d) Rihanna

294. Which soccer player was the inspiration behind the 2012 film Goal! The Dream Begins?

a) Zinedine Zidane
b) Cristiano Ronaldo
c) Alan Shearer
d) Pelé

295. In which 2009 film did former professional footballer Eric Cantona play a major role?

a) Looking for Eric
b) Goal II: Living the Dream
c) The Secret Player
d) Bend It Like Beckham

> **Ultimate Penalty Shootout**
> Answer 5 questions correctly in a row to earn 15 extra points.

296. Which soccer was offered a role in the 2009 action movie The Pink Panther 2 but declined?

a) Thierry Henry

b) Cristiano Ronaldo

c) David Beckham

d) Zlatan Ibrahimović

297. Which music superstar featured Lionel Messi in an Adidas commercial in 2024?

a) Beyoncé

b) Bad Bunny

c) Drake

d) Pharrell Williams

298. Which soccer legend has been featured in commercials for Adidas, often alongside famous actors like Robert De Niro?

a) Cristiano Ronaldo

b) Pelé

c) Lionel Messi

d) David Beckham

299. Which soccer player has appeared as a guest star in the television show How I Met Your Mother?

a) David Beckham
b) Cristiano Ronaldo
c) Lionel Messi
d) Neymar Jr.

300. Which international soccer star is known for his collaborations with fashion brands like H&M and has a prominent presence in the fashion world?

a) Cristiano Ronaldo
b) Neymar Jr.
c) David Beckham
d) Zlatan Ibrahimović

DREAM TEAM DRAFT: Pick Your Favorite Player!

Pick your favorite player from the list of three by considering their skills, achievements, and impact on the game. Think about their playing style and what makes them stand out. Choose the one you'd want on your dream team and see if your friends agree!

Right Winger

1. Arjen Robben	2. David Beckham	3. Sadio Mane

Known for his pace and deadly left foot, Robben was a constant threat on the right wing. His signature move—cutting inside and unleashing a powerful shot—was unstoppable for defenders. He was instrumental in Bayern Munich's success, including their 2013 Champions League victory.	A master of the crossing game, Beckham's ability to deliver inch-perfect balls from the right wing was unparalleled. His skill with set-pieces and precise free kicks made him a global icon, and his leadership helped England during their international campaigns.	A dynamic and explosive winger, Mane was known for his speed, dribbling, and clinical finishing. His role in Liverpool's success, including their Champions League and Premier League victories, made him one of the most impactful forwards in recent years.

YOUR PICK: _____

Left Winger

1. Franck Ribéry

A key figure in Bayern Munich's success, Ribéry was known for his speed, creativity, and ability to take on defenders. His dribbling and precise crosses made him one of the most dangerous wingers in Europe during his prime.

2. Gareth Bale

A powerful and fast winger, Bale combined athleticism with technical skill to become one of the most dangerous players in the world. His breathtaking runs and crucial goals for both Wales and Real Madrid made him a legend in his own right

3. Neymar Jr.

With dazzling dribbling skills and flair, Neymar is one of the most skillful and unpredictable players of his generation. His performances at Barcelona and Paris Saint-Germain have established him as one of the most talented wingers in world soccer.

YOUR PICK: _____

Stadium Spotlight

Get ready to put your soccer knowledge to the test! You'll see a picture of a famous stadium, and your challenge is to name it. If you're unsure, don't worry, three clues at the bottom of the page will help guide you to the right answer. Take a good look and see if you can recognize these iconic soccer venues!

YOUR ANSWER: _____

- The only stadium to host two FIFA World Cup finals.
- Located in the capital of Mexico.
- The site of Diego Maradona's "Goal of the Century."

Trophies in The Shadows

You'll see the silhouette of a famous soccer trophy. Your challenge is to guess which trophy it is just by its shape! If you need help, check the three clues at the bottom of the page. See if you can recognize them all!

YOUR ANSWER: _____

- Awarded to the top national team in North and Central America.
- Its design includes a tall, angular shape resembling a chalice.
- First awarded in 1991.

9. Soccer and Pop Culture - Answers

Easy Questions

267. b) Shakira
268. c) Zinedine Zidane
269. b) Pelé
270. a) Lionel Messi
271. a) Ricky Martin
272. b) Kuno Becker
273. b) LA Galaxy
274. a) Ronaldinho
275. a) Shakira
276. a) David Beckham

Normal Questions

277. c) David Beckham
278. a) Vinnie Jones
279. b) K'naan
280. c) Cristiano Ronaldo
281. a) United States
282. c) Cristiano Ronaldo
283. a) David Beckham
284. c) Paris Hilton
285. c) David Beckham

286. c) Diego Maradona

Hard Questions

287. a) Carlinhos Brown
288. b) Pele
289. b) Roy Lassiter
290. c) Snoop Dogg
291. d) None
292. a) Oliver Kahn
293. a) Shakira
294. c) Alan Shearer
295. a) Looking for Eric
296. c) David Beckham
297. b) Bad Bunny
298. d) David Beckham
299. a) David Beckham
300. c) David Beckham

Bonus Section

1. Estadio Azteca
2. CONCACAF Gold Cup

9. Soccer and Pop Culture - Score

Section	Multiplier	Right Answers	Total Points
Easy Questions	x1		
Normal Questions	x3		
Hard Questions	x5		
Bonus	x10		
Ultimate Penalty Shootout	15 Points		
TOTAL POINTS			

MAX POINTS = 145

If you got 116 points or more you earned the:

Congratulations!

CHAPTER 10

Fan Culture and Traditions

Fan culture and traditions are the heartbeat of soccer, fueling the passion that makes the game unforgettable. From electrifying stadiums to chants that unite millions, soccer fans create an energy like no other. In this chapter, you'll dive into the most exciting rituals and traditions that make soccer fandom truly legendary. Ready to explore the wild side of the beautiful game?

Easy Questions (1 Point Each)

301. What is the name of the famous chant often sung by Manchester United fans?

a) "You'll Never Walk Alone"
b) "Glory Glory Man United"
c) "Keep Right On"
d) "Take Me Home, Country Roads"

302. Which passionate soccer fan groups are known for creating large, colorful "Tifo" banners to show support for their team?

a) Casuals
b) Ultras
c) Hooligans
d) Nomads

303. Which famous song is sung by Liverpool supporters to cheer on their team?

a) "Sweet Caroline"
b) "Take Me Home, Country Roads"
c) "You'll Never Walk Alone"
d) "We Are the Champions"

304. Which German soccer team's fans are known for their 'Yellow Wall'?

a) Bayern Munich

b) Liverpool

c) Borussia Dortmund

d) PSG

305. What is the nickname for fans of the Argentina national team?

a) La Furia Roja

b) The Three Lions

c) La Albiceleste

d) The Azzurri

> ⚽ **Ultimate Penalty Shootout**
> Answer 5 questions correctly in a row to earn 5 extra points.

306. What is the tradition for Italian fans when they score a goal during a match?

a) They wave a white flag

b) They throw pizza

c) They light flares and sing

d) They release white doves

307. Which country's fans are known for throwing toilet paper onto the pitch during matches?

a) Brazil
b) Uruguay
c) Mexico
d) Chile

308. Which fan tradition in Brazil involves banging drums to create a rhythmic, energetic atmosphere during matches?

a) Samba
b) Bossa Nova
c) Carnival
d) Batucada

309. Which soccer team's fans are known for their "Barmy Army" chant?

a) England
b) Germany
c) Italy
d) Spain

310. What is the traditional name for the fan group of Celtic FC, which is known for their passionate displays of support?

a) The Green Brigade
b) Bhoys
c) The Blue Army
d) The Ultras

Normal Questions (3 Points Each)

311. Which team's fans are famously known for their "Ultras" supporters group?

a) AC Milan
b) Barcelona
c) Juventus
d) Manchester City

312. Which Premier League team's fans are known for singing the song "Keep Right On" to support their team?

a) Birmingham City
b) Manchester United
c) Chelsea
d) Tottenham Hotspur

313. What is the fan tradition called when supporters light flares and create a spectacle to support their team, especially in European matches?

a) Tifo
b) Ultras
c) Pyro display
d) Banner parade

314. Which South American country has a tradition of their national team's fans holding massive parades called "La Fiesta" after a win?

a) Argentina
b) Brazil
c) Colombia
d) Chile

 Did you know?
In Argentina, soccer fans are known for their passionate chants, with one of the most famous being "La 12," which is sung by Boca Juniors supporters, filling stadiums with energy.

315. Which national soccer team is most famously associated with the use of vuvuzelas, the loud plastic horns, during the 2010 FIFA World Cup?

a) Brazil

b) South Africa

c) Argentina

d) Germany

316. What is the name of Borussia Dortmund's famous fan section, known for its massive displays of support and standing capacity?

a) Curva Nord

b) South Stand

c) La Bombonera

d) Kop End

317. Which soccer club's fans are known for the chant "Blue is the Colour"?

a) Chelsea

b) Manchester United

c) Arsenal

d) Manchester City

318. Which team's supporters are known as the 'Red Devils'?

a) Manchester United
b) Liverpool
c) Barcelona
d) Bayern Munich

319. Which country's fans traditionally celebrate with a crowd wave during international tournaments?

a) Mexico
b) United States
c) Brazil
d) Spain

320. Which major international tournament has the tradition of 'Fandango' dance performed by fans in the stands?

a) FIFA World Cup
b) UEFA European Championship
c) Copa América
d) CONCACAF Gold Cup

Hard Questions (5 Points Each)

321. Which club's fans are known for their "Gooners" nickname?

a) Arsenal
b) Liverpool
c) Chelsea
d) Tottenham Hotspur

322. Which country's fans are known for bringing inflatable kangaroos to the stadium as part of their game-day tradition?

a) Australia
b) United States
c) Argentina
d) Netherlands

323. What is the name of the fans of **West Ham United**?

a) The Blades
b) The Hammers
c) The Toffees
d) The Red Devils

324. What is the name of the Italian soccer team's fan group that has become notorious for their ultra-passionate and often controversial fan support?

a) Curva Sud
b) The Ultras
c) Curva Norte
d) The Roman Legion

> 📝 **What's your favorite soccer tradition or fan ritual that you love being a part of?** Whether it's a chant, a tailgate, or the atmosphere at a live match, share the tradition that makes soccer more than just a game for you.
> _____
> _____
> _____
> _____

325. Which country's national team fans are famously known for their use of drums, trumpets, and flags to create a vibrant atmosphere?

a) Colombia
b) Brazil
c) Germany
d) Italy

326. Which European club's fans are famous for the "Pride of London" chant?

a) Chelsea
b) Arsenal
c) Tottenham Hotspur
d) West Ham United

327. Which country's soccer fans are known for wearing red and white striped clothing, inspired by the national flag?

a) Brazil
b) Denmark
c) Argentina
d) Italy

328. Which of the following is a fan tradition of Australian soccer supporters, especially those of the national team, the Socceroos?

a) Bringing inflatable kangaroos to the stadium
b) Singing "Waltzing Matilda" during matches
c) Performing the haka before games
d) Marching to the stadium singing "Advance Australia Fair"

329. Which English club's fans are famous for their "Yid Army" chant?

a) Chelsea
b) Tottenham Hotspur
c) Manchester United
d) Arsenal

330. Which club's fans are known for their "Red and White Army" chant?

a) Manchester United
b) Liverpool
c) Stoke City FC
d) Arsenal

331. What is the name of the famous 'fanzine' that Manchester United supporters have published since 1987?

a) Red Issue
b) United We Stand
c) Manchester News
d) Old Trafford Times

332. Which of the following unique traditions is associated with Spain's soccer fans during international matches?

a) Singing their national anthem with lyrics

b) Creating vocal renditions of their anthem without lyrics

c) Lighting flares during every goal

d) Performing a traditional dance before every match

333. Which club's fans are known for their song "I'm Forever Blowing Bubbles"?

a) West Ham United

b) Arsenal

c) Chelsea

d) Manchester City

DREAM TEAM DRAFT: Pick Your Favorite Player!

Pick your favorite player from the list of three by considering their skills, achievements, and impact on the game. Think about their playing style and what makes them stand out. Choose the one you'd want on your dream team and see if your friends agree!

Defensive Midfielder

1. Claude Makélélé	2. N'Golo Kanté	3. Roy Keane

Known as the unsung hero of midfield, Makélélé's ability to break up opposition attacks and his superb positional play made him a crucial figure for both Chelsea and Real Madrid. His role in holding the midfield allowed other players to shine.	A tireless ball-winner and a relentless worker, Kanté is known for his extraordinary stamina and ability to cover ground. His performances in Leicester City's 2016 Premier League win and Chelsea's 2018 World Cup victory made him one of the best defensive midfielders in the world.	One of the toughest midfielders ever to play the game, Keane's leadership, tackling, and commanding presence in the middle of the park were central to Manchester United's dominance in the late 1990s and early 2000s.

YOUR PICK: _____

Center-Forward

1. Pele

One of the most iconic and decorated players in soccer history, Pele was a goal-scoring machine with unparalleled technical skills and vision. His three World Cup victories with Brazil solidify him as one of the greatest strikers of all time.

2. Karim Benzema

Known for his link-up play, poise in front of goal, and versatility, Benzema has been Real Madrid's talisman for over a decade. His ability to score crucial goals and assist his teammates in vital moments has earned him recognition as one of the best strikers in modern soccer.

3. Zlatan Ibrahimović

A larger-than-life character on and off the pitch, Zlatan is renowned for his powerful presence, stunning goals, and supreme confidence. He has played for top clubs across Europe, leaving his mark at Barcelona, PSG, and Manchester United.

YOUR PICK: _____

Stadium Spotlight

Get ready to put your soccer knowledge to the test! You'll see a picture of a famous stadium, and your challenge is to name it. If you're unsure, don't worry, three clues at the bottom of the page will help guide you to the right answer. Take a good look and see if you can recognize these iconic soccer venues!

YOUR ANSWER: _____

- Famous for the anthem "You'll Never Walk Alone."
- Home to a club with deep roots in Merseyside, England.
- Known for its intimate and electric atmosphere.

Trophies in The Shadows

You'll see the silhouette of a famous soccer trophy. Your challenge is to guess which trophy it is just by its shape! If you need help, check the three clues at the bottom of the page. See if you can recognize them all!

YOUR ANSWER: _____

- A sleek, modern design featuring a spiral and a golden soccer at the top.
- First awarded in 1991 to highlight excellence in women's soccer.
- Stands 47 centimeters tall and weighs just over 4 kilograms.

10. Fan Culture and Traditions - Answers

Easy Questions

301. b) "Glory, Glory Man United"
302. b) Ultras
303. c) "You'll Never Walk Alone"
304. c) Borussia Dortmund
305. c) La Albiceleste
306. c) They light flares and sing
307. b) Uruguay
308. a) Samba
309. a) England
310. b) Bhoys

Normal Questions

311. a) AC Milan
312. a) Birmingham City
313. c) Pyro display
314. a) Argentina
315. b) South Africa
316. b) South Stand
317. a) Chelsea
318. a) Manchester United
319. a) Mexico

320. c) Copa América

Hard Questions

321. a) Arsenal
322. a) Australia
323. b) The Hammers
324. b) The Ultras
325. b) Brazil
326. a) Chelsea
327. b) Denmark
328. a) Bringing inflatable kangaroos to the stadium
329. b) Tottenham Hotspur
330. c) Stoke City FC
331. b) United We Stand
332. b) Creating vocal renditions of their anthem without lyrics
333. a) West Ham United

Bonus Section

1. Anfield
2. Women's World Cup Trophy

10. Fan Culture and Traditions – Score

Section	Multiplier	Right Answers	Total Points
Easy Questions	x1		
Normal Questions	x3		
Hard Questions	x5		
Bonus	x10		
Ultimate Penalty Shootout	5 Points		
TOTAL POINTS			

MAX POINTS = 130

If you got 104 points or more you earned the:

Congratulations!

YOUR COMPLETE DREAM TEAM DRAFT

POSITION	PLAYER NAME
Goalkeeper:	
Central Defender:	
Midfielder:	
Striker:	
Right-Back:	
Left-Back:	
Central Midfielder:	
Attacking Midfielder:	
Right Winger:	
Left Winger	
Defensive Midfielder	
Center-Forward	

Write your favorite's coach name or put your own name!

Coach: _____

TOTAL SCORE AND RANKS

Chapter	Score
1. Greatest Matches of All Time	
2. Unforgettable Goals	
3. Legendary Coaches and Tactics	
4. The Underdogs	
5. Rivalries and Derbies	
6. Golden Boot and Records	
7. World Cup Wonders	
8. Women's Soccer	
9. Soccer and Pop Culture	
10. Fan Culture and Traditions	
TOTAL POINTS	

MAX POINTS = 1,355

Ranks

- 0–338: Benchwarmer 🏟️
- 339–677: Passionate Supporter 🎉
- 678–1,015: Mastermind Manager 💬 ⚽
- 1,016+: Legendary Icon 🏆

213

¡Congratulations!

Images Attributions

Soccer Players

1. **Lev Yashin:** [1], Public domain, via Wikimedia Commons

2. **Gianluigi Buffon:** PUMA, CC BY 3.0 <https://creativecommons.org/licenses/by/3.0>, via Wikimedia Commons

3. **Manuel Neuer:** Michael Kranewitter, CC BY-SA 3.0 <https://creativecommons.org/licenses/by-sa/3.0>, via Wikimedia Commons

4. **Franz Beckenbauer:** Panini Group, Public domain, via Wikimedia Commons

5. **Virgil van Dijk:** Ailura, CC BY-SA 3.0 AT, CC BY-SA 3.0 AT <https://creativecommons.org/licenses/by-sa/3.0/at/deed.en>, via Wikimedia Commons

6. **Bobby Moore:** Panini, Public domain, via Wikimedia Commons

7. **Zinedine Zidane:** Walterlan Papetti, CC BY-SA 4.0 <https://creativecommons.org/licenses/by-sa/4.0>, via Wikimedia Commons

8. **Michel Platini:** Panini, Public domain, via Wikimedia Commons

9. **Xavi Hernandez:** Fars Media Corporation, CC BY 4.0 <https://creativecommons.org/licenses/by/4.0>, via Wikimedia Commons

10. **Cristiano Ronaldo:** Student News Agency, CC BY 4.0 <https://creativecommons.org/licenses/by/4.0>, via Wikimedia Commons

11. **Lionel Messi:** Кирилл Венедиктов, CC BY-SA 3.0 GFDL, via Wikimedia Commons

12. **Thierry Henry:** Web Summit, CC BY 2.0 <https://creativecommons.org/licenses/by/2.0>, via Wikimedia Commons

13. **Cafu:** Palácio do Planalto from Brasilia, Brasil, CC BY 2.0 <https://creativecommons.org/licenses/by/2.0>, via Wikimedia Commons

14. **Gary Neville:** University of Salford Press Office, CC BY 2.0 <https://creativecommons.org/licenses/by/2.0>, via Wikimedia Commons

15. **Dani Carvajal:** Football.ua, CC BY-SA 3.0 GFDL, via Wikimedia Commons

16. **Roberto Carlos:** Diario de Madrid, CC BY 4.0 <https://creativecommons.org/licenses/by/4.0>, via Wikimedia Commons

17. **Ashley Cole:** Football.ua, CC BY-SA 3.0 GFDL, via Wikimedia Commons

18. **Marcelo:** Granada, CC BY-SA 4.0 <https://creativecommons.org/licenses/by-sa/4.0>, via Wikimedia Commons

19. **Diego Maradona:** Gerardo Prego, Public domain, via Wikimedia Commons

20. **Andrea Pirlo:** Biser Todorov (original picture), Mess (derivative work), CC BY 3.0 <https://creativecommons.org/licenses/by/3.0>, via Wikimedia Commons

21. **Frank Lampard:** Fars Media Corporation, CC BY 4.0 <https://creativecommons.org/licenses/by/4.0>, via Wikimedia Commons

22. **Ronaldinho:** Darz Mol, CC BY-SA 2.5 ES <https://creativecommons.org/licenses/by-sa/2.5/es/deed.en>, via Wikimedia Commons

23. **Johan Cruyff:** Nationaal Archief, CC BY-SA 3.0 NL <https://creativecommons.org/licenses/by-sa/3.0/nl/deed.en>, via Wikimedia Commons

24. **Kevin De Bruyne:** Кирилл Венедиктов, CC BY-SA 3.0 GFDL, via Wikimedia Commons

25. **Arjen Robben:** Дмитрий Садовников, CC BY-SA 3.0 GFDL, via Wikimedia Commons

26. **David Beckham:** Calebrw at en.wikipedia, CC BY-SA 3.0 <https://creativecommons.org/licenses/by-sa/3.0>, via Wikimedia Commons

27. **Sadio Mane:** Екатерина Лаут, CC BY-SA 3.0 GFDL, via Wikimedia Commons

28. **Franck Ribéry:** Christophe95, CC BY-SA 3.0 <https://creativecommons.org/licenses/by-sa/3.0>, via Wikimedia Commons

29. **Gareth Bale:** Tasnim News Agency, CC BY 4.0 <https://creativecommons.org/licenses/by/4.0>, via Wikimedia Commons

30. **Neymar Jr.:** Ailura, CC BY-SA 3.0 AT, CC BY-SA 3.0 AT <https://creativecommons.org/licenses/by-sa/3.0/at/deed.en>, via Wikimedia Commons

31. **Claude Makélélé:** Web Summit Qatar, CC BY 2.0

<https://creativecommons.org/licenses/by/2.0>, via Wikimedia Commons

32. **N'Golo Kanté:** Кирилл Венедиктов, CC BY-SA 3.0 GFDL, via Wikimedia Commons

33. **Roy Keane:** Irish Defence Forces from Ireland, CC BY 2.0 <https://creativecommons.org/licenses/by/2.0>, via Wikimedia Commons

34. **Pele:** El Gráfico, Public domain, via Wikimedia Commons

35. **Karim Benzema:** Football.ua, CC BY-SA 3.0 GFDL, via Wikimedia Commons

36. **Zlatan Ibrahimović:** Tasnim News Agency, CC BY 4.0 <https://creativecommons.org/licenses/by/4.0>, via Wikimedia Commons

Stadiums

1. Camp Nou
File:Camp Nou aerial (cropped).jpg. (2024, July 10). *Wikimedia Commons.* Retrieved 01:32, February 25, 2025 from https://commons.wikimedia.org/w/index.php?title=File:Camp_Nou_aerial_(cropped).jpg&oldid=896094955.

2. Santiago Bernabeu

File:Estadio Santiago Bernabéu 39.jpg. (2024, October 24). *Wikimedia Commons*. Retrieved 01:41, February 25, 2025 from https://commons.wikimedia.org/w/index.php?title=File:Estadio_Santiago_Bernab%C3%A9u_39.jpg&oldid=948927815.

3. Old Trafford

File:Manchester United Old Trafford.jpg. (2023, October 16). *Wikimedia Commons*. Retrieved 01:42, February 25, 2025 from https://commons.wikimedia.org/w/index.php?title=File:Manchester_United_Old_Trafford.jpg&oldid=812191487.

4. Wembley Stadium

File:Wembley Stadium, London, UK.jpg. (2022, December 13). *Wikimedia Commons*. Retrieved 01:43, February 25, 2025 from https://commons.wikimedia.org/w/index.php?title=File:Wembley_Stadium,_London,_UK.jpg&oldid=714883252.

5. Maracana

File:Maracana stadium, brazil - panoramio.jpg. (2024, November 29). *Wikimedia Commons*. Retrieved 01:44, February 25, 2025 from https://commons.wikimedia.org/w/index.php?title=File:Maracana_stadium,_brazil_-_panoramio.jpg&oldid=963199366.

6. Allianz Arena
File:Allianz-Arena-München.jpg. (2023, August 2). *Wikimedia Commons*. Retrieved 01:47, February 25, 2025 from https://commons.wikimedia.org/w/index.php?title=File:Allianz-Arena-M%C3%BCnchen.jpg&oldid=789358267.

7. San Siro
File:San Siro 2014.jpg. (2022, January 1). *Wikimedia Commons*. Retrieved 01:46, February 25, 2025 from https://commons.wikimedia.org/w/index.php?title=File:San_Siro_2014.jpg&oldid=618303652.

8. Signal Iduna Park
File:Signal iduna park stadium dortmund 4.jpg. (2024, October 31). *Wikimedia Commons*. Retrieved 01:55, February 25, 2025 from https://commons.wikimedia.org/w/index.php?title=File:Signal_iduna_park_stadium_dortmund_4.jpg&oldid=951471990.

9. Estadio Azteca
File:Estadio Azteca desde el aire 1.jpg. (2024, November 1). *Wikimedia Commons*. Retrieved 01:57, February 25, 2025 from https://commons.wikimedia.org/w/index.php?title=File:Estadio_Azteca_desde_el_aire_1.jpg&oldid=951627118.

10. Anfield

File:Liverpool anfield road stadium.jpg. (2024, November 28). *Wikimedia Commons*. Retrieved 01:58, February 25, 2025 from https://commons.wikimedia.org/w/index.php?title=File:Liverpool_anfield_road_stadium.jpg&oldid=962742186.

Don't forget to download your player rating diploma!

https://playmakerbooks.com/player-stats-us

Showcase your score on every single chapter of the book and your achievements to your friends with our FREE player rating diploma!

How do you like our book?

Please consider leaving a review. We would love to hear your feedback
as we are always trying to create better and better books.

Thank you so much, we truly appreciate it.

Have any questions?
Send us an email: info@playmakerbooks.com
Follow us on Instagram:
@playmaker_books

Made in United States
Cleveland, OH
04 February 2026

FIRE STORM

by

Ethan Ross

Shield  Crest

© Copyright 2018 Ethan Ross

All rights reserved

This book shall not, by way of trade or otherwise, be lent, re-sold, hired out, or otherwise circulated without the prior consent of the copyright holder or the publisher in any form of binding or cover other than that in which it is published and without a similar condition including this condition being imposed on the subsequent purchaser. The use of its contents in any other media is also subject to the same conditions.

ISBN: 978-1-912505-32-6

MMXVIII

A CIP catalogue record for this book is available from the British Library

Published by
ShieldCrest Publishing Ltd.,
Aylesbury, Buckinghamshire,
HP22 5RR England
Tel: +44 (0) 333 8000 890
www.shieldcrest.co.uk

This book is dedicated to Elisabeth, her loving family and her tireless enthusiasm.

Other books by the author

Point Of No Return
(Part of the Jack Copeland Series)
(ISBN: 9781912505098)

Executive Protection – The Next Level
(ISBN: 9781911090847)

Forgive your enemies,
but never forget their names

John Fitzgerald Kennedy

Plans are useless,
but planning is essential

Winston Leonard Spencer-Churchill

Courage is what it takes to stand up and speak. Courage is also what it takes to sit down and listen.

Winston Leonard Spencer-Churchill

The price paid by those who seek to make the world a better place, is testament to those who continue in the face of fear and the unknown.

Ethan Ross

Abbreviations

JSC	-	Johnson Space Centre
ISS	-	International Space Station
SMS	-	Shuttle Mission Simulator
STS	-	Space Transportation System
GNS	-	Guidance & Navigation Simulator
SST	-	Single Systems Trainer
SVMF	-	Space Vehicle Mock-up Facility
JGTF	-	Jake Garn Training Facility
NBL	-	Neutral Buoyancy Laboratory
SCTF	-	Sonny Carter Training Facility
LPS	-	Launch Processing System
KSC	-	Kennedy Space Centre
ASCANs		Astronaut Candidates
EVA	-	Extra Vehicular Activities
NASA	-	National Aeronautical Space Administration
VRL	-	Virtual Reality Laboratory
SES	-	Systems Engineering Simulator
SDI	-	Strategic Defence Initiative
POTUS		President of the United States
IMCC	-	Integrated Mission Control Centre
FLOTUS		First Lady of the United States
R & D	-	Research and Development
SVR	-	Russia's Foreign Intelligence Service
Intel	-	Intelligence
IMU	-	Islamic Movement of Uzbekistan
MMPI	-	Minnesota Multiphasic Personality Inventory
SAD	-	Special Activities Division of the CIA
NSA	-	National Security Agency

IMEI	-	International Mobile Equipment Identity
SIM	-	Subscriber Identity Module
CNN	-	Cable News Network
OPF	-	Orbiter Processing Facility
VAB	-	Vehicle Assembly Building
TPS	-	Thermal Protection System
FRR	-	Flight Readiness Review
PoI	-	Person of Interest
WSMR	-	White Sands Missile Range
JTTF	-	Joint Terrorism Task Force
FBI	-	Federal Bureau of Investigation
HRT	-	Hostage Rescue Team
MIA	-	Missing in Action
ICBM	-	Inter-Continental Ballistic Missile
KIA	-	Killed in Action
NTR	-	Nothing to Report

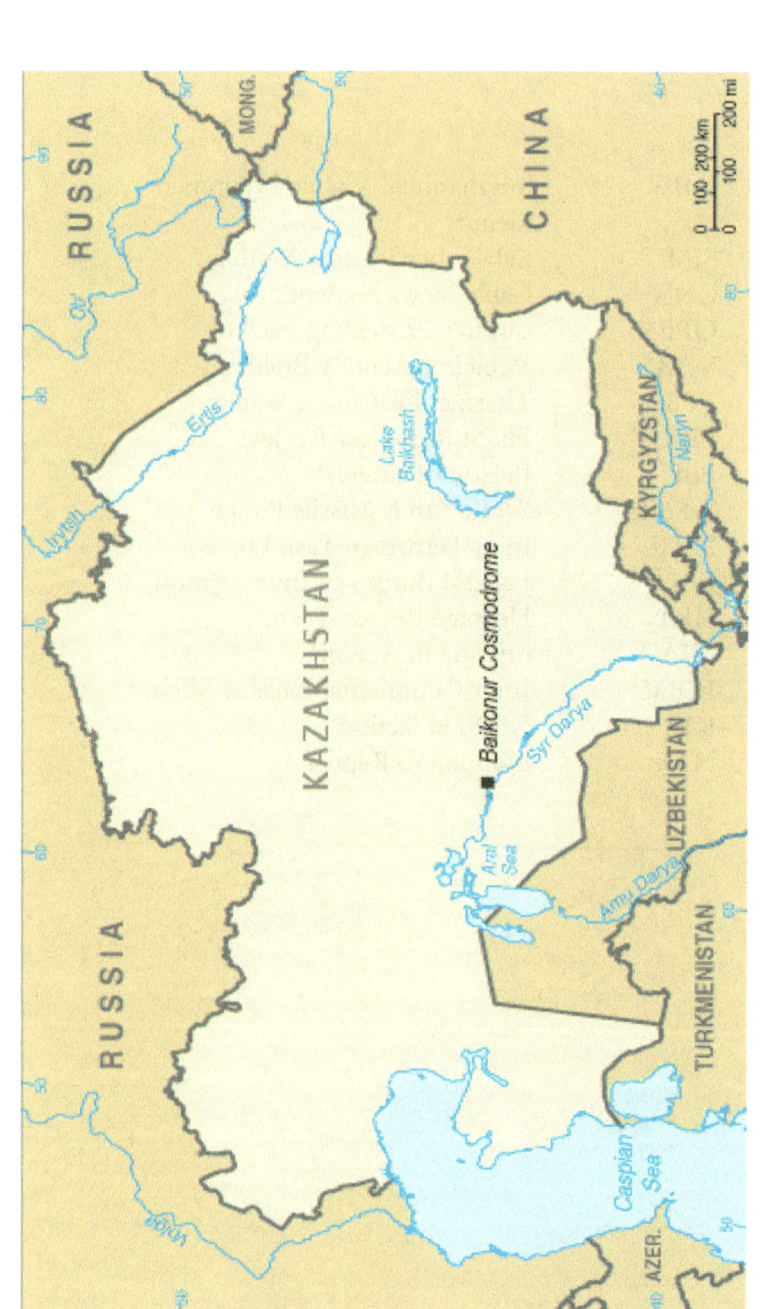

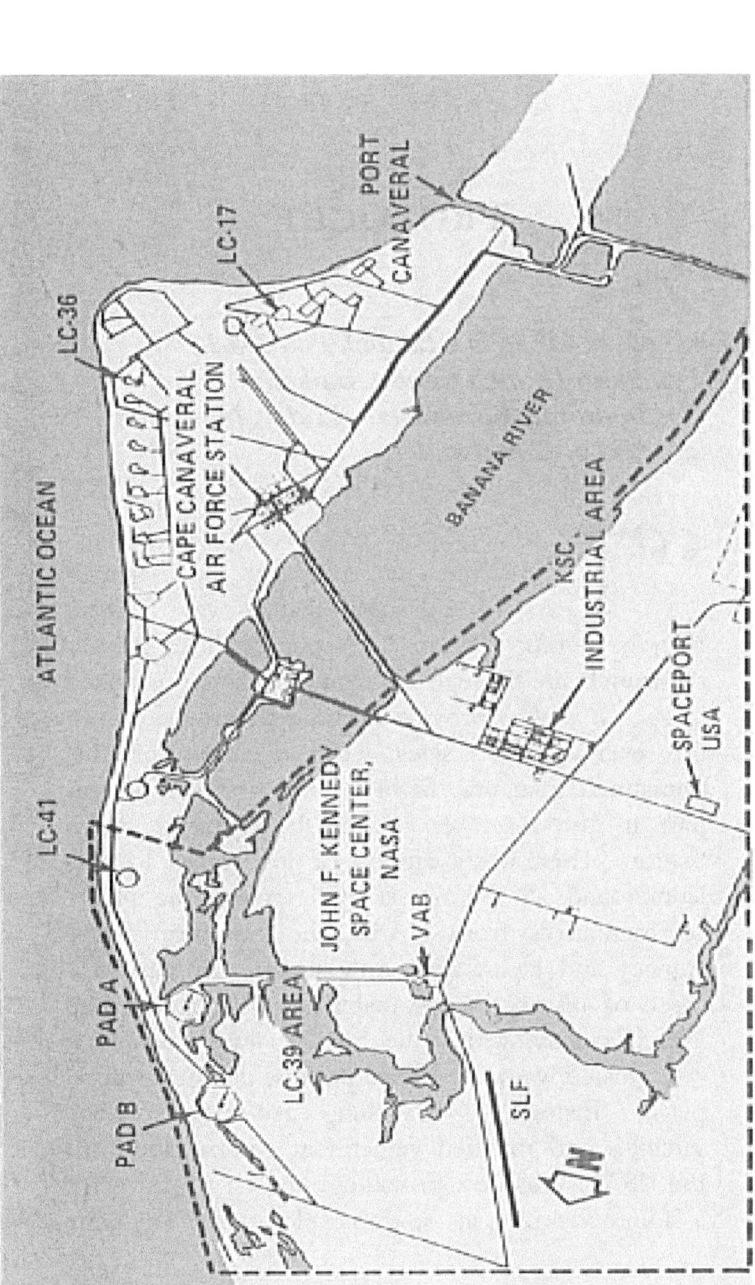

PROLOGUE

45° 63' N 63° 26'E – Launch Pad 333-L, Tyuratam Launch Centre, Baikonur Cosmodrome, Kazakhstan, Friday, November 20th 1998 at 1230 p.m. local

"T*minus tridtsat' odin sekund do zapuska*" came the voice over the loud speaker system indicating that it was *T minus thirty-one seconds to launch*. The sound echoed around the launch site through the many speakers positioned in such a way to provide maximum immersion into the event. The skies were overcast for this unmanned inaugural flight of the first component part in the assembly of the International Space Station. There was a window of opportunity for this launch and all the media eyes around the globe, representatives from NASA, the European Space Agency and Japan were now focused on this new piece of history in the making. This once secret launch facility, which the Soviets always denied it ever existed was now a focal point with a new role to play. Instead of launching geo-stationary spy satellites and manned vehicles in competition with the USA, it was now providing the first platform for a joint venture in space exploration. The one hundred and eighty-foot-long Proton rocket contained in its nose fairing, the two hundred and thirty-eight million-dollar Zarya Control Module, the Russian name for *'Sunrise'* – aptly named to symbolize the dawn of a new era in space. The countdown continued to be controlled and monitored by Mission Control Centre at Korolev, Russia; controllers at the Johnson Space Centre in Houston, Texas were also monitoring this event. Two minutes before the programmed launch time came the words; *"Posledovatel'nost' zazhiganiye"* signifying the start of the ignition sequence. Once the six stage RD-276 engines powered up and reached forty per cent thrust at 1.75 seconds then one hundred per cent at T minus 0.9 seconds then the final countdown would be initiated, *"Pyat, chetyre, tri, dva, odin. Zapusk podtverzhdayetsya T plyus pyat"* came the final words indicating that a successful launch had been confirmed at T plus five seconds and the spacecraft was now airborne and in a positive rate of climb. The six Proton rockets thundered the craft away on a planned trajectory to an initial orbit of two hundred and twenty miles above the earth. Ten minutes after launch, the Proton's third stage separated from Zarya, triggering a sequence of pre-programmed commands to deploy critical communications and rendezvous antennas. Three minutes later, Zarya's large solar arrays unfurled, enabling the module to convert sunlight in to electricity through a wingspan of eighty feet. Zarya at forty one feet long and thirteen and a half feet wide was designed as the ISS's primary link with earth as well as its only source of power, propulsion and control. Its construction was funded by NASA and constructed in Moscow by Boeing and the Khrunichev State Research and Production Space Centre. From inception to completion it took four years. The modules engines and the 36 steering jets would control its orbit around earth with a six-ton reservoir of propellant to fuel altitude and orientation changes. Three hours later, computer commands were sent to Zarya by Russian Mission Control to place the module in an orientation that would provide the essential heating on the spacecraft. The first stage of this 'Space Laboratory' was now in place, which would be used primarily as a passageway, docking port and fuel storage site. The months and years to follow would see at least a further fifty slated STS launches of the US Shuttles Destiny, Hope and Horizon, including the Soviet Proton rockets that would deliver additional components expanding the size and configuration of the ISS. The only thing missing now on this feat of an engineering masterpiece, were its crew.

CHAPTER 1

Washington DC – July 2000

Since returning from his last mission in Africa, Jack Copeland had semi-retired from special ops missions and was now a desk jockey in the capital; something that he always vowed he would never do. Having met Elisabeth though, a CNN reporter on that same fateful mission she had changed his life completely. He was following his heart but wasn't quite sure where it was going and that he was sensing that he was at the crossroads already. He decided to leave his office at Scorpion a little earlier than usual. It was Friday after all and the weekend was looming but he wanted to take Elisabeth away for a break. She deserved one, in fact they both did. Copeland liked Point Lookout State Park at the southern point of Maryland on the west side of Chesapeake Bay. He wanted a break and to do a little swimming, fishing, boating and to camp out under the stars. It's a great historical site and being only eighty-six miles away and a two-hour drive, it seemed a perfect place to get away from the hustle and bustle of city living. The sky was blue; the temperature was in the high eighties; it had all the ingredients of being perfect. The forecast predicted similar conditions over the next few weeks. As he drove along the freeway, Copeland lowered the top down on his BMW convertible and took in the fresh air as he contemplated the weekend ahead. He had stopped en-route at a street vendor selling flowers and bought a bunch of her favourite white roses with a mixture of lilies. He arrived at the apartment still not sure what to do, parked his car in the underground car park and took the lift to the sixteenth floor. Copeland entered the apartment and immediately noticed the trouble to which Elisabeth had gone in arranging the table. It had the hallmarks of some good or bad news. He hoped it would be the former.

"Hey" he said before continuing, "what's this?"

He enquired suspiciously as he handed over the flowers.

"Hi Jack, does there have to be a reason for everything? What happened to spontaneity and good old-fashioned romance?" Elisabeth said defensively with a coy look over her shoulder as she walked towards the kitchen to get a vase for the flowers. Copeland approached Elisabeth and kissed her passionately. He held her hands and looked in to her big blue eyes. Since meeting Elisabeth, the previous year, Copeland had thought that his life had taken a new twist since his divorce and that he had truly found the one person with whom he would long to spend the rest of his life with. He knew that since they were both still young and active, the zest for increased adventure and new challenges would be something that both would have to face eventually.

It wouldn't be easy and it was always in the back of his mind that one day…no surely that's not the reason for the romantic place settings. What he couldn't come to terms with would be the timing no matter how prepared he was. Copeland decided on a pre-emptive strike.

"I know you're about to tell me something, judging by this." he said pointing to the table before continuing "and it is probably something I'm not going to like. Break it to me gently though and go easy."

"It's impossible to keep anything from you Jack. I was hoping you could have waited until we had at least sat down together"

Elisabeth returned from the kitchen and placed the vase on the dining table and slightly adjusted the stems so they splayed evenly.

"Is it good or bad news?" insisted Copeland

"It's good news," she said positively.

Copeland looked at Elisabeth and paused briefly, "For who?" he said hesitantly then realising it might come across in a way he hadn't intended to. "Sorry love, that came out wrong"

He removed his coat and hung it next to Elisabeth's coat on the spare hook behind the apartment door. She told him to sit down at the table, which he did whilst she brought out the meal and wine. Copeland opened the bottle of her favourite Chilean red and poured two glasses. Elisabeth began to help herself to the servings after which Copeland did the same. Above the small talk, there was a sense of quietness as he was waiting for Elisabeth to continue and the bombshell to be dropped. He had found true happiness and it would seem all that was about to change. Copeland was finding it hard to grasp why life could be so cruel sometimes. Was she seeing someone else; is that why she wanted to go away. He inwardly felt as though he was being selfish and not fully understanding her needs and that she had a full and varied career of her own. He didn't want to pin her down nor did he want to lose her and therefore wasn't sure how to fully handle this. Both were career like-minded individuals so had never talked about having children. Copeland was happy not to since he already had a sixteen-year-old from his marriage and a gut instinct told him that Elisabeth wasn't too fussed either way. He looked along the table and gazed in to her beautiful eyes and reminisced about the first time he had seen her in Sierra Leone. He had fallen in love with her then and his feelings were the same now if not stronger. Living with someone energises those feelings and to have them torn away would be the hardest thing he would have to come to terms with. On the other hand, it could strengthen what they have already.

"Okay, what's the deal?" he began

"Jack" she said gathering her thoughts and placing her knife and fork onto the edge of her plate hoping to choose the right words before continuing, "I've been asked if I would like to go back in to front line international reporting."

"I guessed as much. Where this time?" he asked curtly and realising it was a sharp response.

"Russia" she said quietly almost muffling the words.

"Where?" he exclaimed, "Russia. That's the other side of the world. Don't you have to learn a little Russian or something? I mean it would come in handy."

"I know a little Russian to get by, but my bosses will let me attend classes to brush up"

"This is all a bit of a shock, a bit sudden. I could sense though that you weren't entirely happy being in Washington. Itchy feet I think it's called."

"Jack, it's not that at all." Elisabeth interrupted "I love it here and I love being with you but there is so much going on in the world that's being missed and I need to be there to report it."

"If I was to be honest with myself," he paused "then I did expect something like this eventually but never thought in my wildest dreams that it would happen so soon. Russia wasn't on my list of possibilities either. Does it mean promotion? What would you be doing there? Will I be able to contact you or come and see you anytime?"

Elisabeth raised her hands, "Jack sweetie, stop. There are just too many questions to which I don't have the answers at the moment. I haven't gone yet."

"When are you expected to leave?"

"Not for a couple of months." She hoped that the time frame might ease the situation slightly. "So, what do you think?"

"Why are you asking me? It's obvious you've already made your mind up."

"I really need your support on this one Jack. I need to know you're behind me."

Copeland knew that if he said anything else then it might just exacerbate the situation and she would storm off in a huff. He would be sleeping in the spare bedroom and they wouldn't talk with each other for days. That wouldn't resolve anything. He would have to sit tight and talk through what was about to change their lives. He needed to face this head on and either come to terms with it or insist she remain in Washington. The latter was non-negotiable, as he knew he wouldn't win that argument. That left just one option.

"I'm really pleased for you sweetheart. I really am and that was selfish of me to react that way. I won't stand in your way. I love you and you have to follow your instincts. At the moment, yours is in reporting. From some of our briefing notes, isn't Russia a little volatile?"

"I'll have to read up on the bureau notes. Don't know much about Russia. It's a whole new ball game for me. I understand it is now called the Russian Federation and includes lots of satellite states. It's another learning curve Jack. That's about it really. Now what about you? How was your day?" she asked trying to quickly change the subject.

"I'm being haunted by the events in Afghanistan. It now seems that the tyrant survived the blitz and has vowed to take an even stronger revenge. He hasn't said where but I'm sure it's going to be something big. I'm getting agitated Elisabeth. I'm keen to get back too. I started this so I'm gonna have a damn good try at finishing it."

Copeland couldn't believe he had just said that. He began thinking that it was probably with Elisabeth wanting to get back that had prompted him to feel the same way. Could he be on the re-bound or was he really missing the buzz. He continued "This semi-retirement lark is all well and good if all you want to do is play golf all day, but I miss the action and the guys."

"So, why don't you request re-assignment full time?"

"I want the DoD to come to me, then that way I know they can't do without me. I did a good job really in Africa besides the personal sacrifices and costs in human lives and the Pentagon knows that. They won't admit it though. They'll contact me rest assured. Anyhow, let's toast." Both Copeland and Elisabeth raised their glasses.

"You're a stubborn old mule Jack but you're a damned fine soldier and a great lover. What shall we toast?" she asked with a seductive smile.

"Here's to us, our future and whatever challenges there are along the way."

"I'll second that" she said as she clinked Copeland's glass. He felt more relaxed now having discussed matters.

They both moved to the sofa after the meal and toast. Copeland placed his arm over the back of the sofa and onto Elisabeth's shoulder. She began to snuggle up to him.

"So, when did you learn Russian then?" he asked as if he was trying to get to know her all over again.

"At College and as part of my media studies."

"You're a dark horse Elisabeth, have you ever had to use it?"

"No, but I can still remember a fair amount. That's why I was probably asked if I would like to work out of the Moscow office."

"How long though? You must have some idea?"

"I honestly don't know Jack. How long is a piece of string? Don't put any pressure on me though will you. You know how important my work is to me. I know you understand and that's why I love you. You'll get your assignment soon I'm sure and who knows you may be sent to Russia."

"Sounds like some kind of punishment," he said managing a smile before continuing, "we're not drifting apart are we?" tested Copeland

"No, this will definitely test how strong our relationship is. It can only make us stronger if we both work at it." she said reassuringly. "It's not as if I'm incommunicado or anything. We have all the latest techno gadgets, e-mail, telephones, facsimiles, and satellites. The Russians do have telephones you know."

"Yeah, but there all bugged." insisted Copeland

"I'm sure we'll be okay."

"Let's go away for the weekend." He asked hoping she would be as keen as he was.

"That'll be great. Where were you thinking?"

"Do you remember our camping trip to Point Lookout last year?"

"I do indeed. That'll be perfect Jack. Let's leave first thing in the morning. I'll put a picnic together for us."

Elisabeth stood up from the couch, grabbed Copeland's hand and led him towards the bedroom. As they moved through the doorway, Elisabeth turned and passionately embraced and kissed Copeland. She then released herself and walked backwards towards the bed in a provocative and tantalising way undoing her blouse as she went revealing her hidden charms. Copeland wasn't going to deny himself this opportunity of showing how much he loved and cared for her. Whilst unbuckling his belt, he deftly closed the door behind him.

* * *

3 Months later – October 2000
John F Kennedy Airport, New York – Terminal 8

Copeland drove Elisabeth towards JFK for her outbound flight to Moscow via London. Their moods were sombre, no one wishing to speak. The traffic flowed freely along the Van Wyck expressway as Copeland followed the American Airlines departure signs towards Terminal 8 and then the short-term parking lot signs. He pulled in to a vacant slot close to the departure area, unloaded the cases and placed them on to a trolley that he had recovered from a nearby trolley bay. Elisabeth looked at the airport structure as if seeing it for the last time and wanting to have a lasting impression.

"You've got enough clothes here to last years," quipped Copeland as he smiled before continuing, "you may have to pay excess baggage."

"I know but I need to be prepared for all the different weathers they seem to get. I would imagine it would be more inclined to be cold than warm with the chill from Siberia and all that."

"You've got your tickets and passport, haven't you?" he asked as they moved towards the terminal building. He knew that she would have them but just wanted to be sure.

"It's a bit late to ask me now Jack" quipped Elisabeth as she locked her arms in to his. As Copeland pushed the baggage trolley single-handedly towards the terminal they both stepped through the automatic doors and headed towards the American Airlines first class check in desk. Copeland had second-guessed that Elisabeth's bosses would send her first-class. The small queue having subsided, Elisabeth presented her passport to the check in ground hostess whilst Copeland manhandled the luggage on to the scales. The airline hostess tapped in Elisabeth's details.

"You'll be flying American to London then your connecting flight to Moscow will be by Aeroflot. This is a no smoking flight."

"OK. Could I also have a aisle seat?"

"Sure, I'll just check now." Having tapped in her request, she continued, "Yep, that's fine" she confirmed and then began to attach printed labels to the baggage after which the hostess pressed a button on her counter and the cases disappeared onto a conveyor belt behind her. Elisabeth was surprised not to have to pay excess baggage charges but that seemed to be a perk when travelling first class these days.

Fire Storm

"Will my luggage be transferred automatically on arrival in London?" queried Elisabeth

"Absolutely, all you have to do is collect it once you arrive in Moscow." The hostess handed Elisabeth her tickets, boarding card and Passport and then continued with an almost standard script. "You'll be in row 4, seat J and will board at the front of the aircraft. Should board in about an hour. Enjoy your flight and your stay in Moscow."

"Thanks" Elisabeth acknowledged, gathered her documents and moved away from the counter.

* * *

30 Minutes later

Both Copeland and Elisabeth took the time to stroll around the area trying to spend as much time together before the announcement was made. The public-address system came to life.

"American Airlines are pleased to announce the departure of flight AA106 to London Heathrow. All passengers are requested to proceed to gate 9 and to have their boarding cards and passports ready for inspection."

They both walked towards passport control. Copeland wouldn't be allowed passed this point so he stopped, held Elisabeth around her waist and kissed her in a lovers embrace which seemed to last forever. He wanted it to and he would capture and treasure that moment and her feminine taste. He could smell the Tiffany perfume that he had recently bought her.

"Give me a call as soon as you can and let me know what is happening won't you?" requested Copeland

"You bet" she said reassuringly

"Elisabeth," Copeland paused before continuing, "I love you. Be careful out there?" he added.

"I will and I love you too. All good things come to those who wait. Remember that."
She gave Copeland one last kiss, turned and checked through passport control. She glanced back and with her usual provocative and lasting smile, she waved. All Copeland could do was watch helplessly as she vanished amongst the mist of other passengers. His life would be empty now – for a while at least. He had to get back to work to occupy his mind. She'd be okay, as he tried to convince himself. Deep in thought, he walked past the row of telephone kiosks in the departure lobby and heard one caller speaking in a foreign language. Not being familiar with the accent he dismissed it as another tourist. He left the airport building, returned to his vehicle and drove back to DC.

* * *

As Copeland walked passed the tourist at the telephone kiosk, the man on the phone simply said, "Yego podruga sobirayetsya sest' na bort samoleta" informing the person at the other end of the call that Copeland's girlfriend was about to board the aircraft.

Fire Storm

"poyti s ney" came the response instructing the tourist to go with her.

"Da" he simply replied acknowledging his instructions before replacing the handset on the cradle and joining the remaining passengers.

* * *

Copeland had listened to the words of encouragement that Elisabeth had shared with him earlier. He wanted to do something about it and whilst the time was right, he had to do it now. As he drove from the airport, he decided to make the call. He scrolled through the contacts list on the dash console and selected the one he needed.

"Jack, good to hear from you." Came the voice of the US president.

"I want back in Mister President." he simply said.

"That's great news. There are only so many books you can read and rounds of golf you can play." He said with a light-hearted chuckle, "Good to have you back Jack. Let's catch up in a meeting early next week. Give my secretary a call and make the arrangements."

"Indeed sir." Acknowledged Copeland before severing the connection and dialling a second number.

"Office of the President." Came the voice of the Presidents secretary, "How can I help?"

"It's Jack Copeland. I've just been on the line with the President and he asked me to make an appointment for next week. What days would be suitable for him?"

"Hi Jack, well he has a busy schedule Monday through Wednesday but Thursday looks clear at the moment. Would that be convenient for you say around ten o'clock?"

"Perfect. I'll schedule that in. Many thanks." Copeland acknowledged and then cut the call.

Jack was pleased that the President had secured a second term. He deserved another chance and the people of the US agreed with him. He now relaxed and smiled knowing that he had taken the first step in returning to operational duties. He turned the volume up on his car CD player and began tapping his fingers on the steering wheel to the music of Chris Cagle and it's good to be back.

CHAPTER 2

Star City, Oblast Region. North East of Moscow, Russia – Cosmonaut Training Facility 55° 52' N 38° 06' E

Located approximately thirty-one kilometres north-east of Moscow and secreted off a busy highway surrounded by deep copses of birch and pine trees lies 'Star City'; home of the Cosmonaut Training facility and the Pride of Mother Russia. Resembling a US Midwestern college campus, it is the primary training and research facility of the Soviet Space Programme where men such as former German scientist, Herman Grottrup played a key role in advancing the space race and legends such as Yuri Gagarin, the first man in space remains an icon of Soviet heroism. With a population of some six thousand five hundred, including about sixty Cosmonauts, the Russian Space Agency's physicians, engineers, researchers, trainers and support staff are based at this once top-secret military establishment and former Soviet air base and is almost a self-contained town. Star City never existed during the Cold War according to the Soviets but dummy space centres were built to fool high altitude photography of the U2, SR-71 and later spy satellites. The competitive race during this period to establish space dominance had taken a heavy toll on the already crumbling economy of this once great nation and super power. With the demise of east-west hostilities and out of necessity, they forged a new relationship with the United States which would create an opportunity for the Soviets to generate some financial assistance by opening its doors to the west and bringing together varying experiences and knowledge of both pre and post war space technologies. The outcome was the International Alpha Space Station, a technologically advanced replacement for the ageing Soviet Mir outpost. Having the world's most advanced reliable rocket in the form of the Proton and with more experience in long-term space travel than the US, their knowledge would be invaluable to the success of the ISS programme. Cosmonaut candidates would spend approximately two and a half years at Star City and endure between two thousand five hundred to three thousand hours of intensive training to prepare them for the arduous tasks and emergencies that they face during their planned missions. Additional training was now needed for the shuttle missions to the ISS to make them familiar with the differing technologies. A selection process had been undertaken to identify prospective candidates to be sent to the Johnson Space Centre, Florida to train alongside their US counterparts. The first two candidates waited nervously outside the office of the Chief of Cosmonaut Training and Aviation, Pilot-Cosmonaut Lieutenant General Igor Syromokov. Neither of them had any reason to stand outside the office during training but they had an idea what was at stake now. The senior of the two candidates knocked on the leather-studded door, turned the handle and walked in closely followed by the second candidate. Both saluted and stood in front of the General's large, but sparse mahogany desk. A thick Cuban cigar lay in the ashtray billowing plumes of blue acrid smoke, which swirled around the General almost engulfing his face by creating a smoke screen. Syromokov was himself an accomplished Cosmonaut with three space missions under his belt aboard Soyuz spacecraft and the SALYUT-4 and SALYUT-6 orbital stations. Behind the smoke was another figure in a dark suit that seemed to walk out of the shadows from the corner of the room. Syromokov reclined his leather chair and began:

"Comrades, I would like you to meet Michael Wilson. He's NASA's special envoy here in Russia who will validate some of the things I am about to say. He has his own agenda that will become apparent in a little while. Before I let Michael speak, I want to say that you are both testament of one of our greatest moments in space development and your training here has been designed with a difference. The space race programme between our two countries has taken a heavy toll on our economy causing hardships everywhere. The fear we used to instil across the world has had to be watered down as we adopt global concerns over military capabilities and expenditure. The Space frontier is still an area shrouded in much mystery and secrecy, which through human curiosity still presents itself open to investigation. Russia could not pursue such ventures on its own but would actively support an international role in space exploration." Syromokov was part of the old guard and never thought he would be saying these words. He looked across to Michael and simply nodded.

Michael stepped forward out of the shadows. He was dressed in a dark plain suit, white shirt and a thin black tie. He had jet-black hair that was swept back over his head and looked as if it was held in place with some grease. As he moved forward he removed his large dark rimmed glasses from his face with his left hand and a pocket-handkerchief from his right hand trouser suit pocket with his right hand and set about to clean them before replacing them onto his face. Slowly placing the handkerchief back into his pocket, he looked at his audience and then to Syromokov.

"Thank you General." Michael began slowly, "Russia's contribution during the tense times between both our countries provided a lot of valuable information and of course the ability to dock with Mir enhanced that knowledge. What we propose now is to take this one step further by creating something that would be truly international bringing together the wealth of knowledge and experiences in this field. The US alone could not undertake a project of this magnitude without the cooperation of its allies. The costs would be just too exponential. The International Space Station is a stepping-stone to greater things and would benefit both our countries. Your Proton rocket launch facility at Baikonur is already taking part in changing the shape of the ISS by providing the vehicle to deliver necessary parts as the station begins to expand. As the ISS increases in size there becomes a real need for it be occupied so as to monitor the on-board life support and navigational systems. Your Mir project was just the beginning. It has opened up the prospects of a whole new world ready to be explored. We should put behind us the things that have happened in the past and join together in partnership to share the results of the future. It is intended that the ISS will be weaponised in the short term so that Earth can be protected from any hostile intervention. During the Cold War between 1968 and 1983, as you are aware, the USSR deployed a Fractional Bombardment System that contained a nuclear warhead. This was placed in low Earth orbit, with the intention that it could hit any location on the Earth's surface. The SALT II treaty of 1979 signed by US president Jimmy Carter and the Soviet leader, Leonid Brezhnev in Vienna of course prohibited such weapon systems and had to be phased out. However, the primary defensive role of the ISS will be to deflect any space debris in the form of asteroids, satellites or meteorites from being in close Earth proximity, which would create endangerment to the life on earth. This will be a new development and role for the ISS and will be developed over the next year. Science and other fundamental research will of course continue." Michael looked over at Syromokov, smiled as if indicating that he had said enough on the subject and then stepped to one side. "Thank you General." Michael concluded.

Syromokov stood up from his chair and picked up his Cuban cigar from the glass ashtray positioned in front of him. He was a big man, not tall but a little heavy around his midriff, which made his light brown uniform look a little tight. His epaulets were colourful and an impressive array of medals added an air of distinguished authority to him. He took a deep drag before releasing the billows of blue smoke towards the high ceiling in slow controlled movements, which formed into circles. The swirling fan in the centre of the ceiling seemed to be pushing the smoke back down towards Syromokov. After a brief moment, he looked at the two cosmonauts.

"Having qualified as pilot cosmonauts, you have both been chosen to be representatives of the new Russian Federation on this, the first of many such missions involving the Joint Space Training Programme. The future of our commitment to this global venture rests heavily on your shoulders. You know what to do and your training has prepared you well. This is just the beginning. Good luck Comrades."

* * *

The next day

The black Volga made its way towards the front gate of Star City passing the high rise dormitory buildings on either side of the road mixed with wide walkways and separated by large grassed areas. The occupants of the car looked on in silence as they reminisced at the two and a half years that they had endured whilst undergoing training. This had been their home and their family for four and a half years and there had been good times, mishaps and the unfortunate tragedies with the loss of life of some of their comrades. That's the price to pay for realistic training but also to the complexities of space travel. They would be leaving behind their wives and families as they embarked on a new venture for mother Russia for however long it would take. The wooden gate barrier was raised as the car approached the exit and the armed guards saluted the passing vehicle. Both men inside the car returned the salute and looked back in the direction of the wooden guardhouse noticing the Red Star taking its pride and place in the middle of the building with the words 'Peoples Friendship' etched into it. Sitting next to this was a picture of Lenin and his name proudly sitting above.

"Today is the dawn of a new era for Russia Vladimir."

"Of course, Comrade Colonel and there's also a lot at stake for both sides." He paused before continuing," It's hard to imagine that in a short while we will be training alongside our former adversaries."

"This is certainly the beginning of a new chapter." Sergei said quietly as he turned his head and continued to look out the side window as the scenery began to pass by in a blur.

The car headed southwest and sped along the A-103 highway towards Moscow and eventually towards terminal D at Sheremetyevo airport. The distance would be fifty-nine kilometres and the journey at this time of day would take approximately one hour. Their flight from Moscow to London Heathrow was on Aeroflot SU 2580 departing at 08:21. They would need to make a connecting flight in London to American airlines flight number AA51 departing at 0915 hours local from Terminal three direct to Dallas in Texas. The car journey to Moscow would be shorter than normal since the driver knew that no one would stop his vehicle whilst it displayed official government plates. He took the opportunity and increased his speed. His passengers, Colonel Sergei Grigorev and Major Vladimir Popov of the Soviet Air Force had been specifically selected to represent the Russian Federation in the US. His cargo was important and he was instructed to deliver. Their flight time to Dallas Fort Worth, Texas with one stop in London would take approximately sixteen hours.

* * *

Sheremetyevo International Airport, Moscow Terminal D – 0610 hrs. The Same Day

Elisabeth only just made the connecting flight at London Heathrow having to travel between Terminal five and Terminal four. Aeroflot SU244 from London Heathrow landed thirty minutes later than scheduled, but Elisabeth wasn't duly concerned since it seemed like it was still the middle of the night in any case. Having adjusted her watch during the flight she glanced at it now which read ten past six in the morning. Moscow was three hours ahead of London.

She hadn't been to Russia before, let alone Moscow. She collected her luggage, cleared customs and passport control without a problem and made her way through the arrivals hall on the first floor. She was surprised to see only kiosks in place of the large shops she finds at the airports back home. But this was Russia with a crumbling economy and luxuries such as vast sprawling duty-free shops were not a priority. She noted the cleanliness of the terminal and the fact that it was a no smoking zone; which she found surprising since just about everyone in Russia smoked. Smoking would only be permitted outside of the terminal building and she figured that it would be an obstacle course during the day when the airport would be much busier. She left the airport building in search of a cab. Having recognised one in an instance with its distinguishable triangle on the roof and four-digit number after the words 'TAKSI' she headed in its direction. The driver she noticed was leaning against his vehicle smoking a cigarette. As she got closer, he looked in her direction and quickly pushed himself from his vehicle and at the same time he deftly flicked his cigarette into the gutter.

"Otel Novotel na Mezhdunarodnoye Shosse." She instructed.

Almost at the same time, Elisabeth looked over her shoulder and out of curiosity noticed a tall man wearing a three-quarter length dark grey leather jacket walking behind her from the direction of the terminal building. He had no luggage and he instantly averted his eyes once she looked towards him. He continued to walk passed her seemingly oblivious and crossed the road towards a grey SUV.

The cab driver nodded and responded to Elisabeth's request with "Da" in acknowledgement and acceptance of her journey. She then climbed into the rear of the cab whilst the driver tended to the luggage. The vehicle was small and he had to load some cases inside the vehicle as well as the trunk that made it a tight fit inside. Elisabeth could hear the driver struggling as he tried to get some of her cases in the trunk but she was sure that she wasn't the only person who travelled with everything. After loading the luggage in both back and front of the taxi, the driver switched on his meter and began to pull out from his parking slot when they heard a loud car horn sounding to his rear and almost at the same time noticed a car in his side mirror. He slammed on his brakes causing Elisabeth to jolt forward and the driver to curse.

"Tupoy idiot?" Cursed the driver

"Chto sluchilos" Elisabeth asked as to what had happened.

"Some high-ranking government official I suppose. They drive like they own the road." he said rhetorically.

Elisabeth got the impression that he had an issue with government vehicles and that it was a frequent occurrence. The black car passed the cab at speed and headed towards the emergency gates to the aircraft parking areas and disappeared. She noticed two people in the back but didn't pay much attention to them or to enquire with the driver any further. Eventually the cab pulled out and began its journey to the hotel. Elisabeth looked over her shoulder and noticed the grey vehicle drop in two vehicles behind the taxi but put it down to coincidence since there were many other vehicles doing the same. She sat back and relaxed for the short journey.

* * *

Dallas Fort Worth International Airport Terminal D - 1325 hrs. local the Same Day

Their arrival had already been notified to the immigration staff at Dallas Fort Worth International airport so as to limit the amount of time they would have to spend going through the bureaucratic channels. Both Sergei Grigorev and Vladimir Popov were met by an official car from NASA and driven away for the four-hour drive, 265-mile journey to the JSC in Houston, Texas along I-45. The driver gave them a guided tour pointing out different landmarks as he drove. Both Sergei and Vladimir spoke almost perfect English, a by-product of the Cold War and the time they had spent at the University of Moscow. They were also encouraged to continue whilst at the Air Force Academy. Sergei was thirty-six years of age, married with no children and began flying gliders and parachuting at the age of fourteen. He graduated from secondary school in the summer of nineteen eighty-four and enrolled in the Armavir Higher Military Aviation School for fighter pilots located in the Krasnodor Territory on the banks of the Kuban River in south-east European Russia. After graduating as a class one pilot in nineteen eighty-nine, he had been identified as a natural and was destined to have a glittering career in the Soviet Air Force. For six years he had been posted to a front-line fighter Squadron and in nineteen ninety-seven was promoted to Colonel. His career to date has amassed him three thousand five hundred flying hours in more than forty types of aircraft and prototypes. He was an only child whose love of flying was evident from an early age. His room would show posters of Russian aircraft and more sinister ones of the catastrophic effects of Armageddon. His parents supported him and often went without things so that their son could realise his ambition and for them to be proud. Vladimir on the other hand was thirty-eight years of age and considered by many as the best 'Wingman' in Russia. He had graduated from the Balashov Higher Military Aviation School in nineteen ninety and shortly after married his child hood sweetheart, Natalya who gave birth to twins three years later. He had joined the Air Force in nineteen eighty-five, a year later than Sergei and after five years at the training academy he joined a fighter Squadron in Georgia and Czechoslovakia and shortly after moved to the Ministry of Aviations Industry Test Pilot School. After graduating from there, and being promoted to Major, he joined the Gromov Flight Research Institute as an experimental Test Pilot at their research facility in Zhukovsky some forty kilometres south-east of Moscow where he continued to amass some two thousand six hundred flying hours in more than thirty types of aircraft including fighters, bombers, civilian jets and helicopters. In a secret space programme in nineteen ninety he was selected to pilot OK-1K2 (nicknamed

Ptichka - Little Bird) one of two active Soviet Buran Space Shuttles that were similar to NASAs shuttles. He had successfully docked twice with the Mir outpost. After an hour of the journey had elapsed, both passengers decided to sleep until they reached Houston.

* * *

Hotel Novotel, Moscow

After the short journey, the taxi pulled into the drop off point in front of the hotel. Several yards behind, the grey VW tucked into a spare parking bay. Elisabeth paid the fare and alighted but quickly, casually and unobtrusively looked along the street to see if she saw anything out the ordinary that was beyond coincidence or in connection with the airport. As she looked, she saw the sidelights of a grey SUV being switched off and was parked behind other vehicles about fifty metres away. The taxi driver began to remove her luggage and the bellboy from the hotel assisted and had to make two trips to ensure that he had all the baggage. Having confirmed that she had all her luggage, she made her way into the hotel.

* * *

The man sitting in the grey VW was watching as Elisabeth left the cab. He noticed her looking along the street but hadn't made the connection that she had probably seen the vehicle pull in. He picked up his phone, selected a fast dial number and simply gave his location.

* * *

Having checked in and found her room, Elisabeth figured that there was a seven-hour time difference between Moscow and Washington DC, so she decided to take a shower and have breakfast before calling Copeland. Having taken care of her personal admin she called the hotel reception and requested a connection to the number she gave. She'd try the flat first and the connection was made first time.

"Hi Jack." she said realising there was an echo and quite a long-time delay before he replied. She hated the fact that the pause caused both of them to talk over each other and she didn't seem to be getting anywhere.

"Hi Sweetheart. Have you just arrived?" Copeland asked whilst he was half asleep.

"I would have called earlier but I don't think you would have appreciated it."

"What's the time difference?"

"About seven hours ahead and I feel kind of exhausted" she replied

"How long are you staying?"

"Overnight. Flight to Tashkent is late tomorrow evening on the red eye flight and gets in at an ungodly hour the next morning. I'll ring you once I get there. "Oh, by the way." she began before the line was severed. Elisabeth wanted to let Copeland know about the possible tail from the airport but didn't want to worry him unnecessarily. Since meeting Jack, she had become more aware of her immediate surroundings and developed a keen sense of awareness. Since travelling in foreign counties alone she knew this made sense and was concerned about her own personal safety and security. With the connection severed Elisabeth stared at the phone for a while and wished she were back in Washington and with Copeland. For the first time in her life and career she felt alone and vulnerable in a strange country where she knew no one.

* * *

Lyndon B. Johnson Space Centre, Houston, Texas

As the driver approached the outskirts of Houston, he woke his passengers. Twenty-five miles later and travelling down NASA Road 1 and onto East NASA Parkway the huge rectangular sign, positioned at the side of the road announced their arrival at the JSC.

*NATIONAL AERONAUTICS & SPACE ADMINISTRATION
LYNDON B. JOHNSON SPACE CENTER*

At the crossroads, the driver turned right onto Saturn Lane and followed the blue signs for JSC Badging and in particular headed towards building 110 and took the right lane as the sign indicated. At the next traffic lights, he turned right into Second Street for the short distance to the security hut.

The driver stopped at the security checkpoint, handed over his official ID badge and gave the names of his passengers. Once they had been checked off against the list the security guard had on his clipboard, the guard pressed an external button on the guardhouse wall and the barrier was then raised allowing them access to the facility.

As the driver slowly made his way to reception he gladly offered more information about JSC and how famous it is throughout the world as 'Mission Control' that has served as the Command Centre for NASA's human space flights since nineteen sixty-five. He pointed out the low-level building on the left which had aptly been named 'Rocket Park' and that it was littered with the sleeping giants of the past decades of space exploration and the largest of the rockets, Saturn V was situated outside of the 'Rocket Park' building. This rocket was the height of a 30-story building and was perhaps the most accomplished of the rockets with nine trips into outer space, six of which had landed on the moon and carried a total of twenty-seven astronauts. They drove past building 31-N and the driver pointed out that this was the Lunar Sample Laboratory Facility where more than eight hundred and forty pounds of lunar material gathered by astronauts during the six missions to the moon's surface and meteorites, believed to be from Mars are housed within this facility. The driver took a few unauthorised short cuts and pointed out a full-size

Apollo rocket that was showing signs of its age and now housed bird's nests instead of Astronauts.

Eventually they arrived at the Administration building and were met by NASA Administrator, Kurt Davies.

"Gentleman, welcome to JSC. I'm Kurt Davies, the NASA Administrator in other words the guy who takes the fall when anything goes wrong," he said with a wide confident smile and extending his hand.

Sergei and Vladimir smiled at Kurt's humour and accepted his salutations.

"It's a great honour to be here in the United States Kurt and I'm sure both our experiences can be utilised for mutual benefit." Sergei spoke before continuing, "The future of generations to come is in our hands."

"Sure is." responded Kurt. "Hope your driver gave you a good tour of the facility. Leave your baggage in the vehicle and follow me up to the Presidential Conference Room. Just want to give you a quick overview and a few administrational procedures, including your ID badges squared away then you can go across to your accommodation and settle in."

Kurt led the way to the lift area and selected the sixth floor once everyone was inside. The conference room occupied a corner of the rectangular shaped building and had windows on two sides of the room offering panoramic views of the great sprawl of JSC. Both Sergei and Vladimir didn't waste any time and took the opportunity to see their new home. Kurt pointed out various buildings of interest to both

Cosmonauts who seemed awe inspired in comparison with their own Star City.

Looking out the window with Sergei and Vladimir, Kurt began, "All the buildings at JSC are numbered for ease of reference including the street names. We like to keep things simple; it's less of a headache. Joking aside, it's actually a Federal requirement. The one you are in now is building number one, which is the headquarters of JSC. A short distance from here is the chow hall, which is in building number three. Building one hundred and ten is the security hut on the outside of JSC gates. You passed this on the way in. Always show your badge here when re-entering. There are over one hundred buildings on site at the JSC covering some one thousand six hundred acres of real estate that acquired the official nickname 'Space City' back in '67. Here's a map to make things a little easier." Mike hands over two A4 pages representing the JSC map to Vladimir and Sergei. "Make sure you know which building you're in for your SMS training. As a point of note, it's generally in building five. After a couple of weeks, you'll be able to sleep walk around the site." Kurt said with a wry smile before continuing, "for downtime we have the astronauts bar located a couple of miles off site. It's called the Outpost Tavern and a great hangout after a day at the office. You may get quizzed about your bio, but it's all part of everyone getting to know each other around here so don't be fazed. It's one hell of a community and a great family. As a matter of interest, one of our presidents, John F Kennedy said in 1962 that the JSC was once the furthest outpost on the old frontier of the West that will now be the furthest outpost on the new frontier of science and space. He was absolutely right. Any questions gentlemen before we wrap for the day?"

Neither Vladimir nor Sergei asked any questions. They had the mind-set that all would be revealed soon. After the mandatory administrative brief on regulations including fire and evacuation plans, together with a brief overview of their training programme, both had photographs taken for their official NASA pass. Moments later they clipped them to their jackets, left the building and were driven to their accommodation block. They were now officially an integral part of this multi-billion-dollar organisation.

* * *

Inter-Continental Hotel, Tashkent, Uzbekistan – The Next Day

Elisabeth arrived at Tashkent International Airport on time and at what seemed to be once again the middle of the night. She was starting to think that she was becoming nocturnal. She looked at her watch, two fifty-five in the morning. During her brief stay in Moscow she had arranged with CNN Moscow bureau to have a vehicle meet her on her arrival in Uzbekistan. At least she wasn't disappointed when, having collected her baggage, cleared immigration and customs she noticed the familiar white SUV with CNN emblazoned in black letters on the side parked outside the terminal building. She headed over to it, introduced herself and then assisted the driver to load her luggage in the car. The events in Moscow with a possible tail were certainly fresh in her mind and she was starting to think that she was becoming paranoid. Having instructed the driver as to where she was staying, she was whisked away to the hotel and was in her room on the sixth floor within the hour. She'd call Copeland later that day, but what she needed now was sleep and plenty of it.

* * *

Outside the Inter-Continental Hotel, 107A Amir Temur Avenue Tashkent - Same Day

The man in the grey leather jacket was able to take advantage of the late-night flight and was hopeful that the woman he was following would be too exhausted to notice him. On arrival at the hotel, he picked up his cell phone, selected the same fast dial and simply gave his location.

* * *

The White House Oval Office – Four days later

Copeland arrived at the White House twenty minutes early for his appointment with the President. He never liked to be late and always maintained his military discipline to ensure that it remained that way.

He looked at his watch; it read nine thirty-eight. Walking along the corridors of power towards the Oval office and escorted by a Secret Service agent he could feel his stomach tighten as if gripped by anxiety. He put it down to the immense power this building emitted after all it is the people's home of the leader of the free world. Whilst it seemed busy with staff moving around in different directions, he also got the feeling that it was a lonely place to be. He had never been to the White House before and intended to make the most of it. Having been escorted to the first floor, he passed the Cabinet Room, Situation Room and the Roosevelt Room and managed a quick peek as he did so. Dressed in a dark navy-blue suit, light blue shirt and a blue and silver striped tie, he looked as if he belonged in this historical building. He reached the desk of the President's secretary who acknowledged Copeland's arrival. She walked from behind her desk and towards the large wide looking door, knocked once and entered. Copeland followed closely behind giving the secretary little chance to introduce Copeland to the President. He was almost like a child waiting to see the parent. He couldn't wait to get in.

"Jack, good to see you. We missed you. I missed you." Began the President as he moved towards Copeland and shook his hand before sitting on the couch opposite the door in which Copeland had just entered. Jack sat opposite the President. "So, how's Elisabeth?"

"She's great thanks. A few days ago, she headed out to Moscow for CNN, as there is a lot of work to do and some unfinished business that needs to be dealt with. News reporting is a continuous evolving platform. There's always something going on; either good or bad."

"Tell me about it. I try not to look until the Chief of Staff switches it on which is mainly every day now. It constantly reminds me of how fractured our world is."

"I concur sir. Not sure what we mere morsels can do to change that. Elisabeth needed to get back and so do I Mister President. I've enjoyed the break but I now have itchy feet. Not that I didn't before." Both Copeland and the President raised a smile at that comment.

"Yep there's only so much…" The President began before being interrupted by Copeland.

"Heard it all before Mister President." Finished Copeland.

"You've kept you finger on the pulse Jack and you're up to date on global issues. I have no concerns there. You and your boys are a great asset to this country's defence."

"Thank you, Mister President. We're ready to go at a moment's notice."

"Have you been keeping your eye on Russia of late?" The President asked.

"Not specifically. Any reason why I should?"

"I attended a summit in Moscow in June with the newly-elected Russian President. We signed a mutual agreement on strategic stability with a view to reduce offensive arms and would continue to discuss this on the START III treaties. Not sure when that's going to happen as I have a feeling this will be a non-starter Jack and we will bow to the pressure of Russia as we always seem to do. Everyone on both sides talks a good talk. We also signed a Strategic Stability Cooperation Initiative where both Russia and the USA could cooperate to control the spread of missiles, missile technology and weapons of mass destruction. All these initiatives and treaties we keep signing is almost an excuse for a get together but it's also a chance to flex our muscles with our former foes. Very little progress is ever made because Russia is so hard to please. They are the experts in deception with a solid smoke screen of deniability. Keep an eye out on any Russian intelligence that you come across Jack from a military perspective. I think they've gone quiet for a reason. They're up to something and I want to know what it is."

"And I think I have the right person for the job."

"I'm guessing Elisabeth?"

Copeland nodded

"In that case Jack, keep me up to date."

"Yes, Mister President."

Copeland left the White House and headed back to his office. He had work to do and he needed to find some answers as soon as possible.

CHAPTER 3

JSC, Houston, Texas - NASA Astronaut Training Facility

Both Vladimir and Sergei were both picked up from their accommodation building by the JSC shuttle bus at nine o'clock on their first morning and taken to their training block. Although they were both fully qualified cosmonauts in their own right, they had to convert now to the needs of the shuttle programme. During their training they will be exposed to the Shuttle Mission Simulator (SMS) which will eventually prepare them for all shuttle vehicle operations and in all system tasks associated with the major flight phases; pre-launch, ascent, orbit operations, entry and landing. There are two simulators, a fixed base and a motion base, which both Vladimir and Sergei will need to undertake in order to pass the evaluation. The fixed base station will be used for mission / payload training and launch descent and landing training. The motion-based station will be used to train pilots and commanders in the mission phases of the launch, descent and landing. The only thing the SMS can't do is replicate the noise and vibration of launch and the experiences of weightlessness are missing from the simulators. Both Cosmonauts will be expected to build up flying time in the single systems trainer (SST) in order to go through Orbiter Subsystems using checklists similar to those found on a real-time shuttle mission. This training would be designed so that they can carry out corrective actions for malfunctions and will need to be carried out as a prelim before using the SMS. Exposure to microgravity will be scheduled on board a modified KC-135 jet aircraft. Those who have gone before Sergei and Vladimir had aptly named this ride as 'The Vomit Comet'. Here they will experience periods of weightlessness for about twenty to thirty seconds each time the aircraft dives from an altitude of thirty-five thousand to twenty-four thousand feet. This would be repeated forty times per day. Vladimir will build up his aircraft hours and practice Orbiter landings by flying fifteen hours per month in NASA's fleet of two-seat T-38 jets and Gulfstream II business jets that had been modified to perform in a similar way to those of the shuttle craft. Vladimir would receive at least one hundred hours on board a Shuttle Training Aircraft (STA) that would equate to at least six hundred shuttle approaches. Sergei on the other hand would fly a minimum of four hours per month. In the meantime, both Sergei and Vladimir assembled with other ASCANs and had to go through rigorous medical checks before being officially affirmed into the programme.

* * *

Inter-Continental Hotel Tashkent, Uzbekistan

Elisabeth woke after a long sleep and slowly looked at her watch, which she still had on her wrist. It read seventeen fifty-six in the afternoon and she couldn't believe that she had slept for so long. She was mindful of the time difference back home and having worked it out to be plus nine hours between Tashkent and Washington DC, this made it eight fifty-six in the morning on the eastern seaboard. She picked up the room phone by her bed, dialled zero and asked to be connected with the number she gave. After several sounds of clicks and switches, she heard the sound of a connect call. The typical single short burst tone, which sounded several times before it was picked up.

"Hi, this is Jack." came the reply

"Hey it's me. You ok? I'm just checking in."

"Hey. How's it going? Where are you staying?"

"I'm at the Inter-Continental in Tashkent. It's like I'm stuck in a time warp. Water pressure low, Wi-Fi is unpredictable. Food's pretty good though. All the essentials of life we need and take for granted but hey it seems to be the norm round here. What's happening back home?"

"Not a great deal really other than I called the President and asked to be put back on operational duties."

"That's great Jack. What did he say? He agreed hopefully."

"He was over the moon. It was like greeting a long-lost friend."

"There you go, it was easier than you thought."

"How long you staying there?" Copeland asked

"Not sure at the moment. CNN has no bureau here so I'm kind of isolated. Alex the cameraman is here too. He was with me in Africa."

"Is there anything happening down there that I need to know? Something I may have missed?"

"Nothing at all. I'm here just to tie up a few loose ends."

"Okay. Sounds a long way to go just to do that though." He said rhetorically and not expecting a response.

"Comms are terrible Jack. I'll catch up with you later. Love you."

"Love you too." He managed to say before the line was severed.

Elisabeth was pleased that Jack was getting back with the DoD. It gave him a purpose and would certainly occupy his mind while she was away. She missed him for sure but knew that he would always be there for her even though she seemed to be stuck in a time warp and it felt like he was a million miles away.

* * *

JSC, Houston, Texas – 6 Months Later
April 2001

The astronaut training programme would last for over two years for those starting out at JSC and since both Vladimir and Sergei were already Cosmonaut trained they would only complete one year of shuttle conversion training at JSC. Training was progressing well and both Sergei and Vladimir had integrated as expected. Their first few months of training had seen them undertake a variety of tasks from flying to the preparation for scientific research. During their classroom phase they were schooled in shuttle and space station systems along with a variety of other disciplines, including Earth sciences, meteorology, space science and engineering. It was also required that they train in land and water survival, aircraft operations and scuba diving. Vehicle operations using simulators were conducted in both the JGTF and the SVMF buildings. The Garn Facility was used to prepare the ASCANs for launch, landing, payload and ISS operations and rendezvous activities.

The SVMF allowed both Sergei and Vladimir to be exposed to full-sized mock-ups of the shuttle aircraft including the flight deck, mid-deck and one full-sized shuttle mock-up. It was necessary that they train for a combined total of three hundred hours in these simulators to fully prepare them for all possibilities. In addition, they would test their skills in the VRL immersing them into a computer-generated microgravity environment.

Sergei was not a natural swimmer but had managed to get through the training at Star City and now both Vladimir and himself had to endure the world's largest pool, the Neutral Buoyancy Laboratory housed within the Sonny Carter Training Facility. The pool held some 6.2 million gallons of water and was more than two hundred feet long and forty feet deep. It was necessary in order to simulate the weightlessness environment of space and they would train for spacewalks on fully submerged, full-sized replicas of space station modules. Ten hours would be spent submerged for every hour they would spend walking in space.

In the event several crewmembers were immobilised and unable to carry out flight duties, it was deemed essential that all ASCANs should be familiar with the engineering systems of the spacecraft including spacecraft propulsion, thermal control and life support systems. Vladimir and Sergei had already been given schooling in earth observation and astronomy, as these were common disciplines within JSC and Star City. The MIR outpost and ISS shared similar internal events, which all ASCANs must undertake. These are deemed as events that would pose a hazard to their health, the health of the crew, or successful mission outcome. These types were categorised as failure of a critical life support system, capsule decompression, fire and other life-threatening events. Mission outcome on the other hand included training in the form of an EVA, scientific experimentation, or spacecraft piloting.

After the completion of nine months training out of the twelve months ISS and shuttle conversions, the final phase of training would be classed as intensive. This would start at about three months prior to launch and would serve as a preparation for the crew who had been specifically chosen for the mission and designed to provide a dynamic testing ground for mission rules and flight procedures.

* * *

JSC 3 Months Later – July 2001

Both Sergei and Vladimir were now at the nine-month point of their training and left their dormitories at eight-forty-five as they had done for the previous months. They boarded their shuttle bus as normal along with other candidates. Their programme for the day was scheduled as a revisit to building nine – the ISS module mock up facility. The shuttle bus began moving forward but seemed to be heading off in a different direction. Neither of the passengers commented, as there was probably a valid reason for the reroute. After a short while the shuttle bus pulled up outside building 4-S. A plaque on the wall gave the name as 'Mission Operations Support Offices and Flight Crew Operations Division'.

One of the candidates looked towards the driver, "What we doing here buddy? Meant to be building nine."

"I was instructed to bring you all over here. No questions asked. I'm just the driver."

"Right." Came the response from the candidate. He'd have to settle for that.

Everyone gathered their personal things and alighted from the shuttle muttering to themselves and entered the building foyer where the JSC Director, James Hartman, met and introduced himself to them. He was alone.

"Gentlemen, welcome." he began. "I'm Director Hartman. Let's go up to the conference room on the second floor."

James was fit as he expected all his staff and trainees to be. He didn't like elevators and would expect others to take a similar viewpoint and walk upstairs where necessary. He led the way and made the approach to the stairs and was pleased to see that the others had taken his lead and were following closely behind. The candidates had never been inside building four and were awe inspired by the importance of being met by the Director himself. They had never met him so this of course led to a curiosity as to why they had been brought to the building in the first place. Having reached the conference room and settled into the chairs around a large oval shaped smoked glass table, the director took up his position at the head of the table in front of a large TV screen positioned on the wall. The TV was lit and the JSC logo was proudly being displayed in the centre of the screen. The Director looked at those in front of him and paused momentarily whilst he gathered his thoughts.

CHAPTER 4

Command Centre – The Pentagon Same Day

Copeland had been summoned to the Pentagon for a real time briefing on a major event that was so secret that his timings were kept to the very last minute. On arrival he joined several others in the room who seemed to be choreographed to arrive at the same time. Jack looked around the room and counted them all. In addition to himself, there were nineteen other people; some were in uniform and others in suits. He knew most of them, but not all. These were the sixteen representatives of the US intelligence community headed by the Director of National Intelligence himself. Jack had never been to such a high-powered gathering of such prominent people in one room. This meeting was clearly to be intelligence led. They had a total budget of $66.8 billion so it was fair to say they were at the heart of all US interests. The unfortunate thing about so many departments concentrating on the same thing is that they all seem to pull in different directions. Having no clear direction and all out to claim the glory for themselves can often create chaos and confusion when the facts are a little murky in the first place they are often presented that way so that one or more department is sniffing the wrong trail. In the far corner and dressed in military attire was the new Chairman of the joint chiefs, General Peter Gomez. He had taken over from General Walter Zieglar who had decided to retire early, reportedly due to ill health. Jack knew a different story but was happy to let bygones be bygones. Copeland circulated around the room trying to catch what was going on. A snippet here and a snippet there would be useful but being in a room full of intelligence personnel was like trying to get blood out of a stone under normal circumstances. But he also got the feeling and impression that they didn't actually know themselves why they had been summoned. Something kept from the intelligence community, now that had to be a first and it had to be ultra-important too.

* * *

JSC Houston – Building 4 Same Day

"You will notice from your training schedule that there is a period which has been categorised as classified." The JSC director began, "This element of your training has been left until your last three months here and before you embark upon your mission in real time. It has been done that way for a reason and it is important that you are brought up to speed as the whole world will be relying on the ISS should things go cosmic. I will of course explain and unwrap this mystery in a little while. Before I do so I will briefly give some background information as to why this will be happening and why we have arrived at this point."

All candidates in the room looked at each other not quite understanding what was about to be said. It was like a cryptic clue to a crossword. Currently the Director was giving nothing away but merely throwing a teaser into the mix to gain interest and almost leaving you to fathom out the answer for yourself. On this particular occasion though, that was never going to happen. No one in the room had any idea as to the information the Director was obviously privy to. He was playing his cards close to his chest for now. The Director had the attention of everyone in the room. Sergei and Vladimir watched and listened intently to what the Director had to say.

"The USA and Russia have always competed against each other and to be one step ahead whether it be the race to the Moon, military equipment, nuclear weapons. The list goes on. Many treaties that have been signed in the past have been done so because the cost of maintaining a defensive mechanism has spiralled out of control. The only way to bring this back into check is to have both sides sign an agreement to stop or at least reduce certain elements. That way, it allows both countries to regroup and to channel savings to other needy causes thereby controlling expenditure. For those countries that have a suspicious mind however, it could also be seen as a distraction by either the USA or Russia or indeed China that there is something else going on in the background." The Director paused whilst he took a drink of water from the glass on the table in front of him. He continued, "At the height of the Cold War, Russia was ahead of the US in many ways. It was difficult to keep competing with each other like for like without other areas of either countries suffering. Russia had a decent sized nuclear capability that was not only confined to Earth but had encroached into space also. They had a live programme running which we termed as a Fractional Orbital Bombardment System. The concept of this type of system was to provide a weapons delivery system that inserts a payload into an orbital trajectory from which a re-entry vehicle (RV) is deorbited. Russia deployed such systems between 1969 and 1983. The warhead was between two and twenty megatons and would be able to hit Earth within 3 to 5 kilometres of its intended target. This had to be stopped otherwise a space war could realistically have broken out with the Russians calling the shots and Earth held to ransom. The US at that time was not willing or prepared to compete in an arms race that had Armageddon consequences." The Director again paused to gather his thoughts and to maintain the interest of the group in front of him. "A bilateral treaty signed in Moscow on thirty-first of July nineteen ninety-one between the US and Russia under the auspice of the Strategic Arms Reduction Treaty (START) put a halt to any such weapons and with the aim to reduce nuclear weapons overall. START however was never implemented and as such leaves the door wide open for further development. The treaty gave breathing space for the US and now we want to step this up a gear and to become a super power once more. An agreement signed in nineteen sixty-seven was the Outer Space Treaty, which prohibited any weapons of mass destruction from being placed in space. As this is a dated treaty, it has not been revised to take into account today's modern technology. What is interesting is that in November nineteen ninety-nine, one hundred and thirty-eight UN members voted to reaffirm the Outer Space Treaty. Only the US and Israel abstained from the vote leaving the door open for exploration. This is where the ISS comes into the equation today and ready for tomorrow's new world. Slated for launch next month will be a resupply vessel to the ISS with additional cargo on board. This cargo up to now has been classified to the hilt but the US no longer wants to hide the fact that it wants to establish space supremacy. We are at that point in which we are able to do something rather than just words."

Vladimir and Sergei knew where this was heading. They had been briefed whilst at Star City of the US concept for advancement in space technology. What they didn't know was the type of system being deployed.

* * *

Copeland and the rest of the assembled audience listened attentively to the JSC Director as he gave his speech across a live feed from the JSC. All eyes were transfixed to the huge screen positioned on the back wall of the situation room. Everyone was trying to figure out where he was heading. The intelligence community were up in arms demanding to know why this hadn't been tabled before. They felt side lined, misinformed and unable to respond effectively. It was almost as if their hands had been tied and they were blindfolded. Copeland himself was surprised how something like this could've been kept for so long from the eyes and ears of the US community. The whole world thrived on a good leak and this was an opportunity missed.

The JSC Director continued, "The cargo will involve a new type of technology in the form of a laser guided system."

Just about everyone in the room gasped, shuffled in their seats, looked at each other and began asking rhetorical questions to which no one in the audience had any answers.

"This system will have many uses including the overall defence of Earth from space debris to redundant or out of control satellites. As a last resort, it also has the capability to defend Earth from any land-based hostilities. In other words, the ISS will become self-contained in research, life support systems and defence." The Director paused whilst everyone absorbed this last piece. "Any questions?" The Director asked knowing full well that once he opened the floor he would be bombarded from all sides.

"This is Jack Copeland from Scorpion. Are we talking about a weaponised system here Director?"

"Thanks Jack. The US DoD has been developing various types of lasers and has agreed on a particular one using particle beams. So yes, it could be used as a defence weapon system as a last resort.

As I said before, it is not being deployed as its primary function."

Copeland wasn't giving anyone else chance to but in.

"How would it work as a weapon though?" Copeland was pushing for answers now.

"A particle beam weapon would be able to generate power many times more destructive than current laser development. It would compose of two parts; a power source and an accelerating tunnel to accelerate electrons, protons or hydrogen atoms through the tunnel and once charged would fire at a designated threat. The complexities of the science behind this device are beyond myself and the audience."

"That's the text book answer. How does it work in reality?" insisted Copeland.

"The beam once deployed would create a rapid increase in the target's temperature causing the object to explode in a matter of seconds following impact."

"Has this been tested?"

"I'll pass you over to the Director of the SDI's energy office, Air Force Colonel Tom Walker who will have the answers and be able to better explain this for you."

"Thank you, Director." Began Walker, "A neutral particle beam accelerator was launched into space last week from White Sands Missile Range in New Mexico and operated for four minutes. The accelerator was a twenty-four foot, three-thousand-pound beam launched to an altitude of one hundred and twenty-five miles on a Minuteman rocket. It cannot be underestimated or denied that the Earth's orbit would not be the next battlefield."

"What is your budget for this SDI Colonel?" asked the rep from the Defence Intelligence Agency.

"Sixty million dollars." Responded Walker

"Is this Congress approved?" came the next question from the National Geospatial Intelligence Agency

"Indeed, it is. We couldn't do it otherwise." Walker confirmed.

"Why were we never told? Is this an off the book operation?" It was the CIA and NSA at the same time.

"It was never tabled so as to maintain its anonymity."

"I'm guessing POTUS on board?" enquired the National Recon Office.

"Absolutely, it was his inception."

"Who'll be operating and controlling this weaponised system whilst it's in space?" Again, it was the CIA.

"IMCC at Houston. All alignments and target selection protocols will be initiated through Flight Control."

"What about the crew aboard the ISS. How safe will this weapon be and will they be able to take control as an override facility for instance?" This time it was the Department for Homeland Security.

"In the event Earth has a serious problem and the IMCC has been neutralised or compromised, then yes they will be able to respond themselves. There will be various safeguards in place for proper control."

"What about selection of the crew? Has that been taken into account more rigorously to ensure no renegades or mavericks? After all this is a mission with a difference." Copeland asked

"Thorough screening has taken place and the selected crew have been cleared to launch."

"Is this taking technology a little too far though? Space weapons, I mean it's not as if we don't have enough problems on the planet itself." asked the CIA

"We live in unpredictable times and the laser weapon system can prevent advancement of conventional warfare. We can take control from the moral high ground. It will be able to neutralise missiles travelling through space, break up meteorites or disable rogue or redundant satellites and all this at a fraction of the cost. It must be borne in mind however that Article Four of the Outer Space Treaty of nineteen sixty-seven states that Parties to the Treaty undertake not to place in orbit around the earth any objects carrying nuclear weapons or any other kinds of weapons of mass destruction, install such weapons on celestial bodies, or station such weapons in outer space in any other manner. As it stands at this moment, a laser system is not covered by this convention."

"When this gets out you'll create a fire storm. How will you convince other countries that this is a peacetime deployment and not some hostile take-over of the world?" asked Homeland Security

"Good question and well presented. In the eyes of others, it will be classed as some kind of military hardware and convincing them will be difficult to begin with. Given proper reasoning of course the US can and will assist any country in the time of need by the use of this technology which I'm sure they will be grateful that the USA are leading on this and taken the initiative."

"If we are able to laser the earth, is there anything which can fire back at the ISS?" It was the NSA's turn.

"R and D is on-going at the moment. So, at some point the answer to your question would be a definite yes."

"A laser takes a lot of power. How's the ISS going to cope with this and be able to generate enough?" asked the Geospatial Intelligence Agency.

"Making a lot of power comes down to a lot of solar panels which would add size and weight to the existing ISS and would make it difficult to keep the weapon discreet. Currently, the panels on the ISS create one hundred and ten kilowatts of electricity. This quite obviously is not enough, as a laser would need power in the megawatt range. As a note, the panels are charged when sunny side up so in effect, storage could be housed in capacitors for use when on the dark side."

"What about weather?" enquired Copeland.

"The laser would not need a visual to the target. It would be centred on the target by given coordinates from our other satellites. One hurdle that we have had to overcome is getting a laser beam through the air. Air is full of things like water vapour, dust and pollution, etcetera, and all these things presented difficulties by distorting the beam and almost making the weapon ineffective. This was overcome by a marginal increase in the power to the beam which unfortunately made the air around it that much warmer and more noticeable."

"Would a missile not be cheaper and perhaps less noticeable so that more deniability could be applied?" came a question from the US Navy."

"Several countries have missile shields which would be expensive if these were an effective way to destroy an incoming missile. A laser can penetrate these shields with a single burst of energy. With all the tags and labels on missiles these days, these alone will identify a country as much as the ISS using its laser-weaponised system will do. If no further questions, I'll hand you back to Director Hartman at the JSC."

CHAPTER 5

"What the hell just happened?" asked Copeland aloud but to no one in particular. He glanced around the room visibly noticing the expressions of others and listening to the muted chatter, which now filled the room. This was certainly a talking point and one that would last into the night and beyond. This is something that will be on going for generations. Some seemed to be excited whilst others showed some real concerns.

"I'm with you on that Jack." It was the CIA Director who came alongside and whispered in his ear "I'm worried."

"Me too." Said Copeland, "It's a step too far. We're entering into a whole new world that I just don't feel comfortable with."

Copeland was annoyed that this was allowed to happen and to many others in the room, this was a bolt out the blue and a bit of a curve ball. In fact, there wasn't any curve it was vertical. This was a whole new playing field with a different set of rules. It was certainly the best-kept secret in the world; no one saw it coming but everyone knew that it would be a game changer and something the world wasn't yet prepared for. The battlefield lines had just been redrawn."

"As soon as the Russians know about this it'll be open warfare. It'll be back to the Cold War again." Added the CIA Director.

"I'm concerned that proper protocols haven't been put in place to ensure this cannot be used against us. This'll be our worst nightmare, I guarantee it."

"You have a knack of being right Jack, but I just hope you're way off the mark on this one."

"You know when you get a gut feeling, an instinct about something, well that's what I'm feeling at the moment. I hate it when that happens."

"What are you going to do?"

"By the addition of the laser to the ISS, this changes the functionality of the outpost from a scientific laboratory to a military weapon. Other countries will see it that way too. It has a military role to play now and that's where I come in. I'm going to head off to JSC in the morning, have a chat with the Director and see if I can pick up some more information to calm my nerves. I need to be convinced that this is necessary unlike others who seem easily swayed to the idea."

* * *

JSC Headquarters, Houston - Building 1
Next Day

The JSC Director met Copeland outside the headquarters building and exchanged formalities with the cursory handshake. Copeland had had the chance to read the bio of James Hartman whilst on his way to Houston. He was suitably impressed and by all accounts was certainly the right man for the job.

"If the truth be known, I wasn't surprised to get your call yesterday Jack." The Director began, "I'm sure you have a lot of concerns and questions to ask. Let's go up to my office."

Both Copeland and the Director made their way into the building and took the stairs to the third floor and then into the office. It was a large office, well equipped, functional, and practical and gave a feeling of power. As you would expect, there was a variety of model space rockets on most of the desks in the room. When you're the JSC Director you want to know what hardware is at your disposal. There were models of both redundant and current space vehicles.

"Would you like a drink Jack? Coffee, Tea, water?"

"Coffee would be great. Thank you."

"How do you take it?"

"Americano. Straight as it comes."

The Director picked up his desk phone and asked his secretary for two coffees.

"How did the community take the briefing yesterday?"

"That was one hell of a presentation James. You certainly ruffled a few feathers and maximised the attention of everyone. No-one can figure out how you'd managed to keep it quiet for so long."

A knock came on the door that disrupted the conversation. The Directors secretary brought a tray with two coffee cups on top and placed them on the coffee table next to Copeland.

"Thank you, Helen." The Director said to his secretary as she withdrew from the room. He didn't answer Copeland's question but then looked at him, "How can I help you Jack?"

"The addition of the laser to the ISS changes the initial mission profile and now has a military connotation. It has the potential and ability to be used as a military weapon, a lethal weapon and a weapon of mass destruction."

"There is no denying that of course. The perception of people will often be drawn to that conclusion. The addition of the laser would certainly change the mind set of many."

"My concern is that it is up there." Copeland looked and pointed to the ceiling imitating the fact that he was indicating space, "and of course they have the software to override controlling mechanisms here on Earth."

"We have checks and balances at the IMCC so it is virtually impossible for the ISS to take full control."

"No disrespect Director, but I'm a great believer that nothing is impossible. I always plan for the worse and hope for the best."

"If everyone reasoned that way then we would all be living in fear. The equipment has been tried and tested and was successful. The launch next month will include the hardware for installation inside the ISS together with the laser system itself. There will of course need to be EVA's to fully install the laser in the correct place. Good old-fashioned nuts and bolts still need to be attached manually even in space."

"What crew have you identified for this mission?"

"It will be a crew of five. Three Americans and two Russian cosmonauts."

"How did the Russians get involved with this?" Copeland asked with a look of surprise.

"It's part of the new exchange program. We send some guys over to Moscow and in return they send some to us."

"Why did you decide to put the cosmonauts into this program specifically considering how sensitive the cargo is?"

"It's all part of the new world order Jack; openness, transparency. Something even I have to go along with whether I agree or not."

"What are the names of the cosmonauts?" queried Copeland.

Director Hartman tapped a few keys on his computer keyboard and then looked back at Copeland, "Colonel Sergei Grigorev and Major Vladimir Popov from the Russian air force. Both have served with distinction."

"Have all the crew been fully vetted?"

"Yep, they've all been psychometrically evaluated by our in-house doctor and external shrinks. I've also had the medical reports sent to me by Moscow in regards the two cosmonauts. Clean bills of health all round - not even a sniffle."

"Forgive me for being a little sceptical Director, but even the best trained people can go rogue. It just takes a personal issue back home to flip someone to create a moment of madness. Maybe even a financial incentive or they think they're working towards the greater good. The potential consequences here of course are mind blowing. Someone in charge of a lethal weapon could potentially hold the world to ransom. It is not something that I want to happen on my watch."

"Whilst I understand your concerns Jack, we need to protect Earth from external forces. By this I mean meteorites or asteroids. These are becoming more of a common occurrence creating problematic situations. It's like the stuff of doomsday scenarios. Something we can't defend against from Earth alone, hence the need to have an alternative. Back in two thousand there were several close calls with meteorites. On January eighteen in two thousand for instance, one managed to get through our so-called atmospheric shield and exploded over Tagish Lake in British Columbia near Alaska. The explosion had the force of multiple nuclear warheads. Ground zero was above any land mass but if it had impacted it would've been devastating to say the least. We need to neutralise these the moment they are deemed a threat to humanity. We can't afford to have any more close calls."

"I get that." Acknowledged Jack, "and probably I'd be the first to agree. But if something goes wrong in the opposite direction then I'll be called in to pick up the pieces. It's just that I see this as a problem from a different perspective and I sure as hell don't want to be proven right. I want to be convinced enough to be sure that this has been thought through on a rigorous scale and not purely for financial reasons."

"You have my word Jack. It was a consideration during the initial consultation phase with POTUS especially opening up the ISS to our Cosmonaut colleagues. It was something which couldn't be ignored."

"When is the launch slated for?"

"We have several FRR meetings to go through first."

"FRR?" repeated Copeland with a frown.

"Flight readiness reviews. Two high-powered meetings to make sure everything is on track. But to answer your question, it is currently pencilled in for December fifth around twenty-two hundred hours. Just one other thing that may put your mind at ease."

"Which is?"

"You probably won't remember, but back in October nineteen ninety-seven, the US Secretary of State approved the use of the world's most powerful laser to shoot at a sixty million-dollar US Air Force satellite. It was carried out from a secret location in New Mexico and though successful, it was the first time a laser beam had been fired through space. There were two experiments and the whole idea was to test its potential for destruction."

"How was it executed?"

"The beam was six feet wide and a burst of concentrated light lasting less than one second was fired towards the target two hundred and sixty miles above earth. During the second experiment, the laser was charged and fired a pulse lasting less than ten seconds."

"What happened to the satellite?"

"It crippled it without actually destroying it. A longer burst of course would have pulverised the satellite."

"Was anything learnt?"

"Well, the whole idea was to learn the extent to which energy lasers on the ground could blind or destroy satellites in space but of course there has never been any intention to use the laser for offensive purposes but purely as a means to collect data. It was a useful exercise, costly I admit but sometimes you have to speculate to accumulate and the use of real equipment cannot be under estimated."

"Is this public knowledge?"

"Not really. Congressional critics and arms control groups have long campaigned against firing the New Mexico laser."

"Was the satellite a redundant one?"

"Funny you should say that, actually no it wasn't. In fact, the Air Force stated that they didn't require it anymore so in effect, yes it was redundant. However, according to the satellite's makers in Arizona, it had years left in service. The military argued that the test was needed to reduce the vulnerability of other US satellites. However, there has been no acknowledgement that it would ever be used for offensive purposes."

"Would this not set off an arms race?"

"Congress put forward a case that it is likely to set off a race for space weapons that in the long run could increase the risk for the nations satellites."

"What about the arms control treaties? Would this not be in violation of that?"

"Step back a bit. Weaponising space would spoil relations with China and Russia for sure and I can't for one minute imagine they'd want to do that. The control aspect would be governed by the nineteen seventy-two anti-ballistic missile treaty which the US government are keen to abandon."

"Are lasers not included in this treaty?"

"The treaty does prohibit the deployment of weapons in outer space which technically restricts a US military doctrine called "space control'. Nothing has been suggested that lasers are deemed a threat and therefore have not been included."

"That's an interesting point. Well and truly open to interpretation by countries especially if nothing specific has been included. Thank you for your time Director. I think I have a better understanding now."

"Not a problem. The program needs support from all sides to make it work. It can only be built on success and this will be measured at the moment it actually serves its purpose by defending Earth."

Both Copeland and the Director stood up and retraced their steps back to the front of the building. Copeland shook hands with the Director and then climbed into his official car before being driven away. Having cleared JSC, Copeland picked up his phone and dialled a number he had selected from his contacts list.

* * *

Office of the CIA Director, Langley, Virginia
The Next Day

Copeland had arrived at the CIA Headquarters at ten o'clock in the morning having made the appointment whilst leaving the JSC the day before. He was met at the security desk by the Director's secretary and escorted to his office on the third floor. The Director came from behind his desk and shook Copeland's hand.

"Welcome to the mad house Jack." The Director began, "Coffee?" he asked as he returned behind his large mahogany desk. Behind his chair was the flag of the USA draping from a pole in one corner and one of the CIAs in the other.

"Perfect." Responded Jack.

The Director picked up his desk phone and ordered coffee for both.

"How was your trip?"

"Very interesting. Director Hartman gave me the answers that I think he and everyone else wanted me to hear. In an ideal world, what he said was actually plausible. But we don't live in that glass bubble of an ideal world."

A knock on the door was the announcement that coffee had arrived. The tray was placed on the Directors desk and the secretary retreated, closing the door behind her before Copeland continued.

"Hartman is an idealist and is guided by his ideals rather than practical considerations. I think he's in denial. It's a terrible combination to have both though. It leaves no margin for error and it will leave no room for manoeuvre should this thing go south."

"I have my concerns too Jack. To add a laser to the ISS and with all the R and D for lasers that's going on at the moment, how can anyone not think of a worst-case scenario? In my eyes, it's a whole new style of modern warfare that may not play out by the rules."

"Also added into the mix, Hartman mentioned that there would be a crew of five on the next slated launch; three Americans and two Russian cosmonauts. With all the good will in the world, this to me is a red flag." Copeland smiled, "excuse the pun." He added having realised what he had said.

"A major concern and a headache for the intelligence community. Everyone needs to stay on top of this one."

"Wise words. Could you get your guys to find any background intel on the two cosmonauts, Colonel Sergei Grigorev and Major Vladimir Popov. Whilst looking at the Russians may seem the obvious choice, I'd like you also to look at the three astronauts, Tom Anderson, Neil Burgess and Matt Cooper just to be on the safe side."

"We don't normally look at domestic problems Jack. We are an international intelligence-gathering agency. That's not to say that we can't. With regards the Russians however, that's going to take a little while. We're not exactly rubbing shoulders with the SVR at the moment. The collapse of the cold war in nineteen ninety-one was meant to re-write how intelligence was gathered. That was easier said than done as most countries still wish to hold onto information. They see it as the more information they have then the more powerful they are. If I have it and you don't then I have a means in which to deal later on.

"What exactly are we looking for?"

"I'm not sure at the moment. Every piece you get, let me know no matter how trivial."

"Okay, I'll give the FBI director a call and see if we can look into this together."

"Keep it under the radar though." insisted Copeland, "I don't want this getting out just yet."

"You know the astronauts go through a rigorous selection and bio checks before enrolling into the ASCANs programme?"

"Yep, but nothing is infallible. With the reputation of the Russians at the moment, I just want to make sure that this launch is as tight as it can be. You do, too right?"

"Of course, I do. Leave it with me."

"Do your best." Said Copeland, "I'm not sure how much time we have."

CHAPTER 6

JSC, Houston Texas – Mission Briefing Room
2 Months prior to launch – October 2001

"Welcome gentleman." Began the Director of flight crew operations Dean Kelly. "You've reached the part of your training now whereby considerations need to be given as to the identity of both the primary and secondary crews for an up and coming slated STS mission. Whilst crews are generally pencilled in advance, this mission has been under wraps for the last twelve months. It's now time to reveal the names of the crew slated for STS–108A. Pilot and Commander of the Orbiter Horizon will be Tom Anderson. His payload commander will be Neil Burgess and the Flight Engineer will be Matt Cooper. Mission specialists are Sergei Grigorev and Vladimir Popov."

Others in the room began to applaud and personally congratulate those selected.

"Way to go man." It was the stand by pilot who was first to congratulate."

"Hey thanks buddy. Means a lot." Responded Tom with a smile that could've said you've just won the lottery.

"You still have six weeks left of your scheduled training here at the JSC." Dean paused before continuing, "In approximately two weeks you will be transferred to KSC where you will be billeted in the Operations and Checkout building in preparation for your launch. Whilst there, you will all undertake a physical exam called the L-10 and as the name suggests, it will take place ten days before launch. This initial test is to ensure that you are not already infected. After the exam and seven days before launch you will all be placed in quarantine until ready to ride the shuttle bus to the launch pad. You will undergo a second exam, two days prior to launch and then you will be given a brief medical check before you all suit up on launch day. At any stage, if anyone is showing signs and symptoms then you will be removed and rotated out with a member of the secondary stand by crew who will also be quarantined alongside you throughout this period. The date of the projected launch gentlemen is scheduled for December fifth. It will of course be subject to the usual weather variables. Nothing is as straightforward as it seems. Those of you who intend to be the traditionalist and hit the tavern tonight, enjoy. It'll be your last taste of freedom for six months."

* * *

Outpost Tavern, Webster – Same Day
Astronaut Hangout

Prior to all shuttle launches, it was tradition to hold parties and for the Orbiter crews to buy a keg of beer. It was equally a tradition to celebrate a safe return. Both Vladimir and Sergei, having been officially informed of their position on the next slated launch, decided to celebrate in the official manner. On their first visit, the tavern was referred to as building ninety-nine. They both looked on their map that had been given to them by Kurt on their first day but couldn't find any reference to building ninety-nine. When they asked other ASCANs where it was, they would laugh and say it was the Tavern and that it usually caught everyone out. Building ninety-nine doesn't exist on any NASA schematics but was labelled as such when an astronaut returned from a mission and asked where they should have a de-brief and it has stuck ever since.

The old red building seemed a faraway place from the cutting edge advanced technology of the NASA facility at the space centre a short drive away. It had a tangle of bushes growing up the outside wall and a faint smell of sewerage was evident to welcome you on arrival. It wasn't very inviting but push inside through the inner swinging doors shaped liked two bikini-clad women and sentiment and nostalgia wins the day. A great place to swing the lamp and with the walls lined with photographs of smiling, blue suited astronauts you got the feeling of being amongst a different and elite crowd.

Vladimir and Sergei jumped on the shuttle bus along with their newly identified team and standby crew and took the six-minute journey to building ninety-nine. The complete STS-108A primary and stand by alert crews dropped by to fulfil tradition. It was impossible to break that loop and those who were superstitious amongst the crew ensured that it wasn't an option. The last tradition was for the launch of STS-105 back in August. Now it was their turn to live the dream. It was the second home for the engineers who often sketched their ideas on napkins where a burst of inspiration needed to be noted and remembered. Sergei burst through the doors and headed straight towards the bar.

"Here's two hundred dollars for a keg of your best Corona Extra. This is our night."

"Coming up." John the barman replied as he headed outback to collect the keg returning moments later rolling the barrel towards the bar. He knew exactly what Sergei meant and was only too willing to oblige. He'd seen crews come and go and the lucky ones return. The community was close knit and any loss was hard to bear as it was like losing a member of your family. The rest of the crew now began to filter through the swing doors and headed towards Sergei. The area around the bar was small but cosy at the same time.

"When you shipping out?" asked John with a genuine interest as he multi tasked and gathered glasses from under the counter to fill. These people were his family and he treated and respected them as such. The loss of the shuttle Challenger on January twenty-eight nineteen eighty-six decimated the community. It took a while to get over it but life had to go on.

"Slated for December fifth." It was Neil Burgess the payload commander.

"When is the current crew due back?" John asked, as he would need to ensure that he had enough supplies on hand.

"Due to return eleven days after we arrive so once we've taken over you should expect to see them here shortly after. It's only a six-hour flight. Load up with more kegs ready and waiting, they'll need it for sure. It's amazing what you miss when you're in isolation." It was Tom who answered. "Burgers and fries all round John. Don't know what you do to them but they are the best in town." added Tom.

The food arrived shortly after being ordered and before long the keg was flowing nicely and the conversation between the teams became competitive. Matt headed over to the jukebox and selected a song that began to play in the background to the tune of 'Ground Control to Major Tom' by David Bowie.

"Okay, who listed that one?" chuckled Tom as he looked at the others and caught Matt walking back towards the bar, "Nice one Matt."

"Seemed appropriate."

No one talked about the up and coming mission. It didn't seem right or appropriate. There was always apprehension and concern before flights but these NASA guys were legends in getting these things to work and defying the laws of gravity.

John came from around the bar and produced the official photo of STS-108A. He handed it to Tom along with a pen and without a word he began to sign it. Once done, it was passed along the line where all the remaining crew signed the front. Vladimir was the last to sign and then he handed it back to John who proudly affixed it to the memorabilia board taking pride and place along with those who had gone before.

As the night passed by and the keg was down to its last drops, both crews decided the night was over.

"Have a good trip guys and catch you on your return. Stay safe up there." came words of encouragement from John as the crew moved towards the bikini-clad doors.

Once outside they boarded the bus and headed back to the JSC.

* * *

Washington DC – 0600 The Next Day

Copeland woke early at six o'clock as he did most mornings and set off for his daily four-mile loop around the National Mall between the Capitol and the Lincoln Memorial that was lined with a treasure troth of landmarks. Running past the Washington Memorial and behind the White House gave a rare glimpse of an eerily quiet DC. There are twenty million annual visitors to DC who come purely to look at these remarkable landmarks and   Copeland preferred this time of day since it gave him the chance to clear his head and to think things through without having to be distracted whilst he dodged a tidal wave of people. He kept reminding himself of the conversation he had with the Director of the JSC and whilst he tried as much as he could to put to rest his comments, Copeland was finding it difficult to let go. Mulling things over in his mind just created scenarios that almost seemed real like. Having reached his apartment, he decided to take a shower then he would call Elisabeth who he knew was nine hours ahead.

* * *

Inter-Continental Hotel, Tashkent, Uzbekistan 1700hrs the Same Day

Elisabeth was in her hotel room tapping away at her keyboard as she did most nights. It was an opportunity to document the activities of the day and to make a fresh start the following day on other news stories. Whilst looking over her notes on the pad next to her computer, she heard the telephone ring that startled her and broke her concentration. She picked up the receiver after the third ring.
"This is Elisabeth." She answered.
"Hey it's Jack. Just checking in. How's it going?"
"Hey, I need a break. It's so nice to hear your voice. This country is a real mess Jack. They have so many issues that any we have back home seem so insignificant in comparison."
"What's been happening?"
"Where do I begin? The issues with Human Rights for starters is staggering. Uzbekistan gained independence back in nineteen ninety-two and have

advanced consistently in the name of consolidating the peace and security of the region which allowed them to boost health care etcetera. The usual stuff they want to convince you with, but what they don't tell you about is the diabolical Human Rights problem. People here are sphinx-like. They are almost in denial of the treatment they receive. When we ask them questions they are very canny traders of information. Things are not good but not bad either but they are quick to reverse the questioning to ask us what we think of Uzbekistan. They listen without comment or expression. They are very sympathetic towards nine eleven and were surprised at the US being invited to stage warplanes at the Karshi-Khanabad airbase known as the K2 near the southern town of Khanabad. This of course was in support of the Afghanistan operation Freedom that also allowed for overflying rights and the defence of Uzbekistan from fuzzily defined future foes. All of this of course was agreed with the regime of President Islam Karimov once fifteen million dollars had been handed over. We picked up chatter that critics have accused the US of propping up one of the world's most brutal regimes in exchange for the use of the base. Because of a media blackout, not one journalist is allowed to be within two miles of the base so it is very difficult to gauge any proper local response."

"Wish I'd never asked now." Quipped Copeland, "Wow you have been busy."

"Sorry Jack, I didn't mean to pile this on you but I know I can use you as a sounding board.

You're a great listener. I needed to get this off my chest and I needed to vent."

"Anything else going on?" asked Copeland cautiously not knowing whether or not Elisabeth had finished.

"There is a major problem here with terrorism."

"In what way?" Copeland asked

"In nineteen ninety-nine for instance, sixteen people were killed and over one hundred were injured in a car bomb outside Government Headquarters in downtown Tashkent. This was seen in some quarters however as an attempt on the life of President Karimov and blame has been attributed to the IMU although not yet confirmed. This is a nation whose annual salary is about three hundred dollars a year. Corruption is terrible, even worse than it was during the Soviet era. It has been mentioned that the US government has been targeting the Hizb-u-Tahrir group. They are a Jordanian organisation with some ugly ideas and a small following here. The group circulated leaflets criticising the government of cruelty and corruption. Nothing new in that of course but they added that democracy is evil. The regime has taken a harsh stance on anyone in possession of a leaflet and is punishable by a prison term up to twenty years. It's a way of stifling free speech."

"Does any of this affect the US directly?"

"My fear is that the Uzbek government will turn to the US and say *'Help us in countering our internal threats'* and by that I reckon it means help us continue this horrific campaign against peaceful and independent Muslims. Human rights workers are having leaflets planted on them and being sent to hell. I sense that the US government is divided in its loyalty; the State department wanting better human rights in Uzbekistan and the Pentagon wanting bases. All this of course raises the question: 'why can't we have it all'. After all, the US is doing a huge favour for Karimov's regime by seeking out and destroying his enemies in Afghanistan. We are of course paying him handsomely for the privilege. We've already given Uzbekistan some thirty million dollars in aid and that is set to soar now that we have an allegiance to them. With all this support from our side, we could demand that Uzbekistan take some minimal steps forward on human rights, but instead its all been just toing and froing with no resolution in sight. This really peeves me off Jack. There is no reason why the US government can't simply demand that Uzbekistan move forward towards guarantees on human rights. The state department has delayed its release of the annual list of countries that do not respect religious freedoms and I think they should release it with Uzbekistan near the top."

"You really have put your heart and soul into this. I can see and feel your frustration but it will always be an uphill struggle to get these regimes to understand the values of people. This is often the case when they have been in power for so long and have lived a privileged life themselves without being accountable to anyone. They make laws to protect themselves whilst their bank balances become bigger. They have no understanding or interest of human suffering. They want to take as much as they can regardless the state of the country. They also expect the likes of the US to pump money into a crumbling country and economy where we will get nothing in return to show for our support. It will always be one-sided and that is how they work. Governments around the world believe that by throwing money to a problem it will miraculously resolve issues but that is just so far from reality."

"Jack." Elisabeth said trying to change the subject

"Yeah."

"I didn't want to bring this up as I know you will be worried about me. I think I've spotted what you would call a tail. It's become more than a coincidence."

"When did this happen?"

"It all started once I arrived at Sheremetyevo airport, Moscow. I didn't think anything about it at the time but I saw a man with a long grey leather jacket follow behind me from the terminal building without any baggage then jumped into a big vehicle that followed me again. It dropped in two cars behind my taxi."

"That's common trade craft. Why wait until now to tell me though?" Copeland added with a tone of concern.

"I tried to tell you before but the line has been terrible for us to have a serious conversation on this matter. I also saw the same vehicle pull up outside my hotel in Moscow."

"Have you been approached or spoken to?"

"No nothing like that."

"Have you had any messages left at the hotel reception?"

"No."

"Have you seen the man or vehicle since you arrived in Tashkent?"

"No. I'm just so busy and because I haven't seen anyone like that since Moscow I haven't been concentrating on that side of things. It was another reason why I didn't let you know Jack."

"Ok. You did well though to spot the tail. Keep alert and don't let your guard down. Follow the drill I told you before you left the US."

"Will do."

"When you coming home?" asked Copeland

"Not for a while yet."

"I have some leave owing me. I was thinking of coming over. How's next week sound?"

"That'll be great Jack. How can you get away so soon though?"

"Because I have something that I need to do."

"Okay. Sounds intriguing. I miss you."

"I miss you more."

"Impossible." She teased

"I'll let you know flight details when confirmed."

Copeland wanted to say more to her but he was pretty sure that the line wouldn't be secure. He needed to make the visit personal and for two reasons.

* * *

Washington DC – Offices of Scorpion
The same day

Copeland pressed the intercom button on his desk phone.

"Mary, can you find me a return flight to Tashkent in Uzbekistan for next week please. I'm heading out to see Elisabeth. Long overdue."

Mary was Copeland's long-standing secretary who he could trust implicitly. He wasn't sure how he would cope without her if ever she decided to call it a day. She was fifty-five and never married and Copeland was her family. After fifteen minutes, Copeland's desk phone buzzed.

"Jack, there is a flight from JFK to Tashkent with two stop overs, a red eye flight to Frankfurt and then onto Almaty in Kazakhstan."

"Timings?"

"Leaves JFK at nine fifty-five pm for a seven-hour forty flight and arrives Frankfurt at eleven thirty-five am local the next day with a one hour fifty-five lay over. From Frankfurt you take the thirteen thirty flight to Almaty arriving local eleven fifty with a layover of twelve hours thirty. You'll then need to take the twelve twenty flight arriving Tashkent the next day at twelve fifty pm local. All this added together it's a two-day trip Jack."

"Okay. Thanks Mary. I knew it'd be a long haul. I definitely need to go so go ahead and book and clear my diary for a week."

* * *

CIA Headquarters, Langley Virginia
Office of the Director – The next day

Karl Langdon was two years into his tenure as CIA Director. He was a military man and having retired from the marines as a two-star general, it was a privilege to have been chosen by the President himself and offered the post as CIA Director during the last administration poll. He had accepted the post without hesitation.

Having considered the request by Copeland, he now needed to put the request into action. Langdon picked up his desk phone and dialled a number. The call was picked up after four rings. "I need a favour but it needs to be kept off the books and reporting directly back to me."

"Okay, sounds interesting. What's the deal?" asked the FBI Director, Felix Burnette.

"Jack Copeland over at Scorpion has a hunch that there's an issue down at JSC involving the next manned launch to the ISS scheduled for this December. It involves the crew and since it's a mixed international one this time which involves our friends from over in Russia, he wants to make sure that they are as clean as they can be. I can't say any more than that for the usual script *"In the interests of national security"* etcetera. I wouldn't be making this call if I didn't see it from his point of view also."

"He has a hell of a hunch. What do you want me to do?"

"Background bios on the American part of the crew with as much info as you can whether trivial or otherwise.   Nothing will be too small. The Russian angle we'll look after from this end."

"I figure NASA would've done an adequate job of screening their candidates in the first place. Don't they have to complete an MMPI or something and then be evaluated by Doctor psycho this and Doctor psycho that. Everyone else applying for government jobs have to go through the same process. Unless you're a real fruitcake, it's difficult to fail these tests."

"I'd call these checks as belt and braces. It's better to be sure that nothing happens than something does occur and we all have egg on our faces. Wish I could tell you more Felix but I can't at this stage."

"Okay, what are their names?" Burnette finally asked. Langdon gave Burnette the names of the three US astronauts. "You have to be prepared though," Burnette added, "that there is a chance of course that if something doesn't flag up during their bio checks that there probably isn't anything to be found or they were very good at masking any revelations in the first place."

"I concur, but it's the latter part that I'm worried about."

CHAPTER 7

Tashkent International Airport, Uzbekistan
One Week Later

Copeland arrived on time having experienced a two day journey from hell. It took him almost a full day by the time he arrived but he had no regrets. This visit was needed for two reasons. He had arranged with Elisabeth to pick him up and wasn't disappointed when he left the terminal building to see her large white CNN SUV pull up to the pick-up point. Elisabeth had jumped out the vehicle and came around to Jack's side. Running towards him she jumped with excitement into his open arms. She felt like a teenager all over again. Times like this were priceless and being apart was made for moments like this. He looked into her eyes and paused wanting to capture this moment for a lifetime. She looked even more beautiful than the day she left. Copeland was fortunate to have her; in fact they were both fortunate to have each other. They were true to each other even whilst apart which made their bond even stronger.

Having loaded Copeland's small case into the vehicle, Elisabeth drove the short distance to her hotel, the Inter-continental on Amir Street. Having parked the vehicle in the car park at the front of the hotel, they both went to the sixth floor and to Elisabeth's room. Having entered the room, Copeland dropped his bag, embraced Elisabeth and at the same time, closed the door with his right shoe heel. This was a moment of sheer pleasure that he wanted to last forever. The excitement of being close to her was overwhelming. The smell of her distinctive La Perla perfume was both captivating and scintillating. Even though he was exhausted from the journey, he wasn't about to cut short his evening. Whilst they kissed passionately, Copeland removed Elisabeth's pink sweater revealing a white strappy top beneath. Dropping the straps one by one he removed the top, which revealed a white see through lace bra. Her nipples were hard and erect and were standing firm beneath the lace material. Copeland teased each nipple in turn, causing Elisabeth to arch her back to enjoy that sensitive and tantalising moment. Her breathing became stronger and more rapid and moans became louder in response. Copeland reached behind her back and managed to release the clip on her bra the first time and then release it to the floor. He cupped both breasts together and pinched each nipple, which sent Elisabeth into a spasm. Not wanting to enjoy the moment all for herself, Elisabeth removed Copeland's jacket, and slowly his shirt then rubbed her soft hands onto his bare chest and across his now hardening nipples. She needed this. It had been a long time since she left DC.

Pulling Copeland close to her, she felt his desire for her become more intense. As she walked backwards towards the bed and not wanting to take her eyes away from him, she revealed her bodily charms and, in a few moments, both were entwined as one. Elisabeth sat astride Jack and inserted him into her and both began to rise and fall to the point that their inner excitement could be contained no longer. They both rolled over together and before long Copeland had drifted off through both physical and travel exhaustion.

* * *

As Copeland began to stir from his sleep, he rolled over to feel the closeness of Elisabeth. As he reached out there was nothing for him to touch. The sheets were still warm however and he could still smell the scent of her perfume where she had laid moments earlier. He closed his eyes again whilst he thought of the fond memories of the night they had just spent together which brought a sensual feeling in his loins. As his senses became more aware, he could smell fresh coffee and as he looked over to where the machine was, he noticed Elisabeth standing with her back to him and preparing two cups. She was dressed in a lovely black thong and a small strappy white top that revealed all her charms. The perfect outlines of her breasts were pressing against the soft material and her nipples were showing through which excited Copeland even more. His eyes were transfixed as if in a trance. Her body was sculptured from years of training. She looked amazing and he was so much in love with her. Elisabeth sensed movement behind her.

"Hey, morning lover boy." She said with a wide smile, "You've had a good long sleep."

"What's the time?" Copeland asked bleary eyed as he began to sit up in bed, puffed up the pillows behind him then reached across to his bedside cabinet to look at his watch. He felt as though he'd been asleep for a whole day.

"A quarter after eight." they both said at the same time that brought a smile and a chuckle, which lightened the moment. Copeland had just had seventeen hours sleep.

Elisabeth brought the two coffees across placing one on Copeland's side table and walked around and placed the other on her side of the bed. She then drew the curtains back revealing a glorious day of sunshine after which she slid back under the sheets and snuggled up against Copeland by placing her right arm over his chest.

"I know you've only just arrived Jack but how long are you staying."

"I've booked a week off. Heading back next week. Maybe we can have a look around. I'm the tourist and you're the guide."

"This was such a lovely surprise. That sounds perfect. Let's order room service." She asked rhetorically as she leant across to her side cabinet and picked up the menu. They both chose a full breakfast and after Elisabeth made the call to reception, they both laid back and snuggled under the duvet to enjoy the moments of togetherness and intimacy once again.

* * *

With a knock on the door, breakfast had arrived. Elisabeth had signed the slip of paper and the waiter retreated closing the door behind him. Having enjoyed the lazy start to the day, both decided to get showered and dressed. Copeland was keen to get outside and to see the city for himself with the expert guide by his side. The temperature was set to be around twenty-two degrees so both Copeland and Elisabeth dressed accordingly. Copeland wore a white cotton short-sleeved shirt with light blue chinos and Elisabeth settled for white linen trousers and a dusky pink plain strappy vest top. Forty minutes later they were both heading down the elevator and to the front of the hotel where Elisabeth had parked her vehicle the day before. She was happy, she was content and she almost wanted to skip through the hotel foyer but didn't quite buck up the courage to do so. She'd leave that for another day. Having both climbed into the vehicle, she began to drive off.

"I'm going to take you first to the old town. It's so picturesque; you'll love it. I've had to learn quite a lot about Uzbekistan and in particular Tashkent whilst I've been here. Not quite mastered the Uzbek language yet." Elisabeth smiled, "I've had to consider its history which is pretty chequered by normal standards. Besides all their human rights issues, Tashkent is actually a well-balanced combination of a modern metropolis and the unique flavour of an eastern city. It is after all the capital of

Uzbekistan and the largest metropolis in Central Asia. For sixty years, Tashkent was the capital of a communist republic, which helped enormously the city in its socio-economic development, which we can see today. There was a downside to all this of course, since the Bolsheviks were not very kind to the religious architectural monuments of feudalism and capitalism, they tried to set their own monumental buildings to the liking of the soviet era. The further out you go from the city, you will notice that more and more of the monumental architectural buildings have been preserved for example in Samarkand, Bukhara, Khiva and Kokand. Samarkand is the second largest city in Uzbekistan. They all mean nothing to you at the moment but hopefully we may get a chance to see them. The city went through an overhaul after the earthquake of nineteen sixty-six which devastated the area and only a limited number of buildings from the middle ages were left intact. Give the Russians credit though, they began to rebuild and restore the city the day after the earthquake struck."

Copeland kept looking behind their vehicle through the side mirror and wanted confirmation that the tail, which had followed Elisabeth, was still there or had been pulled. If he couldn't see them it didn't mean that they weren't there anymore, it just meant they had become more professional and therefore harder to spot. Copeland couldn't see anything that would warrant more interest and a different approach.

"You have been busy. You're missing your true vocation in life." Copeland teased, "You should've been a tourist guide. You'd be fantastic. What I've noticed so far is that this is one of those places that you know something isn't quite as it should be but takes a little while to figure it out."

"I don't follow. How do mean?" quizzed Elisabeth not quite grasping his thought.

"It's interesting that almost every single car we've seen and passed are all white and there are only several different vehicle makes. They're either a Daewoo, Chevrolet or a Lada. All of which I'm guessing are from the Soviet era."

"I've been here for so long that I never even noticed. Now that you've pointed it out I can see what you mean. How bizarre."

Elisabeth and Copeland spent the rest of the day driving around parts of the Silk Road looking at the hypnotic mosaics, voluptuous domes and glittering minarets. The incredible ancient monument in Bukhara's Registan Square was a place to be visited as was the walled city of Khiva at dawn and Elisabeth intended not to disappoint Copeland over the next few days. Having driven around for a few hours, she decided to stop at the Semo de Roma Italian coffee house on Chekhov Street. Having parked her vehicle on the main road, they both walked up the outside steps onto the long wooden veranda with tables and chairs on either side. The restaurant was one floor up and directly above the Kpacota gift shop. It had a veranda that was covered with a canopy to keep out the daily heat. On the right against the shop window were round tables for two people and on the left were square tables for four people next to a metal four bar fence which ran the full length of the veranda. Attached to the fence were rectangular window boxes at varying intervals to soften the look. Each was filled with small coloured flowers. Elisabeth chose a table for four on the left, which slightly obscured the view back to the road. They both sat next to each other and since the veranda was slightly elevated above the ground their view was looking down towards the road. Having settled down, she attracted the attention of the waiter who promptly appeared next to her and ordered an Americano with no milk whilst Copeland ordered a Latte. Both had asked for two glasses of water. The weather was just perfect. Blue sky, a light breeze and a blazing sun that made for a perfect day. Elisabeth chose the seats carefully to make sure they weren't directly next to anyone else. She also made sure that they both had their backs to the window of the coffee shop.

Elisabeth leant forward "Before you came here," she began in a quiet voice, "you said to me that you had something to ask of me but had to wait until you saw me in person. Now you're here what was the big secret?" she asked with a little excitement in her voice.
Copeland looked around him before he began, "I had a meeting with the President a week after you left DC and he has some concerns about our mutual friends the Russians."

"Oh, such as?" she asked almost disappointingly.
Copeland sensed that she had an expectation of something else but he wasn't quite ready for that. He wanted to for sure and there was no denying that but

he needed to get answers to things which he knew were important to both of them. "They've gone particularly quiet and he feels as though they are up to something."

"That's not unusual. In what way is he concerned?"

"He's not too sure about that part."

"What are you asking?"

"We need to establish some kind of line of enquiry."

"Who's we?" she asked with a suspicious look.

"Well that's where you come in."

"I'm not with you Jack. Is this some kind of riddle?"

"No. I offered your name to the President to see if you could do your investigative journalistic bit and poke around the Russians for a while. He thought it was a great idea. I honestly believe you are the right person for the job given your credentials with CNN. It's a Presidential request but not an order." Copeland hoped that would sway the idea and ease the moment but he knew it was a lot to ask of Elisabeth.

"No Jack. No, please don't put me in that position. I don't work for the government."

"I know but the president is asking; no I'm asking you."

"That's emotional blackmail Jack and unfair. There are around six hundred thousand Russians living in Tashkent. Where am I supposed to begin? How am I supposed to find the time to do any of what you want in any case?"

"Not in Tashkent." Copeland said quietly.

"Oh." She looked puzzled, "where then?"

Copeland paused for a brief moment as he looked into her eyes to sense a reaction, "Moscow."

"Moscow." she repeated louder than she expected and then lowered her voice to continue, "Why Moscow?"

"That's where the seat of power is and where decisions are made."

"Ha ha very funny. When I first came to Moscow you weren't exactly thrilled at the idea."

"That was then and this is now."

"Are you asking me to go into the Kremlin?" she offered with a glint of excitement in her eyes.

During his conversation with Elisabeth, Copeland continued to look towards the street when he noticed a white taxi pull into the rank opposite the coffee shop and drop off his fare. As he kept watching, he continued his conversation, "No, sorry to disappoint you but nothing like that. That would be too risky. The CIA could do that if we wanted to."

"Moscow is two thousand five hundred square kilometres in size Jack. So where am I supposed to go and what am I supposed to do?"

Whilst the US president had his concerns, so too did Copeland whose concerns were more personal by putting Elisabeth into harms way. He decided to follow his instinct to see where it would lead. "The Oblast Region, thirty-one kilometres north-east of Moscow."

Copeland watched the white taxi as it drove away.

* * *

Taxi Rank opposite Semo de Roma Coffee Shop, Tashkent Same day

A white Chevrolet taxi pulled into a space on the rank opposite the coffee shop. He dropped off his fare and the driver looked at a single sheet of paper on his front seat that had two pictures on it, a male and a female and nothing more. Having confirmed what he was looking at on the first floor veranda of the coffee shop were the two people on his front seat, he began to take several photographs of them using a Canon SLR camera with a zoom lens. He was able to look dead ahead whilst taking the photographs so as not to arouse any suspicions. Once finished, he picked up his phone, fast dialled a stored number and reported what he had seen before receiving instructions and driving away moments later.

CHAPTER 8

Washington DC, Scorpion Offices - 7 days later 0900 hrs.

Copeland's visit to Tashkent was successful as far as he was concerned. He had gone there for two reasons and both had been accomplished. He had fully briefed Elisabeth on what was expected of her and he had spent some personal time with her. He wasn't comfortable with changing her schedule and away from Tashkent nor was he happy of potentially putting her into harm's way. He knew he had no choice but using a legitimate cover story of a fully-fledged investigative reporter from the CNN would give it some credibility. Should the Russians decide to look into Elisabeth then no flags would be raised. She is on the payroll of CNN after all and her face is known across the world whilst reporting on the big screen and therefore there would be no need for the US government to issue a strong deniability statement that one of their own was sniffing around. All her travel arrangements, hotel bookings and letter of assignment would be dealt with by CNN alone to ensure that her reason for being there was watertight and legit.

Copeland pressed a button on his desk phone, "Mary, can you bring a coffee in and then put me through to Karl Langdon over at Langley please?"

"Of course."

Moments later Mary had brought in Copeland's coffee and stood in front of his desk, "How was the trip?"

Copeland placed his Mont Blanc pen down onto his desk, "It's certainly a long way as we had already discovered. It may take me another week to get over the lag." he said with a smile.

"How's Elisabeth doing? Must be pretty lonely out there?"

"To be honest, she seems too busy to notice. I'm proud of what she does though and I'm fortunate to have met her."

"You two do make a great couple but being so far apart it must be so difficult?"

"It's certainly a challenge and pretty much a test of how strong the relationship is. We both trust each other implicitly not to do anything stupid to ruin what we do have and what our future holds together."

"What is the future with you both?"

"Mary, is this some kind of a twenty-question challenge?" he said in a teasing way.

"We never really get chance to talk about personal stuff. We've known each other for some time now and I will always be here to talk things through with you. I may be your secretary but I'm also a friend."

"I appreciate that Mary and you would be the first person I would turn to if the wheels came off between Elisabeth and me. Not wishing to push you out of the room but could you now get me Karl over at Langley please."

Mary retreated and a short while later, Copeland's desk phone rang and he picked it up, "Karl on line two." Said Mary.

Copeland pressed line two, "Karl, thanks for taking the call."

"That's fine. Welcome back. How was the trip?"

"Tashkent isn't as bad as we all make it out to be. The Russians did a hell of a job putting the place back together again after the earthquake almost levelled the whole place. "

It's not the top of my list of places to visit any time soon."

"I had to go. As you know Elisabeth is over there at the moment."

"How's she coping?"

"Pretty well under the circumstances. I wish she'd come home though but I can't make that decision for her. I can talk it through with her but she'll know when the time is right, hopefully."

"Yeah for sure."

"I asked Elisabeth to use her position at the CNN to look into something for me. You know I have a gut instinct concerning the ISS launch in December; well I need to find out some information to either negate it or step up a gear and do something about it. The President is on board with it."

"That's great news. We need to get to the bottom of this. I've heard absolutely nothing from the intelligence side of things that may indicate that there is a problem or an expected one with the December launch. No news sometimes is often good news. I'm keeping ears to the ground but if there is anything I can do then let me know."

"There is something you could do Karl. It's a personal request."

"Okay, shoot."

"I'm placing Elisabeth in a vulnerable position to fact find and this is a big ask, but could you supply a couple of your agents from the Moscow embassy to look out for her? She's doing this for the US and she'll have no recognition for this even if it turns out I was right."

"Consider it done. It'll need to be an off the book black op though with total deniability of ever being there. There can be no association with the CIA. We'll be on foreign turf and you know the kind of shit storm that will blow up between the two countries if we are known to operate inside Russia."

"Appreciate it Karl. Your guys from SAD are pretty hot and I'm sure no one will know they were ever there."

"What time line are we working to here?"

"I'm having Elisabeth moved out from Tashkent back to the CNN Moscow Bureau hopefully next week once the paperwork gets signed off at CNN. That'll be her official base from where she will work.

"Do I need to know what info Elisabeth will be collecting?"

"Not at this point Karl. Let's see how it plays out. I'll contact you once she has arrived back at the Moscow office."

"Perfect."

"Just one other thing, any update on the US astronauts?"

"Not at the moment Jack. This may take a little longer than first thought."

"Okay. Keep me posted though with any info you come across. Any snippets you have could be pieces of a jigsaw but I just hope there aren't any missing pieces."

* * *

JSC, Houston Texas 1600 hrs. Wednesday October 24, 2001 – Six weeks before launch

Sergei needed a break from the routines at JSC. He hadn't spoken to his wife since he arrived or anyone else back home. With the launch only six weeks away he wanted to speak with her but he knew that it would be difficult. The restrictions back home meant that he had no phone. He was in the western world now where freedoms were a great privilege and a way of life. He walked out of JSC onto NASA Road One and hailed the first cab available which was driving along. As the cab moved away, a dark grey sedan pulled in two cars behind.

* * *

CIA Headquarters, Langley, Virginia
Office of the director – The same day

"Jack, it's Karl over at Langley."

"Hey, the excitement in your voice sounds like you have something for me?"

"Sort of. Since our conversation regarding our Russian friends at JSC, I put a tail on them and today Sergei may have come up trumps. He took a cab alone from JSC where he was followed to the Baybrook Mall at Friendswood and went to the AT&T shop on level one. It's been confirmed that he bought a burner cell phone with a prepaid SIM."

"A what?"

"Keep up with the times Jack. It's a throw away disposable phone. One that seems impossible to trace and listen into."

"Even for you guys?" questioned Copeland

"It's not impossible but takes much longer than ordinary cell phones. Of course, but it is much quicker if we had the SIM number to start with."

"How would that work then?"

"Many users will use a SIM card once then throw it away but for those who use the same one continuously then potentially they could be located. It also needs the cooperation of the network operator who often obtains information about the SIM card but also the IMEI serial number. Having them on board shaves some time off the trace."

"Sounds easy."

"In theory, yeah. In practice it's a little different. Using these kinds of SIM cards, the traces would only be able to reveal his most current location where he was whilst the phone was powered up and connected to the network. By getting a number of historical locations, could eventually reveal enough information."

"That's great isn't it?"

"In certain circumstances yep. But he needs to mess up by being careless. The main obstacle would be the time when he makes a connection, how long he is active and the speed by which he disconnects. These are important variables. If the shop records the SIM number then we've just won the lottery."

"Did they?"

"Well, the law isn't exactly on our side when it comes to things like this. What was in our favour though is that one of my agents overheard Sergei on another phone registering his new SIM."

"I'm in suspense here Karl."

"He gave the IMEI serial number which is key to tracking and listening. I think this is all new to him as I'm guessing he's never done this before."

"Has he made any calls yet?"

"No but he loaded fifty dollars of air time for the SIM and he has thirty days in which to use it."

"That's a shit load of phone calls."

"Tell me about it. I've instructed Mike Adams, the director at NSA over at Fort Mead to keep their ears pinned for when the phone goes from dormant to active. He'll put his best tech boys on it. It'll have to be around the clock in two shifts."

"Nice job. Has he ever been seen with anyone else off base?"

"No."

"Where is he now?"

"Back at JSC."

"What about Vladimir? What has he been up to?"

"Nothing, just the usual day to day routines at JSC."

"Has he ever been off site?"

"Only to the Outpost Tavern out at Webster. Even then he went on the shuttle bus with all the other guys."

"There's something not quite right here. We're either missing something or we're looking in the wrong place."

"It does seem rather quiet considering your initial gut feeling Jack. I would've expected a lot more activity at this point."

"Me too. Let's keep tails on them for a little longer. There could be a spike in traffic as we get even closer to the launch date."

"I'll bring NSA Director Adams up to date."

* * *

NSA Intercept Room, Fort Mead, Maryland
0830 hrs. the next day

"Hi it's me." Sergei began, "We are ready to launch in a few weeks. Should anything go wrong I want you to know that I have done my very best for you. I feel this may be a one-way trip."

Using the automatic voice translation and interpretation software, they were able to translate in real time the conversation of their target. The controller flicked his fingers towards his supervisor and then waved indicating for him to come over and listen to the conversation. The supervisor put on a set of headphones, "Both Vladimir and myself are ready. We know what we need to do. We have the blessing of General Syromokov who has taught us well."

The NSA duty supervisor picked up his desk phone and dialled a number "Director, this is the day supervisor. We've picked up chatter between the Russian and an unknown female voice."

"Wasn't expecting it to come through that quick. Anything of substance?"

"It's of interest."

"That's pretty vague. Okay, send it across to me."

Director Mike Adams opened up the file and listened to the content. He immediately picked up his phone, "Karl, its Mike Adams over at NSA. "

"What have you got Mike?" Karl sounded excited.

"We've picked up some chatter from the Russian to an unknown female. I'm sending it over to you now. We'll keep monitoring."

* * *

CIA Headquarters, Langley, Virginia
Office of the Director – Late afternoon the same day

Having listened to the audio file, Karl wanted to share the news with Copeland.

"Jack, NSA have come up with an audio file of some chatter between one of the Russians and an unknown female. Sounds interesting and I'd like your take on it. Come over to my office when you can."

Copeland drove the ten-mile journey along the Washington Memorial Parkway and was there, parked his vehicle and sat in front of Karl within forty minutes. He listened attentively to the file and replayed it over several times to try and get a feel as to the tone and the purpose of the conversation.

"Not a lot to go on." Said Copeland, "If it's his wife then there isn't any romance or emotion. Are Russians that cold?" he asked rhetorically.

"Two ways you can look at this." Karl began, "It could be innocent or it could be coded. The innocent part could be a conversation with his wife saying his good byes before launch. To be fair, I'd probably do the same or on the flip side, it could sound like some kind of warning. If it is then we need to analyse this more deeply."

"The problem with words Karl is that they can have several meanings and we could be barking up the wrong tree and looking at this from the wrong angle. We are probably looking for a problem that may actually not be there."

"Well, that just confused the hell out of me."

"Me too, even though I say it myself." Copeland chuckled, "On a serious note he mentions that the trip may be one way. Wow that's a powerful statement to make and got my attention pretty quickly. Reading between the lines doesn't always mean you come up with the right answer each time. I feel that's what I'm doing now."

"Under normal circumstance I'd make a request for him to be picked up and questioned because there are open ended statements he's made. If he is involved in some renegade action, what we don't want to do is scare him but at the same time we need to establish if he has any intentions. We do have a major problem though when he leaves, it's not as if we can knock on his door, he's going to be two hundred and forty miles in the vertical. Currently, all the edges are a little fuzzy. We need more chatter to be able to get a better hold on what is being said. We can't action anything until we have solid Intel."

"I agree. If anything happens whilst on the ISS it'll be down to the crew to assist in resolving issues." Confirmed Copeland.

"We're both assuming here that Sergei has some kind of agenda. For all we know, it could be anyone or no one at all for that matter."

"In the absence of anything, we have to go with what we know. At the moment, everything is pointing towards Sergei unless I'm missing something."

"I was always told when I was at school, be wary of the quiet ones. So far, everyone, less Sergei has not even blinked an eye which means going by that analogy, we should be sceptical of the others and give them due consideration too."

"Point taken Karl."

"Director Adams and his staff are locked into this and are monitoring day and night. If there is anything, they'll pick it up for sure. The Russian made a connection with the name of General Syromokov. We know that he is the head of Cosmonaut training out of Star City but the way the Russian used the general's name it was as if the general had all but sanctioned something. This is a concern for me Jack."

"Let's leave it to play out for a while. We may find the answers soon."

"Okay. Has Elisabeth moved back to Moscow yet?"

"She arrived last week. I sense a question here though."

"Very astute. Could she sniff around regarding this general Syromokov?"

"That's a big ask. Russia is so secret and great at spinning propaganda. Not sure that if she ever did find anything that we could rely on it being anything but false."

"Fair point. But we have nothing else to go on at the moment. We need a lead, a dead end or good luck. No half measures."

"I'll see what I can do."

* * *

Kutuzovsky Prospekt, 7/4 Корпус 1
CNN Bureau Moscow – Two days later

Elisabeth was on the sixth floor of the CNN building with a great view overlooking the wide tree lined avenue of Kutuzovsky Avenue. CNN had expanded its investigative journalism, which had allowed Elisabeth to make the transfer from Tashkent and came with it was promotion to Senior International Correspondent. Her defined role in Moscow was to embed herself with the military and political leaders. If she was true to herself, she preferred the modernised Moscow to the dark ages of Tashkent. Unlike the free press in the modern world we live in and the recognition of free speech, CNN are monitored by the Russian government on a daily basis. This is to ensure that nothing adverse would be printed or released that would probably embarrass the Kremlin. One of her main priorities would be to interview the current Russian President, Vladimir Putin during his first term since he was appointed in two thousand. Elisabeth had been to the washroom and was heading back to her desk.

"Elisabeth, you have an external call on line four." Came the voice of her colleague who picked up the phone in her absence. Elisabeth made the hand gesture as if to ask whom it was but was none the wiser.

"This is Elisabeth." She said having picked up the phone.

"Hey, its Jack. Have you settled in?"

"Pretty much. Didn't take long. How are things back home?"

"Usual stuff. Is your line encrypted?"

"It's scrambled, yep. Why?"

"I need to ask you something. "

"Okay. Why do I get the feeling I'm being dragged into some governmental issue?"

"Because you're very clever, beautiful and you know me too well."

"Wise words Jack. You've got my attention. I'm listening."

"From a conversation we had previously, I understand that part of your remit is to embed with the military and politicians alike. Is that correct?"

"Absolutely. And?"

"Could you have any reason for direct contact with the Cosmonauts out of Star City."

"Where is this leading Jack?"

"I need you to sniff around and maybe do a subject header at this facility."

"What kind?"

"Just general stuff but leaning towards the senior staff."

"Anyone in particular?"

"Lieutenant General Syromokov. Head of cosmonaut training."

"That's straight to the top then? What's he done that's red flagged?"

"Are you familiar with the new joint space programme between Russia and the USA?"

"I'm aware of it, yes. Why?"

"I'd like you to find out as much as you can about Syromokov. He may be a dark horse but I'm hoping he has skeletons in his cupboard."

"I doubt he'll admit them if he has."

"Ask your bosses if you can do an international piece on Star City and this new joint venture. I have a gut feeling that Syromokov is playing some cards close to his chest and I'm hoping he can reveal his hand and intentions. You never know, we may get lucky and if he's had enough of mother Russia he may want to sing like a canary."

"That's a good call. But turning Syromokov will have to be for the CIA to recruit him surely. That's outside of my league and above my pay grade. I'm sure the thought of bundles of US dollars and a new life of his choosing can turn many people. Money talks and that's a fact."

"I will speak with Karl at Langley and see whether there is a need to recruit him. If the US feel he is a small pawn and very little would be gained from his recruitment, then it may be a non-starter."

"I'll ask around in the meantime. Since this is an all-new venture I'm sure the Russians will be keen to advertise their involvement with the ISS. They don't like to miss a trick when publicity is involved. Leave it with me."

"Whilst we're on the subject, there are two other persons worthy of interest namely, Colonel Sergei Grigorev and Major Vladimir Popov."

"What have they done to deserve such interest? And how much time have I got to be able to look into them?"

"Not sure but they are the first two cosmonauts on this exchange programme. You can sell the reasoning behind this investigative reporting as background information on them. Being the first two of course is in the interests of the whole country.

Whilst that is a smoke screen for the real reason, could I ask that you reach out to speak with the wives and try to ascertain whether or not their husbands have disclosed anything to them regarding the up and coming shuttle launch in December. Any good or bad points would be most welcome."

"Do they both have kids?"

"Sergei, no. Vladimir has twins."

"Sounds like you have a hunch about something?"

"I just want to be sure."

"Can't the CIA do something for you?"

"It'll take forever. With you already being there in an official capacity you have one foot in the door and therefore you have the best shot out of them all."

"I'll do my best once I've been given clearance. We'll have to contact the ministry and make the arrangements. Don't expect a reply as quick as back home though."

"Have you found a place to stay yet?"

"I've arranged to look at one later today at four p.m. funny enough. It's a three bed. Pricey, but it looks nice on paper. I'll let you know how it goes. Changing the subject, how you keeping? I do miss you."

"I miss you more."

"Impossible." Elisabeth knew this was a joke between the pair of them and she smiled, "Jack, I've noticed on occasions two people following me at random times. Is this anything to do with you?"

"I asked Karl to look out for you. They are there for your own safety. You're in a strange place where anything could happen."

"You could say that for anywhere in the world."

"But you're not anywhere. You're in Moscow."

* * *

Moscow, 1600 hrs same day
Smolenskaya Street, Moscow

Elisabeth left the office earlier than usual. She had an appointment to view an apartment she had seen advertised in the local paper by 'Landmark' realtors. Tapping the address into her Satnav, she knew that it was just under ten kilometres away and would take her at least thirteen minutes. The traffic was beginning to build up as workers decided to finish early for the day. Having driven away from the CNN offices, she checked her rear-view mirror and saw the comforting sight of her followers in the distance. Knowing they were there, she blanked them out and concentrated on the journey.

Once she had arrived at the address, she parked and went up to the eight floor. Two knocks at the door and the door was opened by a man standing on the inside.

"You must be Elisabeth? Right on time." The man extended his right hand to greet her, "I'm Mikhail Belkin from Landmark Realtors. We spoke on the phone this morning."

Elisabeth accepted his greetings, "Ah yes. Thank you for coming out at short notice."

"No problem. After all you are the customer. Please come in."

Elisabeth stepped into the apartment and initially had a quick glimpse around what she could see. The room was light and airy with a modern feel to it.

"Let me show you around," Mikhail began.

Elisabeth followed on behind and listened to what the realtor had to say.

"It's a three bedroomed apartment which is quite spacious. It comes fully furnished as I mentioned on the phone." Walking down a short hallway, Mikhail continued, "This is bedroom number one; the master with en-suite." He continued to show Elisabeth around the apartment and pointed out various things that she needed to know.

"What's the size of the apartment?"

"One hundred and forty-six square metres."

"What about parking? I have one vehicle."

"Yes, there is underground parking for one vehicle."

"I noticed a desk clerk in the entrance. Is he there all the time?"

"It's twenty-four hours so yes."

"Any movement on the price?" Tested Elisabeth although she knew that CNN would foot the bill but at least if she tried to negotiate it might seem plausible.

"The land lord has fixed his price."

"Remind me again what it is?"

"Four thousand three hundred US dollars per month. Does that work for you?"

"I'm sure that could work. I like the balcony."

"That's one of the attractive pieces to the apartment. It's well sought after and especially being on the eight floor it commands an excellent view."

"How long is it available to rent for?"

"As long as you want it for at the moment."

"Okay, you've got yourself a deal. Send over the paperwork to my email address and I'll get our accounts department to finalise things."

Both Elisabeth and Mikhail shook hands to cement the contract and walked out the building together and headed their separate ways.

* * *

Once Mikhail got back into his car he scrolled down his contact list on his cell phone and selected a number. "Hi this is Mikhail, she's taken the apartment." He simply said and then disconnected the call.

CHAPTER 9

JSC Houston, Texas – The next day
Office of the Director

Director James Hartman was about to walk out of his office when his desk phone rang. He stopped as he reached his office door, looked back in the direction of his desk and pondered whether he should answer it or not. He decided he had time before his meeting and retraced his steps. He placed his briefcase and jacket on the chair in front of his desk and then leant forward and picked up the handset. Having depressed the flashing line button he simply said, "Hartman."

"Director, its Jack Copeland over at Scorpion."

"Hi Jack, I'm kind of busy at the moment. I don't have a lot of time as I have a scheduled meeting I need to attend in about thirty minutes. If it's brief, how can I help?"

"I'll try and make it quick. How easy is it to swap out astronauts?"

"I'm not with you."

"If NASA needed to remove an astronaut and replace him with another, how easy would it be?"

"Ah okay. As you know we have a stand by alert crew ready in the event should that need arise. The alert crew train alongside the primary and are quarantined at the same time too. If one of the primaries' falls sick or something else happens then an alert astronaut takes their place. Do you know something that I don't?"

"I'm just reaching out at the moment to gauge a full understanding as to how all this works. Have NASA ever replaced astronauts with flight assignments in the past?"

"Of course, but it has only ever happened once close to a launch. You've probably heard of the most famous one that occurred in nineteen seventy when the command module pilot for Apollo thirteen moon mission was exposed to measles. He was replaced just three days before launch. The pilot of STS-33 was replaced when he was killed in nineteen eighty-nine flying a vintage aircraft. Two shuttle commanders were removed from flights in nineteen ninety for disciplinary reasons after they violated NASA flight rules in unrelated incidents. The pilot of STS-85 was replaced in nineteen ninety-seven because of a family illness and another astronaut was replaced on STS-98 in two thousand for reasons I can't disclose. So, in answer to your question, yes it can and does happen. I'm sure it will happen in the future too no matter how much care we take not to expose them to the outside world. I'm guessing your reason for the call is to do with the conversation we had at JSC concerning the joint venture programme."

"You've been a great help Director. Thanks for your time." Copeland said without being over committed, "If I need anything else I'll come back to you."

"Just one other think Jack, it costs around three million dollars a year to train an astronaut and to remove one there has to be a very good reason for doing so."

"I understand Director. Thanks again."

* * *

NSA Intercept Room, Fort Mead, Maryland
1700 hrs. The Same Day

The analyst was engrossed in a game of solitaire on his desk computer when he heard familiar chatter through his headphones. He immediately sat up and began recording the conversation. With no introduction of names of those talking, the conversation began, "We're almost done here now. You were correct about the type of training we were to receive. We now have a better understanding about its purpose." The analyst attracted the attention of his supervisor by standing up and waving frantically to him and both were now listening to the conversation on the computer speaker as it unfolded, "You have done well Comrade and mother Russia will be proud of your achievements." The caller severed the call and almost immediately another call began between the Russian and a female. "It's me. Is everything in place?"

"Yes." The female replied
"When will it happen?"
"About eight weeks from now"

The supervisor phoned his Director and forwarded the file as requested.

* * *

CIA Headquarters, Langley, Virginia
Early evening – Same day

Karl Langdon was working late to cover the fallout from the September eleven incident in New York that rocked just about every community in the US and beyond. All agencies were at stretching point to narrow down the source of the incident. No stone was to be left unturned until the evil minds behind this barbaric act had been found. This was a presidential order. Whilst typing his interim report, an email with an attachment came through from the NSA. Having opened the document and listened to the attached audio file he needed to pass this on to others. "Jack, our Russian friends have been busy again."

"What do you have?" Copeland asked

"Another NSA intercept has come through. I'm sending it over to you now. Listen to it then get back to me."

Moments later Copeland received the email with attachment. He decrypted the file and then listened to it. He then returned the call to Karl moments later.

"Interestingly, the first conversation was between two males. If I were a betting man, to which I'm not by the way then I would hazard a guess that the other male was Grigorev. To confirm this, can you do a voice analysing match on Grigorev?"

"Yep, I can ask Mike at NSA to follow that through. I'm sure he's onto that in any case."

"Sergei talks about his training is nearly finished and he has a better understanding about its purpose. What is he referring to? Better understanding about what? Is it his training or the laser? Why is he being praised for something? Christ, I was never good at crosswords. You guys are the experts in all this cryptic speech. What do you make of it?"

"Same as you at the moment. There are so many unsolved questions and with nine-eleven having happened we are all jumpy about anything so everything will be seen as being a potential problem even if it turns out to be innocent."

"I get your point. Can't your guys at the embassy in Moscow try to recruit Grigorev and tease him with a bunch of Uncle Sam dollars? Everyone likes to earn a bit more on the side whether legal or otherwise."

"It's not that easy Jack. For one thing Grigorev is a hard liner and loyal to the communism way of life. He'd be out of his depth if we gave him a new one. Russia will never forgive him either if he sells out. He'd have a life imprisoned and looking over his shoulder every day. Yes, we'd get what we wanted but then hang him out to dry. Another thing, it takes time to gather all his background stuff before we can even begin to initiate a first meet. We'd have to find his weaknesses to develop anything. Don't get me wrong, all Russians in power have a skeleton somewhere which can be worked on but not overnight."

"I get that. Worthy of a try though?" Copeland pushed the question.

"I'll put a request through and see where it leads and whether there is any chance. No promises though."

"None taken. At least we can say we tried. The second call was interesting too between Sergei and the female. They talk about something happening in eight weeks' time. That's when the Russians will be on the ISS. Are they all related or in isolation of each other? Is it his wife he called and they have planned something for that time whilst he's away? Or is it something more sinister?"

"That's a million-dollar question and I wish I had the answer." Langdon tried to offer Copeland the words he was looking for but was currently at a loss.

"I've asked Elisabeth to look into something for us to see if she can try and get a better understanding of Sergei's words about planning something."

"What's the ask?"

"Meet with the wives' of both Sergei and Vladimir and hopefully they will reveal any plans that they may have."

"Official or unofficial?"

"Official from CNN's point of view alongside an unofficial US government's one of interest."

"Good luck with that one." Karl said with a genuine concern.

"If I had to apply through official channels, it would take forever and since Elisabeth can run independent, it makes sense."

"I totally get where you're coming from Jack."

"I know it'll be a difficult task for her but she's good at what she does and is popular around the world so I feel she has at least a chance, in fact a better chance than most. The media have a knack of being able to get to places and sniff around far more productively than say if your guys went in. They're not representing any particular government or countries so are not deemed a risk to the host's national security. She'll have to go through protocol in any case to get permission, which will leave things hanging in the balance for a while. I'm not entirely sure what time line we are working to hear. Moscow doesn't seem to be able to rush things through unless they gain something from it themselves. I'm keen to get this information sooner rather than later. Time is running out."

* * *

Kutuzovsky Prospekt, 7/4 Kорпус 1
CNN Bureau Moscow – Three days later

Having spoken with Copeland regarding meeting with the wives of the Russian Cosmonauts Sergei and Vladimir, Elisabeth drafted a request letter to the Ministry of Foreign Affairs requesting to run a feature on the first Cosmonauts to go through the US space programme and to serve on the ISS. That was three days ago, today she had received a reply giving her the permission she needed from the Russian government who also offered any other assistance she would need for the report; Elisabeth wasn't just delighted, she was ecstatic. Not just by the agreement but the speed and efficiency in which she had received authority. *'This had to be a first for the bureaucratic system of Russia'* she thought to herself. Overcoming her delight, she read further down the letter and noticed a caveat that stated she would have to be accompanied by a member from the Defence Ministry. She figured that would be the case and wasn't surprised. This was mother Russia after all where openness was frowned upon and oppression deemed as the normal way of life. She just hoped that she would get what she needed and the wives were able to extend a sense of pride for their husbands without feeling intimidated. Being accompanied seemed a way for the government to censor what the families were saying and what was being reported. She wasn't convinced that her chaperon would be military, more likely to be from the Domestic Intelligence Service. Either way, she knew the interviews were not going to be easy.

CHAPTER 10

Kennedy Space Centre, Merritt Island, Florida
Six weeks prior to launch

The Orbiter Horizon had arrived at the KSC having piggy backed a ride on the back of a modified NASA 747 aircraft from Edwards AFB, California two weeks previous. Once it had been removed from the 747, the Orbiter was rolled into the OPF and raised off its landing gear and levelled. An elaborate arrangement of scaffolding and platforms were erected around the aircraft to provide access to all parts of the vehicle. Every single component would be inspected, removed, repaired or replaced as needed. The thermal protection system (TPS), certain structural parts, landing gear and other systems would be inspected for damage. Any damage to the TPS – including the twenty-five thousand tiles that cover much of the Orbiter's body – will be repaired before the vehicle launches again. All consumable fluids and gases would be loaded aboard and the final step in the OPF Orbiter processing would be weighing the Orbiter to determine its centre of gravity. This will be the inevitable fine balance between success and failure.

Two weeks later and six weeks prior to launch, the Orbiter was towed to the VAB transfer aisle, a fifty-two storey one hundred and seventeen-billion-dollar vehicle assembly building, then raised to the vertical position, lowered onto the Mobile Launch Platform and then mated with the massive external fuel tank and the two solid rocket boosters. The only thing left now was to move the Orbiter to the launch site.

* * *

Russian House – Ten o'clock the next day

Elisabeth had received a call yesterday on her desk phone instructing her to go to an address in Skhodnia about twenty-four miles outside Moscow where the military liaison officer from the interior ministry would be there to meet her. On receiving the call, she informed her cameraman, Alex to get everything ready that he needed to take with him. If it wasn't needed then it was to be left behind. She had checked a map to orientate herself where the address was and the area she would be heading into. She would take the M-10 motorway and then navigate towards the location. She worked out that it would take at least forty minutes and therefore to make allowances for the morning traffic, she decided that they would depart at eight thirty. Looking at the map, nothing seemed out of the ordinary except it looked a remote area with very little around or nearby except a small town. She accepted it for what it was and figured the family were private people. Driving away from the bureau, she followed the instructions she had been given during the call. Glancing through her rear mirror, she felt the comfort of knowing Copeland's men had dropped in behind and were instinctively following but oblivious as to where they were heading. On the flip side, Elisabeth herself wasn't familiar with the area so was a kind of blind leading the blind.

Elisabeth had covered nearly twenty-four miles and travelled for nearly an hour when she pulled up outside the house which had been described to her, looked at her watch and noticed she was ten minutes early. Taking the opportunity to glance around from inside the vehicle she wanted to see if she could see any other vehicles that may have had either the liaison officer or the astronaut's wife in them. Following the advice of Copeland, who often said to her about the option for a quick escape, she left the engine running and she would do so until her contact arrived. No names had been given during the call so Elisabeth wasn't sure which one she was visiting first or the name of the military liaison. It felt to her like a clandestine meeting and one of secrecy. '*But why*', she asked herself. These meetings were all about publicity so as to let the world know that Russia had teamed up with the US to create a joint space programme; a new venture and a new beginning. Elisabeth sensed that her security team were in the area although she couldn't see them nor hear them. Not that she expected to. These people worked in shadows after all and would be there if she needed them – hopefully. Feeling confident but against her better judgement, she climbed out of the vehicle leaving Alex to gather his equipment and then began to walk closer towards the house.

The house was a wooden structure and nothing like what she had expected. It was in the countryside of course but hardly something you would want to advertise how your hero astronaut lives. The building looked derelict and in a state of disrepair. *'Perhaps they expected her to report on the poverty plight of the Russian people.'* She thought to herself but soon dismissed the idea, as Russia wouldn't want to admit to that. The house had a lean too attached to the right side with a pair of wooden windows looking back along the driveway. A small window was fitted above the porch over the veranda and front door. A small chimney elevated itself above the roofline at the back of the house. There was no smoke billowing out which would signify someone maybe at home. To the right of the front door, recently cut logs were stacked eight rows high and six deep. As she began to walk up the wooden stairs at the front, she heard a sound, a distant sound. She stood in silence for a brief moment with her head to one side so as to figure out what it was and more importantly where it was coming from. Suddenly she realised it was the sound of a vehicle approaching. Retracing her steps, she headed back to the vehicle and almost at the same time noticed a black car driving towards her at a reasonable speed and creating a dusk cloud behind it; almost like a smoke screen and reminiscent of something out of a movie. The vehicle stopped short of Elisabeth's and the windows were blacked out. The dust cloud from the track continued after the car had stopped and enveloped both vehicles covering them with particles of grit like dust. Elisabeth wafted her hand in front of her face to try to minimise the amount of dust she would be breathing in. Too late, she began to cough. In the end she turned her back momentarily to let the cloud settle. Once she turned back, she looked at the number plate, it showed that they were government plates by the number A 001 AA and followed by the Russian flag on the right side. She stood by her vehicle and waited for the occupants to make the first move. Alex came around to Elisabeth's side to get a better view for himself and to give some morale support to her.

After a brief moment and once the dust had settled, the rear door opened and out stepped a tall lean man dressed in a dark business-like suit and sporting sunglasses. Both Elisabeth and the man began to walk towards each other almost at the same time. The man removed his sunglasses and extended his right hand to which Elisabeth reciprocated, "My name is Andrei Vasiliev from the Ministry of Interior. Elisabeth, I presume?" he offered in excellent English.

"Indeed, it is. Elisabeth Young from the CNN Moscow Bureau." She began and then turned to Alex," and this is my assistant and cameraman, Alex Wilson." Andrei nodded in acknowledgment in acceptance of him being there. "Thank you for this opportunity Andrei. I'm really excited to be able to report on such an historic moment. Your English is very good I must say. Far better than my Russian." She added as if embarrassed.

"It's proof of the high level of education we receive and testament to our excellent universities. English by far is often our second language followed by German. Our constitution allows for us to learn a second language. It is a necessary means of today's lifestyle and business opportunities. Let us now discuss why we are here."

"Indeed. Thank you." Began Elisabeth, "The success story of the Russian cosmonauts working alongside their US Astronauts, I felt it would be a good opportunity to promote such an alliance between our two countries. As a first, they will also be living and working on the ISS for six months."

"Yes, this is a great achievement for mother Russia. How can we help you?" offered Andrei as if he already knew the answer.

"It would be great if we could speak with the wives of both Vladimir and Sergei and to do a piece on each. They must be very proud of their husband's achievements."

"Who would you like to speak with first?" Andrei was straight to the point

Elisabeth pointed to the house, "Are we not here already? I thought this was..." She stopped short having realised it sounded a ridiculous idea.

"No. I asked to meet here as it is equal distance to both houses." Andrei pointed to the house, "These are typical dacha's that people have as their second homes. These are national characteristics of Russia. In other languages, no such word exists. It is derived from the eighteenth-century word 'give'. The dacha was a haven for a private life and therefore offered a brief respite from the hustle of city living. It's sad to say that in post-soviet Russia the dacha is dying."

These were houses of nondescript and couldn't believe people would want to escape to somewhere like this no matter how quiet and unassuming it all was. Some of the houses looked like they belong to a horror movie set but she was equally sure that some were at the other end of the scale too. "Can we begin with Sergei's wife please?"

"Of course. Follow me; it's about a forty-minute drive towards Razdory. This is also a Dacha village."

"Okay. Can you tell me a little about her before we get there?"

"Her name is Oksana. Aged at thirty-four with no children. Anything else you may ask her."

"Excellent. Thank you."
Both walked back to their vehicles and Elisabeth took this as an indication to ask anything she wanted. She would push the boundaries as most reporters generally did.

* * *

Having completed a dogleg of a journey to leave Skhodnia, they eventually joined the E-105 highway heading south. Andrei wasn't holding back on speed now he was on the highway. A speed limit of eighty miles per hour meant nothing as he increased speed to at least ninety. Elisabeth suspected that being a government official he had the credentials to get out of the situation if stopped by the police. After approx. thirty-five minutes they had crossed the Moscow River, still heading south. At junction fifty-nine, they turned right onto a slip road to join the A-106 two-way road. Elisabeth looked at her dash wish gave a compass heading of southwest. After travelling just over three miles along a tree-lined road with pines on both sides, they turned right.

Right on cue and after a forty-five minutes' drive and nearly twenty-four miles they arrived on the outskirts of Razdory. Elisabeth continued to follow Andrei along a narrow lane to a high wrought iron gate with a privacy screen attached. She noticed two cameras, one either side of the double gates. *'Clearly someone was concerned about security'* she mumbled to herself. A metal six-foot high fence continued around the property either side of the gates, which no doubt would cut in at some point to border the property. Andrei left his vehicle and went up to the intercom on the left side of the gate, pressed a buzzer and having quickly spoken into the speaker, the gates opened. Moments later they both drove through and the grounds opened up in front of them. It seemed so quiet and peaceful and certainly seemed like a place to get away from it all. This definitely was a Dacha village with several small wooden houses dotted throughout the countryside. To the rear of the house was the Moscow River and the other copses of trees and in the middle was a magnificent house. *'Now we're talking'* she said aloud to herself causing Alex to look at her in case he needed to answer or to look animated. A blank stare from Elisabeth was all that he needed. Andrei pulled his car in front of the house and Elisabeth pulled in behind him. As she stepped out of her vehicle, she looked around to take in this magnificent view. It was a modern house by Russian standards to which Elisabeth was in awe. What a lovely weekend retreat this would be. Eventually and having back to the reason she was there, she followed Andrei towards the front door. Alex was in tow and carrying all his camera equipment. He looked like an over packed donkey.

Andrei pressed the doorbell and moments later the door was opened and the doorway filled with an elderly man dressed in what seemed to be a butler's attire. "May I help you?" he asked slowly in English and eloquently pronouncing every word as he spoke.

"I'm Andrei Vasiliev from the Ministry of Interior. Oksana is expecting us."

"Just a moment please." The butler then turned around and slowly headed back into the house. After a brief moment a woman's voice was heard in the background and then she appeared at the door.

"Hi, I'm Oksana. I apologise for Albert. He's part of the family and great company when Sergei isn't here."

Elisabeth looked towards Oksana and noticed how beautiful and striking she was. She was tall, at least five ten, long blonde hair, high cheekbones and an hourglass of a figure. Not what she had imagined, in fact she hadn't even thought of what she would look like. Elisabeth extended her hand, "I'm Elisabeth from the CNN Moscow Bureau." She then turned to look behind her, "and this is my assistant, Alex. Thank you for taking the time to meet with us."

"It's my pleasure. Please come in." Oksana invited with a hand movement and lead the way towards a reception room on the left of the entrance hall. There was a large chandelier hanging in the hallway, highly polished wooden floor throughout the downstairs and pictures of modern art that would make Sotheby's proud. "Please take a seat." There were two light grey coloured sofas stacked with neutral cushions and a single chair in the room. They were configured in a square shape in front of an unlit open fire. There was a large grandfather clock to the right of the fireplace, which was ticking beautifully and chiming on cue. It reminded Elisabeth of the clock that her father had given to her some years previously, which momentarily brought back fond memories and a slight swelling of the eyes. Andrei sat on the single chair and Elisabeth on one of the spare sofas with Oksana sitting in front of her on the opposite one. Alex was stood behind Elisabeth and began to set up his equipment. "I was surprised though when I received a call from the government asking if I minded to give an interview with regards to Sergei. That is all they told me. I was curious of course. How can I help?"

"We are keen to do a piece on Sergei in light of the successful space programme between the US and Russia. It is a world's first of course and therefore in the interests of everyone. Do you mind if I call you Oksana?"

"Not at all. Please do."

"Alex will be filming the interview throughout." Elisabeth looked behind her to see if he was ready to begin and with a single nod she turned around again to face Oksana.

"How rude of me. Forgive my poor manners. May I offer you all a drink of something? Coffee, tea, water before we begin?"

"That would be most welcome, thank you." Elisabeth asked for an Americano without milk but with less water. Alex a latte and Andrei water with ice. Oksana picked up a bell from the coffee table in front of her and rang it once. Elisabeth began to think this was like something from an old English movie with Jeeves the butler. As if programmed, Albert appeared and Oksana gave him the requests and he then retreated in the direction of the kitchen mumbling to himself as if trying to remember the drinks list.

"How did you two first meet?" Elisabeth began.

"It was a fairy tale beginning." Oksana smiled, "Sergei was training at the Armavir aviation school and graduated from there in nineteen eighty-nine. It was summer of eighty-nine and as top of his class he was invited to the Gagarin air force academy in Monino and to the aviators' summer ball. This is where we met and it all began with a kiss." Oksana blushed a little before continuing, "He looked dashing in his uniform. How could I resist."

"How could any girl resist indeed. That sounds so perfect and romantic. Do you have a picture of Sergei?"

"Yes, I do somewhere." Oksana stood and walked over to a small cabinet under the window behind Andrei and retrieved a picture from the top drawer. "Here it is. It's a few years old but he hasn't changed." Oksana handed it to Elisabeth and sat back down again on the sofa.

"Thank you." She looked at the photo, "I can see why you fell for him. He is dashing." Elisabeth momentarily had a memory flash back to when she first met Copeland in his uniform. He too was dashing and although not at an officer's ball, the moment was still a romantic one nevertheless. "A girl always likes a good romantic story. When did you decide to tie the knot?"

"We instantly knew we were meant for each other and we were married after a year. It was in the spring of nineteen-ninety. It may have seemed quick to some people including my own family. I was always a believer in taking opportunities when you can so as to avoid disappointment later. Do you think that is the right approach Elisabeth?"

"I do indeed. I travelled along the same path. How about children?"

"Sergei wasn't able to have any. He was seriously injured once whilst on a flying mission. He didn't tell me much about it but it affected him down there." Oksana pointed to her groin area, "I've adjusted to a life without children though. It's simple, not complicated and I have to say that I'm used to it now. You don't think that I'm being selfish do you Elisabeth?"

"Not at all. You should only have children if you truly want them. They do change your lives. They can be so demanding that some days you just want to pull your hair out with frustration."

"Given your description I think I have made the right choice."

"Has Sergei always been an aviator?"

"It's in the family blood. His father was an aviator too and encouraged Sergei as a child to follow in his steps. His interest began at the age of fourteen when he was flying gliders and parachuting."

"Would you want him to give up flying?"

"I'm a proud woman with a privileged background and it was important to me to find someone who had a career that I could be proud of."

"What were your thoughts when he decided to become a cosmonaut?"

"I didn't really understand much about what it entailed. I knew it meant travelling away from our planet but I hadn't given the dangers any thought."

"Did Sergei ever discuss this with you?"

"Not in so much detail. He probably knew the dangers but didn't want me to worry so we never crossed the subject."

"When he went to Star City." Elisabeth began and then noticed Oksana look towards Andrei. Elisabeth quickly glanced towards him and saw him nod officially to Oksana. "Did I miss something there Oksana?"

"No. I just want to make sure that I can speak freely about things that the government often call national security. Please carry on Elisabeth."

"You must be very proud of him once again. Representing Russia is a great honour and a fantastic achievement."

"I am indeed."

Fire Storm

"Whilst he was at Star City, was he able to come home at all?"

"Most weekends he was able to travel home but it is so expensive. He wasn't able to use an official car or driver so I probably saw him every few months."

"That must've been difficult?"

"It was at first then I sort of became accustomed to him not being here. Strange really."
Elisabeth sensed some sort of marriage fragility but then dismissed it as normal way of life. She was after all in the same position. As the conversation began to flow, Albert brought in the drinks and placed the tray on the coffee table to allow everyone to help themselves.

"Thank you, Albert." Oksana said gratifyingly and then dismissed him.

"Tell me about yourself Oksana."

"I'm thirty-four and an interior designer by trade."

"I can see that. Did you design the furnishings for the house?"

"I did. I've tried to mix both feminine and masculine touches to balance out the colour schemes. What do you think?"

"Impressive. I like it. I may need you to do ours. What about your family? Any siblings?"

"I have an elder brother Alexei and a twin sister Anna. My mother passed away when I was young. I miss her very much. My father is still around."

"What does your father do?"

"He owns one of the largest gas companies in Russia. He is an oligarch I think you call it."

"I can see why you have this house. Away from prying eyes and well secluded. You have a lovely view over the river. I dream of looking out on a morning and seeing that. I have to make do with the metropolis of both Moscow and Washington DC these days."

"I love it. It used to belong to my parents until my father remarried and moved out to start another life. To keep it in the family, he handed it to me along with my butler, Albert."

"It's lovely that your father can do that for you. The times Sergei came home from Star City, did he ever discuss what he was doing there?"

"He wasn't allowed to discuss nor did I ever feel the need to enquire."

"Both Sergei and Vladimir have of course both been chosen to take part in the joint space programme in the US. Did Sergei know Vladimir before they went to Star City?"

"No, they didn't. Well at least I don't think so. Sergei never mentioned his name until Cosmonaut training."

"Now they are both in the US, do you know what they will be doing there?"

"As far as I know they are training for a year to prepare them for travel to the space station for six months."

"Have you had any contact with Sergei in the year he has been training in the US?"

Elisabeth could sense that Andrei had leant forward in his chair "Why are you asking this question? It is almost like an interrogation," insisted Andrei

"I'm asking so that I and the viewers can get a feel for family life. Being apart is traumatic in itself and I want to see if the valour of this cooperation brings the family together."

Andrei flipped his hand in a dismissive gesture and didn't comment further but merely sat back in his chair.

"Could you please answer my last question Oksana?"

There was a momentary pause as she looked over to Andrei seeking his silent permission to answer. She received the obligatory nod, "Yes." She confirmed.

"How does he contact you? Phone or email?"

"We don't have email. It is normally by phone."

"Do you know if it's a cell phone or a land line?"

"Strange thing is, he never had a cell phone but I think he is using one."

"When was the last time you spoke with him?"

"A few weeks back. Why, is he okay?"

"Yes of course. He's perfectly fine and looking forward to the mission. You can certainly be proud of him."

"I am proud of him and my father likes him a lot."

"Do you recall the conversations you have had with Sergei recently?"

"There hasn't been much to say really, just normal conversation. He did say that everything was prepared now."

Elisabeth had to be mindful not to give too much away in her questions with regards the conversation between Oksana and Sergei otherwise she will think that their conversation was being listened to. She's a bright woman and Elisabeth had the impression that she wouldn't miss a trick.

"What do you think he meant by that?"

"That his training has now finished I presume."

"Was there any strain to his voice or excitement or maybe worry that you may have noticed?"

"Not that I heard. It was difficult to tell as the connection was a little scratchy."

"Is he excited about the launch?"

"Of course. I would think he is nervous too."

"Why would he be nervous?"

"In case something happened on the launch or in space itself. Sergei has always provided the best for us and I'm very much looking forward to his safe return."

"And we are too. Do you have anything planned whilst he is away?"

"Such as?" Oksana asked with a curious frown and almost defensive like as if wondering if Elisabeth knew something.

"You may have wanted to keep yourself occupied so that your mind isn't focused all the time on the dangers the crew face."

"I have an operation I need to attend in a few weeks' time. It's bad timing with Sergei being away but I have no choice."

"I'm sorry to hear that. Is it serious?"

"Yes. It is a personal matter. Can we move on please?" There was a slight tear running down the cheek of Oksana. She pulled a tissue from under her cuff and wiped it away.

"Has Sergei ever mentioned General Igor Syromokov?"

"Yes, he has. The General was his mentor and Sergei looked up to him for inspiration to better himself in everything that he did whilst flying. Sergei knows that he wouldn't be where he is today without him."

"Do you know why General Syromokov chose Sergei to go to the US?"

"Because clearly he is the best at what he does."

"Have you ever met the General?"

"No, I haven't."

"Did Sergei manage to get back home the weekend before he left for the US?"

"Yes, we had a wonderful weekend. Around here you don't need to go too far to enjoy beautiful nature."

"Yes, I can well imagine. Do you know if the General has ever asked Sergei to do something specific whilst in the US or on board the ISS?"

"Such as?"

"To learn something new or to act on something?"

"He will always learn something new. He is that kind of person."

"The launch will be in a few weeks' time and the eyes of the world will be focused on it. Has Sergei ever said what he will be expected to do whilst on the ISS?"

"Nothing in particular. I have no idea what an astronaut is supposed to do. I've seen them walking outside and floating around on the inside which I must say it all looks fun. I guess that's what he'll be doing."

"Has Sergei ever mentioned to you about a special piece of equipment that will be going to the ISS?"

"No. What is this equipment?"

"It is nothing of importance. Have you met Vladimir's wife?" Elisabeth looked towards Andrei for the name.

"Natalya." He offered.

"No, I've never met her. Where does she live?"

"About twenty minutes from here. I'm sure Andrei can arrange for you to meet." Elisabeth said as she looked at Andrei who nodded his approval almost reluctantly and rolled his eyes almost in despair.

"Oksana, you have been a great help with this interview and thank you for your invaluable time. If you think of anything else that may be useful then please call me on this number." Elisabeth handed her CNN business card to Oksana.

Oksana took the card, looked at it briefly and simply replied, "Thank you. I will."

Fire Storm

Oksana's guests left after baying their farewells.

"We have three very prominent regions around here for our wealthy businessmen and politicians. Razdory as you have seen, there is also Barvika about three minutes away and Zhukovo around seven minutes. And did you know that the Russian President, Vladimir Putin has a house in this area." Offered Andrei as they walked back to their vehicles.

"No, I didn't. How very interesting."

"So too does another prominent name in the gas industry, Mr Abromovich. I'm sure you've heard of the name."

"Yes, I have and well, that really doesn't surprise me. I may have been a little concerned if he didn't have one."

* * *

Once the guests had left, Albert picked up the phone in the kitchen and dialled a number, "The reporter from CNN has just left." He said, "She was asking questions of Oksana about Sergei. I think the reporter is suspicious of something."

"Thank you, my friend. You have done well. Where are they heading now?"

"I think to Natalya's house."

As Oksana came out of the sitting room she heard Albert speaking from the direction of the kitchen and went to see whom he was talking to, "Albert, who are you talking to?" she asked in a decisive tone.

"Just ordering some more groceries." He replied without a flinch or giving any suspicion of being disturbed, "We're out of milk, vegetables and fruit. They'll be here tomorrow."

"I thought there was someone else in the house. Okay. Thank you, Albert. I don't know what I would do without you." Oksana accepted his response and headed back to the sitting room.

* * *

Elisabeth again followed Andrei. She had no idea where they were heading. She didn't mind. After all, it was just great to get out the office and to see the real Russia. Oksana's house was fantastic and she hadn't imagined such a house existed in Russia. Being wealthy though or from a wealthy background was a plus in any country. Checking her mirrors as she drove away and back onto the A-106, she was confident of the car that had dropped in some distance back. They were her chaperons and she was quickly getting used to the idea. Whilst she had the comfort of knowing they were there, she inwardly hoped they wouldn't need to step into anything. If they weren't there one day then she would be worried. What she hadn't seen was another vehicle that had dropped in some distance further back. Violence was never her thing and was of the mind-set that it should be used as the very last resort. She knew that Copeland would be worried for her safety and accepted his concerns whether warranted or not.

* * *

Fire Storm

A dark coloured VW SUV was parked next to a blue waste disposal van in the small car park near the T-junction with Rublevo-Uspenkoye Shosse. The driver noticed the white CNN suburban drive from the road to his right and then turned left back in the direction towards Moscow. Moments later he observed a Mercedes SUV with two males that had joined the road from the opposite side having been parked there for some time. As the VW SUV pulled out and behind the Mercedes SUV, the passenger in the VW made a call, "We have a complication." He simply said.

"In what way?" came the reply.

"It looks like she has a security team of two people."

"Do not worry comrade. This is a temporary inconvenience. Let's stick with the schedule. When the time is right, we can consider our next action."

"Da." Responded the passenger in acknowledgement.

* * *

Thirty minutes later and having traversed the winding country roads, they finally reached their destination, the Solntsevo District on the west side of Moscow. The contrast between Oksana's house and Natalya's couldn't be any more different. Elisabeth was looking at a series of white concrete apartment blocks. These were definitely reminiscent of the soviet era when they were built to solve housing problems when buildings, which were damaged during the war, were razed. Both vehicles pulled up outside the apartment block and stopped alongside the yellow and black kerbstones. As they approached the large wooden door on the ground floor, Andrei looked for the name Popov on the intercom list, which he noticed, was to the right of the door. Having identified who he was, Natalya pressed her buzzer to release the front door. "I'm on the sixteenth floor." She said, "The lift will be in front of you." Andrei acknowledged and the lift quickly but noisily took them to the apartment. A knock on the door and with introductions made, they were all invited into the house. Elisabeth noticed that the apartment was very spacious, tidy and almost unlived in; like a show house. By Russian standards it was very modern with clean lines and bright. Judging by the size of the interior, Elisabeth guessed that it would be a three bedroomed apartment. The layout of the furniture was almost symmetrical and with a little fen Sui for that calming influence and less busy effect. Elisabeth stepped towards the window and looked out, "You have an amazing view." She said to Natalya even though all you could see were rows and rows of the concrete jungle.

"It's not much to look at really." She admitted, "The view never changes. I would love to live by the sea, but that is my dream."
Elisabeth walked back towards the triple seated sofa and began to sit down, "Anywhere in particular?" She asked trying to put Natalya at ease.

"There is a beautiful area called Lake Turgoyak. That would be wonderful."

"Anywhere by the sea I can only imagine would be magical. Where is the lake?"

"Near the city of Miass, on the east side of Moscow."

"Have you been before?"

"When I was a child, my parents would take me. I can remember the fragrance of the pine trees, the lapping of the water against, what would you say?"

"The shoreline." Elisabeth quickly added

"Yes, it is so soothing."

"Sounds like heaven."

"It truly was."

"Would you go for the weekend? Is it nearby?"

"We would go in the winter months when the lake was completely frozen and you could walk over to the islands of Cajka and Vera. It takes nearly twenty-two hours to drive so we often went for at least a week if not more. On Vera there is an old monastery which my friend and I would often go to and spend the day. It was cold but it was much fun. It's a shame we have to grow up, do you not agree?"

"I do. It sounds so exciting. The kind of things us girls would do."

"Can I get anyone a drink?" Natalya finally asked.

Elisabeth, Alex and Andrei asked for water. Natalya left the room to get the drinks returning moments later. Alex had set up his recording equipment in the meantime and Andrei had sat himself on a single dining chair towards the back of the room. Natalya was now sitting on the double sofa opposite Elisabeth.

"Your English is very good Natalya."

"I was educated at the Moscow State University."

"They have done you proud."

"Thank you. That is a lovely compliment. After so much talking how can I help you?"

"Were you given any information as to why we would be visiting you?"

"Only that you would be from the CNN and asking questions regarding my husband. Is that correct?" Natalya quickly glanced towards Andrei almost seeking confirmation. He made no comment only jerked his head upwards in a single motion.

"Yes, it is and at least that makes it easier to begin. We are putting together a broadcast in respect of the joint space venture involving Russia and the USA. This is a big story for both countries and we are all hoping that it'll be a success story too. Let's start with a little bit about you Natalya. How old are you?"

"Thirty-eight years."

"Are your parents still alive?"

"Yes they are but I don't often get the chance to see them. They are too far away."

"Tell me about Vladimir and yourself. How did you meet?"

"We were both child hood sweethearts and even went to the same schools. You could say we grew up together."

"When did you marry?"

"Vladimir finished his flying training after he graduated from the Balashov Aviation School in nineteen ninety. We kept in touch and met up shortly after. He proposed and well the rest as you would say is history." Natalya finished off with a smile as if reminiscing.

"Children?"

"After we had married and within three years we had twins, a boy and a girl. The girl is Tasha and our son is Viktor."

"How lovely. How old are they now?"

"Both seven years old."

"How did Vladimir become involved with the Space programme?"

"He's flown with his friend Sergei many times and Vladimir has the label of being the best wingman in Russia. When Sergei was asked to go to Moscow he immediately recommended that Vladimir join the team too."

"That was very noble of Sergei to do that."

"I think it was more to do with trusting someone you know to be around you. They both think alike. It's uncanny."

"How hard has it been for you whilst Vladimir was away training in Moscow for the space programme?"

"Very difficult, especially bringing up two children. I don't work so I rely on money from my husband to support us."

"Was he able to come home during training?"

"Not sure if he was able to. I didn't see him during the training years."

"Were you able to see him before he flew away to the US?"

"No, I didn't."

"Have you spoken to him since he has been in the US?"

"No. I didn't think we are allowed to. I'm sure the cost would be too much."

"Have you ever come across the name General Igor Syromokov?"

"Yes. Vladimir mentioned his name before he went away to Moscow."

"In what context?"

"I don't understand, how do you mean?" Questioned Natalya

"For what reason did he mention his name?"

"Sergei had said to Vladimir that they both would be working for the General. They both look up to him as being iconic in Russian aviation. They saw it as a great honour and a privilege."

"Did Vladimir express any concerns to you regarding the General?"

"Nothing at all. If he had any then he kept them to himself. Should I be worried?"

"Not at all. Was Vladimir excited about starting the space programme?"

"Very, he saw this as an opportunity to better humanity. He always wanted to make a difference with anything he did."

"He'll certainly be making a difference here, that's for sure. Did Vladimir know much about Sergei before they went to Moscow?"

"As I mentioned earlier, they had flown together. I wouldn't say that they were best pals or anything like that but had similar interests and that was flying."

"Tell me a little about Vladimir when he was younger."

"He was so cute that I knew I wanted to be with him for the rest of my life. We grew up in the same neighbourhood and did most things together. He kept looking at planes when they flew overhead so I knew that he had an interest in flying from those early days. He was very cheeky but confident and I knew other girls would be looking at him. It made me jealous but it made my feelings stronger and I knew I had to work harder to keep him."

"Sounds like your hard work has paid off."

"With all the heartache I have with him not being here, I wouldn't change any of it. I know it is his job and that he has to go away. I respect that and I am totally loyal to him forever."

"Will you be watching the launch next month?"

"I wouldn't miss it. I'll be very nervous because anything can happen. I will be praying for his safe return so we can be back as a family once again."

"Sounds like you have it all worked out. Maybe then you can think of going back to your ideal place by the water."

"Those are our plans, but many plans do change."

"Do you know Sergei's wife at all?"

"Oksana, yes I have met her. It was many years ago."

"Can you remember where?"

"Let me think. In fact, I may have a picture somewhere." Natalya left the sofa and moved towards a side cabinet against the back wall of the room and opened several drawers before she found what she was looking for.

"That would be helpful, thank you." Elisabeth looked towards Andrei who shrugged his shoulders with indifference. He didn't seem bothered that Oksana had said that she hadn't seen Natalya.

"Here we are." Natalya sat next to Elisabeth and showed her a picture in the photo album. That was definitely Oksana. The beautiful woman Elisabeth had seen in Razdory earlier that day. She hadn't changed that much at all. Maybe money had brought her the continued looks. "Where was it taken?" Asked a curious Elisabeth.

Natalya pulled the picture out from the plastic sleeve and turned it over. It simply gave the date that was hand written, "Nineteen-ninety."

"Do you know where?"

"I couldn't forget such a date, it was Vladimir's graduation from the Balashov academy."

"There are five people in the picture. Can you describe them?"

"Yes, the two on the right are Sergei and Oksana. The two on the left are of course Vladimir and myself. The one in the middle let me think." After a few moments whilst she gathered her thoughts, "Do you know I do believe that is General Syromokov."

"Are you sure?"

"Absolutely, I'm positive. I'd completely forgotten that I had met him before. I remember now, he was in charge of the air force and handed Vladimir his wings on graduation. It was a lovely day and most families were there to support their husbands. Vladimir speaks highly of him."

Elisabeth looked towards Andrei whilst she was preparing to ask the next question. She knew that it would be explosive and raise an eyebrow or an interruption but she wanted to ask in any case. Still looking at Andrei to gauge his response, "Natalya, how loyal is the General to Russia?"

Andrei shuffled uneasily in his seat and couldn't believe a question like that could be asked. "ne otvechay." he said to Natalya warning her not to answer.

"Zachem." replied Natalya asking for the reason why she shouldn't.

"We do not question the loyalty of high ranking members." He continued in Russian.

Elisabeth's basic Russian allowed her to capture some of the words being used and to her they seemed like threats. "Natalya should be allowed to speak freely Andrei."

"This is Russia. We do not question the legitimacy or loyalty of high-ranking government or military personnel. It can be seen as treason with a penalty of a lengthy incarceration."

"I thought oppression was a thing of the past Andrei. Openness is how we change the world, not dictatorship."

"I think your time is up now. Please finish off." He said as he looked towards Elisabeth then Natalya.

"I think we're done here in any case." Elisabeth said reluctantly as she knew there was more to come from Natalya given time and space from

Andrei, "Thanks for your time Natalya, it has been most enlightening. Should you think of anything else of course please call me any time." Elisabeth shook hands with Natalya and in doing so discreetly handed her business card to her. Elisabeth was confident that she would call her at some point.

CHAPTER 11

Offices of Scorpion – Washington DC
10 a.m. - Two days later

Copeland needed to speak with Elisabeth; he didn't want to pester her but he needed answers. Conscious of the time difference he worked out it would be ten hours ahead of DC and after a quick mental calculation he figured it out to be eight in the evening. He picked up his desk phone and dialled her cell number which was answered after three rings, "Hey it's me. Everything okay?"

"Hey you. Everything's good."

"You sound tired."

"It's been a manic couple of days."

"I've been meaning to ask; how did you get on with your apartment hunting?"

"I liked the first one I looked at so I decided to accept. When you get chance, after all the things which are going on at the moment, pop over for a break."

"I certainly will sweetheart. Any news on your interviews?"

"Actually, yes. After we spoke, I went through the official channels to get authority to speak with the wives' and was pleasantly surprised to get the clearance through within a couple of days. That's generally unheard of. Anyway, I've spoken with Oksana already."

"Oksana?"

"The wife of Sergei."

"Ah, okay. Anything of interest or useful?"

"Surprisingly no, other than she has a hospital appointment in several weeks' time, which she says is an urgent one. She was emotional whilst telling me so it could be to do with female problems."

"Did you sense that maybe that could've been a rouse?"

"No, I didn't. It seemed genuine."

"Did she tell you what the appointment was for?"

"No. I asked her questions similar to what you had asked me to do but to be honest; I don't think she knows anything at all. Now that's my gut feeling as a reporter coming into play here."

"How strong is your gut feeling?"

"Probably not as strong as yours but she gave nothing away that would've raised any suspicion. There was a representative from the Ministry of Interior, a chap called Andrei Vasiliev who tagged along."

"Could he have silenced her by being there?"

"Possibly. She seemed to look towards him several times to seek approval before she answered. She did seem uncomfortable of saying something that the government may not approve of."

"There you go then. She's holding something back. Now that's my gut feeling here." Chuckled Copeland. "What about her family?"

Elisabeth passed on details about Oksana's father and siblings. She also shared details about the house and Albert, the inherited butler and family treasure.

"She has the ideal life style. Did she admit to making contact with Sergei at all?"

"She admitted to speaking with him, yes. She feels that he was using a cell phone that he has never had or owned and seemed rather surprised. She is very proud of Sergei and doesn't feel the need to ask him too many questions. Jack, is it possible that you may be looking at something that isn't there?"

"Believe me, that's a question I keep asking myself and I do sincerely hope that I'm wrong here. But there is something which keeps niggling at me and telling me not to let up."

"Nobody could ever accuse you of not being thorough. You are persistent and stubborn sometimes."

"Thanks for the compliments. It's a great confidence booster." Copeland said teasingly, "Only you are allowed to tell me that though otherwise powers that be may start questioning my sanity and those guys in white coats start knocking on the door sooner rather than later."

"One other thing which may be of interest, Oksana and Sergei live in a massive house overlooking the Moscow River in the suburbs of Razdory. This is not your typical Russian house, far from it."

"Why is that of interest?"

"It's what you would call millionaires row. Abromovich and Putin live in the area."

"Nice. Any clues?"

"Well, she did say that her father owns one of the largest gas companies in Russia. She didn't expand on that but called him an oligarch. This maybe where her wealth comes in."

"Interesting and it's a great way to disguise something. Changing the subject, what about Vladimir's wife?"

"Natalya, well that was an interesting twist and I think more productive that meeting with Oksana."

"Go on." Insisted Copeland

"Oksana had said that she had never met Natalya and yet Natalya said that they had met."

"Why would she say that?"

"Unless she had forgotten."

"That's possible. When did they supposedly meet?"

"Nineteen-ninety."

"Well it is eleven years ago and I'm not sure my memory would serve me well if I had to look back that far."

"Natalya had acknowledged straight away that she had seen Oksana. It just seems strange that's all that she wouldn't acknowledge that herself."

"Anything on Syromokov?"

"Another twist, Oksana said that she hadn't met the general but Natalya said that they both had."

"Can we confirm that they had?"

"Well interestingly, Natalya showed me a picture with five people on it."

"Who were they?"

"Sergei, Oksana, Vladimir and Natalya."

"That's only four. The fifth one being?"

"General Syromokov himself."

"What was the picture about?"

"It was an awards ceremony where he had awarded Vladimir's wings on graduation."

"When was this?"

"Nineteen ninety. Seems like the point at which everyone had met for the first time. Another interesting point was that Andrei had told Natalya not to answer one of the questions I put to her."

"What was the question?"

"Do you think the General is loyal to Russia."

"Wow, that could've created a firework display. Good on you to ask though. What kind of response did you get?"

"Andrei shuffled unceasingly on his chair and I'm almost positive that Natalya would've answered given the opportunity. I discreetly gave her my card when I left and I've got a feeling I'll be hearing from here soon."

"That's great work sweetheart, I'm impressed. Are you able to interview General Syromokov any time soon?"

"That's on my list of things to do. It may take a little longer to arrange especially after what Andrei had said to Natalya. Andrei may speak with the General and in which case this may be off the agenda before it even gets the green light."

* * *

CNN Moscow Bureau – Same Day

Elisabeth decided that whilst it was fresh in her mind after the meetings with the two wives', she would make an official request to meet with Syromokov. She submitted her letter through her editor who agreed it should take place and then subsequently forwarded it onto the Kremlin. She wasn't confident that it would come back as speedily as the last one and nor would she be surprised if it authority didn't come back at all. All she could do was hope and wait.

* * *

1200 hrs. The same day – Scorpion offices

Copeland picked up his desk phone and dialled the direct number to the CIA Director, "Karl, I've just had an interesting conversation with Elisabeth."

"Fill me in."

Copeland explained everything to Karl that Elisabeth had told him. He left nothing out.

"Now that is very interesting indeed. There is certainly some intrigue here. I think there is more to this than we imagined."

"I'm with you on that Karl. Just don't know how deep it goes. And why the secrecy of Oksana?"

"It certainly begs the question but I don't have the answer at the moment."

"Oksana had confirmed that she had spoken with Sergei and acknowledged that something had been arranged in a few weeks' time but that was for a hospital appointment, which is personal to her. That may have been what Sergei was referring to. It certainly sounds very plausible."

"Are you starting to have second thoughts?"

"Not likely. I'll be watching everything like a hawk until Horizon leaves and comes back and then everything in between whilst the crew is on the ISS. This is going to be six months of sleep deprivation. I'll be booking a bed at the Pentagon until this is over."

"Rather you than me Jack."

"Any news on the other crew members?"

"Not as yet. We seem to be heading up blind alleys. At the moment they all seem squeaky clean. We're comparing the NASA documents when they first joined the Astronaut Corps with info being collated recently. Any updates or changes, I'll come back to you."

* * *

KSC – Launch Pad L-39A, Merritt Island, Florida 8:30 p.m. EDT - Four weeks from launch

The eighteen-wheeler crawler transporter powered by two, two thousand seven hundred and fifty horsepower diesel engines inched its way from the VAB to its final resting point at launch pad 39-A. It was a journey along the crawlerway, a distance of just over five thousand five hundred metres in a process termed as a *'rollout'*. Shrouded in brilliant xenon spotlights, it was a beacon of hope and an example of today's technology; it was also an icon of inspirational determination. At a maximum speed of one-mile per hour, it typically took six hours to cover the three-point five-mile journey with a burn of one hundred and fifty gallons of diesel oil per mile. Whilst the flight crew prepare to be quarantined, the Orbiter began a month's final preparations for flight including loading the hypergolic propellants and hosting the crew for countdown rehearsals.

* * *

KSC – Twenty-three days prior to launch

With the Orbiter Horizon firmly secured to its launch pad, ground crews began to perform a 'tanking test' to make sure the shuttle's external tank would be both safe and robust enough to fly. X-ray scans were taken of the Orbiter-facing side of the intertank section. With rigorous tests being carried out, the Orbiter was fuelled and ran through a regular countdown sequence. Stresses on the tanks are immense and the data collected would determine whether there is a 'go for launch' or put back for another day.

* * *

KSC – Twelve days prior to launch
TCDT – Countdown Rehearsals

The crew of STS-108A travelled to KSA to begin their two-day TCDT. Dressed in their pressurised launch and entry suits, they began practice run-throughs of the countdown and launch procedures and also received emergency training. It is after all their last chance to run through everything prior to lift off. The one thousand two-hundred-foot-long 'slide wire' would be their means of escape from the shuttle in the event of a mishap and aptly named as the launch tower escape system. This would whisk the astronauts away from any danger at the launch pad in baskets to an emergency evacuation bunker nearby. The commander and pilot practiced landings at the Shuttle Landing Facility using modified Gulfstream aircraft to simulate the shuttle's approach and landing. Once completed, they returned to JSC.

* * *

JSC Press Briefing Room
Mid-day - 10 Days prior to launch

"Good morning ladies and gentlemen." Began the director of flight operations, "It's good to see so many of you here on this exciting day today. The final executive meetings of the Flight Readiness Review have now taken place here at JSC and I am pleased to announce that STS- 108A is on schedule to be launched at twenty-two hundred hours, Sunday December fifth from launch pad thirty-nine Alpha. A launch window of course is timed to ensure that the Orbiter will be in the correct position in orbit to rendezvous with the Space Station. Bearing in mind they will have to travel at seventeen thousand miles per hour to stay in orbit and at a cost of four hundred and fifty million dollars per launch we need to make sure we get this right. It will be the first launch to the ISS involving our partners from Russia as we open up the space programme to them for the first time. This is not a new concept however, you may recall that in nineteen ninety-three, Russia had become a full partner in a renamed International Space Station together with Europe, Japan and Canada. US astronauts have been using the Mir outpost whilst the ISS was being built. The Russian space agency, RKA have first-hand experience in space exploration and it seemed the right thing to do by bringing this knowledge and experience together and to harness the vision that both countries have in making a better and safer world. The space station is here today because of the determination of others. In nineteen ninety-three, President Bill Clinton was advised to cancel the space station programme due to the exponential and spiralling costs. It was also behind schedule and the decision could quite easily have been an easy one to make. But thankfully the correct decision was made.

President Clinton emphasised the subject of the ISS cooperation in nineteen ninety-eight saying that, *'This is a promising moment, instead of building weapons in space, Russian scientists will help us build the*

ISS'. We are delighted to have them with us today. Space is a new frontier and worthy of further investigation. All current tests on the Orbiter Horizon are still on going as is the normal pre-launch checks to ensure that we have a 'Go for launch'. To confirm the crew, they have been chosen as follows; the commander and shuttle pilot will be Major Tom Anderson US Air Force; Mission specialists will be our partner colleagues, Sergei Grigorev and Vladimir Popov together with Neil Burgess as the payload commander and Matt Cooper the flight engineer. After this press conference, the crew will head over to the medical facility to begin their quarantine phase and then seven days before launch they will be quarantined over at KSC in the final preparation. The stand by alert crew will also be quarantined to provide for a secondary crew should anyone on the primary become too ill to travel. I'll open up the floor now for any questions you may have."

"How long is the mission Director?" it was the NBC reporter, John Williams who broke the ice

"Hi John, this one will be six months duration." The director added

"When will the Orbiter return?" John continued

"Approximately in two weeks. Dependant on how long it will take to unload all the equipment and supplies."

"How's the weather looking for the launch Director?" asked Glenn Jackson from Fox news.

"Currently it looks perfect. A great window but we know how these things are extreme and how quickly it can change. We'll be monitoring this right up to the point of countdown. Any change we will let you know."

"How's the shape of the crew looking?" asked Amanda Giles from CNN.

"They're in great shape. Ready for the off and excited as we all are. Having the Russians on board makes the space station truly international."

"Do you have any concerns opening up the space station to Russia? They were our enemy at one point and the ice from the cold war era still hasn't melted." Amanda added.

"Not at all. This is the thing; we must put those differences to one side for the sake of humanity. Space exploration isn't the same as wanting to dominate the world. This is a shared focus and with shared interests. It is also a shared expenditure in order for both countries to harness the same results. It would be difficult for one country to go alone on this. The race to the moon was a prime example. Equally of course, and as I have said earlier the space station now has an appropriate prefix - international."

"Who will be the flight director for this mission?" questioned Ian Cummings from the Washington Post.

"It will be Matt Roberts. A seasoned veteran of twenty-three years with NASA."

"What's the window time for this launch Director?" posed Tim Neal from Sky news.

"To answer this one in the correct way, I'm handing this one to the Flight Dynamics Engineer, Mark Owen. Mark."

"Thanks Director. I'll try and keep this as simple as I can. We have the launch period and the launch window and both overlap each other. We simply look at the launch period as the collection of days that the orbiter can reach its intended orbit and the launch window is the time period on a given day that the orbiter can be launched to reach its intended orbit. This can be as short as a second or even the entire day but is generally limited to no more than a couple of hours. As you know it's not weather permitting but where the ISS will be so that we can come in behind it and dock. As we all know, the earth rotates at one thousand and thirty-five miles per hour but an objects orbit is fixed in space. This means that the orbital path of the ISS passes over a different part of the earth on each ninety minute, seventeen thousand miles per hour orbit and therefore the stations 'ground track' is always shifting to the west. If you can image that on one orbit the ground track of the ISS may cross near KSC but when it comes back around ninety minutes later, Earth will have rotated and the orbit will cross at a point about one thousand miles due west. The result and to answer your question, there is only one plane window per day for a rendezvous mission because it takes about twenty-four hours for the target orbit to return. The other component of the launch window is the phase window, which is a period during which launching the shuttle will place it behind the ISS and on schedule to rendezvous at a specified time, usually three days after the launch. Fuel constraints limit the launch window to between two and a half minutes and ten minutes for a rendezvous. Any longer and the shuttle will not have enough fuel to catch the station. It's interesting to note, that those shuttles which are held on the launch pad for hours before launching didn't have a scheduled rendezvous. To close on this question, whilst the launch window coincides with the space stations orbital path, launch isn't necessarily timed for the exact moment the station flies over Kennedy. Engineers factor in multiple orbits over several days before agreeing on a schedule. A rendezvous could happen on launch day but the crew need time to adjust to weightlessness and to prepare for their mission. The orbiter therefore takes a lower orbit at higher speed, possibly lapping the ISS and then burns its engines to increase altitude, slow down, and creep up on the station from below and behind on the third day. The good thing is, they usually know it's coming. The launch window has become so critical that we have a dedicated team of engineers specifically on this task alone to ensure we get it right. It's a long answer Tim, but I think we covered what you asked." Mark looked back at the Director implying that he was handing back the podium.

"Wish I'd never asked now." Replied Tim which brought the room into rapturous laughing.

"Will the astronauts stick with the traditional steak and eggs breakfast before launch?" it was the turn of the New York Times reporter, Catherine Miller.
Those in the room chuckled.

"Absolutely." The director paused and smiled before adding, "It produces less waste to get rid of when they are in zero gravity conditions."

"One for all the space cadets out there, what exactly does the T stand for during a countdown? Many believe it stands for time." Asked the NBC reporter John Williams

"It took me a while to figure this out myself John when I came to NASA. You hear us talk in the Launch Control Centre about T minus nine minutes, T minus twenty minutes, etcetera and so the assumption is that T stands for time. I joined the space programme some eighteen years ago and I asked my elders the same question. It turns out that T actually stands for test because it is not always related to time. And so, in the early days of the space programme back in the Mercury and Gemini days and indeed Apollo, T stood for test. This again is because not all tests are based on time. It could be the start of a particular test in our OPF that is independent of the time of day. A very good question. I like that one. Any others?"

"To ensure that no damage had been caused to the Orbiter on launch and therefore safe for its return journey, do you think it would be a good idea for the Orbiter to do a flip manoeuvre to inspect the under belly and other surfaces?" pitched the Washington Post reporter.

"The correct term that we like to use is the *'rendezvous pitch manoeuvre'* or more commonly known as the RPM. It's not something we are planning on doing at the moment."

"How soon after take-off does the Commander or the pilot have control of the Orbiter?" It was Copeland who fired this one.

"The entire shuttle system is computer controlled from lift-off until it reaches orbit, so it's really like autopilot for the commander. There are some situations and certain abort procedures that the crew could get into which would require them to take over the flight controls of the vehicle which we have never done in the history of the programme. But there are those possibilities and so there is a remote chance that the commander might have to fly the shuttle during ascent and an emergency return to Earth. For the most part, it's fully automated. Landing day is a bit different, it's mostly autopilot from de-orbit burn until reaching the Florida area and over the Shuttle Landing Facility when the commander does take over the Orbiter and flies it in on its final approach to touchdown."

"How long will the journey to the ISS take?" questioned the USA Today reporter, Nancy Williams.

"Hi Nancy, thanks for your question. For all the mathematical genius out there, the ISS is two hundred and forty miles above earth. We have eight and a half minutes to get the Orbiter from zero to seventeen thousand miles per hour and into orbit. The longest part is the docking process. All things being equal, it will take approximately six hours from entering orbit to a sealed dock. After one and a half hours, the shuttle will be seventy-six kilometres behind the ISS. With three hours to go it will be fifteen kilometres behind. The last four hundred feet will be incredibly slow and may take forty minutes to complete. The speed between the two has to be manageable and the rendezvous has to be zero tolerant. The station safety rules dictate a cautious approach. One mishap and we have a catastrophe. If there are no more questions, then we can move on to the photo shoot with the astronauts before they head over for their medicals."

"One last question if I may Director," it was Glenn Jackson again, "Why did the Orbiter's external tank change from white to orange?"

"A good question to finish off with I think? You press don't miss a trick, do you? Originally the white paint was used to reflect the UV rays which helped to keep the liquid oxygen and liquid hydrogen fuel cool after being filled prior to launch. Well, the boffins over at Lockheed decided that they could save an extra six hundred pounds of weight if they reverted the tanks back to their original insulating foam's natural tone which is rust orange in colour. It'll be the same colour you'll see as we move towards launch day. The extra saving in poundage could then be used to increase the payload for the missions. A reasonable compromise I'd say. Thank you everyone."

With all five astronauts lined up and the click of cameras sounding like a cat walk, the photo shoot lasted approximately forty minutes before they headed off to the clinic to start their pre-launch medicals.

CHAPTER 12

Offices of Scorpion, Washington DC - 2 p.m. Same Day

Copeland listened attentively to the press conference being broadcast live from JSC. Astounded that the crew hadn't been swapped out but he understood the concerns given by the JSC director. Without factual information that a crewmember posed a particular threat to the mission he was powerless to do anything. All he could do was wait and that waiting was painful. As the camera panned across each of the crew, he looked at them to see if he could see any flaws in their expressions that may give them away, but there was nothing. Just smiles all round. Copeland picked up his desk phone and dialled a number, "Karl its Jack."

"Are you watching the JSC press conference?"

"That's what I'm ringing about. What do you make of it?" probed Copeland

"There's nothing out the ordinary. Just seems like all the other ones. It looks normal."

"That's what worries me. What's the status on the info regarding the flight crew? Any update?"

"I've had nothing at all from Felix over at the bureau. Seems like we have no leads, just dead ends. They all seem squeaky clean which I would've expected and hoped for. Anything more from Elisabeth regarding Syromokov?"

"Nothing as yet. I'll ring her later. Not sure if she has made contact as yet. I would've hoped she would tell me if she had. If she has, then perhaps there was nothing to report. Do you think I'm being paranoid Karl? Be honest."

"It had crossed my mind. The checks and balances to get a flight crew in the first instance is thorough enough so when you said you had a gut feeling it came as a little surprise. I was hoping there is no way it could happen but you got me into thinking about it. I agree with the philosophy that you can never say never and with this new addition to the ISS, it has a way of making you sit up and to look at it from a different perspective. Funny thing is, it's making make me paranoid too." Langdon chuckled.

"Glad it's not just me then. We'll be heading off to the shrink together if this turns out to be nothing. Keep me apprised."

* * *

2101 Nasa Parkway, Houston
JSC Flight Medicine Clinic - 3 p.m. EDT Same Day

Directly after the press conference and photo shoot, the crew of STS-108A were transported to the medicine clinic to begin their first day of a ten-day medical evaluation and quarantine process termed as L-10. Swabs were taken and blood drawn to ensure that they weren't already infected. Over the next two days, their results would be known and if the all clear is given, they will fly out to KSC where they will begin the full quarantine process four days before launch.

* * *

White House – Pennsylvania Avenue, Washington DC Office of the US President – Same day

"Jack, good to hear from you." Began the President having picked up his desk phone, "Thought you'd gone silent on me and I was beginning to think you'd gone back into retirement again."

"Not a chance in hell Mister President. You'd be the first to know if I intended to."

"That's good to hear. So, what's on your mind?"

"A while back, do you remember asking me to keep an eye on our new-found allies, the Russians?"

"I most certainly do. I don't have Alzheimer's yet. What do you have?"

"That's good to know and the country will be pleased about that. I'm not sure what I have at the moment. I'm a little anxious about having this laser on-board the ISS with our Russian friends."

"Go on?" encouraged the President.

"I just have a gut feeling that something isn't right here."

"Are you talking about the crew or the laser?"

"The crew." Copeland began before adding, "Or maybe a combination of both."

"The Russian crew were personally hand-picked by the RKA and confirmed by General Syromokov himself. Top of their class, couldn't argue with that. The ASCANs are home bread and scrutinised to the hilt. I don't see a problem here Jack."

"The consequences of this falling into the wrong hands are immense and just to be sure Mister President, I've asked the CIA Director to have a second look into their backgrounds. If they come up clean then I'll back off."

"You know the CIA has no jurisdiction at home?"

"Yes sir, so I've involved the FBI in this for that reason. CIA will look into the cosmonauts."

"Sounds like you've got your teeth into something here. The agencies priority at the moment is the after math of nine eleven. I don't want them distracted on a whim when there's no evidence to suggest any wrongdoing. Keep it low key Jack but let me know if you find anything."

"Indeed, Mister President."

* * *

NSA Intercept Room, Fort Mead, Maryland
One hour later - Same Day

"Hi its me." Came the words from Sergei as he dialled a number that was answered after several rings.

"Hi, how is everything?" came the voice of a female.

"We just had the Directors briefing and confirmation of the flight crew."

"Are you nervous?"

"Of course. We are on the verge of something new."

"Sergei, I had a visitor several weeks ago, a reporter."

"Oh yes." He asked in a suspicious tone, "What did they want?"

"Asking questions about you and our family."

"What did they say?"

"They wanted to make a story about you and Vladimir."

"In what way?"

"They see it as a major story because you will be travelling into space with the Americans to their space station. I thought it would be okay."

"It's fine. Do not worry."

"There was a man from the Ministry of Interior with them. It all seemed very official."

"Did he say his name?"

"He left a business card; his name was Andrei Vasiliev."

"Did you mention about the event whilst I'm away?"

"I said that it was a hospital appointment."

'Perfect. This will be my last call now as I am going into quarantine soon. You will see everything on the news."

"Please be careful. I'm worried about you."

"This success of this mission is in the hands of others."

* * *

Offices of Scorpion – 4 p.m. same day

The desk phone rang with a deep shrill in Copeland's office, which brought him out of a semi trance. He looked at it as if it was some valuable object that he was admiring. He wasn't in any particular mood to pick it up but he still had a lot of outstanding matters that needed to be resolved and figured that the call may just be one solution to many of his problems. Copeland relented and picked up the receiver, "This is Copeland."

"Hi Jack, it's Karl. I nearly rang your cell as I was thinking you may have been out the office."

"Had a few bits to do. Any news?"

"Just had another intercept on Sergei's phone. I'm sending over the audio file to you now. Have a listen then get back to me."

* * *

Fifteen minutes later

"This guy is so full of cryptic I need a translator to decipher. You lot are the spooks Karl, what do you make of it this time?" began Copeland

"Whilst he may feel that his words are innocent they do come across as a bit of a concern. The language he uses may seem normal in his own country, but to an out sider listening in it has a different meaning. I'm seeing this the same way you do Jack at the moment. Any news regarding Syromokov?"

"Not as yet. Elisabeth did say that it would take a little longer than it did with the wives'."

"What do you want to do next Jack?"

"My hands are tied at the moment. The President has put this on a low priority, which means there won't be any swap out as we have nothing concrete to go on and the crew have now entered their quarantine phase over at KSC. I'm going to let this play out in the absence of anything-solid Karl. It's certainly keeping me up at night trying to make sense of it all."

"Okay. We'll still keep digging around at our end."

"Appreciate it."

Copeland reclined back in his chair and listened to the audio file once again. Not sure what he hoped to find but he felt the need to at least analyse it once again. He remembered when he was younger and the times when he went back to watch a movie two or three times over and each revisit he picked up something different from the previous one. He figured the same philosophy could work here too. After each play back, Copeland wrote notes down on his yellow desk pad as if trying to break down each part of the conversation to make sense of it. He was struggling to comprehend any of it, which added frustration especially when he was starting to think that he might be looking too deeply into this. In the meantime, Copeland's clock was ticking but down to what or where he had no idea.

* * *

Three days later – seven days prior to launch

A clean bill of health came through for all five astronauts from the flight surgeon at JSC. Ecstatic, thrilled and eager to go, all five boarded three of NASA's two-man T-38 pristine white supersonic jets over at nearby Ellington Field and headed to KSC for the one-and-a-half-hour journey. Here they begin their final preparations and entered into medical quarantine for the last few days and before joining the elite men and women who have gone before. Two days prior to launch, all the astronauts would undergo a second exam. Nothing could be left to chance and the consequence of any of the crew becoming ill whilst in space was serious. A final once over would happen before they all suit up on launch day. On arrival, they were met by the centre director, Bob Taylor and retired astronaut Tony 'Slim' Harris who welcomed them to their new home, even though for a short time.

* * *

Kutuzovsky Prospekt, 7/4 Kopnyc 1 - CNN Moscow Bureau – Mid-day on the Same day GMT+3

Elisabeth had just returned from her lunch break when her desk phone rang, "Elisebeth Young." She answered.

"This is Igor Syromokov, General Igor Syromokov."

"General, this is a surprise."

"I don't see how. You've been making enquiries about me have you not?"

"Well yes. Um, it's just that I didn't expect you to call me directly. Isn't this against protocol?"

"Maybe."

"How did you get my direct number out of interest?"

"This is Russia."

"Of course. Nothing happens without the Kremlin knowing about it."

"Indeed. You have my attention so what can I do for you Miss Young?"

"I would like to interview you in relation to the space programme initiative currently taking place between the US and Russia."

"Why me?"

"Because you were instrumental in making it happen."

"I cannot take all the credit for this."

"Nevertheless, I would like to speak with you. It is a milestone and an achievement between our two countries that we should embrace together."

"You have a nice way with words. I will give you your meeting as there is something I need to tell you but I cannot until after the launch."

"You can't just give a reporter a snippet of information and leave it hanging there. It begs a handful of questions. It'll be like dangling candy in front of a baby then taking it away."

"I not with you."

"You're teasing me general."

"I will contact you to arrange. It's been very good talking with you Miss Young, goodbye."

Elisabeth was about to speak but the line was severed. She continued to look at her hand set momentarily before placing it back on the cradle as if hoping to make sense of what he was trying to say to her. All it achieved was a blank stare with many unanswered questions.

* * *

Elisabeth knew that it would be three o'clock in the morning back in DC but she needed to call Copeland. Her contact with Syromokov was worthy of a wider audience. She made the call and was surprised that it was answered after only several rings, "Hey it's me. Sorry to wake you at this ungodly hour."

"Hey no worries. Is everything okay? You okay?"

"I'm good thanks but missing you."

"I miss you more but I sense you're ringing for a different reason than to tell me that."

"I had an interesting conversation with General Syromokov a short time ago."

"You managed to make contact with him then?"

"Strange thing is he called me at the bureau. I'm still waiting for the green light from the Kremlin to make it official."

"So, what happened?"

"He rang to tell me something then he didn't actually tell me."

"I know it's early but am I supposed to make sense of that?"

"His exact words to me were that he will give me my meeting with him because there is something that he wants to tell me but not until after the launch."

"Was that it? Nothing else?"

"I thought it was important."

"I didn't mean it that way. It's both important and interesting, absolutely. It's just that I was wondering whether or not he had expanded on what he'd said at any point."

"I tried to probe him but he just said that he will contact me to make the arrangements and then cut the call."

"How did he sound? I mean was he flustered, calm, excited or worried maybe?"

"It was difficult to gauge, however he seemed expressional as if he was in control of something and wanted to share it with me but at his pace."

"This was certainly a curve ball Elisabeth. I never expected this."

"Me neither, he caught me by surprise. I could've asked him more questions if only I knew. One other thing though, it may be nothing but I sensed that he wanted a private meeting. He didn't say anything to suggest that but just his words *'I will call to arrange'*. I also sensed that he made the call off book without Kremlin's approval or knowledge."

"Just a thought, but did you try to ring the number back?"

"There was no number to call. It was obviously withheld or he had a disposable SIM. He didn't want me to call him back I guess. Another part of his control maybe."

"We talked about turning Syromokov and this may be our opportunity. When something comes out of nothing it's like being given a life line."

"Are you making progress with anything else Jack?"

"All the roads go nowhere at the moment, dead ends. It's annoying and frustrating to say the least. I know all the agencies have other priorities with the aftermath of nine-eleven so I can't expect them to drop everything on something that isn't a sure bet."

"I just hope you're right on all of this Jack. As things come together, I'm starting to see it from your point of view though however, I'm not sure if that's because I'm biased in all this."

"More and more things are making sense. It's basically like a jigsaw. We just need to find the right pieces."

* * *

CIA Directors Office, Langley 9 o'clock a.m. Same day

"Morning Jack, you sound exhausted." Began the CIA Director, "What's the latest?"

"You're not going to believe this, but I had a call from Elisabeth in the early hours."

"How would that be unusual? You two are together right?"

"Yes of course we are." Copeland responded indifferently, "Nothing to do with that but she had a conversation with Syromokov yesterday."

"How did that come together?"

"He called Elisabeth directly at the bureau. The interesting thing is that he has agreed to a meet but not until after the December fifth launch. He confided to her that he has something to tell."

"Did he say what?"

"No."

"Do you think he's genuine or playing us?"

"Elisabeth sensed that he may have made the call without knowledge from the Kremlin and she has a feeling that he wants a private meeting."

"The interesting thing here is if something is going to happen why would he wait until after the launch to tell us. I mean clearly he must be wanting to talk about that."

"That's a strong assumption. It sounds plausible and I'd like to go along with it in the absence of anything else. Speaking of which, any more updates Karl?"

"Nothing I'm afraid. I get weekly emails from the FBI with NTR written on them. If it was sent by post, I'd say it was a waste of paper."

"Until Elisabeth has the meet with Syromokov, I don't think we should pull the background checks from the Astronauts just yet. It may not pan out to anything with him but we need some hope."

"Unless something happens soon Jack, I'm going to have to pull the plug on this. Pressure from above and all that."

"I understand, but I don't not necessarily agree."

CHAPTER 13

Launch Pad 39A – Eighteen hours before launch

Located on the west side of the pad's flame trench, stands the Rotating Service Structure which acts as an umbilical tower and had provided access to the Orbiter over the last month. Incorporated within the tower is an elevator allowing maintenance and crew access that also facilitated the loading of Horizon's cargo – the laser. In preparation for the launch, at T-18 hours, she was rolled back but three of the umbilical's connected to the Orbiter for stabilising, remained in place. This would be needed in the event the crew had to evacuate one hundred and ninety feet down in an emergency and would only be released five seconds from launch, which would swing away from the Orbiter to prevent any damage. Situated on top of the orange external tank sits the vent arm with a 'beanie cap' as a vent hood. Seven 'slidewire's', each one thousand two hundred feet in length extended from the Orbiter access arm level to the ground on the west side of the launch pad. Suspended from each wire and surrounded by netting was a flat bottom basket capable of carrying up to three people. Designed to quickly take the astronauts to the emergency shelter bunker located west of the pad. It was every astronaut's worse nightmare but one which they practiced relentlessly.

* * *

JSC Spaceflight Meteorology Group
9 hours before launch

Tanking would only begin if a twenty-four-hour average temperature on the day was below forty-one degrees Fahrenheit and that the wind was not expected to exceed forty-two knots. Since it would take around three hours to load about five hundred thousand gallons of cryogenic propellants of liquid hydrogen and liquid oxygen into the external tank, the monitoring of weather was on-going. If there was a twenty per cent or greater chance of a lightning strike within the first hour of tanking and within five nautical miles of the launch pad overall, then the order to stop the countdown would be given. The telephone rang in the office of Neil Brody, the Meteorologist in charge at JSC, "Neil Brody." He answered.

"Neil, its Matt Roberts. How are things doing?"

"Hey Matt. Currently it's looking good. We've confirmed everything with the guys over at the forty fifth Weather Squadron and we're on track for tonight as scheduled."

"That's good to hear. Run it by me again the max wind allowed for launch. Keep it simple though."

"Sure, no more than thirty-four knots."

"That sounds pretty good."

"Depends which way you look at it. If the wind direction was between one hundred degrees and two hundred and sixty degrees then the max speed may be as low as twenty knots because of cross winds. That would seriously ruin your night."

"What's the direction at the moment?"

"Forty-five degrees."

"Speed?"

"Twenty-eight knots."

"Perfect, we're in the larger margins. What about precipitation?"

"None expected on the pad or the planned trajectory. As you know we can't fly if there is any chance of it."

"Indeed. Temperature at the moment?"

"Sixty-eight degrees."

"This is what I call a perfect night."

* * *

T minus 5hours and 20 minutes and counting

The countdown was stopped and a standard two-hour hold initiated. The ice inspection team were sent out to inspect the external tank's insulation to ensure that there was no dangerous accumulation of ice on the tank caused by the super-cold liquids loaded during the tanking process. These liquids had to be maintained at a constant minus four hundred and twenty-three degrees Fahrenheit. A challenge for anyone considering that the outside of the tank is sat outside in the Florida sun and then reaches as hot as six hundred degrees during its ascent before being jettisoned. All this protected by a one-inch thick coating of spray-on polyisocyanurate. At T minus three hours the countdown was resumed paving the way for the astronauts to leave the Operations & Checkout building after suiting up and heading out to the launch pad. During the next two and a half hours, the astronauts arrived at the white room located at the end of the Orbiter access arm and entered the Orbiter. Once inside, all air-to-ground communications were tested and checked off with the LCC and MCC. At the same time, the Orbiter hatch was closed and a hatch seal and cabin leak check were being carried out. One final check of the IMU was carried out which then allowed the white room crew to evacuate and the close out crew proceeded from the launch pad to the fall-back area. At the same time, the primary ascent guidance was transferred to the backup flight system. As the white out crew departed, they gave the thumbs up to the Orbiter crew signifying everything was well on the outside.

At T minus twenty minutes, another hold was initiated but this time for ten minutes after which the on-board computers were commanded and programmed to their launch configuration and all fuel cell thermal configurations began. The Orbiter cabin vent valves were closed and the backup flight system transitions were moved into launch configuration.

At T minus nine minutes, another planned ten-minute hold was implemented. Just prior to resuming the countdown, the NASA Test Director situated at his console facing into the firing room, requested a 'Go for Launch' verification from the launch team responsible for the test, checkout and monitoring of the flight hardware and ground support equipment. This was to ensure that the criteria had been met in order to commit the Orbiter to launch. Once confirmed, the Ground Launch Sequencer was turned on and the terminal countdown resumed. From this moment, all countdown functions were automatically controlled by the Ground Launch Sequencer.

* * *

Smolenskaya Street, Moscow - Elisabeth's Apartment Midnight Moscow Time

Elisabeth had been in bed and asleep for almost three hours when she heard a vibrating noise. Not recognising what it was immediately, she lifted her head off the pillow to get a sense of direction of where it was coming from. *'Surely it can't be the alarm already'* she said to herself. Half asleep and bleary eyed, she managed to switch on her side light which almost blinded her momentarily causing her eyes to squint and dilate at the same time. Having now focused and accustomed to the light, she looked towards her phone, which she had placed on the bed side cabinet and noticed that it was lit up and ringing but with no caller ID. She looked at her watch; it read midnight. Ordinarily, she wouldn't answer a call which showed no number but at this time of night it had to be something of importance. At least she hoped it was otherwise she would probably be venting down the phone at the caller. Having accepted the call, she wearily said, "Hello."

"Is this Elisabeth?" questioned the caller

"It is. Who is this this?"

"It's Natalya, Natalya Popova."

There was a slight pause whilst Elisabeth took in what she had said. This was completely out of the blue and whilst Elisabeth expected her to call at some point, she never expected her to take her up on that offer and certainly not at this time of night, "Natalya, are you okay?"

"Yes, I'm good thank you. I am very sorry to wake you at this time."

"It's no problem really. This is a surprise though. What has happened?"

"Nothing has happened. You asked me to call you if I wanted to speak."

"I did, yes but didn't expect anything at this hour."

"I can ring back tomorrow if better?"

"No, no it's fine. Were you having trouble sleeping?"

"I have things on my mind which I need to talk about. I cannot rest until I have said my piece."

"Okay, sounds intriguing. Is it to do with our meeting?"

"Yes."

Elisabeth could sense that Natalya was crying as her words came out, "Why are you crying? Has something happened to your children or Vladimir?"

"No nothing like that."

"Natalya, I'm in suspense here. Why did you call me?"

"It is to do with Sergei."

"Oksana's husband?"

"Yes. I have something to say."

"Okay, you now have my full attention." Elisabeth plugged into the phone a recording device and pressed record to begin recording the conversation.

"I think Sergei is planning something whilst he is in space."

"Okay, could you be more specific?"

"I heard him on the phone one time to Vladimir and they were discussing things like what would it be like to take over the space station."

"This is significant Natalya. Do you think that was just them having a prank maybe?" Elisabeth asked as if trying to play down the comment and to give Natalya chance to think about the seriousness of what she was implying.

"No, I do not think that."

"Could you say why you feel that way?"

"Because they were saying things like how to disable the override which allows ground to control the station."

"Why have you waited until now to tell me this though?"

"It's not that easy in our country to speak openly. You don't know what it is like. I'm scared even talking with you now. Someone is probably listening and I will have the FSB knocking on my door and I will never see my family again. Siberia is so inhospitable this time of year as it is most of the time. I would not survive in prison. I would be too weak."

"You've come this far and have done well Natalya. It takes a lot of courage to speak out but someone has to if any wrongs have to be made right again. Did you hear anything else?'

"Vladimir at times was speaking quietly so it was difficult for me to listen properly. But I think it had something to do with what they are taking with them."

"What do you think they were referring to?"

"They talked about using the space station to do something on earth."

"Do you know what they meant by that?"

"No, I don't. I do not understand all this jargon. It's almost like a code."

"When did this conversation take place?"

"About three weeks ago."

"Was it in your house?"

"Yes."

"You told me that Vladimir hadn't been home during his time in Moscow. Are you telling me now that he had been?"

"He did, but he wasn't supposed to. That's why I didn't say anything at the time and with that government man there, I didn't want to get Vladimir into trouble and to spoil his chance of going into space. He deserves a chance like this."

"Did Vladimir say anything about what cargo they will be taking into space?"

"I only caught part of it but he mentioned that it was a secret weapon. What he was referring to, I don't know. The rest I couldn't here as I had to see to the children."

"I'm struggling to figure out here what they'd gain from all of this?"

"This is what I can't understand."

"Sorry to ask this Natalya, but do you have any financial worries?"

"Sorry I don't understand."

"Are you able to pay all your bills on time and do you have enough to live on? That kind of stuff."

"We are not as privileged as Oksana if that's what you mean. We make it work with what little we have."

"People do lots of strange things when it comes to money. Even if you think you know someone close to you, if money is offered for something in return then it is surprising what they will do."

I'm worried now that he might be doing something stupid. I can't look after our two children alone on the money I will get from the government if anything happened."

"To who, Vladimir or Sergei?"

"Both."

"I can't believe we're talking like this. It's as if we are assuming that Vladimir and Sergei are hostiles."

"I'm just giving you what I have heard."

"What about General Syromokov?"

"In what way?"

"Have you heard his name mentioned at all?"

"Briefly I did, yes."

"Can you remember in what context?"

"I heard Vladimir saying '*has the general approved this*'."

"Do you know what he was referring to?"

"No, I don't."

"During this conversation, do you know who Vladimir was talking to?"

"Sergei."

"How do you know?"

"He mentioned his name as if referring to him."

"Do you think you may be making more out of this than what was actually said?"

"Do you not believe me?"

"It's not that Natalya. There is a lot to take in here and I just need to try and understand what possible motive could be in play. I need to make sure that what you are saying is enough to pass on."

"You asked me to call you and I have done so at great risk to me and my family."

"I really do appreciate that. You've been a great help Natalya. Thank you for coming forward and telling me. Please call me again if you think of anything else. I know it must've been a difficult decision to make, but you did the right thing."

"I hope so."

* * *

Elisabeth quickly looked at her watch and realised she had been on the phone to Natalya for at least an hour. The time in Washington would be early evening but she needed to speak with Copeland whilst things were still fresh in her mind. She gathered her thoughts and made the call. The phone rang several times but then went to his voice mail. Frustrated, she left a message asking him to call back whenever he picked it up. In the meantime, she turned off the side light and curled back under the duvet. Before long, she had drifted back into a deep sleep.

* * *

Command Centre – The Pentagon

Copeland sat at the end of the long table in the command centre and watched the huge screens on the wall as everything unfurled in front of him as the countdown continued. He listened to all the communications and chatter between the crew, LCC and MCC but nothing stood out as being of any concern. Everything looked normal and whilst that was good thing it didn't help Copeland at all. He wanted something abnormal so that he could prove that he was right all along – again. The picture he was looking at was a full image of the external side of the Orbiter Horizon and was shrouded in lights as a symbol and beacon of humanity. This was a magnificent piece of engineering and one which tested the boundaries of every concept faced by designers, planners and scientists alike. The room was filled with people from all the services with some in uniform and others in suits.

"Fancy a coffee Jack?" came a familiar voice behind Copeland. He turned around and saw the CIA Director, "Best offer I've had all day." Replied Copeland, "Good call." Copeland stood up and they both made their way to a percolator situated on a table near the back wall. They both picked up a styro foam cup, filled them from the coffee pot and headed back to the table. Copeland returned to his seat with Karl taking a seat next to him.

"So, what's the latest?" enquired Karl.

"If you can call normal something then that's where we're at."

"We're still looking into the backgrounds of the US astronauts but it's like looking for a needle in a hay stack. We have a population of two hundred and eighty-five million and all we need to check on is five people. You wouldn't consider that being difficult, right – wrong."

"Sounds like you've had a bad day?"

"Could've been better. I'm expecting something in the morning at some point regarding the home-grown astronauts."

"What have you heard Karl? Don't leave me hanging"

"I don't want to speculate."

'Fair enough. Just make sure it's water tight so we can act upon it if there's anything of substance."

Karl nodded and at the same time they both looked towards the monitors on the wall and noticed the countdown clock, it read five minutes.

* * *

T minus 5 Minutes and counting

Auxiliary power units were started, the SSR's were armed and the Orbiter's aero surface profile test was initiated. At T minus three minutes and fifty-five seconds, the main engine gimbal profile test was started. At T minus two minutes and fifty seconds the connecting arm which was used for emergency evacuation and attached to the Orbiter, was retracted. T minus two minutes and the crew closed and locked their visors. The transfer of power from ground to internal was initiated at T minus fifty seconds. At T minus thirty-one seconds, the ground launch sequence was a go for auto sequence start. The launch pad sound suppression system was activated at T minus sixteen seconds. At the moment the main engine ignition begins, three hundred thousand gallons of water is released to protect the Orbiter and payloads from acoustical damage reflected from the launch pad. T minus ten seconds, the main engine hydrogen burn off system was initiated and then at T minus six point six seconds, the ground launch sequencer commanded the main engine start.

* * *

Copeland continued to watch and listen attentively to the live commentary being broadcast from the launch site. All the team leaders gave their flight status and everything in between. Then came the flight readiness checks from all twenty-three representatives from the likes of Lockheed Martin and the United Space Alliance followed by the Senior Staff Check and then the Payload Readiness Check. Once all these had been signed off came the familiar words from Matt Roberts, NASA Flight Director, *'You are go for launch'*. The clock hit zero seconds at which point the SRB's ignited which provided seventy one percent of the thrust needed to lift off with the three main engines providing the remaining twenty nine percent. These engines now provided seven point eight million pounds of thrust to launch the fully loaded one million six hundred and six thousand pound Orbiter on a trajectory to the ISS. The commentator described the fact that since the SRB's are solid rocket engines, once they are ignited, they cannot shut down and therefore are the last component to light at launch.

Copeland swung his chair around so that he was looking in the opposite direction and away from the screens, "I can't watch this." He said aloud to himself but he sensed others in the room looking towards him who would've heard his remark but no-one commented. They either felt the same way or they were a curious bunch who expected something to happen."

The lift-off was a perfect text book launch and once airborne, Copeland heard the transfer of all ground control of the space shuttle systems being taken over by JSC. He swivelled back round to see the Orbiter burning its way through the night sky. He didn't intend to take his eyes off the screen for a moment from now. He wanted to follow this visually as far as he could and then listen to the areas that he couldn't see. This was one of many crucial points identified by Copeland where the Orbiter was at risk of what, well he hadn't quite figured that out as yet. After two minutes of flight and a distance of forty-five kilometres, the SRB's had burnt out and jettisoned from the Orbiter and back to the Atlantic Ocean. After a further six minutes of flight and with the propellant used up, the external tank was jettisoned just over ten seconds after the Main Engine Cut Off and once it had reached almost one hundred and thirteen kilometres above the earth whilst travelling at a speed of eighteen thousand miles per hour. Copeland figured that the flight part to the ISS would be the safest part during which the crew would be travelling with a g-force of three up to the point where the gravitational pull is zero and then the crew would enter in to microgravity. He was sure that during this part of the journey he would have a chance to get his head down for a couple of hours. Looking around the room, Copeland noticed Tom Walker, the Air Force Colonel in charge of the SDI programme and headed over to him.

"Tom." Copeland announced as he approached him.

"Jack, good to see you. Another successful launch?"

"Indeed. I'm always on edge when these things start. I have a question and since you're a geek

Fire Storm

in all this space stuff, I figure you might be able to answer it for me."

"Fire away."

"I'm intrigued as to how long it'll take to get to the ISS. Any clues?"

"You'll be looking at about six hours. Why?"

"That's cool. I just wanted confirmation. I remember the Director of Flight Ops saying the same. Thanks for your help. Catch you later." Copeland decided to head off and catch up on some sleep. He had a temporary office in the Pentagon not far from the Command Centre with a sofa and he certainly intended to use it tonight. Having reached his room, Copeland pulled out his cell phone and realised it had run out of juice. '*Damn technology*' he vented to himself. Once he had plugged it into a socket on his desk, he picked up his desk phone and asked one of the orderlies to wake him in the event something was to happen within the next six hours. He had no reason to believe that to be the case however, in the meantime, he needed sleep and he intended to make the most of it.

CHAPTER 14

Pentagon - *The next morning, Dec 6, 2001*
Launch Day Plus One

Copeland started to disturb after his night's sleep on the sofa in his office when he heard a muffled knocking at the door. "Yes" he commanded. The door opened slowly.

"It's oh seven hundred Sir." Came the voice of the orderly. "You asked for a wakeup call."

"I did, thank you. Anything happen last night?"

"Not that I'm aware of Sir."

"That's welcome news at least. Could you grab me a coffee please?"

"Roger that." The orderly retreated, closing the door behind him. Copeland lay on the sofa for a while longer gathering his thoughts and trying to play this out in his mind. It was obvious now that nothing would happen during the launch. It wouldn't have achieved anything if it had. A bit of a mess and a clean-up operation but there was a wider scenario that was being considered. No, the best time is going to be once they reach the ISS and the cargo has been fitted, tested and aligned. Whilst everything would be done in slow motion out in space other than travelling at eighteen thousand miles per hour, he knew it would be time consuming as no doubt there would need to be a spacewalk at some point to set things up. Copeland wasn't sure how all this would pan out nor did he understand how it all fitted together. This was one area where he knew that he would be out of his depth. Having gone to his en-suite washroom he returned at the same time his coffee was brought to him. Sitting at his desk, he powered up his cell phone and almost immediately a missed call alert came through from Elisabeth saying that a message had been left. He called his voicemail, listened to what she had left for him and then looked at his watch before dialling Moscow. The phone rang for several rings, "Hey it's me. You okay? Just picked up your message. Sounded urgent."

"Hey honey. I'm fine thanks. It was and I guess still is urgent."

"Phone ran out of juice last night. What's the urgency sweetheart? Are the Russians launching an invasion and they've caught me napping?" he asked with a chuckle in his voice.

"That's not funny Jack."

"Okay, you got me. Did you see the launch last night?"

"We all did at the bureau. Couldn't have been better. Does that put your mind at ease?"

"Momentarily, yes. I'll be keeping an eye on things once they start to unload the cargo."

"What's the window?"

"The Orbiter which transported them, will probably stay for around two weeks then return to KSC with the returning crew and any rubbish they need to bring back. Okay, changing the subject, what was it you wanted to speak with me about?"

"I had a call late last night out the blue from Natalya."

"Natalya?" quizzed Copeland as he repeated the name slowly as if trying to remember where he'd heard the name before.

"Vladimir's wife. We must've been on the phone for the best part of an hour."

"Take it she wasn't calling for some nonsensical chit chat?"

"Absolutely not. We had a very interesting conversation though. She is convinced that both her husband and Sergei are planning something whilst they are on-board the ISS."

"Whoa! She just came out with that?"

"Yeah."

"No prompting?"

"Nop."

"Was she serious?"

"I think so."

"That's priceless."

"Thought you'd be pleased."

"How convinced are you though? I did sense a bit of doubt in your response."

"That's the thing, part of me thinks that what or, I should say if they are planning on something then it would be very difficult for them to do anything. So, I'm pretty sceptical on that point since everything is monitored from JSC but on the other side, she was very emotional and pretty much convinced me towards the end that she was serious. By the way, I recorded our conversation."

"That's great. Are you okay with this?"

"Yeah, it's just that she put herself at risk by calling me and she's worried that maybe she could be hauled away and sent to prison for speaking out."

"Freedom of speech isn't Russia's strongest area so I can see her point. This could be the turning point and the break through that we needed."

"I suppose." She said almost dejectedly

"Okay, let's get back on track." Copeland responded as if he wanted to take her emotional side out of it, "Can you send me a copy of the script? I'll work through it during the day and try to pick up any flags or anything else that may stand out."

"Will do."

"By the way, do you still have your security team?"

"I guess so. Why do you ask? I thought you would know."

"Just curious." Copeland knew that she was doing her job but also knew that he was putting her into harm's way.

"I haven't seen them. Is that good or a bad thing?"

Copeland paused briefly whilst he contemplated her answer, "It's probably good in a way," he said reassuringly and not wanting to give her any alarm signals, "It's normally done that way so that no one else can see them either. I'll speak with Karl and confirm. I'll let you know when I receive your email. Miss you."

"Miss you more."

* * *

Pentagon – 1000 hrs. Same Day

Copeland knew that he would be spending more of his time now at the Pentagon so he showered, had breakfast and then decided to get on top of things once again. He picked up his desk phone and dialled a number, "Karl, it's Jack."

"Morning Jack. I was about to call you. How was your night on the sofa?"

"To be honest, it wasn't half bad. Okay, you go first."

"I had some info back from Felix over at the DC field office which may be something or not. We can mull this over together if you like?"

"What have you got?" Copeland asked excitedly

"Run through the names again as to whose doing what on the current ISS flight crew."

"Umm, okay. Matt Cooper is the flight engineer, Tom Anderson is the pilot and commander, both Sergei and Vladimir are Mission Specialists and Neil Burgess the Payload Commander. What are you thinking?"

"Matt and Tom are pretty much clean. Nothing out the ordinary there. Usual stuff when they were younger. We've all been there."

"Okay, next."

"The Mission Specialists you're looking into along with our own guys. But interestingly, the last astronaut Neil has a coloured past."

"How's that?" asked an intrigued Copeland

"Well, to begin with he's never been married."

"Nothing wrong with that surely?"

"Correct, but he could technically be classed as a loner."

"No girlfriend?"

"Nop, lives with his mum currently or he did prior to becoming an ASCAN and heading out to the ISS."

"I'm not following any of this Karl. How's any of this make him a PoI?"

"He was involved with the highly classified test firing of the MIRACL back in nineteen ninety-seven."

"You've lost me."

"MIRACL is the Mid-Infrared Chemical Advanced Laser which was successfully fired against a US imagery satellite in low-earth orbit from the White Sands Missile Range in New Mexico."

"Working there isn't a problem is it?"

"In its self no. But he has advanced knowledge of laser systems. He's a real tech geek."

"Are you telling me this is new stuff that was never found when he first applied to be an ASCAN? Or are you just filling me in with background info?"

"It's background info and it was known at the time he applied and that was the basis on how he was recruited."

"Okay, so JSC knew of his previous employer and with the idea of launching a cargo specific to lasers he was chosen and recruited to be the lead specialist on this programme, right?"

"Correct. But in addition, new info has come to light by someone within his previous employers' organisation that he was working on an ultra-secret programme."

"For the US government I take it?"

"Not entirely." Responded Karl sheepishly.

"There's a gap here Karl which needs filling. Who else was he working for?"

"The Russians."

"You're kidding me?" responded Copeland with a hint of excitement as well as disappointment, "Well, that puts a whole new spin on things. Government or commercial entities?"

"Whoever was the highest bidder. I'm sure both would out bid each other depending how valuable the technology was to them. We're talking about Russia here so I'm pretty sure the government would be involved somewhere along the way. They're not one to let others have the upper hand and certainly nothing as powerful as this. They can't be seen as second best."

"Well, this is a bit of a curve ball. Never saw this coming."

"Me neither."

"How did this employer squeal?"

"It's best you don't know."

"I can see why it wouldn't have been found during his preliminary checks for JSC. So, out of all what has been said, what are you saying Karl?"

"Neil is going to be one to watch."

"As well as the Russians?"

"Until we know otherwise, yes. One other thing, he was also on the R and D staff over at Lockheed working on a laser defence system in low-earth orbit."

"This just gets worse. Only wish we had all this info before they launched. He's got so much going on in the background that's right in front of everyone's nose and yet he still manages to elude even the best agencies. I'm at a loss for words Karl as to why this has never come out before. It kind of changes my initial thoughts against the Russians, but not entirely. It makes sense really, he's in the right place, has the right knowledge and experience but what we don't have is a motive if he intends to do anything stupid."

"Indeed. But we can't jump to conclusions. Yes, we have his background now but this could also relate to millions of other Americans."

"But they're not in space and aboard the ISS, Neil is."

"Point taken." Admitted Karl

"I'm beginning to wonder who we can actually trust? We've identified three people of interest and with a crew of five, can we take the risk to inform the ISS Commander, Tom Anderson that he has a potential rogue crew onboard? Or is he involved too?"

"I think in the interim we should let this play out and see what develops, if anything. The other two may be involved even though they have come back clean."

"Hard one to call without creating panic. I'll need to bring POTUS up to speed at some point."

"Okay, your turn now."

"For what?" queried Copeland

"You rang me to discuss something, remember."

"My side pales into insignificance following your revelations. Are your guys still shadowing Elisabeth in Moscow?"

"Is that your question?"

"What, no. It's just for my own sanity."

"Yes, they are, but not sure for how long I can keep it going under the radar."

"Appreciate your help Karl. Anyway, I had an interesting call from Elisabeth last night. It might be nothing after what we've just been discussing but nevertheless it's another piece of the jigsaw that needs to be considered amongst all this."

"Okay, I'm listening."

"Natalya, the wife of Vladimir Popov rang Elisabeth to express her concerns about her husband and Sergei. She feels that they are planning something whilst aboard the ISS. She wasn't able to be any more specific as to what but General Syromokov's name was also mentioned as an agreeing party to whatever was going on."

"This just gets better Jack. I'm not sure you could write this script. This is things that movies are made of. We've got potentially a maverick crew of three aboard a five-man outpost with a weaponised system to ruin someone's day. The odds from where I'm sitting look pretty much stacked in their favour."

"Do you have any fall-back options if this goes south?" questioned Copeland

"None which currently spring to mind."

"I think I have an idea, but a slim one at that."

CHAPTER 15

Office of the JSC Director – 1400 hrs. Same Day

Copeland made the call from the Pentagon and was hoping that he'd be better placed once he knew what he could or couldn't do, "Director, this is Jack Copeland. Sorry to disturb you." Began Copeland as he spoke with the Director at the JSC.

"Hi Jack. No worries. How can I help?"

"What would an ideal turnaround time be for a returning Orbiter to Earth before it could be launched again?"

"Roughly around four months. Why?"

"That long?"

"It's not a commercial airliner. It's going into space and requires a different approach."

"I get that Director. Could you run through for me the procedure when one returns to Earth?"

"Well, the shuttle generally lands back at KSC all being well and then is taken to the OPF where she is stripped down and reassembled. Everything comes off and put back on again. This takes at least three months. Nothing can be overlooked here. After the OPF, she is taken to the Vehicle Assembly Building to marry up with the external tank and

SRB's again. It's a recurring process but shortcuts are not even a consideration. We aim to at least make three launches per year per vehicle. Realistically, we probably send each shuttle twice per year. This time line also allows us to make any final adjustments to who the crew are likely to be. Why, what's on your mind Jack?"

"This space programme is a whole new ball game to me and it's almost like I'm in the deep end and treading water. I have a lot to learn. So, there is no possible way that a shuttle could be launched within the four months?"

"Not a chance. There is more than just the destruction of the shuttle if anything goes wrong. It is likely the crew would perish and not forgetting that other countries rely on the US shuttle programme to launch their own equipment into space. It's a multi-billion-dollar delivery system and if something goes wrong, it will set the programme back several years all because things were rushed and the necessary safety checks were overlooked. I wouldn't even be signing off on that no matter what the emergency. I have the final call."

"Thanks Director for your candour. Oh, one other thing, when do you expect the payload to be unloaded?"

"An EVA is scheduled in six days' time."

"You've been a great help Director, thanks again."

As Copeland cut the call, he looked defeated. Whilst he probably knew the answer before he even asked the Director, he had hoped that there may be some fine adjustments that could be made. He reclined in his chair and took stock of what had just been said. Whilst disappointed, he now knew that if anything happened aboard the ISS, a rescue ship could not be launched for four months; at the earliest.

* * *

Command Centre – The Pentagon, 1500 hrs. Same Day

Copeland walked down the short corridor to the Command Centre. Stepping inside the room, he noticed how eerily quiet it was. The sound on the screens wasn't emitting any and the room was devoid of many people. Looking at the screens, they were showing external shots of the ISS, and he could see the Orbiter Horizon was safely anchored to the docking port. A further shot revealed that the cargo hold doors were open but the cargo hadn't yet been removed. Horizon was due to return in two weeks' time so he would expect the cargo to be unloaded within this period. Copeland looked around the room and spotted an Air Force Colonel next to a computer. He headed over to the Colonel and as he approached, he simply said, "Colonel."

"Yes General." He acknowledged and then stood up when Copeland was nearby.

"Stand easy Colonel. When did the payload doors open?"

"They open when the shuttle is on approach to the ISS."

"Is that safe?"

"Standard procedure. Idea being that as soon as orbit is achieved, the doors are opened to allow exposure of the environmental control and life support system radiators for heat rejection of the Orbiters systems. In other words, it's normally done to cool the space craft on approach to the ISS."

"Oh, okay. So, you described it in forty-eight words, so how about if I described it in just five words, it's a big venting system? Would that do it?"

The Colonel nodded in acceptance of the simplistic words describing a complex procedure.

"Thanks." Copeland then retreated with a smile on his face and headed back to the monitors. It was day one and not a lot was going on inside the ISS. There was a lot of bumping around as the new crew familiarised themselves with the layout in zero gravity conditions. Copeland left the Command Centre and headed back to his office.

* * *

Smolenskaya Street, Moscow – Elisabeth's Apartment 2200 hrs Washington Time, 0800 Moscow Time + 1 day

Elisabeth had showered and was getting herself ready to head off to work when her cell phone began to ring. Heading over to the chest of drawers in her bedroom, she looked at the screen, *'Withheld Number'*. She hesitated for a brief moment but then realised that if she didn't answer then she would never know if the call was important or not. And as a reporter, she couldn't take the risk. She picked up the phone and accepted the call, "This is Elisabeth."

"Good morning Elisabeth," said the caller in English but with a strong Russian accent.

The voice sounded familiar and it took Elisabeth a short while to connect the voice to an earlier conversation and instantly recognised the caller, "General, good morning. You've caught me nice and early. Have you had time to reflect on a meeting?"

"That is why I am calling. Meet me at the West 4 coffee bar at ten o'clock."

"I don't know where that is General"

"Search in the directory. There is only one."

"How will I recognise you?"

"I will find you." Came the curt response from Syromokov.

Before Elisabeth could answer, the call was cut. As a reporter she was intrigued as to what it was that he wanted to reveal and more so why it should be done under clandestine circumstances. What was he hiding? and what was he scared of? All sorts of questions were now running through her mind; did he want to defect but surely that would be done through different channels. Was he about to reveal something concerning the space station or was it to do with Sergei or Vladimir. This was deeper than she imagined and, in a few hours, she will know the state of mind of General Igor Syromokov.

* * *

1000 hrs. West 4 Coffee Bar, Moscow – Two Hours Later

Having decided not to go into the office on her way to meet Syromokov, Elisabeth quickly looked through the phone directory and as Syromokov had quite rightly pointed out to her, there was indeed only one. Having tapped in the address to her Satnav, she knew that it would take her approximately seven minutes to cover the distance of just over one and a half miles. She wanted to give herself plenty of time so she left her apartment just after nine thirty. The traffic was reasonably quiet as she expected it would be at that time of morning. The journey was straight forward and having turned left off the main highway into a one-way street, she confirmed by looking at the street name on the wall that it was the correct one as shown on her Satnav. Immediately on the left she noticed the coffee shop at the last minute, with the words West 4 above the entrance door but beneath an awning which was retracted and as luck would have it, she was able to park in a free bay almost directly opposite the bar. Having parked her vehicle, she looked at her watch, it was almost nine forty-five. Glancing back towards the bar, the outside looked tacky and dingy and almost seedy like which gave her an uncomfortable feeling of not knowing what to expect on the inside. A lone blonde female going into a coffee bar on her own was disturbing. Turning the engine off, she decided to go into the coffee bar and wait. At least it was daylight which gave her some comfort.

Walking through the door and then into the open space on the inside, she was pleasantly surprised how light and airy it was. There was plenty of light throughout the room, mostly from low hung ceiling lights. Over to the right was a brick counter with three sides, and a glass cabinet atop with cakes inside. To her surprise, the room was empty. Not one customer. Ahead of her were several small wooden tables and a long reddish coloured couch against the left wall. Elisabeth headed towards the far end of the room and towards the toilets and chose a seat which looked back towards the entrance so she could see who would come into the coffee bar. Elisabeth had no idea what Syromokov looked like so anyone who walked through the door could potentially be him. After a short while, the barista approached Elisabeth, "Can I get you anything? You seem to have been here a little while."

"I'm waiting for someone. I'll wait until they arrive. Thank you."

"Okay. Give me a shout if you change your mind."

Elisabeth smiled as if to acknowledge then anxiously looked at her watch again which read ten fifteen. Syromokov was late. She took her phone out of her hand bag and checked to see if she had any missed calls or messages; nothing. No reason why or an explanation, just nothing. Was he playing games and he had no intention of meeting with her because he had nothing to give. Was it a ruse or was there a genuine reason for his lateness? What if he had been involved in an accident and she was being judgemental as to selfish reasons why he wasn't there. She wasn't sure what would be the normal grace period before she would decide to leave. Another ten minutes she thought would be reasonable. Time was up she thought to herself, bade her farewell to the barista who looked confused and headed back to her car. Once inside, her phone began to ring. Looking at the screen, it was a withheld number again and since Syromokov used a similar tag before, she felt that she needed to answer it, "This is Elisabeth." She cautiously answered.

"My apologises for being late and for not contacting you sooner. I will not be meeting you there. Please come to the Four Seasons Hotel."

"Are you giving me the run-around General? I don't play games and this is wasting my time."

"Please be patient. I will explain when we meet. Come now."

Elisabeth sat motionless in the car for a few minutes gathering her thoughts. He knows how to throw bait and Elisabeth needed a story and felt she needed to follow this through. She took the bait and decided to see where it would lead. After all, Copeland had asked her to fact find on Syromokov and there were indeed some lose ends.

CHAPTER 16

Four Seasons Hotel, Moscow – Same Day

After an eighteen-minute journey and around the houses, Elisabeth arrived at the hotel. First impressions were that the hotel looked like some government monolithic building which had little character. You could've quite easily have been mistaken to think of it as a bank in its former life. Whilst it was grand on the outside, it was definitely palatial on the inside. The transformation was immense and whatever thoughts she had before she came through the doors, they were soon evaporated. Elisabeth was immersed into the splendour and trappings of the high life that this hotel could offer. *'Now we're talking'* she said quietly to herself as her eyes widened on looking around the expanse of the reception area and to figure out what to do next. The overwhelming feeling almost made her forget why she was there in the first place. In a corner, she spotted a seating area where a couple were sitting and chatting. It was either a business meeting or some kind of liaison. Body language somehow dictated the latter. She headed over and sat looking back towards the entrance door. Some sort of advance warning when he turned up would be useful so that she wasn't taken by complete surprise. The fascinating thing about a hotel is that you can do a lot of people watching. So much goes on in such a small place and you begin to wonder about their lives. Equally, it's easy to criticise couples together as a miss match and people's somewhat disastrous dress sense. People came in and went out and Elisabeth was getting bored with this now when suddenly, a man came through the door which made her sit up. He was large and rounded and dressed in a light-coloured shirt and dark chino's. She imagined Syromokov to be someone like that but then he made a bee line towards a woman standing by the reception who was clearly not his wife. An embrace suggested lovers'. Each to their own she thought to herself.

Elisabeth dropped her shoulders in disappointment and sat back in her chair once again. This gave her chance to think of Jack and how wonderful it would be to be in his arms right now instead of the other side of the world and alone. Being here gave her the opportunity to rethink her own life and she most certainly wanted to be with Copeland for the rest of her life but when that would be, she wasn't entirely sure. For now, though this waiting game wasn't something she was comfortable with and being at the behest of others, was outside of her control. Moments later, there was a voice behind her, "Elisabeth."

She quickly turned around to see a slim man of medium height with short dark hair and tanned as if he had just come back from holiday. He wore a dark suit, white shirt and dark tie, very official she thought to herself. Caught by surprise she answered, "How did you, oh not to worry. Yes, it is." She knew the answer before she asked, "Are you Syromokov?" although she doubted that it was since the voice didn't match the one during the phone calls. Even then it could've been masked.

"No, please follow me."

Elisabeth knew that there was no point in asking any questions since it was unlikely that he would answer them, so she followed the man through several internal doors and then to the lower ground car park where there was a black Mercedes standing alone and outside the lines of normal parking spaces. This was clearly someone who was powerful and defied laws or thought they were above reproach. As Elisabeth approached the car, she could see that all the windows were blacked out with privacy glass so was unable to see anyone inside. The man she was following opened the nearside rear door and stepped to one side ushering her to step into the vehicle. Elisabeth knew she was here to meet Syromokov, or at least she thought she was and by stepping into the vehicle would bring closure to this particular chapter and she would have all the information she needed. She was now entering voluntarily into the unknown world of clandestine operations.

* * *

Langley, Virginia – Same Day
0400 hrs. US time, 1100 hrs Moscow Time

The perils of being the CIA Director is that you are always on call. Karl was tired and soon dropped into a deep sleep which was soon disturbed by the vibrating of his cell phone on his bedside cabinet.

"Yeah."

"Sir, sorry to bother you, It's Jon from the Moscow office."

"What is it Jon?"

"We were following the target and she went to a random place, a coffee shop about four clicks from the Kremlin. She met no one, stayed for almost an hour, didn't even order a coffee. Once back in her car she picked up an incoming call, then headed east towards the Kremlin."

"And...?"

"The thing is, I think this was a test to see if she was being followed. It had all the hallmarks, but the clincher was when a small black Mercedes van pulled in front of us hitting another vehicle which then blocked the road impeding our passage."

"What are you saying?"

"This was no accident, it was staged for sure."

"Am I missing something?"

Jon hesitated, "We lost her."

"Damn it."

"I'm guessing that if she was meeting someone, then it had to be nearby."

"Reason being?"

"To allow her to come off the main road without being seen. I'm sure the target is within a click radius."

"Keep me apprised."

* * *

"I'm very pleased to meet you at last Elisabeth. I apologise for the way in which we are meeting. I'm Igor Syromokov."

"This is very clandestine stuff General" began Elisabeth. "Why the need for secrecy?"

"Since I work for the government, I had to be sure that you were not being followed. You were in an empty coffee shop so anyone would stand out. You also drove two routes so any followers would be fairly obvious. As it is, you were being tailed by two people in an SUV. My boys ran a little interference. Were you aware?"

Elisabeth was caught on the hop with that question. She knew she had a tail but had never seen them for some time and yet Syromokov's boys managed to find them in a few hours. "The interference or being followed?" she tested.

"The latter."

Not knowing how to answer this, she began, "Well, umm, yeah I suppose." There was no point in denying it as he already knew the answer. "Could we not have met in a coffee shop rather than in an underground car park? It seems just a little seedy."

"I'm a very private man and not one for public areas. I find it easier to talk away from the watchful eyes and ears of everything above ground."

"I take it this young man is your driver?" asked Elisabeth as she pointed to the man outside the car.

"Yes, Yuri is my long-standing driver and is very loyal and trusting servant of mine."

"I'm on the clock here General. You said that you had something to tell me."

"One thing at a time Elisabeth. There is no rush. Please call me Igor."
Elisabeth felt a little repulsive at the fact that he was calling her by her name more often than she was comfortable with and it was as if she was a dear friend or one of his liaisons. Currently, she couldn't wait to get out of the car and away from this close proximity. He looked like a dirty old man and a predator, "What can you tell me about Sergei and Vladimir?"

"Before I begin, I would like to be protected by the Americans."
This was something she had vaguely considered as to why Syromokov wanted to meet in person but never thought of it as a viable option or one that would come to fruition, "Wow, are you wanting to defect?" she asked with a little excitement. She'd never been in a situation like this before. She could see herself as a CIA agent.

"I think that is the word we use, yes. Can you help me in return for information?"

"This is above my pay grade General." Elisabeth corrected herself, "Igor, but I can make a few calls. I will need to know what kind of information you are willing to impart though. The information would have to be, sensitive, secret, invaluable to the US and above all actionable. What can you give me now to take away and discuss with the US?"

"I was part of the old guard of the KGB up to when it ceased operations in nineteen ninety-one. I was reluctant to move to its successor, the FSB in Lubyanka Square. Since I knew nothing else besides this clandestine world that we lived and worked in so I continued as if nothing had changed."

"What does this have to do with Sergei and Vladimir?"

"I don't know why you are fixated with them."

"Are you telling me that the US do not have to be concerned about them?"

"No, I mean yes. I will not say anymore until I have an assurance."

"So, you have nothing of real value except your own history?"

"It is not about me. Although I admit I would like a better life for myself and my family."

"I see nothing of any real substance here Igor to take away with me. Give me something at least."

"It is one of your own."

"Which one? Can you tell me that at least?" asked Elisabeth impatiently.

"Not until I have an assurance of my safety as well as that of my family."

"I'll see what I can do Igor."

"Whatever happens from now Elisabeth, the security of the world will be in your hands."

"No pressure then." She concluded with a hint of concern.

"I will call you in two days' time."

As if on que, the door opened and Elisabeth was gestured out of the vehicle. Yuri climbed behind the wheel and drove off leaving Elisabeth standing there thinking about what the hell had just happened. The meeting with Syromokov gave Elisabeth a little more confidence. She felt more in control of the situation considering he wanted something of importance to him, but also, there were unanswered questions and she would have to wait two days until she knew anymore. She was sure that they would be two very long days.

* * *

Karl couldn't get back to sleep after the call from his Moscow agent. Things were running through his mind. He had promised Copeland that he would make sure Elisabeth was safe, at least for the time being and now she's off the grid. An hour after the initial call, his cell vibrated again. Since he was expecting the call, he quickly picked up the phone.

"Tell me you've got some good news?"

"Yep, we picked the target up again coming out the Four Seasons car park. I reckon they were running interference whilst the meet was going down. Now we're mobile and looks like she's heading back into town."

Karl sighed an element of relief at the news as he knew Elisabeth was an integral part to what was going on and without her involvement, they would be running blind.

CHAPTER 17

Pentagon, 0700 hrs Same Day

Copeland had a good night's sleep considering what was going on. He was getting used to his new sleeping quarters and at oh seven hundred each morning, the orderly brought him a cup of his favourite coffee. Right on que, there was a knock on the door. Even though Copeland knew who it was, he still said, "Yeah."

The door opened and in walked the orderly, "Coffee sir."

"Thanks Mike. How's your family?"

"Very well thank you. Vicky is expecting our third child anytime soon."

"Congratulations. I think to keep the population down, I may have to arrange for you to work here more often."

"That'll be a blessing sir. But she wants more."

"More, as in more?"

"I was in shock too. Not sure I can cope with a full soccer team. It's wearing me out just with the two at the moment." he said with a smile. "They're great kids. Wouldn't change it and if it keeps Vicky happy, then I'm happy too."

"Hope everything goes well Mike."

"Appreciate it sir."

The orderly retreated and left the room. Copeland picked up his cell phone from his desk and checked for any messages or missed calls, nothing. He was keen to get one from Elisabeth but he knew that she was busy. He was missing her for sure. As he began to drink his coffee, his cell phone rang. The laws of averages had an eerie way of doing something at the moment you had a thought. Having seen who the caller was, he accepted the call, "Hey, you okay?"

"It's been manic out here."

"What time is it your end?"

"Just after two in the afternoon."

"So, what's been happening?"

"Where do I begin?"

"From the beginning would be a good start."

"Ha-ha Very funny Jack. I eventually met up with Syromokov. What a mission that was."

"In what way?"

"He gave me the run around. Go here go there and then finally we meet in an underground car park near the Kremlin."

"Well, that was unexpected. What did he have to say?"

"The interesting thing which was key during the meeting, was that he wanted to defect."

Copeland choked on his coffee and spat it out over his desk, "He wanted to do what?"

"He wants to defect in return for information he can give us."

"What's his end game?"

"He wants security for himself and his family in the US."

"Only the President can sign that off. Did he give you anything as a taster of what he has which may be useful to us?"

"He says that we are looking in the wrong direction so to speak. We shouldn't be concentrating on Vladimir or Sergei."

"Really. Any particular reason?"

"He says we have a problem with one of our own. He knows the name, but he won't divulge until he has an assurance that he will have a new life."

"Is he referring to an astronaut or something else? Did he elaborate at least?"

"No. He wasn't willing to say anything else. It was all about him really."

"I'll have to run this past the CIA Director as he'll want to look into this himself as he may run him as an asset. Equally, the President will need to know."

"Syromokov said he'd call me back in two days. So, he's expecting a result by then one way or the other. If we don't, then we lose any info he has and we'll be no further forward with finding out who or what our problem is."

"Are you okay with all this? You're entering into a different world."

"I am now. In a funny way, I quite enjoy the thrill of this clandestine stuff. You probably know already, but he offered up that he used to be part of the KGB old guard and now is working with the successor, the FSB."

"I didn't know that until now, but I did have my suspicions. It's very rare that anyone in a high-ranking position within the government hasn't been at some point a member of the secret services. You've done a hell of a lot sweetheart. It's invaluable what you've achieved in such a short time. How's your new apartment by the way?"

"It's great. I'd love for you to see it. Gives me so much independence away from the office but there is something missing to make it complete and to make it a temporary home for now."

"I'm with you on that. Miss you too."

* * *

White House 0900 hrs The Same Day
Office of the US President

The President was in his office early as he had one important event he needed to finalise, practicing his putting technique along the carpet of the Oval office. Having made twelve out of fifteen puts successfully, he decided that was enough for the day. Sitting back at his desk and rummaging through official documents that he needed to sign off, his desk phone came to life. He accepted the call, "Mister President, Jack Copeland is on line three."

"Thank you." The President pressed the light on line three, "Yes Jack. What's happening?"

"Elisabeth has met with General Syromokov and there's an interesting twist to all this."

"I'm listening. Go on."

"He wants to defect."

"The whole world wants to come to the US. What makes him different and what's he offering in return?"

"Well, the bottom line is he will give us the name of someone who is up to no good."

"Is this still to do with the ISS? We're not still on with this crusade are we Jack?'

"Mister President. It involves General Syromokov, the head of Cosmonaut training at Star City. There must be a connection with the ISS or space in general. He has some actionable intelligence that we need to consider. I've been looking in the wrong direction according to him."

"Have you run this past Langley?"

"Not yet, he's my next call."

"Okay. Get Karl to come back to me once you've done it. Thanks Jack."

* * *

CIA Headquarters, Langley Virginia
Office of the CIA Director – 1100 hrs the same day

Karl was at his desk reading through and signing off bureaucratic paperwork when his desk phone rang, "Yeah." He simply said whilst he carried on reading.

"Karl, it's Jack. There's something I need to run past you."

"Sure, go ahead. I need a break from all this paper work stuff in any case. I didn't join the agency to push papers around. Guess it comes with the territory though."

Copeland explained the conversation he had with Elisabeth earlier and the outcome from her meeting with Syromokov.

"This is hot. Was he serious?" questioned Karl

"Absolutely. In fact, he went out of his way to make sure the meeting was as secret as possible."

"If he's useful, then technically he can become an asset. He'd need a handler to develop him if that's what he wants. This takes a bit of time though to set up and initiate meets etcetera."

"That's something we don't have. He's calling Elisabeth back in two days and he's expecting a positive response. I need your help with this Karl. It's deeper than any of us initially thought."

"What do you need?"

"To make sure we do this the right way, can one of your agents from the Moscow office go with Elisabeth for the next meet?"

"Reasonable request. Have you run any of this past the President?"

"Yep, he wants me to get back to him once I've brought you up to speed."

"Okay, let him know that I agree with a sign off and I'll arrange liaison out of our Moscow site."

"That's great Karl. Thanks for your help."
Langdon didn't have the heart to tell Copeland that the tail on Elisabeth had temporarily lost her. He didn't need to know and as far as Karl was concerned, it was a missing hour but in the bigger scheme of things, it was a small glitch that happens.

* * *

"Mister President." Began the CIA Director, "I've had a back brief from Jack and I think we have a go with Syromokov."

"How certain are you that he's going to be useful?"

"I'm not, but we need to make a start to see where it leads. Sounds like he knows something and if we can dangle a carrot, then hopefully he can give us some actionable intelligence. Jack is convinced there's a problem, and currently, I'm inclined to agree. The edges are a little fuzzy at the moment because we just can't see it. Whatever it is, I hope we can catch it in time."

"Okay, I'll give you some lateral movement with this Karl, but if it looks like a waste of time and resources, you pull the plug. Understood?"

"Yes sir. I'll speak with the head of station out of the Moscow office and get things arranged."

* * *

Pentagon Command Centre – 1400hrs Same Day

Copeland continued to watch the large screens and listened to the ISS crew speaking with Mission Control back in Houston.

"ISS, this is Houston. We have a scheduled EVA for you tomorrow at eleven hundred. This will be for Sergei and Vladimir."

"Thanks Houston. Good to know. How we looking down there?"

"You'll be pleased to know that everything's where it should be."

"What's the task?" queried the Commander, Tom Anderson.

"Payload removal from Horizon to the ISS."
Copeland looked around the room and again saw the Air Force Colonel tapping away at his laptop computer, "Colonel." Shouted Copeland to attract his attention.

"Yes sir?" replied the Colonel

"Step over here please."
The colonel stopped what he was doing, closed the lid to his laptop and headed over to where Copeland was stood. He wasn't sure if he was in trouble or a question was needed to be asked. Luckily, it was the latter.

"Colonel, what's an EVA?"
Copeland knew the Colonel wasn't one to give short answers and clearly, he wasn't going to be disappointed this time either.

"From a space point of view, it is anything which would describe an activity for which any crew member has to leave the protected 'shirt sleeve' environment of the Orbiter's crew cabin. In other words, it is generally termed as Extra Vehicular Activity."

Sensing the Colonel was pretty gullible, Copeland plied on the questions.

"Great. Tell me, why does Houston give twenty-four hours' notice when they want an EVA done? Can't they just say go ahead and do one?"
The Colonel was on a roll now. He was confident and he was in his element. He had the audience of a General who took an interest in his intelligence.

"Well sir, the process leading up to a spacewalk can take almost an entire day. It's not because of the items that make up the space suit but it is the time the astronauts need to go through decompression. Pretty much the same as cave divers use when returning from the depths of the ocean. Anything else sir?"

"What are the space suits pressurised at?" Copeland threw this into the mix to see how knowledgeable the Colonel was.

"Because there is a lack of pressure in space, a suit is normally pressurised at twenty-nine point six kilopascals during a spacewalk. This is about one third of the pressure inside the ISS."

"I'm not going to ask what a kilo thingy, what did you call it?"

"Kilopascal."

"That's the one. What else do I need to know Colonel to get a better understanding?"

"Well, the astronauts breathe pure oxygen for one thing."

"Why?"

"Simply because the amount of oxygen in air at such a low pressure isn't enough."

"One question I've always wanted to know the answer to and that is, is it possible to don a space suit quickly?"

"Not entirely. If an astronaut donned a space suit in fifteen minutes for instance and promptly exited an airlock, he or she would go through decompression sickness. You probably know this as 'the bends'."

"So, you're telling me that's not a good idea?"

"No sir. I mean yes sir."

"Where does the decompression take place?"

"Inside the airlock on the mid-deck section."

"What's the procedure? The quick one."

"To give you the shortened version, the airlock is a small cylindrical area of only one point six metres in diameter and roughly two-point one metres high. The hatch from the mid-deck leads to the airlock, and the airlock is connected by another hatch to an unpressurised payload bay which eventually leads to outer space. Once in their suit, the astronaut shuts himself off completely from the outside atmosphere. The inner hatch of the airlock is sealed and the pressure inside is gradually decreased. Once the area reaches the appropriate pressure, the astronaut can then pull himself through the outer airlock hatch into the payload bay and finally begin their EVA."

"Was that the abridged version? It seemed quite lengthy to me." Copeland asked teasingly knowing that the Colonel would take it as a serious question.

"Yeah. More goes on besides that though."

"How do you know so much of this stuff?"

"I'm a bit of a space techie." He said proudly.

"Clearly. I'm impressed. Okay, what time zone does the ISS use considering it's all over the place?"

"That's an easy one."

"May be for you."

"They run on GMT."

"Reason?"

"It's half way between the two controlling stations of Moscow and Houston so they use UTC which is equivalent to GMT."

"Simple as that uh?"

"Yes sir. Not everything is complicated."

"How long can they do a spacewalk for? Twenty minutes or so?"

"That was the old days." He replied with a smile, "We've moved on since the early years. Now they can last from anything between five and eight hours. It's dependant on the task of course."

"Thanks Colonel. It's been most enlightening." said Copeland genuinely as he dismissed him.

The Colonel looked disappointed having been dismissed. He was set to be there for a while. It was almost as if he had been cut down in his prime. Needless to say, he understood.

CHAPTER 18

International Space Station – 1100 hours GMT
The Next Day

Both Sergei and Vladimir were suited up and already pressurised. All they needed now was clearance from Mission Control which came shortly after.

"ISS, this is Houston."

"Go ahead Houston."

"You are good to go for your EVA."

"Roger Houston. EVA is good to go." Acknowledged the ISS commander, Tom Anderson. Both astronauts went through the airlock and into the open payload bay of the Orbiter Horizon. The payload bay was just over eighteen metres in length, over four and a half metres wide and had payload attachment points along its length which currently secured the cargo preventing it from dropping into space. Houston would be monitoring all the vital signs of both Sergei and Vladimir to ensure they stay within acceptable limits. There would be no margin for error. Both astronauts carried the tools they needed and since there was no gravity, they were tethered to anchor points. Sergei headed over to the robotic arm. This would be used to lift the cargo out from the payload bay. He used the pistol grip tool with a nut attachment to attempt releasing the securing bolts of the arm. The arm was capable of lifting thirty thousand kilograms of weight on Earth or up to two hundred and sixty-six thousand kilograms in the weightlessness of space and at speeds of up to sixty centimetres per second. It had an accuracy of placement within five centimetres of a designated target. Manoeuvrability in space was a lot easier than on earth but was more time consuming and tiring.

* * *

Pentagon Command Centre 0600 hours - The Same Day

As Copeland watched the unfolding of the EVA in front of him, he could never stop marvelling at this incredible structure of engineering which was the most challenging ever attempted. The fact that it was in space with zero gravity, made it even more of a masterpiece. He never fully understood what went on there but he had the utmost respect for those who travelled there and, in some cases, sacrificed themselves for others. To him, they were true believers and heroes. Everything looked normal to Copeland. Nothing seemed out of character. Not that he would instantly know even if it was.

He was looking at two Russian Cosmonauts who, according to Syromokov were not persons of interest but nevertheless were still on Copelands watch list until proven otherwise. He was finding it difficult however to believe that any one of the others could be involved. He sincerely hoped that tomorrow would bring a better understanding of what actually he should be concentrating on and that it wasn't some kind of distraction by Syromokov. This waiting game was time wasted and the fact that it was in the control of Syromokov, agitated Copeland even more. He was calling the shots whilst the rest had to bow to his demands. Whilst there was nothing out of the ordinary actually happening on the ISS, that had to be a good thing, but Syromokov wanted to wait two days, which Copeland began to think to himself, that at least nothing was going to happen until after that period. This was certainly a comforting thought; at least for the time being.

* * *

CNN Bureau, Moscow - 2 p.m. the next day

Elisabeth had stepped out of her office to grab a bite to eat at the staff canteen on the third floor. After she had finished, she grabbed an Americano to go and took the elevator back to her floor. On walking back, she heard what sounded like her desk phone ringing. Quickening her pace, she reached her desk and picked up the receiver, "Elisabeth Young." She answered. The line went dead. She was either too late in picking up the receiver or it was a drop call. Placing her coffee cup on her desk, she heard the vibrating noise of her mobile. Scrambling through her hand bag, she retrieved her cell phone. On looking at the display, it read '*Unknown Caller*'. Accepting the call, she hesitated before speaking, "Elisabeth Young." She said briefly.

"This is Igor. Please listen to me. I do not have much time. I will not be meeting with you today as I fear someone knows about my plans. I will contact you again soon."

"But…" Elisabeth was cut short as the line was severed. Syromokov's voice sounded strained like that of a worried person. If someone did know what he was about to do, then he had every right to be worried. She hoped that he would contact her again soon and that he wasn't about to end up in the Moscow River at the hands of the FSB. She felt hopeless, but there was nothing she could do. He always withheld his numbers so she couldn't contact him and nor did she know of any hangouts he may frequent. The ball was yet again in his court and on his terms.

* * *

Moscow, 3 p.m. The Same Day

"Jack, it's me." Began Elisabeth as she made a direct dial to Copeland

"You okay? You sound worried."

"I had a call from Syromokov about an hour ago. It didn't go the way I expected it to."

"Sounds ominous. How did it go then?"

"He said he wasn't going to meet me and that he would call again."

"That's probably not unusual in his situation. Did he say when?"

"No."

"Did he say why?"

"Not exactly."

"That's a little vague. Did you sense maybe a change of heart?"

"I don't think so. I was only on the phone for a short while and there wasn't a lot said. He mentioned that he feels someone knows about his plans. He sounded worried too."

"This may change things slightly?"

"In what way?"

"Means we may have to move quicker than expected."

"Didn't know you had anything planned."

"For your next meet with Syromokov, I've arranged with Karl for him to send one of his spooks from the embassy in Moscow with you, so this can be made more official."

"Did the President agree on Syromokov's defection then?"

"Only if the information he provides is tangible. If it is, then the US would honour his request for a new life. If it isn't, then he could theoretically end up in the Moscow River as you suggested because his safety concerns have turned out to be valid. By sending the spook with you, I also want to confirm that his intel is legit before we all become totally distracted by all this furore."

* * *

White Sands Missile Range, Las Cruces, New Mexico – Sunday Two Days Later

White Sands was in the middle of nowhere and located in the Tularosa Basin of south-central New Mexico with the Organ Needles as a back drop. It's a half-way house to nowhere and being off highway Route 70, it is one place that you could quite easily pass and not realise you'd been there. The only clue would be the red and white signs as you approach the facility warning of live missile testing. Fifty-six miles to the south was El Paso in Texas. To the north one hundred and seventy-four miles was Albuquerque. Three hundred and forty-eight miles to the west lay Tucson in Arizona and heading east for five hundred and sixty-five miles was Fort Worth in Dallas. White Sands is run by the US Military and has its own little self-contained community from a middle and elementary school to a post exchange and a commissary. It also had its own police station, the WSMR PD. With a population of some six hundred active service employees, over one thousand six hundred family members and three thousand six hundred civilians. It was in all intents and purposes, a small town.

Mike Reynolds was a security guard supervisor at the facility and had been for eight years. Prior to that, he was a traffic cop with the LAPD before transferring to the White Sands PD for a couple of years. An opportunity for a security supervisor hit the internal vacancy board, so he decided to apply and he's never looked back since. He's married with two daughters and lives with his wife, Mariana on the base in a small house situated on Jupiter Avenue and located at the far end of the compound. He's in a job that he loves and he thrives on the responsibilities he has. He knew everyone by name and what they did within the facility. Although he was fifty-five years of age, he kept himself fit. He jogged five miles each morning along the flats within the base and off site. He had a small gym in his garage and worked out after each run. He was as strong as an ox and as fast as a cheetah. As a supervisor he typically worked the day shift although, on occasions he would pull a night one to ensure things were happening the way they should. After all, he was responsible for the security of the base as to what came and went. Today was Sunday and he was doing the day shift in the base checkpoint. He also had two mobile patrols in a 4x4's covering inside as well as outside the base. One of the mobiles had just checked in over the radio relaying that his sector was secure and as he returned the call to acknowledge, Mike saw a white vehicle approaching from the area of Route 70. Sunday was normally a quiet day and it was unusual to see any traffic or stragglers along the route. It was a day when everything happened on base.

As the vehicle approached, Mike noticed it was a white SUV and they took the right slip road and headed towards him at the control checkpoint. The car stopped alongside the security kiosk and with the barrier retained in the downward position, Mike stepped outside to establish who the meanders were. "Hey guys, what brings you all the way out here?"

Fire Storm

questioned Mike considering it was just over three and a half miles from the main road.

"What is this place?" asked the passenger in the SUV as he looked down at the name badge on the security guard, "Mike."

"Clearly, you're not in the right place. Where you heading?"

"We're after the MTR."

"This is the MTR." Confirmed Mike. He checked his clipboard for the list of visitors for the day, "Are you here to meet someone?"

"Yeah." Acknowledged the driver. He pulled a sheet of paper from his glove box, "Bradley Hernandez."

Mike knew that Brad was an equipment specialist missile engineer within the MTR. He worked on the MIRACL project and it wasn't uncommon for other engineers to visit but rarely did this happen at a weekend.

"Sorry guys but I don't have you listed. When were you scheduled?"

"Today."

"Have you got some ID? I'll need licence, insurance and vehicle registration."

Both visitors pulled out documents and handed them over to Mike. The driver was Ramirez and the passenger Diaz. Mike recorded their details on his visitor's log. "Let me give him a call." Mike headed back into the kiosk and made the call to Bradley. "Hey Brad, I've a couple of guys, Ramirez and Diaz at the gate saying they have an appointment with you today."

"Oh yeah, I forgot Mike. It's been a busy week."

"You know the rules Brad. No notification means no access. You're supposed to send in your requests in writing. You received the memo last week reiterating that point. So, what's the deal?"

"They're both software engineers and I need them on site to assist in a project we have on-going at the moment."

"How could their scheduling be missed if they're important to you? It's unlike you Brad to be forgetful."

"Give me a break Mike. I'm under pressure."

"How long they staying?"

"About two weeks on and off. At the most three."

"You need to get down here and sign them in otherwise I'll be turning them around. Comprender?" Mike asked in Spanish if Brad understood.

"Loud and clear. Thanks Mike. That gets me out a whole load of shit. Owe you one. I'll be down in ten mikes."

Brad arrived in eight, signed his visitors in the register and left the kiosk with his guests following behind. Mike felt uncomfortable about these two visitors and equally the body language when Brad saw them. If he was expecting them then he sure as hell looked uncomfortable having them around. Having two patrols at his disposal, he knew that one of them was on base. Mike pressed his radio button on the hand set fastened to the front of his shirt, "Papa one this is control."

"Go for Papa One." came the immediate reply.

"Just had two unannounced Hispanic visitors to Lima Charlie gate for Brad Hernandez." Mike was following them visually as he looked through the kiosk window, "They're in a white SUV currently on base and heading south along Headquarters Avenue. Meet them and do a lose follow and see where they end up. Brad signed them in and he's leading the way in his own vehicle." Mike's suspicious mind gave him the edge but he thought it a little premature to raise a concern at this point. It may come to nothing.

"Ten-four. Thirty seconds out. Currently on Aberdeen Avenue." After a brief pause, the patrolman continued, "I have visual. Behind them now and continuing south."

"Received. Keep me apprised."

* * *

As instructed by his supervisor, the patrolman followed the white SUV at an appropriate distance. Once they began to approach the end of the town limits, they turned right and headed along the perimeter road. Moments later, they turned left and into the car park at the side of a building. The patrolman stopped his vehicle in a second car park across the road and monitored what was happening. Since there was nothing untoward, he radioed back to Mike, "Control, this is Papa One."

"Go for Control." Responded Mike.

"Nothing going on here. They've stopped at the Frontier Club, unloaded their vehicle with a couple of average size cases and headed on inside. Brad shook hands in the car park and has left. Looks like they're gonna be guests here."

"Did you notice anything suspicious at all?"

"Nothing out the ordinary. I'm sure they were aware that I was behind them and I figured they'd noticed that I was across in the other car park. They turned slightly so their backs were facing me so they could talk with Brad before parting with the shake of the hands, but nothing else."

"How did Brad look?"

"His usual self. A little jumpier than normal I'd say though. Besides that, it all looked kosha."

"Okay, I'll log it for now. Resume your sector patrol."

Mike made a note in the occurrence book with a reminder for him to check on Ramirez and Diaz during the week and with Brad's boss. He wasn't expecting anything to come back but it would satisfy Mike's curiosity and put closure to this occurrence.

CHAPTER 19

CNN HQ, Moscow – 11.30 a.m. The Next Day

The office was busier than usual with phones ringing in all corners of the floor and voices raised over each. Almost like a competition to see who could be the loudest. Elisabeth was sat at her work station going over some notes with her colleague from the Asian desk when a loud shrill of a ring tone on her phone broke up the conversation. Picking up the phone from her desk top, she noticed the call was withheld. She had an inkling as to who it might be. She looked at her colleague and lifted one finger before saying to her, "Give me one minute please." Her colleague left Elisabeth who then accepted the call, "How did you…" she began, "oh never mind." She knew the answer in any case even before she knew who the caller was.

"Elisabeth?"

She recognised the dulcet tones of the voice once again. She was pleased that he had called but was frustrated that she had no control when he did and therefore wasn't prepared. "Yes Igor. Have you had a rethink?"

"No. I'm just being really careful. I think I am being watched. Nothing surprises me about this country anymore. I would like to meet sooner than later now."

"Okay, that sounds positive. I'm good with that. Your call once again I take it?" Elisabeth realised she sounded condescending.

"How do you mean?"

"A meet of your choice as always."

"I know this country far better than you Elisabeth and I will choose places on what I know as being safe areas. Is that too much to ask?"

"No, no, not at all. Sorry it sounded like an off the cuff remark. It's been a hectic morning so far. I will meet you wherever you decide."

"I will send you a text within the hour." The line was severed as quickly as it connected. Before placing the phone back on the desk, Elisabeth looked at it and spoke softly to herself that she was still no wiser than before. She expected to be given the run around as seemed to be the norm, but inwardly hoped this time would be more positive. The next hour she was sure would be an anxious and distracting time.

* * *

White Sands Missile Range, NM
Headquarters Office – Monday

Brad was in the office earlier than normal. Whilst it wasn't unusual when projects were on-going, it was strange however that he was going through the cabinets and drawers in the sensitive and restricted drawings room. He was looking for something but clearly was having trouble in finding it. The door suddenly opened catching Brad by surprise. Coming through the door was Hank Shepherd, the building janitor pushing his cleaning trolley with his head phones on and immersed in a different world. Catching a sudden glimpse of a figure in a corner of the room he quickly removed his head phones, "Hey, whose there?" he said as he gradually moved forward armed with his mop. Hank was a larger than life guy. He knew his limits and always stayed away from trouble, "Oh, it's you Brad. You scared the shit outa me. I was about to hit you with my mop." They both had a little chuckle at that comment. "Anyway, how'd you get in here? It's restricted access at this time."

"I've a big project I'm working on at the moment. You know, one of those top-secret things." Brad demonstrated with two closed fingers at each side of his head indicating quotation marks, "Just needed some papers."

"I know everything in here. What you looking for. I'll see if I can find it."

"That's okay Hank. It's not super urgent. I'll grab it another time." Brad walked past Hank and headed to the door, "See you Hank." He said without looking back.

"Yeah for sure." Hank replied with a confused look on his face. Brad didn't seem his usual chirpy self. Hank headed over to the cabinet where Brad had been loitering when he initially came through the door. It wasn't immediately obvious to him what he'd been looking for but he eventually found a loose piece of paper partly hidden under the cabinet which had probably dropped from a file Brad was looking at before he was disturbed. As the janitor, he had the responsibility of cleaning things up and a piece of paper on the floor was deemed as his responsibility. As he picked it up, he noticed it was from the US State Department and flagged as TOP SECRET in red which had been stamped across the centre. Hank knew what went on in the drawings room and had been given special privileges by the Base Commander, Brian Chevez. For the time being, he put the paper into the miscellaneous file and continued with his work. Having pieces of paper lying around, Hank knew was a breach of security protocols and would report the matter later. In the meantime, he put his head phones back on and for the time being, carried on his janitorial work.

* * *

32.632°N -106.332°W, Test Range 22 miles NE of WSMR, New Mexico – Same Day

Brad, Diaz and Ramirez left the base just after nine. All three travelled in Brad's vehicle and signed out at the gate lodge with a destination of simply 'the Test Range'. Mike was in the lodge and made a note of where they were heading. Because of patrol scheduling, Mike knew that the external patrol would be close by the range. Once Brad and his guests departed through the barrier, Mike picked up his radio, "Papa two from control."

"Go for two." Came the reply

"What's your twenty?" Mike asked for their location.

"Route seventy near the test range."

"Head over to the test range and wait there until Brad arrives. He has guests with him so just monitor what they do. No interference, understood?"

"Received."

After twenty minutes, the patrol noticed a vehicle heading their way along the track from Highway seventy. As the vehicle entered the open compound, they parked near a dome shaped building. All three, quickly left the vehicle gathering two small cases as they went. Ramirez and Diaz quickly glanced back over their shoulder towards the security vehicle before they entered the side of the building and disappeared. The patrol knew that the building housed the SeaLite Beam Director which had been used during the MIRACL Laser project in October nineteen ninety-seven. They also knew that Brad had authority to be there due to his position at WSMR as a missile engineer. What they were unsure of, was the role being played by the other two. "Control from Papa two."

"Go for control."

"All three are now in the dome. Shall we wait here or resume?"

"Wait in situ for the time being."

* * *

CNN HQ, Moscow – 12.30 a.m. The Same Day

Elisabeth's phone vibrated with the notification of an incoming message. Even though she had expected one, it still made her jump. Her initial reaction was to rush to pick the phone up, but she decided to try and be a little more in control herself. Slowly she picked the phone up and opened the message. Noticing that it was a withheld number again she opened the message which simply read, '
Elisabeth rang the number Copeland had given her when they spoke last time. He also gave her some information she would need to use as a means of ID. It was to be used only when Syromokov had arranged his second meet.

"US Embassy. How can I direct your call?" Came the response.

"Access code, Echo Yankee one, nine, six, two."

"Connecting now."
After a slight pause and a few switches and clicks she'd been connected, "Elisabeth. Karl over at Langley said you'd be calling at some point. I'm agent Neil Johnson.

"Is that your real name?"

"I'll leave you to be the judge on that one. I understand by the call, you've received some instructions from our mutual friend?"

"Yeah. A short time ago."

"What was the message?"

"We are to meet at eleven tomorrow morning by the Kutafiya Tower at the north end of Alexandrovsky Garden."

"That's close by the Kremlin. He's playing that close to home and in the open. It'll be quiet around that time with very few people nearby. I'm suspecting though that it won't be the final meet point. Spy trade craft dictates that it'll be a place to check to see that you aren't being followed."

"He did that last time too, so it won't be a surprise. By the way, he knows that I have a security vehicle following me. He made a point of letting me know."

"The guys filed a report on that. I expected that would happen. If he's serious about doing what he is suggesting, then he'll take all the necessary steps to minimise the risk of exposure. We'd do exactly the same if someone is looking at changing sides from our end. Does he know that you'll have someone with you this time?"

"I'm not aware. Certainly, I haven't said anything."

"That's not a problem. I didn't want him to be spooked but he will need to understand that his reason for meeting will involve another person at my level who can assess and validate what he has to offer. I'll give you my direct cell number to pass me his next message."

"Is that safe?"

"All our phones are encrypted."

"I wasn't thinking about yours."

"What do you have?"

"Blackberry."

"They're pretty secure. In fact, it's what we all use. However, if you're still concerned, then stick with the current contact method."

"As long as you're sure. I've come this far, I don't want to mess it up by compromising what we're doing."

"Stick with the plan and we'll be good. I'll wait for your next message to let me know where to pick you up."

* * *

Test Range WSMR – 12 p.m. later that day

The security patrol remained in location for several hours when Brad came out the dome alone. As he walked back towards his vehicle, he dialled a number on his cell. The patrol couldn't hear what he was saying but by his actions, he was a little agitated. Gesticulation of his arms suggested that things weren't quite as they should be. He was either venting at someone for not doing something or he was making a point about something else. Brad was pacing up and down alongside his vehicle for several minutes whilst he let loose his frustrations and what seemed like anger. After he cut the call, he walked quickly back towards the dome. The expression on his face implied that the matter hadn't been resolved.

* * *

The Kremlin, Moscow, 7 p.m. same day

The Defence Minister was sat behind his desk when the sound of a cell phone disturbed the ambience.

Since he didn't have a personal cell, he knew what it was. He opened the bottom right drawer of his desk cabinet and having picked up the phone, he accepted the call. He knew who it was. "Yes." He simply began.

"Why did you send me that text message? You know I'm busy."

"We need to bring the timings forward."

"That's impossible. We're not ready yet."

"You're not in a position to dictate."

"I'm the one doing the work. We'll be ready when I say so. If I'm not ready, then the whole thing will fail and it'll all have been for nothing. Is that what you want?"

"The window of opportunity is getting close. We'll miss it if we delay for too long."

"I have to test it once the algorithms have been uploaded. It can't be rushed. One missing piece of code can make the difference between success and failure."

"You have been paid handsomely to deliver. I expect results in the time frame given. Is that understood?"

"Clearly." Brad said reluctantly and with resentment.

* * *

Brad returned from his rant outside and entered the dome. Both Ramirez and Diaz were busy tapping away at their laptops. Diaz's laptop had the orbit interface of the ISS as it flew around the globe in real-time and Ramirez was tapping in information and instructional codes along with algorithms which would control the outcome. As the outer door slammed shut, Diaz looked away from his laptop towards Brad, "You've got a face like thunder. Take it didn't go too well then?" asked Diaz sarcastically.

"It's okay for you. I'm the one under pressure although shit rolls down hill and you two are in the firing line."

"Woah, keep me outa this. We were sent to do a job and these things can't be rushed." added Ramirez without looking away from his laptop.

"What was said then?" questioned Diaz

"He wants to bring the date forward."

"What's he thinking?" asked Ramirez

"A week at least."

"Impossible. We're nowhere near ready. The time line he gave us originally was only just enough in any case."

"I agree but we may have to work longer each day to at least get ahead of ourselves."

"Coding isn't something that can be put together overnight. It requires off-line testing before it can go live. I'll guarantee that there'll be some erratum in the code and there'll be tweaks needed before we're ready."

"We've been paid a great deal to do this so we have to give it a go and it would be an expectation. We knew it would change at some point, nothing ever goes according to plan." Brad looked over towards Diaz, "Where's the ISS at the moment?"

"Latitude twenty-seven point eight eight, longtitude minus one hundred and twenty-six point thirteen."

"Do I look as though I have a map in my head? Where's that in English?"

"If you look at the screen it'll show you but in essence it's almost overhead, but to the north of us."

"Thank you. That wasn't difficult." Brad replied condescendingly and with a look of disgust before continuing, "How long does it take to do a complete cycle?"

"A full earth circuit is ninety minutes from west to east. Why?" asked Diaz

"So, what you're saying is that every ninety minutes, the ISS will be above us"

"Yeah"

"Okay, at that point then, it will be known as zero for the purposes of calculations."

CHAPTER 20

White Sands HQ – The Next Day

Mike Reynolds decided to drive around the facility and rostered himself to be base patrol for part of the day. Driving along Headquarters Avenue, he saw Hank Shepherd walking out the main HQ building and along the side walk pushing his cleaning trolley but in the opposite direction from where Mike was driving. As usual, he was in his own little world with his head phones on and jigging to whatever music he was listening to. Mike liked Hank. He was hard working, came from an under privileged background and always had a smile on his face. He led a simple life and never asked for much. He was happy with what he had. Mike pulled his vehicle alongside Hank and tooted his horn. Hank didn't hear it at first but nearly lost his trolley on the second blast.

"Christ Mike. I nearly fell off the kerb. Are you trying to give me a heart attack?" Hank said as he stopped his cart and pulled away his ear phones.

"I'm surprised you don't get run over Hank."

"As long as I have my eye sight, I'm good."

"Point taken. Everything okay at your end?"

"Never realised how busy cleaning was until I started here."

"This is your sixth year now. How time flies. How's your sister?"

Hank's sister was thirty-eight, three years younger than him and suffered a serious fall from her horse four years ago. An MRI scan showed she had bleeding on the brain due to a fracture of the skull. It has affected her physically and suffers badly from seizures.

"It's pretty hard sometimes. She has good days and some bad ones."

"Give her my best Hank. Catch you later."

"Thanks Mike. Will do."

As Mike began to drive away, Hank shouted towards him. Mike stopped and Hank walked alongside, "It's probably nothing."

"What's on your mind Hank?"

"Yesterday, Brad was in the Drawings room at HQ at seven in the morning. I opened the door, and as I walked in, I saw him in the corner by the cabinets."

"He is allowed in there."

"I know, but not really at that time of morning."

"So, what you saying?"

"He looked a little sheepish."

"He probably didn't expect anyone in at that time of morning and you surprised him."

"I guess, but there's something else which was bothering me."

"Go on, I'm listening."

"There was a piece of paper on the floor half under a cabinet. It was by the area where Brad was standing."

"What was the paper?"

"It was from the State Department and flagged as Top Secret."

"What did you do with it Hank?"

"Popped it in the miscellaneous file as procedures say."

"Do you know what was on it?"

"It was to do with the replacement for the MIRACL laser system."

"Why didn't you tell me yesterday?"

"It totally slipped my mind. And as I said, it didn't seem that important at the time. But now, I don't think it was a coincidence that he was in there at that time of morning. He was certainly there for a reason, I'm sure of it."

"Did he say anything to you?"

"Well, I offered to find whatever he was looking for but he dismissed the idea and said that he would come back some other time."

"You did the right thing Hank."

"Hope so."

* * *

Kutafiya Tower, Alexandrovsky Garden, Moscow 11 a.m. the same day

Elisabeth had arranged with the CIA agent, Neil Johnson to meet her at her office and would travel together in her car. Her car was on the radar with

Syromokov and anything out the ordinary, may just spook him to retreat. His watchers would be looking out for her car as well as her security detail, so made sense to keep everything simple. Elisabeth parked her vehicle in one of many spare bays by the National Library. Both Neil and Elisabeth walked the short distance to the Kutafiya Tower and waited. As expected, the area was quiet so it would be easy for both Syromokov to see any tails and also for Neil to do a little bit of counter surveillance. Thirty minutes had lapsed when Elisabeth turned and looked at Neil, "He's not coming."

"This is standard stuff. All about playing the mind. See who gives in first."

After another thirty minutes, Elisabeth's cell vibrated indicating that she had received a message. She opened it and read out loud the message to Neil, "Meet me on the bridge by the Tree of Love on Luzhkov Most. I see you have a friend."

"That's an open place too. That's not where the meet is going to be either. There's somewhere else after this one."

"Are you sure. I only had the run around for two places last time and met him on the second."

"Well, we're a little further on now from the first meeting so becomes more serious. With that, comes more precautions. He's clocked me so must be comfortable with that arrangement otherwise he wouldn't have agreed another meet. Anyway, let's go. We have to cross the river. It's on the other side and traffic I'm sure will be a bitch."

Both Elisabeth and Neil returned back to her car and headed towards the south and over the Moscow

River. The traffic was particularly bad, but they arrived after a thirty-minute drive. Elisabeth parked by the European Commission building and they both walked the short distance to the next point, the Tree of Love.

"It's like being in a game." Elisabeth said, "Go to this point here and that one there. The only thing missing, are the clues."

"The clues in this case are the text messages." Several people walked over the bridge. No vehicles were allowed so it gave both sides the opportunity to be cautious. This time, forty minutes had elapsed when the familiar vibration noise on Elisabeth's cell indicated a text message. Becoming a little impatient now, she grabbed her phone and quickly opened and read the message.

"Cathedral of Christ the Saviour in twenty minutes."

"Let's go." Neil urged Elisabeth as they returned to her car.

After a journey of eighteen minutes, Neil directed Elisabeth to a partly covered lover level car park to the north side of the Cathedral. From here, and with seconds to spare they walked towards the main entrance.

"He's playing this by the book." Said Neil

"How's that?" questioned Elisabeth

"Making timings at each location tight. If we are serious about him then we will make sure we arrive at wherever he wants us to be. This is what he wants to be sure about."

"Have you seen a picture of him?"

Fire Storm

"Yes, we have a dossier. Quite lengthy actually. It's one of the things we do at each station, build up profiles of all prominent people."

Whilst Neil and Elisabeth were engaged in conversation, a tall man wearing a baseball cap and a dark coloured Nike tracksuit walked passed and simply said, "Follow me."

Looking at each other in surprise, Neil nodded to Elisabeth to indicate it was okay to follow. Neil took the lead and they both walked quickly in an attempt to keep up with the mysterious man. Both headed to the area behind the cathedral and towards the east side where the monument of Alexander II was standing. The man in the tracksuit had stopped in front of the statue and simply pointed to the ground. Both approached cautiously and stood by the steps on the left side. Moments later, a gruff voice was heard from behind them, "Elisabeth."

Both Neil and Elisabeth turned at the same time to their rear and the round figure of Syromokov was walking slowly down the steps. He looked older than she had remembered from their earlier meeting. Stress induced she thought to herself.

"Igor, this was a bit of a run around. Wasn't sure if you'd make it." Elisabeth began

"I'm serious about my intentions. Who have you brought with you? I'm guessing CIA."

Neil didn't say anything to agree or disagree but he didn't need to, as Syromokov knew the game himself.

"I thought so. You probably know a lot about me in any case."

Elisabeth was quite happy for Neil to ask all the questions since the subject was a little outside her depth of knowledge.

"General, I need to know what you have before we can offer something in return."

Syromokov turned sideways and looked towards the monument, "Do you know anything about the great Alexander the Second?"

"I'm sure you're about to educate us General." Responded Neil.

"He was a great icon of Russian imperialism. His great reforms stood out as the most significant events in the nineteenth century of Russian history. He was known as the 'Tsar Liberator' mainly because he abolished serfdom in eighteen sixty-one. Ironically, he was assassinated twenty years later. He stands here today for what he believed in yesterday. The modernisation of Russia, but since he failed, he paved the way for revolution."

"You're playing this pretty casual General?"

"I am an old man. I have nothing to lose. Russia isn't the same anymore. The old guard has gone and Russia seems stuck in a time warp. I want to make good before it's too late."

"So, what's on the table General?"

Syromokov paused whilst he looked towards Elisabeth, "As I mentioned to Elisabeth at our last meeting, I would like a new life."

"To defect?"

"That belongs to another era but if that's what you choose to call it, then yes."

"In return for what?"

I have information which I'm sure you will find most useful. As I said before, I want to do some good before my time is up."

"You've got to give me more than that General."

"Have you come with the assurance of the President himself?"

"That's being worked on as we speak."

"I need to see the letter first."

"Why did you choose this spot General?"

"There are no cameras around here and very few people at this time of day ever pass by."

"But it's close to the Kremlin."

"No one ever thinks that you will shit on your own door step. I think that's how you say it."

"Granted, smart move. Meet me half way on this General. Give me a teaser."

"You need to be wary of your own people."

"That's kind of vague. The US is a big country. Which area should we be looking in?"

"That would be too easy."

"Your information has to be proven solid intel if the US is ever going to give you a new start. You do realise that if we recruit you, you will never be able to return back to Russia."

"Yes, I am aware."

"You'll be looking over your shoulder for the rest of your live."

"I don't have much left so it's of little importance to me."

"Your position within the government is head of cosmonaut training in Star City. Is that correct?"

"You should know. It's Pilot Cosmonaut, Lieutenant General."

"So, that being the case I'm suspecting that the information you have but won't yet divulge has something to do with the International Space Station. Is that a fair assumption?"

"Yes."

"Are we talking on-board the ISS or somewhere else."

"If I say anything else, I will be of no more use to you and you will feed me to the wolves. Is that a fair assumption?"

"Does it involve the Americans or Russians?"

"I'm saying nothing more."

"I hope you can understand it from our point of view General. We can't just take someone off the street at face value because they say they have something of real importance. It has to be tangible, significant and worthy of the hoops we'll be jumping through."

"Believe me, you won't be disappointed but I need to see the letter of assurance from the President first."

"You drive a hard bargain General. Is our word not good enough?"

"We are former adversaries who have been brought together by global change. It doesn't mean to say that I like you, it just means that I have a better chance of undoing the wrongs that I see are emanating from within by people who are attempting to gain global supremacy by individual acts alone."

"That's quite a strong statement to put out General. You sound very bitter."

"I've had my moments."

Elisabeth saw this as an opportunity to turn things around and take back some control for themselves. Syromokov was on the back foot and was likely to say something if he was pushed a little harder or a little empathy was introduced, "Where would you like to settle in the US General, given the chance?"

"Washington."

"Nice choice, but I figured you would've wanted something in the country and away from the masses of people. We have Russians in the US and you may be best placed to live outside of major cities so you wouldn't be easily identified."

"Washington would be my dream but I know the reality. I will be a prisoner in my own home for a while whilst I establish myself within the community."

Neil interrupted, "We're talking here like you've already been accepted into the US. There's still some way to go yet. The ball is in your court General. What information you give us next, will determine whether we have any use for you."

Elisabeth pulled Neil to one side, "I'm guessing there'll be another meet after this one."

"For sure. We don't have anything to go on at the moment."

"Can't we do the next meet at the embassy?" she suggested.

"Too risky."

"Why?"

"The embassies are watched for things like this. It's not a smart move. If he's seen, then he'll either be in the river with a concrete slab around his body or shipped out to Siberia. I know which I'd prefer."

They both moved back towards Syromokov.

"We're not making any progress here General." Continued Neil, "It's not for the lack of trying and I understand your situation. You want guarantees, that's fair enough and quite understandable, but we can't do anything and nor are you willing to say anything until I've received the letter from the US President himself. I think we're done here. It's been good to actually see you in person. Good bye."

Syromokov felt that he was losing a bit of control. He's always been the one calling the shots, "But what about another meeting?" he asked in a alarmed voice.

"We'll be in touch."

"How will you find me?" he asked with a clear hint of concern.

"We're the CIA remember." Neil finished with a smile as he and Elisabeth turned and walked away.

CHAPTER 21

Las Cruces Gate, White Sands Missile Range
The Next Day

"Hey Jez, it's Mike over at Las Cruces. How you doing?"

Jez was Brad's boss over at the Special Projects Division at WSMR. It also had an in-route to the Electrical and Computer Engineering department of the University of New Mexico. If anyone knew about Brad, it would have to be him.

"Hi Mike. Not seen you around for a while. I guess we've all been busy. I'm thinking the call isn't a social one?"

"Not really. I just wanted to throw something past you. I may be reading too much into it though."

"Once a cop always a cop."

"I guess you're right."

"How can I help?"

"Brad is over at the Dome at the moment and I'm guessing that's okay with you."

"Yeah, the Dome was shut down after the MIRACL project in ninety-seven as the data which we had recovered from its usage wasn't sufficient enough to continue the project so we decided to terminate it."

"Was the inside dismantled or is it still in a usable state?"

"It's still in a usable state."

"Is Brad authorised to use the facility still?"

"Yeah for sure. He's working on another project which is classified and unfortunately I can't discuss with you other than it's the step up from the MIRACL project."

"Yep, I understand that Jez. The thing is, Brad had a couple of guys turn up at the gate on Sunday last. The guys were called Ramirez and Diaz."

"Never heard of them, although it's not unusual. We use a lot of sub-contractors."

"It wasn't scheduled as a visit and the memo was sent out the previous week reminding staff to let security know of any visitors. It's unlike Brad to forget something as basic as that. He knows the score."

"Yeah, I agree Mike, it is unlike him. He is under pressure on this new project from the Air Force at the moment."

"If that's the case, security needs to be tighter. There's no excuse" Insisted Mike

"Absolutely. We all forget something at some point. I always forget my wives' anniversary."

"Surprised you're still married." Mike said jokingly.

"She's used to it, in fact she never even reminds me anymore."

"You've got a goodun there Jez."

"Wouldn't be without her."

"So, what you're telling me then, is that it's not unusual for two guys to rock up like that?"

"Not at all, especially when projects work to deadlines."

"So, Brad and his visitors are legit to go into the Dome?"

"Yep."

"Okay Jez, thanks for clarifying things. Puts my mind at ease now. Thought we had some strangers in town, but clearly not."

"Mike, you must bring Mariana over sometime for a get together and we'll throw some burgers on the fire and have a catch up with a couple of Budweiser's."

"Excellent plan Jez. I'll hold you to that. Have a good day."

Mike adjusted the patrol roster and decided to include the Dome only twice per day for future sector patrols.

* * *

Pentagon – 3 p.m. The Same Day

Copeland was in Command Ops and watching the large screens in front of him. The unloading of the laser was time consuming. It had to be positioned exactly as modelled. Several EVA's were planned to ensure that maximum time was spent in putting this in place. There could be no margins for error, no twisted threads on the bolts and no spare parts left over. This had to be precision engineering at its best, and its construction was out of this world – literally. No-one could doubt that this was a major upgrade and for Copeland, it was a game changer, it changed everything. It was the beginning of a new order and would eventually change the shape as to how warfare was engaged regardless of how the politicians try to sell and spin it. Copeland wasn't convinced and he wasn't sure that he ever would be. He looked around the room and hoped he would spot the Air Force Colonel. To his disappointment, he was nowhere to be seen. Copeland headed over to the percolator and poured himself a coffee. As he did so, the door opened and to his delight, the Colonel walked in followed by a female Army Captain. Were they together or was this coincidence? He hadn't seen him with anyone before. But hey, good luck to him.

"Colonel, sorry to tear you both apart, can I have a word." He wasn't sorry at all but the Colonel felt on edge as if he had done something wrong; again.

"Of course, sir." The Colonel made his apologises to the Captain. She had a look of disappointment but understood. The Colonel caught up with Copeland and walked towards the screens.

"I'm not a fan of such advancement in technology." Began Copeland as he pointed towards the screen and the picture of the ISS and the cargo, "I'm a military man Colonel through and through but I'm also sceptical. I feel that over the short to medium term, this will open a Pandora's box of global reactions in which other nations would develop their own laser weapons in turn threatening US aircraft. It's a reasonable prediction do you not think?" Copeland asked rhetorically and then continued. "No-one wants to be behind the curve, it's all about being one step ahead and having the upper edge on your foes. Do you agree Colonel?"

The Colonel wasn't sure whether this was another rhetorical question so decided not to answer.

"Colonel, what do you think?" Repeated Copeland trying to engage him in conversation.

"Sorry General. In a way yes. But if we didn't do it then as long as eggs remain eggs then others would do it in any case. In our eyes that just wouldn't be fair game."

"Well-reasoned. I like that. You're an intelligent man Colonel, so when would eggs not be eggs?"

The Colonel looked baffled and was stumped for the first time since he engaged with Copeland. He didn't know what to say, he had no answer to give.

Copeland could see the expression of worry on the Colonel. He wanted to stretch it out for a bit longer but thought better of it, "Only teasing. I had you, there didn't I?" Teased Copeland with a confident smile. "You're into all this space techie stuff as you've already admitted, what's the real purpose of this laser? You know, in a way I can understand it."

"Layman's terms?"

"Yep, that'll do."

"Well, this laser is the sister one to the MIRACL project fired from the US several years ago. It's the same generation model but has more funky bits."

"Funky bits. I like that." Copeland repeated since he was admiring his choice of tech words in a simplified way.

"Yeah, it's been fine-tuned too. The original MIRACL failed to provide relevant data which would've been used to determine the effects and vulnerabilities to satellites. Since then however, the new MIRACL has been improved so that its beam is steady enough to track targets. The uncertainty remains regarding atmospheric turmoil created by the beam whether this would weaken its punch."

"How's this going to be tested then? I'm assuming it hasn't yet been tested?"

"Certainly not in space. It's gone through several live tests on the ground and was thought reliable enough to give it a shot in space. It is likely that the test objective would be to slowly increase the laser's power to gauge the brightness at which the ground object would fail, rather than trying to ruin the object in a blinding flash. It's still in its infancy and data would still need to be collated to ensure that it's deployment is a viable and worthwhile option, not forgetting the immense cost involved."

"Is there a target on the ground that's been identified?"

"You're the General."

"This isn't yet in the military's arsenal so it's not crossed my desk as yet. It's still a civilian asset."

"I'm not aware of any as yet sir. It works going upwards, so the theory is it should work downwards too."

"Is that what's called on a wing and a prayer?"

The Colonel looked a little unsure to what the General was referring to, so Copeland felt obliged to simplify the wording, for a change.

"When you need it, you hope it's gonna work."

* * *

It had been a couple of days since Copeland had spoken with Elisabeth and he wasn't sure how much she had picked up in relation to Syromokov, if anything at all. The clock was ticking and he needed some good news. He looked at the wall clocks to the right of the monitors and particularly the one which had the wording, Moscow underneath. It showed one o'clock in the morning, the next day. He knew she wouldn't mind him calling her so decided to take the initiative. He looked at his cell phone and used the fast dial facility to make the call. He was surprised how quickly it was answered which caught him by surprise, "Hi sweetheart, I didn't expect you to answer so soon. You okay?"

"Hi Jack, yep all okay this side thanks."

"What's new?"

"I met up again with Syromokov, this time with a CIA agent from the embassy. He was there to validate his story."

"So, what happened?"

"He still wasn't forthcoming with anything of use. He kept on stonewalling until he receives the letter from the President acknowledging his reasoning, value and the protection of the US in his new life."

"Doesn't want a great deal then?" he said with a hint of sarcasm, "Did he give anything away at all? A snippet here or there?"

"He assured us that it has something to do with the ISS but wouldn't quantify whether or not it was a land or space threat."

"This clearly requires another meet. Did he say he'd get in touch again?"

"This time, the CIA agent took control and said that he would get in touch with Syromokov when ready. It was funny to see, as Syromokov thinks that he's the only one who can work under the radar and find people but I hope the CIA guy wasn't calling his bluff and that he can actually find him. When you coming out Jack?"

"As soon as I can, I promise."

CHAPTER 22

The Dome, WSMR – The Next Day

Brad was under pressure to provide the results but he knew he couldn't push Ramirez or Diaz. They needed time to be able to do what they do best and that was computer programming. Brad knew that lines of code would take time to input but equally, if Ramirez and Diaz were as good as he had been told they were, then timings should be of little consequence to them and they should be able to work under pressure regardless. He had never met either of these two before until they arrived at the base check point. His hands had been tied and he was under instructions to work alongside them until the work had been done. After which, he would never see them again. Brad had every confidence though that they would be finished on time and he knew that his work in the Dome was fully justifiable which meant little or no disruptions.

"Ramirez, how's it looking?" Brad asked almost as if testing his temperament.

"If you stop pestering me then I can finish it sooner." He snapped back, "As it is, I'm thinking another three days just to finish up the coding."

"What's the hold up?"

"The code which was used for its original purpose is slow and not robust enough to prevent a catastrophic failure. I've had to rewrite the algorithms to ensure that all eventualities are covered. Is that okay with you?"

Brad ignored his outburst to the annoyance of Ramirez, "Will it be finished at the same time as the one on the ISS?

"I'd say so, yep. As luck would have it, because it takes about three days to unload and zip tie the MIRACL on the ISS, they still have to reset the software. Currently, we have the advantage over the ISS, but if we slip, then that advantage will lessen gradually. The worst-case scenario will be that we, at this end will end up behind schedule."

Brad always knew there would be tension between the nerds who thought the world couldn't do without them and saw themselves as indispensable. A kind of arrogant attitude that came with the territory. He didn't like it, but he knew that the work had to be done so he had no choice but to accept it. It was after all, a compromise.

* * *

Pentagon – Command Ops, Three Days Later

Copeland had been listening on and off to the chatter between the ISS and Mission Control. The EVA with Vladimir and Sergei was going according to plan and there was a chance that they may be ahead of their initial schedule. Nothing to date had jumped out at Copeland which suggested that the Russians were up to something. It all looked normal as they went about their daily routines. Copeland still hadn't figured out what Sergei and his wife Oksana were up to. Whatever it was, it was going to happen two weeks after the launch according to their last conversation. Copeland did a quick calculation, *'Shit, that's today or tomorrow. Goddamn it.'* Without knowing, it puts Copeland and everyone else on the back foot and no control, in any shape or form, to change the outcome. Copeland realising what he'd just worked out, needed an immediate response. He picked up the desk phone in the middle of the briefing table and dialled a number from memory.

"Karl, it's Jack. Listen to me, do you remember the last conversation between Sergei and his wife, Oksana?"

"Vaguely, fill me in."

"He said that something was going to happen a couple of weeks after the launch."

"Yeah, I seem to remember that bit, and…"

"That time is now. Or it could be tomorrow."

"Is it two weeks already? Christ. Any ideas as to what he might be up to?"

"None at all. I've drawn a complete blank. I was hoping you may have come across anything."

"It's a green light all the way from my end. We're on standby but we have nowhere to go."

Copeland was disappointed, "That doesn't help Karl. I'm going to have to keep an eye on Sergei over the next forty-eight hours. It might be nothing but I need to see or hear what's coming our way."

As Copeland stepped away from the screens, the chatter continued. But something caught his attention and he quickly turned around to listen.

"Mission Control this is Sergei."

"Go ahead Sergei."

"We need to cancel the EVA scheduled for tomorrow."

"We're on a tight schedule Sergei. That's not possible. For what reason are you citing?"

"Personal."

"You need to be more specific."

"I need to speak with my wife in the morning at ten o'clock."

"Yep, that's um kinda specific, yeah. Okay, we can do that. I mean you can make the call whilst on your EVA."

Copeland was as confused as hell. He had no idea what he was referring to. He was helpless and all he could do was follow this through. He brought Karl up to speed and he also agreed that nothing could be done until we knew anything else. What the end game was would've been useful. This is going to be an interesting twenty-four hours of being in the dark.

* * *

ISS – 10 a.m. The Next Day

Sergei began his EVA as scheduled and tethered himself to the side of the ISS as was protocol. He'd been outside, along with Vladimir for nearly fifteen minutes.

"Mission Control, do you have my wife on comm?"

"Yes Sergei, go ahead. You're on speaker."

"Thank you, Houston. Oksana, it's Sergei."

"Why are you calling me from there? Are you Okay?"

"Yep, all good here. Your results should've come through today. Is there any news?"

"Yes, I've had the abortion and the cancer is spreading and I need to have some further tests and possibly radiation."

These were personal revelations which caught everyone by surprise and almost speechless. There was a silence everywhere.

"Sergei, this is Houston. You have just spoken to the whole world. Not sure that was a good call."

'I'll decide if it is or not. My wife is dying and I needed to know what was happening."

"I get that Sergei and we're all routing here for you both. You're in space and have a mission."

"Oksana, I love you from earth to infinity and our times together have been so memorable. I only wish I'd done more and been able to father our own children. I feel a failure and I've let you down."

"What do you mean Sergei?" questioned Oksana with concern in her voice.

"I can't live without you but I can't see you suffer either. I said this would be a one-way trip. I shall meet you again soon. I love you and I always will. Good bye my love."

* * *

Pentagon Command Centre

"Whoa, what just happened?" shouted Copeland to anyone who was nearby, "What does that mean?" he said as he looked around the room.

Copeland continued to look at the screen and watched speechless as Sergei unclipped his tether and pushed himself away from the side of the space station. Vladimir was on the opposite side so was not able to use the length of his tether to reach out and grab Sergei. The picture continued to follow Sergei as he drifted further and further away from the ISS and towards the blackness of space. There was nothing anyone could do. The ISS couldn't stop and turn around as it was travelling at seventeen thousand miles per hour nor was there time to suit anyone else with a jet pack to pull him back in. He was doomed and on his own. Copeland looked around the room again and saw the Air Force Colonel.

"Colonel." Copeland shouted.

The Colonel sensed the anxiety in Copeland's voice and ran over to his side, "Yes Sir."

"How long does oxygen last in the space suit?"

Well it uses one hundred percent oxygen instead of air. Each EMU…"

"Stop, what's an EMU?"

"Extra Vehicular Mobility Unit."

"Ok, go on."

"They have two tanks that work with a carbon dioxide removal system to allow a six to eight-hour spacewalk. Without the ability to remove carbon dioxide, the oxygen tanks would run out more quickly."

"The answer is?"

"It depends on the Astronauts metabolic rate. The life support system holds other things that get consumed during the walk. These include a battery and cooling water. Again, these allow for a walk of six to eight hours. But in comparison, without a space suit, he'd last for fifteen seconds before losing consciousness but with his suit he'd have enough oxygen for several more hours."

"Thank you, Colonel."

Copeland reached over to the phone on the desk and dialled a number, "Mister President, It's Jack."

"Jack, what's going on?"

"The Russian Cosmonaut on-board the ISS has just untethered himself from the ISS."

"What you saying Jack"

"He doesn't want to come back, he's ending his life."

"I'm not with you. Give it to me straight."

"He made a call to his wife who has now revealed that she has cancer and had an abortion. He said that he can't see her suffer and would see her soon."

"Meaning?"

"He's expecting her to die soon and they will meet each other in heaven."

"Any attempt on a rescue. Surely he wasn't doing an EVA by himself."

"Vladimir was also on the EVA but was on the other side of the ISS so was not able to drag him back. It would take too long to suit anyone else up. He planned this right if that's what he intended."

"My Chief of Staff has just switched on the news. You couldn't get much more of a live broadcast than that. So, your concerns with the Russians were a little off the mark Jack."

"Yeah, but I had every justification to think that something was going to happen and I still do. This was a bit of a curve ball Mister President. I sure as hell wasn't expecting this outcome.

* * *

Office of the US Ambassador, US Embassy, Presnensky District, Moscow - The following Day

Jennifer Hart had been the US Ambassador to Moscow for two years. She was married to another diplomat who was currently the US Ambassador to the UK. Both were career minded people and had never thought about the prospect of having children. Their life style suited their needs and was their life as a whole. Her career has been up and down and she managed to weather a storm regards an accusation of an affair whilst she was the Deputy at the US Embassy in Paris four years previous. Her current role was more sensitive and she was seen by some as a top tier diplomat. POTUS had agreed her nomination without hesitation. A test of her leadership came when she had to deal with the fallout from the expulsion of fifty diplomats being expelled by Moscow in 2001 after they were accused of spying. This was the largest expulsion since the collapse of communism which had followed the arrest in Washington earlier in the year of a suspected Russian spy who turned out to be an FBI agent who had been passing information for the past fifteen years. The last time anything on this scale had happened was in nineteen eighty-six when President Ronald Reagan expelled eighty soviet diplomats from the US. The removal of so many staff this time plunged relationships to an all-time low and inhibited some more sensitive operations. Jennifer was sifting through her daily electronic memo's when there was a knock on her door.

"Yeah." She simply said whilst continuing to read her computer screen.

The door opened and Neil Johnson filled the doorway, "Morning Ambassador, can I have a quick word?"

"Sure Neil, what's on your mind?"

Neil came into the room and sat in the chair which was facing Jennifer's desk. She had a large mahogany desk which was topped with leather. There were book cases fitted to the wall behind her desk and filled with all sorts of books necessary for her role. To her left was a cabinet with ornaments and photographs both personal and official. Behind Neil as he sat was a round table which he guessed she used for smaller meetings or to spread out her paperwork. The office was a fair size and uncluttered.

"We have an asset that I'm trying to recruit but he's playing hard ball."

"Okay, fill me in."

"His name is General Igor Syromokov the head of the Cosmonaut training facility at Star City."

"That's a huge catch. How did you manage to reel this one in?"

"He came to us actually. He's had enough of the old way of living and wants to give a better life to his wife."

"Don't they all? What's he offering?"

"Information in exchange for details regarding something which is going to happen involving the space station."

"That's kinda vague. Did he say what?"

"Not yet."

"How many meetings have you had?"

"I met him the other day but Elisabeth Young, General Copeland's girlfriend has met him on two occasions after a cat and mouse round robin trip. Nothing has come about which would lead us to do anything at the moment. He won't speak until we have the letter of assurance from POTUS that the US would guarantee his safe passage to the US and a new life."

"What's your thoughts?"

"He's a senior official who must have some government connections and I'm sure he has something to bargain with. Time is running out if we need to prevent something happening. I get the sense though that Syromokov doesn't want whatever is due to happen to actually happen. If it does then he has to be aware that any offer on the table would be rescinded if there is some kind of attack or whatever else."

"So, what's your ask?"

"If you can apply some pressure to the White House and get this single page letter. That'll be a good start. Once you have it then I can go ahead and arrange another meet. Without it, it's pointless."

"I'll see what I can do."

Neil thanked the Ambassador and dismissed himself closing the door behind him. He wasn't sure how long it would take but he knew she would try her utmost. She was strong willed and determined and always put a good case forward so he had a gut feeling that once she had her teeth into something, she would persevere. The US government would need to take Syromokov's offer seriously as an incident on the ISS would be an attack on many countries.

CHAPTER 23

Neil had found a weakness in Syromokov. He loved his vodka and woman as most of Russia did. It took a small amount of investigative work to find out his local haunt of which he was about to turn to his advantage. He'd established that Syromokov visited his establishment at least four times per week and tonight was one of those nights. It was a secluded place with nondescript markings above the door and highlighted with a single lamp fixed to the wall above. The only entrance was down a dingy alleyway which smelt of urine and had used condoms scattered on the floor. It was a dive but an ideal place for Syromokov to do his discreet business. The alley was only wide enough for one vehicle and Neil knew which vehicle that would be.

Having parked his own transport further along the main road, Neil walked back to get a better look at the place. He was used to clandestine ops but needed to feel comfortable in a place that could turn hostile at any moment when everyone spilled out later on. Going into this on his own, he needed a way out if what he intended to do went wrong. He walked past the entrance to begin with but glanced down the alley as he crossed the road to see for

Fire Storm

himself how narrow the alley was which offered limited space for him to do anything.

Neil looked at his watch, it read eight thirty in the evening but he knew the place wouldn't start coming to life until around nine at the earliest. There was a coffee shop directly opposite the alleyway that was still open and he expected it would be until ten at the latest. He went in and found a table by the window which gave him a great view across the road. He ordered an Americano which arrived a short while later. He figured he'd be there until closing time.

As he looked at the clock behind the counter in the coffee shop, it read nine thirty-five p.m. and he realised he'd been sat there for just over an hour. As he turned his head and back to looking out the window, he saw a black Mercedes slowly approach and then stop as it passed the alleyway. Reversing lights came on and then it disappeared down towards the end of the alley. Neil was now squinting to see clearly. The light was bad but he saw a heavy silhouetted male get out the car and walk into the club. There was only a tiny glimpse of the head as he passed under the light. It had to be him, this was his night.

* * *

The waitress in the coffee shop agreed with Neil to stay open for a further thirty minutes. He asked her nicely so she smiled and genuinely agreed. He'd ordered a further two coffees in the time he had been sitting there so the waitress wasn't too fussed.

As Neil continued to look out the window, what Neil thought was Syromokov's vehicle hadn't moved and lights were out. Ten thirty came and the waitress came over to Neil,

"I need to lock up now and get home honey."

"Sure. Thanks for staying open a little longer. Appreciate it. Do you have far to walk?" He asked with a sincere concern.

"About twenty minutes."

She was a pretty girl, probably in her early thirties, slim, good figure with blonde hair and fastened at the back in a bun. The streets weren't exactly well lit around this neighbourhood and for her to walk home alone must be a scary thing for her, her boyfriend or mum et al. If he wasn't here for a different reason, then he would escort her home. He didn't let on what he was doing, but merely gave the impression that he was lonely and had no reason to rush home.

"Where do you live?" the waitress asked

"About thirty minutes that way." He indicated with the point of a figure in a general direction hoping it wasn't where she was going.

"That's a shame, we could've gone together. I go the other way."

"Yeah it is. Maybe some other time." He said casually and he could see the disappointment on her face.

They both walked out the shop together.

"Hope you get home okay." Neil said, "Been nice talking with you."

"Thanks. Likewise. See ya."

Neil walked away from where he needed to be just to give the impression to the waitress that he had to go that way. Once he realised she was out of sight, he turned back and was now on the other side of the road and approaching the entrance to the alleyway. He quickly peered around the corner and saw the Mercedes with all lights off. The driver was probably taking the opportunity to have a nap whilst his boss was having a good night. Neil kept his back to the wall and used the cover of darkness and shadows to blend in. As he approached closer to the vehicle, the music from the club increased so it muffled any noise Neil made. He stopped momentarily as the door opened and out came a waiter followed by the loud thumping of the music. He emptied bottles from a bucket into a skip behind the vehicle and then went back in closing the door behind him. The driver must've been well out as he never disturbed. For Neil to get into a good position, he needed to get behind the car and be hidden by the shadows. On arrival, Syromokov got out the left side of the vehicle which clearly, he would get back in the same way as it was too tight on the other. There were shadows formed by the wall on the other side so Neil took the initiative and quietly but purposefully walked over to the other side and gradually moved towards the rear of the vehicle. There was just enough space to walk by, but as he got towards the rear of the vehicle, the inside light came on. Neil paused momentarily until the light was extinguished a moment later. He was probably checking the time, Neil thought to himself. He continued until he was at the rear of the car and alongside the skip used earlier by the waiter. This gave him extra cover and as was usual in clandestine ops, all he could do now was wait.

* * *

Standing for so long and in one position had the tendency to make your legs ache so the smallest of movements down to moving toes was necessary to keep the blood flowing. Neil unobtrusively looked at his watch, it read twenty-eight minutes past eleven. He had no expectation that Syromokov would be coming out anytime soon. After all, he only went in over two hours ago and the party would just be beginning. He knew it would be a long wait and he was prepared to wait for as long as necessary. Close to midnight, the driver switched on his display screen and began to watch a movie. All Neil could see were the flashing coloured images as the pictured changed. He hoped that it didn't shine on him but to be sure, he stepped further back into the darkness and once again blended into the shadows.

The driver had settled down to watching his film and was immersed into the story. He missed the door opening and the bright light which emitted lighting up the area around the man who came out. The uncertainty that Neil had before was now confirmed and who he was looking at was indeed Syromokov. Attached to his left arm was a tall leggy brunette who may as well have not been wearing anything. Her clothes were tight and skimpy which left nothing to the imagination. His driver still hadn't made a move and his boss was close by the rear of the vehicle. Syromokov now had his back to Neil who edged his way forward, removed a pen from his inside pocket and was now directly behind Syromokov. He pushed the end of the pen into his back which caused Syromokov to freeze.

"Guess who?"

"You found me." Said Syromokov without a flinch, "Well done."

"It wasn't difficult. Lose the escort. We need to chat."

Syromokov bade his farewell to his lady friend and still stood motionless waiting for the next move. His driver, realising that there was something happening next to his car, debussed.

"You okay boss?"

"It's okay Yuri. You can sit back in the car. This is a personal matter."

After the female escort had left and 'Yuri' had climbed back into the car, Neil made his presence. He allowed Syromokov to turn around so Neil could see his face once again.

"What would your wife say if she knew where you were tonight or the other three nights?"

"You've been doing your homework. She understands. It is how we do things here."

"I need answers General otherwise I'll expose your other weakness."

"Hiding in the dark and jumping out the shadows, it seems like you are trying to frighten me."

"Far from it General. We need to meet again."

"You came out all this way and at this time of night to tell me that. I am honoured."

"Don't flatter yourself. It was proof that I can find you anywhere I want. I did promise you that."

"You did indeed. So what next?"

"Meet me at the Taras Shevchenko monument in Congress Park at eleven p.m. tomorrow night."

"Where is that?"

"You'll find it. You're resourceful. Come in through the entrance opposite the Radisson."

"What if I don't turn up?"

"You have a lot to lose. Your actions alone so far will be seen by your government as treason. Your new life will be over before it ever begins."

Syromokov opened his car door, and then turned as if he wanted to say something but decided against it. He climbed in and was driven away. Neil waited for the dust to settle and then retraced his steps back to his own car.

* * *

US Embassy, Moscow – 0800 next day

Neil was in his office when the phone rang, "This is Neil." He answered as he picked up the receiver.

"It's the Ambassador. I've had the letter from POTUS for Syromokov. You can drop by and collect anytime today."

"That's great news. I'll get on to that straight away. I knew you'd pull it off. Thanks."

Neil now had a bargaining chip which he hoped Syromokov would take and hand over his side. It

Fire Storm

was a lot to ask but that's what he wanted in return for information. While he was excited at the information, he looked at the business card Elisabeth had given him and dialled the number at the CNN headquarters.

"This is Elisabeth."

"Hi it's Neil over at the Embassy. Good news, we've got the letter for Syromokov signed by POTUS."

"That's a step I thought we'd never get. We need to arrange another meet with him to discuss."

"Already set up."

"How did you find him?"

"It's a long story."

"So, where and when?"

"Tomorrow night at eleven p.m. at the monument to Taras Shevchenko. It's in Congress Park and is actually close by you. Shall I pick you up or are you happy to drive down?"

"I'll make my own way. It's easier when we leave after the meet."

"Okay, Park in the car park in front of the Radisson Hotel. I'll see you there."

* * *

Elisabeth pulled out a map from her desk draw and checked the location she was given. Neil was right, it is close by, in fact it was just under two miles and would be an eight-minute drive at that time of night. She finished her day up then headed home. She had so much to speak to Copeland about but she'd wait until after the meet tonight which hopefully would be the last one.

CHAPTER 24

Outside the Radisson Royal Hotel, Moscow
10.30 p.m. local time

Elisabeth arrived ahead of time. To her, even a few minutes was late and this had been drummed into her by Copeland. '*Arrive early and you can scout the lay of the land and have an advantage over your opponent*' she could hear him say. Although she didn't see Syromokov as an opponent, this was unknown territory to her so any local awareness she could encapsulate would no doubt be worthwhile. She pulled up at the orange ticket machine on the central island and took a ticket. It was automatic as her vehicle number was taken on approach by the camera behind the machine and then a ticket was printed. She placed the ticket behind her visor and drove towards the entrance of the Radisson and slightly beyond. She found a space on the left before the down ramp and reversed in so that she had a means of escape should the need arise. She knew that Copeland wasn't a fan of those who drove into spaces as it limited their manoeuvrability and these words echoed around her head. Everything he said, always made sense but to everyone else, it was an alien concept. Having a white SUV with CNN emblazoned on the side was like having a belisha beacon and advertising, '*Here I am*' but it's all she had.

Even though she was thirty minutes early, she began to think that even Syromokov was likely to have arrived in good time to probably do the same. All she could do was go with the flow and see what happens. After getting out of her vehicle, she walked through the car park and found the entrance to the park as Neil had suggested. There were several lights on either side of the path which gave her a better sense of security. She continued to follow the path around to the left which then became an open space. She could see the only monument which she took as the Taras Shevchenko and their meeting place. Elisabeth went beyond the monument to the edge of the park and noticed a wide concrete staircase dropping back down to the main road. She went down the steps and back up again and counted thirty-two steps. The park had a magnificent back drop of the huge façade of the Radisson with its central tower dominating the whole structure.   Everything around the area was well lit and didn't seem like the sort of place to have a meet of this importance. '*Abnormal as well as normal places I guess do happen*' she thought to herself. On her return, she noticed two people walking through the park, a man and a woman who seemed to be together by their body language. There was no sign of Syromokov as yet and as she thought about it, there was no sign of the CIA agent, Neil Johnson either. Was she in the right place, although having checked the map there was only one monument of that name. Elisabeth began to slowly walk back to the monument and climbed several small flights of steps and began to look at it from an interesting point of view. It seemed to have been sculptured out of a single piece of granite although she was sure it would've been bronze. It was lit with ground lights which gave an eerie look and since the top third had no light you got the feeling that he was looking down on you. Directly behind the monument, the rooftop of the Radisson was lit with yellow lights and gave the impression that it was painted in gold. As she was immersed in the aura of the moment, she heard footsteps behind her. She quickly turned and saw it was Neil.

"Hey, sorry if I scared you."

"Okay, I was just trying to get a feeling what was going on here." As Elisabeth pointed to the monument.

"Have you heard of Taras Shevchenko before?"

"Can't say that I have, but to have a monument made in your memory, he must've done something right."

"He was actually Ukrainian and a writer and poet. The monument captures him walking with his hands behind his back whilst thinking. It was placed here in nineteen sixty-four in honour of his hundred and fiftieth anniversary of his birthday. It was cleaned and restored last year in two thousand."

"Impressive. What does the inscription of words on the stone down below read?"

"You don't speak Russian?" Neil queried

"I wouldn't have asked if I did." Replied Elisabeth and then realised that her tone was sharp but unintentional.

They both walked back down two flights of steps and looked back at the stone and Neil looked at it for several moments as he translated the words in his head,

"It simply reads, in the great family, in the free family, in new family don't forget pray for me with kind and quiet word."

Having absorbed the simple words, they both walked back up the steps and as they did so, a shadowy figure appeared from behind the monument which stopped them in their tracks. The large figure was certainly the size of Syromokov but it could also have matched many others too.

"Syromokov?" questioned Neil in a way to establish confirmation.

"Yes." He acknowledged and then walked forward towards Elisabeth and Neil.

"What is it with you spooks always hiding in the shadows." Elisabeth asked with a sense of curiosity.

"We couldn't do our jobs if we didn't. Isn't that right General?"

"I no longer work for the KGB or FSB."

"Once a spy always a spy. It's drilled into you."

"You asked me to come here. Do you have news for me?" Syromokov asked deftly changing the subject.

Neil pulled out a folded piece of paper from inside his jacket pocket and opened it.

"I have the letter here from the President of the USA granting you a new life in effect." Neil waved it briefly, "It will not be honoured unless you tell me what you know."

"What's to say that once I give you the information that you will not kill me?"

Neil folded the letter again and placed it back in his inside jacket pocket, "Nothing, but whilst you've touched on that, if anything does happen to you, then it won't be from our side."

"Well, that's comforting to know. The alternative isn't much better either."

"There's lots at stake here General. You either know something or you don't. We've kept our side of the deal, now it's your turn to deliver."

"Before I begin, did you hear the awful news that Colonel Sergei Grigorev had killed himself on the International Space Station?"

"Are you serious?" Neil queried

"Call yourself an intelligence agency. It's across all news networks."

"When was this and is this a scheme that you knew about that you were going to reveal to us?"

"No. He untethered himself and drifted into the black after he spoke with his wife. This was not planned. It was a complete surprise to me also. He was one of my brightest students."

"We're sorry for your countries loss General, truly."

"Accepted."

"So, let's move on to why we are here. The clock is ticking General and unless you begin, then we'll walk away and your new life will be in tatters."

Syromokov took a deep breath and released it with a sigh, "It all began around four years ago. I was summoned to the Kremlin and treated like a king. Suspicious in its own right I know, but I went along with it. It's unheard off in our government so wanted to see where it was leading to."

"Who was in the meeting with you?"

"The President, Michael Wilson an American from NASA, and two others dressed in suits. Although they were never formerly introduced, from the look of them, I would say FSB."

"What was their brief?"

"It was highly anticipated that, even then a laser would be installed on the Space Station. Our country wanted to use it as a weapon and to dominate the world."

"What was their end game?"

"Global dominance. All satellites would be destroyed and the world would be blind. The only ones left standing would be our very own."

"Wow, a master piece."

"I wouldn't have called it that." Interrupted Elisabeth. Neil looked at her in surprise and then back to Syromokov.

"What involvement had Star City in all of this?"

"I was asked to choose two Cosmonauts who were hard liners and would be honourable to their country. Both Sergei and Vladimir fitted the criteria very well."

"At which point were they briefed about all this?"

"It was in their last year at the Cosmonaut training facility. Neither flinched an eye lid and both had a very strong allegiance to our country. They would do anything they were told to do."

"Okay, so when is this global dominance supposed to happen?"

"Within two weeks of the laser being installed and aligned." Syromokov admitted.

"Losing Sergei, does this change anything?"

"It will obviously have an impact and delay things. EVA's will be put on hold for a short period whilst everyone comes to terms with the loss of a crew member."

"Understood. What's the target on earth?"

"Anywhere. The ISS takes ninety minutes to go around the earth, so everywhere is vulnerable."

"Jesus Christ." Blasphemed Neil, "Are any of the US astronauts involved?"

"No. They have no knowledge."

"Can Vladimir do this himself?"

"Control the laser you mean?" queried Syromokov.

"Yeah."

"It's possible, as long as he knows how to punch in the target coordinates."

"Sounds like something out of a movie General."

"Believe me, this is for real."

"The ISS has over ride systems back at Mission Control in Houston. How's it gonna work? It can be scuppered by a few key strokes from earth surely?"

"That's the other thing."
"What is?"

"Sergei or Vladimir were to install over ride hardware into the laser so if Houston tried to regain control, they wouldn't be able to."

"Are Houston aware of this capability?"

"They never factored this in, although your General Copeland questioned before launch why there wasn't such a fail-safe system in place to prevent this from happening at all."

Elisabeth's ears pricked up at the mention of the name Copeland. She knew that he'd be concerned from a security point of view. It was down to the penny pinchers on the hill who no doubt cut corners.

"Is there anyone on Earth pulling the strings here?"

"It would be impossible to do any of this alone. As to who they are, I do not have that information."

"If this failed, was there ever a back-up plan?"

"Yes." He simply answered

"General, this is like pulling teeth. It's painful. So, what was the back-up plan?"

"I wasn't involved with this since it wasn't considered that it would fail. What I couldn't understand myself though was that the space station would be destroyed in the event of the primary mission failure."

"How was that ever going to happen?"

"From a land-based facility somewhere on Earth."

"Missile strike?"

"No."

"Another laser?"

"That would be my guess." offered Syromokov.

"All of what you have said of course will need to be verified before the next step for you can be set up. I'll be in touch soon."

Neil and Elisabeth bade their farewells to Syromokov who turned and disappeared once again into the shadows from whence he came.

CHAPTER 25

Pentagon – 3 p.m. US time

Copeland was sat in his office trying to figure out whether or not he'd missed something. He went through all the information he was in possession of, but whilst there were more parts which suggested something was going to happen than not, he still had no idea what, where or when. The loss of the Cosmonaut was a terrible tragedy caused by personal issues rather than anything sinister. He needed a stroke of luck soon otherwise he would be tempted to pull the plug and head back to DC. Whilst he was contemplating, his cell phone vibrated on his desk. Having picked it up, he recognised the number.

"Hi Elisabeth sweetheart. This is late. I'm guessing it's one in the morning there. You okay?"

"Jack, listen. I'm okay thanks but missing you like crazy. We have a major problem and I've found out what it is."

"What do you mean by we?"

"The US. I met with Syromokov again last night and the CIA agent from the embassy was with me. Syromokov unravelled a whole load of stuff which you're gonna need to sit down for."

"Okay, go for it."

Elisabeth went through everything that Syromokov had detailed that night and missing no parts out whatsoever.

"You could say then that it's a mission failure already with the loss of the Cosmonaut. If none of the US astronauts know anything about the Russians intentions, then with only Vladimir left, it's only fifty percent effective."

"All Vladimir has to do is install the over-ride and its game on."

"I still think it'll be difficult for one person to carry this out." Copeland began, "He could quite easily be over-powered by the other Astronauts. I have this gut feeling again that there's something else going on and plan B is being set up and about to be activated."

* * *

Pentagon Command Centre – Same Day

Copeland left his office and walked the short distance to the Command Centre. As he entered, he quickly looked around the room and caught the attention of the Air Force Colonel.

"Follow me Colonel." He said as he passed him.

The Colonel did as he was instructed and dropped in behind Copeland as he headed over to the briefing table.

"We have a situation Colonel."

"I'm not aware of one sir."

"You're an intelligent man Colonel and I'm going to be looking to you for some answers."

"Okay." Replied the Colonel with a confused look.

"I'm still interested in the laser system concept."

"In what way sir?"

"Well, for starters, give me some background?"

"Easy version?" tested the Colonel with a wry smile.

"What do you think?"

Seeing the expression on Copelands face, there was only one answer he could reply, "Yep, that's exactly what I thought too." He gathered his thoughts and composure, "The concept of lasers isn't new. The US military began working on lasers in the mid-nineteen sixties and the idea of a space laser has been around since nineteen seventy-seven. These are multi-million-dollar contracts for the private sector."

"Not interested in the cost, that's for the pen pushers. Are there any land-based laser facilities that can fire into space?"

"Yes, as you would expect. Tests have been fired from several places across the US."

"Namely?" requested Copeland subtly.

Copeland could see that he caught the Colonel off guard momentarily before he recovered, "Um, well to begin with, there's the TRW San Juan Capistrano test facility on the edge of Camp Pendleton in California."

"What happens there?"

"Initially conceived to develop and test various rocket propulsion systems. Its remit expanded dramatically since it's conception in nineteen sixty-three to include space-based high energy laser weapons systems as well as advanced radar and satellite communications systems."

"Okay, next."

The Colonel had no notes to refer to so was having to rely on his memory to provide Copeland with the answers he was looking for. "WSMR in New Mexico. Here in nineteen ninety-seven, the US government conducted a 'laser dazzler' test against one of our own Air Force satellites using the MIRACL DF laser. The year before, a land launched missile was also hit from the laser at this site."

"What happens there now?"

"The project was shut down purely on the grounds that the feedback from data wasn't sufficiently conclusive to be worthy of any further experimentation."

"Is the WSMR complex still an active site regardless of the MIRACL project being shelved?"

"As far as I am aware General, yes, it is. I'm not aware of them working on anything else though."

"That's okay, next."

"There's the High Energy Laser Centre in El Segundo in California run by Raytheon Electronic Systems. They're a sub-contractor to Lockheed Martin Space Systems."

"What do they do?"

"In June this year, they test fired the first Track Illuminator Laser as part of the Air Force

Airborne Laser programme. They're still analysing the results so nothing else there at the moment."

"Is the place still an active site?"

"Yes sir."

"Do you have any more Colonel?"

"There's the Stennis Space Centre in Mississippi."

"And…?"

"December last year, it was chosen as the preferred site of the Space Based Laser performance test facility. It's never fired anything at the moment."

"Who controls all these sites Colonel?"

"US Space Command, based out of Peterson Airforce Base, Colorado."

"Who's in charge?"

"Commander John Skinner, US Air Force."

* * *

Base Commander, Peterson AFB, Colorado
5 p.m. The Same Day

Copeland returned to his office. He still needed answers to questions that hadn't yet been asked and the information revealed by Syromokov, suggests that whatever is going to happen, it involves space somewhere along the line. Copeland found the number for the base Commander at Peterson AFB and decided to make the call. The call was picked up after several rings.

"Peterson." He answered

"Commander John Peterson?" Copeland asked seeking confirmation.

"It is, yeah. Who's this?"

"Commander, it's Jack Copeland over at the Pentagon."

"Well Jack, this has to be a first. Good to hear from you. That was bad news about the Cosmonaut. Suicide in space, that has to be a first."

"And hopefully the last."

"Yeah, for sure. How can I help?"

"Does your department control the sites where these space lasers are being sited and tested?"

"Who's asking?"

"I am, on behalf of the President."

Copeland knew that the President wouldn't mind his name being used, even if the Commander spoke with the President to confirm, he figured he would agree and then ring Copeland to ask what the hell he was doing. But he doubted it would get to that point.

"Yes, we do. They are secretive sites for obvious reasons. Although we have an annual budget of six billion dollars billed against President Reagan's US Ballistic Missile Defence system, you'd think someone would want to know where its being spent."

"For sure. Anyway, the reason for the call is that I want to establish which of the laser sites under your missile defence programme are still active ones. Is that something you can share with me?"

"Not over the phone Jack. As you can appreciate, there's snoops everywhere. Listen, if it's urgent, I'm over in DC tomorrow so I can drop by on my way through."

"It's actually ultra-urgent Commander and appreciate your time. Look forward to seeing you tomorrow.

* * *

'The Dome', WSMR – The Same Day

Brad was feeling the heat in more ways than one. It was hot in the dome which only seemed to cool when the lid was lifted off and the pressure from Moscow was unrelenting. The loss of the Cosmonaut gave them a little more breathing space to finish up but the urgency was still there nevertheless. Diaz continually monitored the location and axis of the ISS, whilst Ramirez continued coding. Brad was in an agitated state and couldn't wait until all this was over. The temperament of the others wasn't any better either.

"Ramirez, how's it looking?" asked Brad in a tone that was equal to the request.

"Should be finished by tonight."

"Good timing. We're nearly done here."

Brad went outside the dome to get some fresh air. He needed to clear his head.

CHAPTER 26

On-board the ISS

The loss of Sergei Grigorev, the Soviet Cosmonaut from the ISS was a devastating blow to the space programme, the likes of which has never been seen before in such detail. Whilst his departure was intentional, it was watched by billions around the world and had a profound effect on the remainder of the crew; it also put into doubt the remainder of the mission. EVA's had been suspended and wouldn't resume for several days. There was even talk at Houston to ready another crew to replace STS-108A. This was dismissed before it even reached the Flight Operations Director's desk. The Flight Surgeon back at Mission Control had decided that the best remedy would be to keep the remaining crew as active as possible. Being in the bleakness of space and mourning wasn't the best of combinations. It would be down to Tom the commander to motivate his crew and to remind them of the importance of the mission and the time lines in which to complete their tasks prior to returning to Earth. Vladimir seemed to be the worst effected and Tom figured to be for one of two reasons; was it because it was his buddy, or maybe since they were on the same EVA together that he felt as though he could've done more. There was always a human guilt and Tom knew that it was something Vladimir would carry with him for some considerable time.

* * *

Pentagon – 9 a.m. The Next Day

Since Copeland slept in his office, he was always at work. Up at seven, coffee from his orderly then showered, dressed and behind his desk by eight-thirty. At nine o'clock, his desk phone rang.

"General, it's the front security desk. I have a Commander John Skinner to see you."

"Thanks Marine. Yep, he's expected. Can you direct him to my office?"

Copeland hadn't notified the desk of an impending visitor as he wasn't sure what time he would be turning up and nor if he would at all. Good thing he did as this was a discussion which needed to be addressed. By the time the Commander had processed through security and been badged he still had to walk around part of the building which would probably take him a little over five minutes. Right on cue, there was a knock at his door.

"Yeah." Copeland simply said.

The door opened and in walked his visitor. Copeland had never met the Commander who was dressed in a dark blue suit, white shirt and red tie. He looked distinguished with short silver hair, tanned and looked athletic.

Fire Storm

"Jack, good to meet you." The Commander extended his hand to Copeland who had stepped from around his desk.

"Likewise." Added Copeland, "Coffee?" asked Copeland as he walked back to his seat.

"That'll be great, thanks. No milk or sugar." Copeland pointed to the chair in front of his desk inviting the Commander to sit there. He pressed a button on his desk phone which was linked directly with his orderly and requested two coffees.

"Nice office Jack." Commented the Commander as he looked around the room.

"It's also doubling up as my sleeping quarters at the moment too."

The Commander had a frowned look on his face as if waiting for an explanation.

"It's a long story and I won't bore you with the details."

There was a knock at the door after which the orderly entered and placed a silver tray on the coffee table by Copeland's sofa.

"Thanks Mike." Copeland said to the retreating orderly who nodded his acceptance before closing the door behind him. "Commander, we're in a bit of a situation."

"By we, who do you mean?"

"The US. I cannot give you as much detail as I would of course like to at this stage, but like you, the Pentagon works under a cloud of secrecy too which of course, those outside are not privy to."

"It's a wonder anything gets done around the world with all this secrecy. Okay, how can I help?"

"I know the Air Force have been involved with Space Based Laser projects for a number of years, but what I'm interested in are those which are land-based."

"These are classified Jack."

Copeland contemplated his response. He had to get the Commander on side and therefore he would need to divulge to him what he knows already, or at least some of it. Having an understanding of the problem, would hopefully cut through some of the red lines.

"If I was to tell you that we have credible threat with reliable intel concerning the laser projects which are about to have a direct impact on the US, could you reveal some of its secrets?"

"Possibly, and to use the coin of phrase, if it was in the interests of National Security then all options are open."

"That's good to hear and thanks for your understanding. The source, which I cannot reveal but needleless to say is a credible one and is CIA led has intimated that the MIRACL upgrade that was launched on board the Shuttle Horizon, was to be used as a weapon to create global dominance by a foreign power."

"I take it that's the Russians you're talking about since they're on board the ISS?"

"Very astute Commander. One change to all this that I can see, is that with the loss of the Russian Cosmonaut, who had a personal agenda by the way adjusts the focus from space based to land based. I have my reasons for this and is linked to the intel received. My question to you Commander is this; can you identify to me likely active land-based laser

Fire Storm

facilities that may have the capacity to inflict damage to the ISS or to any other orbital system, satellite or otherwise?"

"There are probably two which spring to mind. All the others are either in their development stages or used for other reasons."
Copeland didn't want to sound too excited about the prospect that there were at least two areas of interest.

"Which two?"

"Okay, the first one is the White Sands Missile Range over in New Mexico. The second one operates out of El Segundo in California."

"Are they both government owned?"

"The budget is from federal funds and staffed by a mixture of both military and civilian personnel. The latter one is run by a civilian defence contractor."

"So, what you're saying is yes?"
The Commander simply nodded his response.

"If you were a betting man Commander, which would you say would be the most likely site?"

"There is nothing between them as both are active sites and capable of hitting targets in space."

"Just one last question, does either of them have an airfield?"

"Holloman Air Force Base is near the White Sands facility. Any particular Reason?"

"Curiosity."

* * *

Once Commander John Skinner had left Copeland's office, Copeland sat back in his chair and considered what had been said. It was hard to imagine that anything like what they'd discussed could actually turn into reality. Nothing was impossible and everything was possible. All options were on the table. It was all coming together but Copeland still had the uphill struggle of convincing others that there was a sinister plot in play with the ability to do serious harm. Having the responsibility for the security of the USA and its global interests, Copeland wasn't about to turn his back on this. He was convinced that something would turn up in the short term. He needed first to eliminate the New Mexico and El Segundo facilities from any involvement before he could consider his next options. Being federal facilities, it would be an FBI task force responsibility. Copeland tapped in some numbers to his desk phone.

"Felix, it's Jack Copeland."

"Jack, hi. Normally when you call there's something going on and this is one of those calls I'm guessing. You have a problem that needs fixing, right?"

"That's why you're the FBI Director."

"Very good. What's on your mind?"

"In the interests of national security etcetera, etcetera, there are a couple of federal sites that have popped up on our radar recently that I think are worthy of looking into. They may possibly be terrorist related."

"So, this'll be a Task Force deployment with the Joint Terrorism Task Force taking the lead."

"Yep, that sounds about right."

"Currently, we've thirty-five JTTF's across the US, but just so you know, we're still up to our necks in the nine eleven after math. I know that's not what you wanted to hear so, I tell you what Jack, send me an email with all the details and we'll get to it as soon as we can. I can't say when but maybe in a couple of days. That's the best I can do."

"That's good enough for me. I'll attach the details of the MIRACLE laser which your boys will be looking out for. If it's there, they won't be able to miss it."

Copeland knew that the next step was in the hands of others and he had no influence over their priorities. His hands were tied but he knew someone who may be able to untie them and to move things along a little quicker.

* * *

Copeland picked up his secure desk phone and dialled a number from memory.

"Mister President. I need to bring you up to speed"

Copeland back briefed the President on everything he knew. He missed nothing out but added a couple of embellishments to enhance the problem hopefully making the President see this as a major concern and take the handcuffs off him. The President hadn't always seen the side that Copeland was looking at and often wouldn't make commitments that Copeland deemed were necessary.

"So, what you're saying Jack, is that the ISS don't pose a threat as you originally thought?"

"Yes sir."

"And you now think it's land based?"

"Yes, Mister President."

"This is serious stuff Jack. How solid is the intel from Syromokov?"

"Very, the whole thing is time sensitive. We don't have much time. I do believe this is the real deal."

"What are you asking for Jack?"

"These two sites are federal facilities under government jurisdiction. We have to eliminate these from any potential involvement in hostilities and therefore, I am asking for you to authorise the FBI task force to conduct a search and seizure of the two identified sites."

"That's a lot of manpower. They're still heavily involved with hunting down the mastermind of nine-eleven. I think you may be way off the mark with El Segundo though. From my recollection, it doesn't seem capable of anything like this. It's also the home for toy maker Mattel which makes it an unlikely site."

"A lot of things can be hidden under the noses of people even more so when there are innocent looking companies nearby. We could have a bigger problem if we sat back and did nothing. There will always be something running parallel with other incidents and we can't ignore everything. El Segundo was offered as a possible site by Commander John Skinner from US Space Command. I take his judgement on this as he sees it as a potential site."

"Okay, but equally, we can't investigate everything either. You might want to look at the Western Range at Vandenberg AFB which does come under the op centre of El Segundo. It has the capacity; however, I get your point with everything else Jack. Leave it with me. I'll speak with the FBI Director and sanction the JTTF. If the clock is ticking, I just hope you can find what you're looking for in time. Best speed Jack."

CHAPTER 27

The Next Day

Copeland was confident that the President would come through with what they spoke about yesterday. Felix at the FBI knew what he would be looking for. If anything was there, then he was sure they'd find it. He just hoped it wasn't the case of looking for a needle in a hay stack. Most federal sites weren't small places and would need a coordinated effort to search sectional areas. The JTTF was such a department and with a coordinated effort supported by other law enforcement agencies, they'd be able to saturate the area with mass numbers. Throughout the day, Copeland was on edge. If nothing found at El Segundo then enthusiasm will tend to drift and motivation may slip before moving on to the next. All search teams wanted to find something as this was often a boost of confidence and a real test of their techniques. It was getting late in the afternoon and Copeland was fidgeting with things on his desk whilst he waited for the call from Felix, positive or otherwise. To cap it all, the comment from the President was playing on Copeland's mind. He had doubted El Segundo as a possibility but suggested Vandenberg as a more viable option. '*Of course, that made sense*' Copeland thought to himself. The JTTF were searching or about to search the wrong place. He began to suspect what the President thought and suddenly, he had that sinking feeling in the pit of his stomach.

* * *

When the call came it startled Copeland even though he was expecting his cell to ring.

"Jack, it's Felix. Bad news I'm afraid."
Copeland knew instinctively what he was about to say. "Break it to me gently."

"Searched El Segundo, nothing. Not even a frying pan to make an omelette."

"Are there any obvious signs that something was there recently but has since been moved?"

"Nop, everything's there that should be there."

"Did the President mention anything to do with Vandenberg?"

"He offered the suggestion of Vandenberg but didn't make it a priority. What you thinking?"

"Having realised too late what El Segundo actually was, Vandenberg came up as an option as it has the facilities, capacity and capability for this kind of activity."

"I'm ahead of you Jack. When the President called me yesterday, I immediately picked up the ground plans of Vandenberg and overhead images. We're heading over their tomorrow at dawn."

* * *

The Dome, WSMR – The Same Day

Brad stepped outside the dome and walked casually and confidently towards his vehicle leaving Ramirez and Diaz inside to finish up. Taking his cell phone from his trouser pocket, he rolled through his contacts and dialled a number.

"It's me. We're all done here."

"You are ahead, well done. The ISS isn't aligned yet which is in our favour."

"What do you want us to do next?"

"Wait for now. You will receive further instructions tomorrow."

Waiting around wasn't something Brad was comfortable with. There was a risk the whole thing could be compromised and people would become suspicious as to what they were doing. He had never met the man who he spoke with but as long as he was paid, he didn't care who it was.

* * *

Command Centre, Pentagon – Same Day

Copeland wasn't sure which way the suspected threat would go or whether there was one at all. Either way, he would need to gather the military staff around the table and discuss options in dealing with it. Until he had some evidence to support his theories though, he couldn't do a damn thing about it since no one could see what he potentially could; it was all speculation to others. He just wished that all these do-gooders had the confidence in his convictions. But it was like anything else in life, if it didn't affect you, then you wouldn't be too concerned about it. He's never been wrong before and he certainly wasn't about to start now. All he could do was watch the activities onboard the ISS and listen to the frustrating but many conversations going on elsewhere. When the time would come, and Copeland was sure that it would, he knew that his Scorpion unit were ready for anything at a moment's notice.

* * *

Command Centre, Pentagon - The Next Day

Copeland was up, dressed and in the Command Centre before five a.m. He was looking at the screens which were showing the JTTF live feed for their assault on Vandenberg AFB. Helicopter fast rope drops, pincer movements of the law enforcement agencies to flush out anything that shouldn't be there. Timing was essential which would ultimately give the team the element of surprise and the upper hand. All the JTTF personnel were dressed in black and faces were covered with balaclavas. If you woke and stared at one of these, you'd probably think your world was about to end. The search was systematic as they went from building to building. As the search progressed, Copeland was starting to feel that this was about to become another cluster. One more building to go and he didn't hold out much hope of finding anything, again. But he knew he was close to something, somewhere.

* * *

The disappointment of not finding anything on two major sites was frustrating, not only to Copeland but to those who executed the search. The adrenalin rushes through the body when it's at a high with a great expectation in the hope of finding something, but then is left deflated when the box comes up empty. Copeland wasn't about to give in. He knew that this was merely a temporary blip. The JTTF were heavily involved in the aftermath of nine-eleven and their availability couldn't always be counted on but Copeland couldn't do this without them on home soil. He needed a stroke of luck to gain some more momentum. He looked around the Command Centre and spotted the Air Force Colonel by the entrance door as he was about to leave the room.

"Colonel." Copeland shouted

Having heard and recognised the voice of Copeland, he turned and headed over to him, "Sir." He asked.

Copeland looked towards the name badge the Colonel was wearing, "After all this time, I've never known your name." he paused, "Johnson."

"That's correct General. How can I help?"

"Give White Sands a call would you."

"What do I ask?"

"Speak to anyone, security to start with maybe and ask if anything unusual has happened recently. Bit of a long shot but you never know. Keep it brief. I'll be in my office. Don't want them to get too excited that the Pentagon has called. It might be the only excitement that happens down there."

* * *

Colonel Johnson turned away from Copeland and headed to a spare desk and began the search for the contact details at WSMR. It was often best to start with security as they're the ones who keep their ears to the ground and eyes on the horizon. They also patrol the facility which was an added bonus.

"This is Air Force Colonel Ian Johnson from the Pentagon. I didn't catch your name."

"Mike Reynolds, the security supervisor Sir."

"Mike, I'm calling all the facilities so this is just a routine call. The wonders of being at the Pentagon eh. I have a box to tick so I won't take up too much of your time."

"Sure, go ahead Colonel."

"Have you had any security issues recently at White Sands?"

"Nop, pretty quiet really."

"That's good to hear. Just one other question, what about any strangers?"

"Same. Not much happens down here. Peaceful little town."

"Okay, Mike, thanks for time."

Mike paused briefly and remembered Ramirez and Diaz, "There may be something, but probably nothing."

"Let's go with it. What do you have?"

"A couple weeks ago, on a Sunday in fact, two Hispanics came to the gate and asked to see Brad Hernandez."

"Whose Brad?"

"Bradley Hernandez."

"What's he do there?"

"Equipment Specialist Missile Engineer."

"Why was it suspicious?"

"It was Sunday and no-one drops by. It's the weekend and nearly everyone is chilling out. Also, they came without an appointment which was unusual. They all know the procedure."

Mike continued to explain they were met by Brad and were accommodated on base. His boss was happy for them to be here. He hadn't seen anything wrong with that as Brad was working on another project."

"Where are they working?"

"Over at a place we call the Dome."

Mike explained where it was and how far it was from the gate lodge.

"I guess it's on your patrol sheet?"

"Not any more. I took it off the routine sheet and left it as random since they came back as being legit. As I mentioned, we make random visits now and again but they're not scheduled."

"Do they sign out and back in again?"

"Yeah, every morning and night. They head out with Brad and back in again later on. I wasn't too happy with their reasoning. I'm an ex-cop from the White Sands PD. I have a curious mind." Mike confirmed.

"What's inside the Dome?"

"It's a high frequency laser. Other than that, I don't know what it does."

"Is it active?"

"Sort of, it was shelved after the MIRACL project in ninety-seven but according to Brad's boss, he's working with it on another project. I don't ask too many questions about what they do."

"Fair point. Did they say how long they'd be at White Sands for?"

"Not really, probably a couple of weeks."

"Thanks for your time Mike. I had one box to tick when I called, now I have a full report to write." He finished with a chuckle.

* * *

Colonel Ian Johnson III gathered his notes together and headed down the corridor to Copeland's office. With a knock on the door and the invite to enter, Johnson walked in. With a gesture of an open hand, he was directed towards the seat in front of Copeland's desk where he sat and began his preparation.

"What did you find?" Copeland began

"Well, I wasn't expecting anything to be honest but we may have something."
Johnson laid everything out for Copeland sparing no detail and the look on Copeland's face whilst he was relaying the information, said it all.

"Christ, not to get ahead of myself but I think we've hit the jackpot, well done. That's the most prominent lead we've had and something that I needed pretty quick."
Colonel Johnson excused himself and Copeland, not being able to contain his excitement, punched the air alternatively with both fists and beamed a broad smile which simply said, '*Gotcha.*'

* * *

Acting quickly on the information Colonel Johnson had gleaned from White Sands, Copeland dialled a number on his desk phone.

"Felix, It's Jack."

"Hey listen." Felix began as if to gain some forgiveness, "We tried our best but there just wasn't anything."

"Don't worry about that. Appreciate your help though. Couldn't have done it without you. I have something else," Copeland paused, "Which I think you're gonna like."

"What have you got?"

"Some new intel which I believe maybe our saving grace."

"Where is it?"

"White Sands Missile Range, New Mexico."

"Yeah, I know where it is. Do you know how big that place is?"

"I'm sure you're about to tell me though."

"It's over three thousand square miles and spread over five counties. That's a lot of manpower and resources to coordinate the assault in one hit."

"I know where you're coming from but you won't need to search the whole area."

"I'm not with you."

"It's only buildings that you'll need to look at and everything is above surface. No underground stuff."

"Sounds like you've identified something."

"One building has sprung up which by the sounds of it, maybe be a positive hit."

"Not sure I like the sound of maybe."

"Nothing is ever guaranteed Felix until it's over and done with. However, this is far stronger than the other two which suggests to me this is the one."

"Are you sure this is the right approach?"

"Not with you."

"You're the military man Jack. Putting all your consideration into one building when there are just too many to count at White Sands. Is it wise to single out just one?"

"What are you saying?"

"What happens if your intel is off?"

"The intel is solid Felix. It's certainly a reliable source."

"All I'm saying is that what if its bigger than you think. That the spread is greater at White Sands. It'll take a hell of a lot longer if we had to search all the buildings."

"That's why I'm going with the original plan. It's simple and effective and it'll hit them where it hurts."

"I hope you're right Jack. However, I can't do anything for a couple of days."

"How about if I use some of my guys? A joint operation."

"You'll need POTUS to sign off on that one as it's outside of Scorpion's jurisdiction."

"Understood."

"Email me the details Jack and let's get a plan in motion. If you're right, then we need to move quickly."

CHAPTER 28

Outside Elisabeth's Apartment, Moscow – 7 a.m. local time the next morning

Elisabeth decided to go into work early. She drove out from the underground car park as she did most days and followed the same route to the CNN Headquarters. As she looked at her fuel gauge, an amber light on her dash flashed indicating 'Low Fuel'. *'Damn it'* she said to herself. Although she figured she would have enough for the journey, she didn't like the tank to go too low in case she had to dash off somewhere and it would hinder her if she had to stop. She quickly glanced in her rear-view mirror, and as the roads were exceptionally quiet, she was surprised to see a black van drop in behind her from a side street. Whilst it was some distance back, it unnerved her. Copeland had always insisted to her that if she ever had a problem or suspicion whilst driving that she should go straight to a safe house, either a police station, government building, US embassy or place of work. The latter for her would've been the best option but she still needed to get some fuel although her instinct told her to go straight to the safe house of the CNN. Not listening to her own words, she decided to pull into the gas station hoping that the van would go straight on by. She pulled onto the forecourt of the World Fuel Services and stopped by the pumps where she watched as the van drove slowly by. Once it had passed, she then got out the vehicle and began to fill her fuel tank but looking around her all the while for any hint of a problem. Having filled only half a tank, she went into the kiosk to pay, glancing over her shoulder as she went through the sliding door.

* * *

Elisabeth's escort team had been on duty since six that morning. They had been instructed to monitor and follow Elisabeth wherever she went or watch the apartment block whilst she was at home. They'd just picked up a coffee from a roadside kiosk when the gates to the underground car park opened. The distinctive white SUV with CNN emblazoned on the side appeared and they recognised the driver as the one from their initial brief. Keeping the cups in the cup holders, the driver fired up the engine after the second attempt much to his annoyance. They never knew from one day to the next where she was heading but on regular trips they would make best guesses as to where she was likely to go given time and distance appreciations for previous journey's. As they drove away heading south, Elisabeth had gained some distance already. Travelling at a distance behind a target vehicle, always gave other road users the opportunity to tuck in between. Today was no exception as a black Ford Transit van did exactly that and came in between the target vehicle and their own. They had lost sight momentarily of the target vehicle but then saw Elisabeth take a right from the main highway to cross over the Moscow River. By travelling this route, the escort crew took it that she would be heading in to the office.   Having crossed the bridge, Elisabeth and the van turned right onto a slip road which came back on its self to a T-junction. She turned right followed by the van so that the Moscow river was on their left. As the escort vehicle pulled up to the junction, the driver looked to his left, "Oh shit", he managed to shout before they were side swiped by a lorry which was almost on top of them giving them no time to react. The sheer force pushed their vehicle for several yards before coming to a halt after hitting the bridge support pillar. The SUV caved in and the passenger looked over to the driver and noticed that he was slumped against the wheel and slightly listing to his left. He took the full impact and he knew instinctively that he hadn't made it. The passenger himself was in no better shape. His head was a mess with blood dripping down his face and over his eyes making him lose focus. His head was pounding and his body felt like they'd just been hit by a steam train. Leaning forward and pushing his body through the pain barrier, he picked up the handset for the radio and simply said, "*Broken Arrow*".

* * *

Stepping out the shop Elisabeth consciously kept looking around her as if she had an instinct that something wasn't quite right. She was nervous, on edge and almost in a state of panic. She was frightened but at the same time, she needed to be level headed. *'Why wasn't Jack here. He'd know what to do.'* She muttered to herself. Quickening her pace back to her car, the same black van came onto the forecourt from her blind side and quickly stopped with the screeching of tyres. The side sliding door was opened and she was grabbed having had a black sack put over her head and dragged quickly, whilst she was kicking and punching the air, into the van before it sped away and back onto the main highway.

* * *

Copeland's Office at the Pentagon 2 a.m.

Copeland was in a deep sleep to the point that he could hear himself snoring which at times caused him to roll on his side several times. Although he snored, he wouldn't openly admit it to anyone, including Elisabeth. She had threatened to record him one night but fortunately hadn't got around to it. Whilst rolling over, he heard a faint humming noise. He lay there for a short while trying to figure out what it was and more to the point, where it was coming from. Was it a distant fire alarm, or the humming of the air con unit? As his sleep was now fully disturbed, he sat up on his make shift bed, the sofa and suddenly realised that it was his cell phone that had come to life. Whoever it was, was most persistent. He picked it up and looked at the screen. After rubbing sleep from his eyes and a stretch to waken his senses, he thought he'd recognised the number but wasn't sure.

"This is Copeland."

"Jack it's Karl."

"What time is it?"

"It's two in the morning."

"Don't you ever sleep?"

"It seems that way these days. I have some bad news."

"Christ, is it the ISS? What's happened?"

"It's not the ISS. Jack, I'm sorry."

"For what?"

"There's no easy way to say this but Elisabeth has been taken"

"Taken, what's that supposed to mean? Is she ill?"

"No, no nothing like that. It's worse, she's been kidnapped."

"I'm not with you. What, as in kidnapped? Is this some kind of sick joke?"

"Believe me. I wish I didn't have to make the call."

"From where, what the hell happened, why Elisabeth. She's only a reporter."

"She's more than that Jack as you are fully aware."

There was silence for a moment as Copeland picked up his cell phone and began to make a call.

"If you're phoning Elisabeth you're wasting your time Jack. They've either destroyed the phone, took it from her or it's been lost during the kidnapping."

"God damnit Karl." Copeland said as he put his cell phone back down, "I asked you to keep an eye on her so nothing like this could happen. Where were the team in all this?"

"They were with her but were ambushed. Both agents down Jack. One dead and the other one managed to get a call in to report the incident. He didn't make it in the end either."

"I'm sorry Karl. When I asked you, I never for one moment thought anything like this would happen. This changes everything. Do we know if she's okay? Have you heard anything? Where did it happen?"

"One thing at a time Jack. No, nothing heard as yet. I wouldn't expect anything for at least twenty-four hours."

"I think they're after me for something and they're using Elisabeth because they know how much I care about her."

"That's possible, unless she stumbled on something which stirred a hornet's nest. It may have nothing to do with you."

"Oh, believe me Karl, it has everything to do with me."

"How do you know and what makes you so sure? Is there something I need to know?"

"I'm the head of the special ops team, Scorpion who are at some point going to kick some arse of those involved with the ISS. They'll be using this to get me or the team off balance and out of focus. It's only going to make it worse. I won't let anything happen to Elisabeth Karl. I'll do everything I can and use whatever means I have at my disposal to bring her back – alive. They really don't know who they're messing with. Where did it happen?"

"The report the agent sent through is a little sketchy. He did well considering what he'd been through. I guess it was his last breath. The embassy has a grid square taken from their personal tracker which was the last reported position of the team. That's all we have to go on at the moment."

"I need to go to Moscow."

"That's not a good idea Jack. You're mixing your personal life which is making you emotional. That's not good at all. You're needed back here which is where you'll be far more useful."

"I'll be no good. I can't think straight."

"What would Elisabeth want you to do?"

"Stay focused, find the guys who did this which would eventually lead to where she is."

"There you go. Simple as that. Let's listen to her for a change."

"You're right. But I feel useless."

"Let's wait and see what comes through then we can decide what action to take next. If an op is needed, then of course POTUS will need to sign off on it. The agency will help wherever we can Jack. You have our full support."

* * *

Pentagon Switchboard – The Next Day

"Pentagon, how may I direct your call?" came the robotic words of the operator.

"Listen to my words very carefully young lady." began the caller, "Tell Jack Copeland to back off and stop interfering. If he doesn't listen, the pretty face of his girlfriend will suffer the consequences." The line was suddenly severed as quickly as it was connected.

CHAPTER 29

Khodynka, 4.3 miles NE of Moscow – 8 a.m.

Opening her eyes, she scanned the room. It was small and felt cold. There was one window which was cracked and a single door which was closed. There was also a single four-legged chair against the wall to the left of the door. The room looked derelict and worn with the passage of time and neglect. The walls were blistering and the ceiling in places was beginning to sag as water leaked its way through the roof. She sat up on the bed and rubbed at her eyes. She looked at her wrist to see the time but there was no watch. She also realised that the pebble bracelet which Jack had bought her from Tiffany's the first year they met, was also missing. She looked around the bed area to see if it had fallen off – nothing. They must've been taken or dropped off when she was kidnapped. She had no idea of the time. She checked herself over and was thankful that she was still fully clothed. '*At least she hadn't been attacked*' which was an uncomfortable thought that had crossed her mind. Sliding off the bed, she crossed the room to the door and tried the handle. It was locked and by the look of the hinges, it was a door which opened outwards.

That meant to her that it was either a storage room or some kind of military facility. Stepping back towards the centre of the room, she moved the chair under the window and stood on it. The window was slightly higher than her height and the chair together. Grabbing hold of the window ledge, she was able to pull herself up and take a peek outside. She realised that she definitely wasn't on the ground floor and was maybe two or three floors up. The area outside seemed abandoned with old vehicles and aircraft scattered in all directions. Could it be an old abandoned airfield she was in. She couldn't see a runway and she had no idea of the country but knew she hadn't travelled far so it would make sense that she was still in Russia and more importantly, Moscow. Stepping back off the chair, Elisabeth had that sinking feeling that she had been kidnapped and was now being held a prisoner. As thoughts began to run through her head trying to figure out why she was now in this position, she heard movement outside the door then the insertion of a key into the lock. She quickly moved the chair back against the wall and moved over to the bed and sat on its edge looking back towards the door. As soon as she had sat, the door was swung open and what she saw next, widened her eyes and left her at the point of being speechless.

* * *

1015 p.m. the same day

General Syromokov continued to visit his usual evening jaunt. He gave nothing away to anyone who may have been suspicious of his current activities. He was a smart cookie, but he was a man of routine who liked the simple things in life. He also liked the things which were necessary to mankind – women and Smirnoff Vodka. His lifestyle made him predictable and easy to figure out. Not a great combination for someone in his position. Syromokov wasn't sure how many more days he had left in which to go to his club considering he had been given a new life in the USA. He knew it was presumptuous but nevertheless it felt great. His actions were treacherous but necessary. His driver Yuri, having reversed his vehicle into the small alleyway, got out of the vehicle and put his hand on the rear door handle. As he did so, a dark coloured van reversed at speed into the alleyway and hit the front of the Mercedes knocking Yuri off balance and jolted the vehicle backwards. Before the van had come to a halt, three figures all dressed in black jumped out from a side door and one grabbed Yuri around his throat in an armlock and after being asphyxiated, he fell to the ground. One of the men in black opened the back door of the Mercedes and saw their target was a gibbering wreck. He was in a situation which was clearly outside of his control. He laid down on the rear seat and curled up into the foetal position as if defending himself from an imminent attack.

He was dragged by his feet from the rear of the car and as he bounced onto the floor his left shoulder hit with a thud, a black bag was placed over his head and his hands were bound behind his back with plastic ties. He lost a shoe in the process which was picked up by the third man and thrown into the back of the van. Syromokov's bulk meant that he had to be man handled by two of the men who grabbed him by his restrained arms and pushed and dragged forcibly towards the side of the van and hustled him into it where he rolled onto the floor grimacing as his head hit the metal floor causing a gash to his left temple and the pain repeated itself on his shoulder. Two of the hooded men jumped into the back of the van and the third climbed into the front next to the driver. Before the doors were closed, the van drove off as quickly as it had come. Syromokov had just been lifted unceremoniously and under the cover of darkness by whom he was yet to find out.

* * *

CIA Black Site, Moscow 1 hour later

As the van approached its location, a sliding metal gate was opened and the van drove through and into a cavernous derelict building. Syromokov was again dragged out the vehicle and ushered towards the corner of the building and into an old office where he was dropped onto a chair in the middle of the room. His hands were still tied behind him and the bag remained over his head giving him a feeling of disorientation. Not being able to see or do anything often created a sense of panic amongst those in similar situations. There wasn't a word said, a noise made or any indication that there was anyone else in the room or in the building. To Syromokov, this was unnerving, uncomfortable and frustrating. He was now in a role reversal from his previous life that he never expected.

"Hello." Began Syromokov, "Can anyone hear me?"

There was silence

"Is there anyone there? Why am I here?"

More silence.

Everything was playing through his mind, every scenario and reason for being here. Had he been rumbled and the FSB had lifted him and now they were punishing him for his deceit. Syromokov had interrogated many people throughout his career and as he cast his mind back to his days in the KGB, he knew there could only be one outcome from this. His chance of a new life was over before it had even begun. Was it the Americans who had turned him in. They had their information and now he was of no use to them. With the passing of each second and minute he sensed that it was going to end badly.

"You know I am former KGB and I know your game. I have nothing to say. I have done nothing wrong."

In the shadows and from the corner of the room behind Syromokov, stepped a tall heavy-set man who walked slowly towards him. There was no rush, there was no urgency, there was no noise. Silence and stealth was their working ethos and the tools of their trade. The man stood behind Syromokov for what seemed like several minutes sensing an air of panic and anxiety in him. There was an uncomfortable shift in Syromokov's posture as he sensed someone directly behind him to which he couldn't yet see. He continually tried, but in vain to look from side to side to get some kind of visual image which he knew was never going to happen. The weaving on the bag was too tight for one thing and for another, there didn't seem to be any light in the room either.

"I know you're there. You can't scare me that easily."

The bag was suddenly pulled from the head of Syromokov and at the same time, several arc lights were powered up which had the desired effect of making their guest squint to control the burning sensation of the light which had just transformed night-time to daylight in Nano seconds. His hands were still tied and therefore wasn't able to protect his eyes. All he could do was to open them slowly, gradually and to focus on near objects. The light was so intense that he had trouble making out any objects near or far. Syromokov was unable to speak as he tried to get a perspective where he was and how many were in the room. He knew that wasn't going to happen anytime soon and nor was he in any fit state to even consider a way out of all this. They probably had guns, he didn't. They were undoubtedly fit, he wasn't. Realising that he had very little in his favour, he knew that his options for escaping were diminishing as quickly as he had thought of the idea.

"General Igor Georgi Syromokov, what a pleasant surprise." Came the confident voice in an American accent.

"No one knows my middle name."

"Your father was a farmer, am I correct?"

"Yes. How did you...?"

"Georgi translates into farmer so it was an obvious guess."

"You are Americans, yes?" questioned Syromokov with a hint of both surprise and delight. Whilst torture was the same in any language, he preferred his odds of survival in the hands of the Americans rather than his own countrymen.

"Do you have any idea why you are here?"

"I have no idea where I am and no I don't. Please enlighten me."

"I'm going to ask you some questions and depending how you answer them, will depend whether or not I let the dogs lose."

Syromokov hadn't seen nor heard any dogs so he took it that he was referring to his heavy handlers. They were the inflictors of pain and anguish and the ones who would change his appearance free of charge after which, those who knew him probably wouldn't be able to recognise him again.

"Where is she Igor?"

"I don't understand. Where is who..." he answered as if genuinely surprised. He hoped his training would give him the edge.

"Don't play the innocence. You're full of BS. You know whom I'm talking about. You've been playing us all this time. You expect us to give you a new life after what you've done. You knew all along what was going to happen but you decided to keep it to yourself. That was a big mistake Igor"

"Believe me, I have no idea. Other than what I have already told you before, I have no idea what is going on. I wish I had never trusted you Americans now. You never stick to your deal."

The heavy man turned around and simply nodded. Two other men came from the same shadow and stood in front of Syromokov. They both wore a woollen mask which only revealed the menacing look in their eyes and lips. They each wore leather fitted gloves and came armed with the standard issue towel and bucket of water.

"One last chance Igor before I let the hounds lose."

"I told you. I have no idea what you are talking about."

Again, another nod and the leash were off the wolves. They each struck Syromokov across his face with their fists causing his face to shudder with the impact and the thick spillage of blood from his mouth and nose was released.

"Tell me who you mean and I will tell you if I know anything." Came the muffled words of an embattled Syromokov.

"Elisabeth Young. The CNN reporter."

"I met with her only a few days ago." Syromokov paused, "What has happened?"

"She's been kidnapped and you're going to tell me where she is otherwise you'll never see your family again or the light of day. Do we understand each other General?"

Syromokov nodded uncontrollably and was sweating like an agitated pig that he was.

"Come on Igor. This can be a lot easier if you cooperate."

The man nodded again signalling a silent command and in moved the wolves who punished Syromokov for his silence, he was hit and he was drowned but, in the end, resistance would be futile. Syromokov slumped his head as if in defeat. His eyes had begun to swell, his nose already broken and his teeth at the front had been smashed. Blood trickled down his face and onto his neck and finally began to soak into his shirt. He was a shell of his former self but stubborn at the same time. He was no longer the powerful military man that he was. He was now subservient at the behest of others.

"These kinds of conversations we're having here Igor you never walk out the same as when you came in. You of all people should know that. I'm sure we're both on the same page here, man to man and one professional to another." The man paused before continuing, "What's the game plan here Igor? What's the bigger picture?"

"You've no idea who you're dealing with."

"Are you talking about yourself or someone else?"

"It's bigger than what you think."

"Oh, I can see where we're heading with this Igor. So, we're now talking about a government connection, are we? Interesting how things develop from nothing."

Syromokov shuffled uncomfortably in his seat as if to imply that the question had been correct. His silence was also confirmation.

"We're on a roll here now Igor. By your silent admission, we know that there's a government connection with the disappearance of the reporter. What we don't know is who gave the order for her to be kidnapped and more importantly, why. But I'm sure we can change all that. You're an intelligent man who has a liking for the simple things in life. Do yourself a favour, give me what I need to know and you can go back to enjoying your seedy life. If not, it could all end here and now."

Syromokov listened attentively but remained silent. He'd heard it all before. He used to use the same tactics. The interrogator was right though, he did enjoy the seedy part of his life. He'd reached the crossroads and whatever direction he takes next, would determine his fate, not just for now but forever.

The interrogator was losing patience, "Last chance Igor. I don't want to be just as much as you don't. We can all go home and be with our families. Isn't that what you want?"

Nothing but silence from Syromokov but he was mulling over the words of his interrogator. Was he teasing or was he genuine with his remarks.

Syromokov tried to pull himself together and mumbled something which was incoherent. He was having trouble speaking through swollen lips and a blocked nasal passage and the foaming of the blood over his mouth.

The interrogator moved closer and put his ear in front of Syromokov's face, "What did you say?"

Syromokov struggled to open his mouth.

"What did you say? Say it again."

Finding his reserve strength, Syromokov managed to utter the word *'Khodynka'* and *'Orlov'* before rolling with his chair onto the floor and closing his eyes.

CHAPTER 30

Khodynka, Moscow - midday same day

The man who walked into the room brought with him a tray with water and a sandwich and placed the tray on the chair by the wall. He wore a woollen ski mask, blue jeans and an outdoor field jacket but there was something underneath this exterior which was disturbing her. He looked directly at Elisabeth but never spoke. His eyes looked familiar, but surely it can't be. It was an impossible scenario but she had to know. As the man turned and headed back towards the door, she began to speak.

"Neil, is that you?" she asked with a dread of not really wanting to know if she was right. Neil Johnson was the CIA agent who'd been with Elisabeth the few times she had met with Syromokov. This was unthinkable but the body language suggested that she may have been correct. The man stopped in his tracks as if caught off guard. He turned and stared directly at Elisabeth. Silence was confirmation enough. He didn't need to speak as his actions spoke louder than any words.

"Why are you doing this Neil?"

Still silence as he continued to look in Elisabeth's direction. Perhaps his rouse had been seen through sooner than he had thought and he hadn't been prepared for such confrontation at this early stage. Elisabeth wasn't about to give in. She needed to take some control to try and ease her situation and, in some cases, get the upper hand. Knowing her captor could give her an advantage.

"Where am I and why am I here?"

The man was still standing by the door almost wanting to speak but not finding the words or he just didn't want to have the empathy of his prisoner at this point. He turned and finally left the room closing the door behind him and locking it as he went with the single turn of the key.

* * *

US Embassy, Moscow – 10 a.m. the next day

Rob Cummings was the CIA station chief at the embassy. He'd been on the phone for nearly an hour whilst he was given information by the interrogators who had been speaking with Syromokov. The information was hot, sensitive and undeniable which needed to be passed to Langley at the earliest opportunity. This was actionable intelligence and as Rob began to write his report, he was disturbed by an incoming call. He picked up the handset without looking.

"Yeah." He simply answered whilst trying to do two things at once.

"When was the last time you saw him?" he asked whilst tapping away at his keyboard and trying to listen at the same time. Cummings stopped and gave the call his full attention, "Is he following a lead on anything at the moment?"

"No, just don't let the Russian government know. Keep it in house for the time being."

Rob held onto the handset and was momentarily lost for words. He locked his computer screen and having made several calls to follow up on the information he had just received, he hit the extension number for the Ambassadors secretary, "Is she in?" He received the reply that he had hoped for and quickly left his office and headed straight to Ambassador Jennifer Hart's office. With a simple nod to the secretary, and a tap on the Ambassador's door, he let himself in.

"Come in." said the Ambassador almost sarcastically as she looked up from her desk when the door opened. "Sounded important. What is it?"

"One of my agents has gone MIA."

"Explain."

"He was on task to meet with a possible asset and hasn't been heard from in the last forty-eight hours."

"Is that unusual?"

"Well, yeah. Contact should be made every day unless they are in deep cover."

"Name?"

"Neil Johnson."

"Is that the same Neil who was trying to turn Syromokov?"

"The very same. You know about that?"

"He came to see me. How are you dealing with this?"

"I tried to get hold of Elisabeth Young at CNN but no one has heard from her either. I also tried Neil's cell too; nothing. It's not looking good I'm afraid."

"Have you been to his apartment? He may just be under the weather."

"It's out of character. He's never ill. I'll send a team round just in case though. What if he isn't there?"

"Let's not jump to conclusions. When your team get back and they report he isn't there, then send a flash signal to Langley, Top Priority. We can't have a rogue agent running loose in Moscow. If the Russian government find him first, he'll be more valuable to them than winning the Powerball lottery."

* * *

CIA Safe House, Moscow – later that day

Two black SUV's pulled up outside the apartment block and two teams of three got out and ran straight to the front door pulling their side arms as they went. Short circuiting the entrance access panel, they opened the front door and climbed the stair case to the fourth floor. Having identified and confirmed the apartment number, the lock was picked and entry gained. Moving stealthily through the apartment, room by room, they confirmed that it was empty. There was no Neil Johnson anywhere to be seen. In fact, the apartment looked like it hadn't been touched for a couple of days. The team leader picked up his cell and fast dialled a number, "All clear." He simply said.

* * *

To the frustration of Rob Cummings, the news was bad. He'd never lost an agent in the field and he couldn't understand what had happened here. Neil was one of his better agents, a little creative and wayward sometimes but he always managed to get results. Had the risks to get Syromokov on board been worse than originally thought or had they rushed it without thinking it through properly? The unknowns were eating away at Cummings. He sent the Flash Signal to Langley and all he could do now was to wait for the fall out. All hell would break loose back in Virginia for sure and shit would most certainly be hitting the fan before it rolled back down hill to Moscow where a few heads were likely to topple as a consequence.

* * *

The Dome, White Sands MR, New Mexico 1130 a.m.

Brad Hernandez was sat in the dome and taking an early lunch. All his preparations had now been completed. Both Ramirez and Diaz were busying themselves playing computer games against each other and on-line. Their task was almost over. There was only one more event they needed to do.

Fire Storm

As Brad was about to take another bite out of his sandwich, his cell vibrated in his pocket. Dropping his sandwich back into its container, he took out his phone, looked at the number and having recognised it, he walked out the dome before accepting the call.

"At last, I've been waiting for your call. It won't be long before questions start to be asked."

"How easy would it be for you to arrange a test?"

"A test to do what?"

"I want to be sure that what you have actually works."

"What am I supposed to test it on?"

"A missile."

"Really? Seriously?"

"Absolutely."

"Okay, so which country is this gonna be fired from?"

"I thought you were an intelligent man Brad. It's the US of A of course. Can you arrange for one to be fired from where you are?"

"I've told you before not to use my name over the phone and no, it'll need to be launched from another site."

"Very good. Let me know when it's done."

"Missile tests just don't happen overnight. They take time to fuel and set up."

"You don't have time. Just make it happen."

* * *

WSMR HQ – Later that day

After taking the call, Brad decided to finish up for the day and head back on base. He drove Ramirez and Diaz back to their accommodation and then carried onto the HQ. Having parked his vehicle, he headed into the building and up to the third floor. He found the office he was looking for and having knocked he had the invite to enter.

"Hey Brad." Came the voice of his boss, Jez, "How's the project? I've not had much time to get over and see it."

Brad was a little taken back by that comment. He always knew Jez would leave him alone and for him to even think about checking out the site was a little concerning. "It's going great. Almost done actually."

"Good to hear. Listen, I'll pop over to see you in a couple of days. Just so much to do over here at the moment." Jez figured that Brad wasn't just passing by, "Did you want something?"

"I need to be able to test the equipment so that if there are any adjustments needed before we ship it out, then at least we'll know that it works and we can say with hand on heart, that it was good when it left."

"Good call. What do you need?"

"A missile."

"Just like that." Jez had a little chuckle, "It's not as if we have many laying around."

"I know that, but these tests have to be made so that we can gather data."

"Okay, let me see what I can do. It may not be from here though. I'm thinking Vandenberg."

CHAPTER 31

Khodynka, Moscow - The next day

For many years, Elisabeth had never had a decent night's sleep. Even when sleeping with Copeland, she would always wake up around three or four in the morning and then get to work on her emails so she could keep on top of things for the rest of the day and then be exhausted again at night. This morning however she was sleeping like a baby, almost making up for lost time. Whilst facing towards the wall, she sensed that she had heard a slight noise in the room. She quickly rolled over and saw a man with his back to her placing a tray on the chair. She'd been dead to the world since she never even heard the door open. She was either mentally or physically exhausted. Either way, she had let her guard down. He turned and looked towards her as if he was about to say something, but nothing. He was the second person not to say anything and she was beginning to think they were all mutes. Quickly focusing, she was sure that it wasn't the same one who had brought her tray the previous day. He was wearing the standard intimidating ski mask but he was shorter, almost the height of a jockey for one thing and the eyes were almost black. He'd be known as widget from now on.

"Where's Neil?" she tested for a response.
No response, silence.

"I know it was him who brought my tray yesterday. What I don't understand is why I'm here. Can you tell me that at least?"
Widget came slightly closer and stopped. She knew he was about to do or say something. "Your boyfriend is in the way." He simply said with a deep European voice which had an accent but she wasn't able to place it.

"What has he done or more to the point what are you doing that will make him get in the way?"
There was the non-committal silence again.

"I need the bathroom and I need to shower."
Widget still stood there which was beginning to make Elisabeth more than uncomfortable. She also began to wonder whether or not there would be any running water especially being an old building. If not then she wasn't expected to stay here for long or she would be moved to another building elsewhere.

"Unless you want me to pee and crap on the floor then I would suggest you let me go." She insisted with a tone that hopefully would come across as being desperate.
The man considered her request for a few minutes whilst he figured out whether she was telling the truth or something else. He figured the former due to Elisabeth crossing her legs and moving her body in an uncomfortable way. With a nod of the head and a single wave of the hand he signified that he was happy with her request. Turning on his heel, he

headed back towards the door with Elisabeth following closely behind.

The guard simply knocked once on the door which was then unlocked and swung open revealing the inner part of the building. Elisabeth was alert to finding out more about where she was being held. As she left her room, she could see that the room was office like in its design. It was spacious and with windows along three sides with a closed door leading to a possible stair case on the left wall between the windows. Where there was once tables and chairs in the room it was now devoid of anything. Just loose cables hanging from the ceiling. Having seen the abandoned vehicles and aircraft on the outside yesterday, she was convinced this was certainly an abandoned building. The guard on the outside of the door, which she hadn't seen until now looked menacing as he carried a rifle slung across his chest and held by a sling. He was stretched tall, probably around six six. Not being familiar with guns, she knew that the Kalashnikov was popular in Russia and assumed that is what he was carrying. The small guard purposefully kept Elisabeth against the fourth wall so that she wouldn't have the chance to look out the windows. As she was being ushered towards the toilets, she quickly glanced towards the windows and with the advantage of height, she was able to see something which confirmed where she was being held. Not so much the location, but she saw a runway which suggested an airfield, abandoned or otherwise and probably government owned at some point. She also noticed a long rectangular box in drag olive green military colours placed under the window overlooking the runway. Some of the wording on the side had faded away but the letters 'N C H E R" were visible with a series of numbers and letters underneath the words. The box was closed with the lid securely fastened with at least three metal clips so she wasn't able to see its contents but had to be some kind of military hardware for them to use or if not, it was out of place otherwise considering the rest of the floor was empty. Having reached the toilet, she glanced back to the guard and simply said, "Some privacy please." He stood fast as she went through the door. Surprisingly, the toilet had everything she needed from towels to washing soap.

Elisabeth did what she had to do and was then escorted back to her room. She'd only seen two guards but the third one, the one she took to be Neil was missing. Where was he? Has he decided to quit early on because he'd been rumbled. She doubted that as he looked like someone who would carry out his duty to the end whatever the outcome, life or death. He didn't seem like a quitter. In fact, Elisabeth suggested to herself, that it wouldn't surprise her if he wasn't the ring leader himself. The door was again closed and locked and Elisabeth lay on her bed contemplating what she'd seen and making a mental picture of everything.

* * *

WSMR HQ – Same Day

Jez had made several calls to varying departments within the US Space Command on behalf of Brad. As he was about to give up on the idea, his luck changed. It came not from any space programme but from the Ground-based Midcourse Defence Segment which he knew was formerly called, National Missile Defence. He received confirmation that the launch would be carried out in two days' time at around nine fifty-nine in the evening from Vandenberg AFB in California and they were quite happy for the WSMR to play its part. Armed with this good news, Jez called Brad,

"Brad, it's Jez. I have some good news."

"Okay, let's go with it."

"You can have a minuteman missile but not for two days."

"Is that the earliest test date?"

"Yep, and it's out of Vandenberg."

"That's great. Timings?"

"Scheduled for nine fifty-nine in the evening."

"Any daytime launches?"

"None listed, why?"

"Nothing of importance really."

* * *

After the call with Jez, Brad connected another call,

"It's done. The test will be a night launch in two days' time."

"I'll be watching"

* * *

Khodynka – 1 p.m. The same day

Not wanting to be caught out a second time, Elisabeth heard the sound of the key being turned in the door and the creaking of the hinges as it was pulled open. She sat upright on the bed with her back against the wall and pulled her legs up tight to her chest and then folded her arms around them. The guard came in with the standard tray of water and a sandwich which she figured must be around lunch time. The movement of the guard gave her confidence and as the guard turned towards her, she saw the eyes once again and realised that it was the CIA agent. She needed to latch onto this and to try and figure out what was happening.

"Neil, why are you doing this? In fact, come to think of it, is that your real name." Elisabeth started to vent, "Probably not. You're a liar, a deceiver and a fake."

No response, but she knew that she'd get under his collar if she continued and the outcome may be violent and confrontational. Not something she was keen on happening.

"You'll be caught out in the end and the consequences are for you to only imagine. Although you already know what they are, correct? Are you working for the other side or both?"

He shifted uncomfortably from one foot to the other as if wanting to say something. Elisabeth knew she was about to get under his collar.

"Why am I here? Is it to do with Syromokov?"

"You've got no idea, have you?" the silence had been broken much to Elisabeth's surprise and ultimate delight. "We've been following you ever since you left Washington when you said goodbye to Copeland. We were also with you in Tashkent when Copeland came to stay with you and also here in Moscow. You live in your own little world cocooned from the outside. The world is in turmoil and everyone is sitting back and allowing it to continue. There's a difference to be made here and I want to be on the right side."

"So, it was you or a rogue outfit working for you. Now it all makes sense. I must say that I hadn't seen anyone for a while. Anyway, if you think switching sides is going to make things right then you're very much mistaken and misguided. You're on the wrong side Neil and the further along you go the worse it'll become for you. There is no justification for doing this. Why do you think the world is in turmoil?"

"The US control everything but that is about to change."

"I'm not with you. In what way?"

"You will know soon enough." He said confidently.

"What are you doing that Jack is interfering in?"

"He's the one who is likely to stop our action plan. He's the obstacle that we need to remove."

"Ah, I see now. That's why I'm here as a bargaining chip isn't it? Makes sense. God, why have I been so stupid not to see this before."

Elisabeth moved off the bed and stood a short distance from the guard, "It's not too late to stop this."

"I'm a believer but I'm not a quitter."

"What are you planning on doing to change the world?"

"You'll hear about it soon enough. It'll make the world sit up and take Russia seriously once again."

"Clearly you believe that. Look at it from the other side, if it all goes wrong, which I'm sure it will, then the whole world will be against Russia. It's all going to end in failure and tears. You've given up a great career with the CIA. You'll be hounded for years to come if you get out of this alive."

"Don't push your luck. You're only here because of Copeland."

Elisabeth was hoping that Copeland was by now thinking something wasn't adding up and that if he couldn't get hold of her, he would initiate an action plan. She also knew that it would take time to put something together. But hey, she wasn't going anywhere anytime soon. She had a hunch that the guard was losing confidence in his plan as Elisabeth began to delve more and more into what was supposed to be happening and he began to reveal more than he should.

"I always knew that I was a good reporter and had the gift to be able to smell when there was a good story, but I can honestly say that I never saw this coming. That was well concealed. You had me fooled as I thought being from the government you should be trusted. How wrong was I?"

There was no reply.

"How long am I supposed to stay here cooped up?"

"As long as it takes."

"Was meeting Syromokov a ploy?"

"No, that was genuine. I needed to know what he knew but, in the end, he knew nothing."

"What do you mean in the end? Is he dead?"

"It was a figure of speech."

"Did you turn Syromokov in to the authorities?"

"He's done that himself. Luckily we found him first though."

"Explain."

"Does he think that the meeting places weren't covered by the FSB. They know everything, they are everywhere. In the work place in the streets. Wherever you go there is someone watching you."

"Tell me Neil or whatever your real name is, how long have you been working both sides?"

"None of your business but let's just say I caught the CIA on their blind side and they never expected it and they still don't suspect it."

"A master plan I'll certainly give you that. Even I never expected it for one minute. You can't be working this alone though. There must be someone else calling the shots, a financial backer maybe or someone on the inside of government."

Elisabeth realised she had hit a nerve with the guard. He turned and headed for the door whilst Elisabeth stood still. "Which government?" she questioned, "US or Russia? I'm guessing Russia since we're here already."

As he knocked on the door, he turned and simply said, "Nice try. That's the beauty of clandestine ops. Total deniability. You become a ghost."

"Not quite true, you are merely the pawn which means that you take the fall and pay the price, whilst others in the background walk away into the shadows and get to live another day. If you go down, it makes sense for you to take him with you."

CHAPTER 32

US Embassy, Moscow – Ambassadors Office – Same time, same day

"I've got this horrible feeling that Johnson has gone rogue." Began Rob Cummings as he briefed the Ambassador, "We have a traitor in our midst."

"Let's not get ahead of ourselves here Rob. I'm sure there's a simple explanation to all this."

"I wish I had your confidence. In the absence of intelligence, we have to assume the worse and hope for the best. He doesn't drink so it's unlikely he fell into the river. Has he been compromised and lifted? It's likely in this day and age."

"What happened to his tracker?"

"Disabled."

"Brilliant. You couldn't write this script, could you? Supposing he has gone rogue, the CIA doesn't need this exposure again. In fact, remind me, what was the name of the last one?"

"Ames, Aldrich Ames. It was a huge trial and he was convicted of espionage back in ninety-four and is now serving his time at a penitentiary in Indiana. He spent thirty-one years at the agency as a counter intelligence analyst so he had a wealth of knowledge. What a waste and what an idiot."

"The thing is, he's not the first and he certainly won't be the last. We're going to have to tell the Russians at some point. They'll be annoyed but they'll also make us the laughing stock of the intelligence community the world over. You can just see the headlines caption can't you, '*CIA lose an agent in Moscow*'" said the Ambassador whilst using both hands to imitate a banner.

"Yeah for sure."

"How was Ames found out?"

"He had a salary of around sixty thousand dollars a year but his lifestyle seemed way over that. So, people got a little suspicious and began digging. The cheek of it all, he had a five hundred and forty-thousand-dollar house in Arlington and the dumb ass paid for it in cash. He had a fifty-thousand-dollar jaguar and he spent a further ninety-nine thousand dollars to remodel and decorate his house. Unless he won the lottery, he was out of his depth in the normal scheme of things. He got greedy and he also flashed the cash which clearly didn't do him any favours."

"Clearly."

"I sent the flash message to Langley yesterday. I've had nothing back. They should've been all over this by now. You heard anything?"

"Nothing but given the circumstances, I reckon they're trying to get their head around it to figure out how it got to this point in the first place."

"Sometimes no news is good news but on this particular occasion I would say it's bad news."

"It's that bad uh?"

"Worse. Unless we find him, he won't be getting his star on the wall of fame at Langley any time soon."

"Any more updates on Elisabeth?"

"Nothing. I've got everyone out trying to tap into our assets to locate them both. We've come up empty at the moment."

"What about Syromokov?"

As the question was asked by the Ambassador, there was a knock on the door.

"Yeah." Acknowledged the Ambassador.

The door opened and an analyst popped his head through.

"Apologise Ma'am." As he looked towards the Ambassador and then glanced towards Cummings, "But I need to speak with the chief."

"You can say what you have to say in front of the Ambassador."

"Okay. We've just received information from the Pentagon that an unknown call came into the DoD switchboard with a warning for General Jack Copeland to back off otherwise his girlfriend will suffer the consequences."

Cummings nodded to the analyst who stepped back out the door closing it as he went.

Cummings looked back towards the Ambassador.

"What do you make of that?" she asked.

"That's an answer to one of the questions. At least we know she's probably alive but in the hands of captors. Where, clearly, we don't know. Oh shit…"

The Ambassador could see the worry on Cumming's face, "What is it?"

"Because we had no idea where Elisabeth was, I put a snatch team on Syromokov to try and get him to talk. We took him to a black site that we have nearby to persuade him. I started my report and completely forgot about it when this came in about Johnson. Damn…"

Cummings was annoyed with himself for not following it through

"And did he?"

"What?"

"Talk"

"Uh, yeah, eventually. He simply gave us the word, '*Khodynka*'."

"Any guesses as to what he was referring to?"

"There is an area nearby with the same name."

"Get on it and see where it leads."

Cummings stood up and was about to turn to head towards the door.

"Oh, and by the way, he also mumbled the word Orlov. Does that mean anything to you?"

"Nothing stands out. Keep on it."

* * *

Briefing Room, US Embassy Moscow
Thirty minutes later

Cummings gathered all his agents into the room.

"Okay, this is a level one top priority request. Get your keyboards working and contact your assets and get me as much intel as you can on the word Khodynka. Also look into the word Orlov too. That's it. Let's get to work everyone. Back here in two hours."

* * *

Two hours later

Cummings opened up the floor, "Okay, let's get started. What do we have on Orlov?"

"There are several uses of the word Orlov." Began the analyst, "To begin with, it's a town in Russia and the administrative centre of Orlovsky District in Kirov Oblast and is located on the right bank of the Vyatka River. Been a town since seventeen eighty."

"Where is it in relation to Moscow?"

"It's roughly twelve and a half hours to the north east of Moscow."

"Discount that one. It's too far. They're going to be in Moscow for sure. What else?"

"It's also a popular family name."

"Interesting. Popular to who?"

"Military leaders, politicians, artists, footballers, sculptors and many more."

"Military leaders eh." He paused as he thought about that, "Okay, I have a hunch which is nothing more than that at the moment but check through the Kremlin register of staff will you and see if the name exists." The analyst left the room to work on the request. Cummings looked at another analyst in the room, "This may be heading somewhere else and if I'm right, it could open a Pandora's box. What about the other word, Khodynka?"

"The name Khodynka was given to the Coronation Cup to celebrate the coronation of Nicholas II in eighteen ninety-six." Began an analyst.

"Nope, not that. Next." Cummings waved with his right hand as if moving something along.

"I came up with the Khodynka Field." Began another analyst, "It's an area of open space in the North-West of Moscow."

"Yep, possible. Bank that one. Next."

"There used to be a river by the same name. This has now dried up."

"Next." Cummings dismissed the idea. "There must be something. Come on people, you're the brains of the agency."

"There was the Khodynka Tragedy in eighteen ninety-six on the Khodynka Field which resulted in the deaths of one thousand three hundred and eighty-nine people."

"Next." Cummings said impatiently.

"I came across the Khodynka Aerodrome."

"Okay, go on."

"It's just over four miles northwest of Moscow."

"Is it an active site?"

"Not commercially. That finished in the late nineteen forties. What is interesting is that it is due to close in two thousand and three for redevelopment. Currently, it's used for shipping out new aircraft and also a grave yard for the old."

"Military or civilian aerodrome?"

"Currently in the civilian domain but used to be military when it used to store both the Sukhoi and Mikoyan-Gurevich aircraft. One other thing, the aerodrome has several names. It goes by Khodynka Aerodrome, but officially it's called Frunze Central Aerodrome but is often referred to as the Tsentralny Aerodrome. By the way, it's in the Khoroshyovsky District." The analyst added for good measure.

"Christ, why make it so bloody difficult." Cummings said rhetorically, "Anyway, this sounds like our baby. Get me some aerial shots from live feeds and let's see what's happening out there. At least it's a start. Thanks everyone."

* * *

Pentagon, 10 a.m. the same day

Copeland sat at his desk but all he had was a blank stare. He'd been on tender hooks ever since he received the devastating news of Elisabeth's kidnap. He felt useless at not being able to do anything and he also felt that he had let her down. He was the head of a tactical military unit for god's sake and if he knew where these bastards were, he'd unleash his military might. The ringing of his desk phone broke his thinking.

"Copeland." He simply said

"Jack, It's Karl. How you holding up?"

"It's difficult to keep going and I just hope she's okay."

"She's a tough cookie. It'll take a hell of a lot to break her."

"Hope you're right." Copeland wanted to change the subject, "What can I help you with Karl?"

"It's something I've got for you. We've had a break through."

"Go on."

"Syromokov gave us the name '*Khodynka*' as a possible location of Elisabeth. We're checking it now."

"When did this happen?"

"A couple of days ago."

Copeland was losing patience and was fuming. He almost wanted to vent his frustration and anger but knew it would be unprofessional to do so and probably wouldn't achieve anything in any case. He remained calm, "How come this is the first I know about it?"

"The station chief was typing up his report but then we received some other top priority news."

"And..."

"It seems one of our agents has gone rogue."

"As in."

"Probably working for the other side."

"Jesus, I take it the agent is in Moscow? Is any of this connected with Elisabeth's kidnapping?"

"Not sure, it's too early to speculate, but it's a line we're taking at the moment. It is coincidental I have to admit."

"This is like a syndicate, Syromokov, your agent and Elisabeth. Too much of a coincidence here."

"I agree. There's one other thing."

Karl Langdon gave a brief over view of the call which came into the DoD switchboard with a warning to General Jack Copeland.

"I've stirred a hornet's nest then. But I don't understand which part I'm supposed to be in the way of. Did they say anything else?"

"Nothing. Look at it from their side, if something did happen then it's likely that you'll be called upon to sort out the problem and that could be your position in all of this. Without you at the helm, there'd be a command and control issue which would buy them some time to do what they wanted to do."

"It's all a bit vague Karl, but in some ways makes absolute sense. They took Elisabeth to get to me."

"Seems that way."

"Okay, thanks for the reassurance. Keep me apprised."

Copeland sat back in his chair and was momentarily lifted by the news which Karl had just imparted to him. He needed to remain positive to get through this and not to allow it to cloud his judgement. He needed to be focused throughout. He had a thought and dialled a stored number on his desk phone,

"Mister President."

"Jack, I've just heard." Came the voice of the US President, "Devastating news. How you holding up?"

"So far." Copeland hesitated, "Yeah all good." He wanted to reassure the President that he was still in control of his emotions even though deep down he was hurting. Not for himself, but for Elisabeth.

"How can I help Jack?"

"Director Langdon shared with me a name which had been revealed by Syromokov as a possible place where Elisabeth is being held."

"Your point is?"

"I'd like to be part of the op that goes in."

"It's on foreign soil Jack."

"All my ops are on foreign soil mister President. Why is this any different?"

"It involves the Russians. You know how difficult it is for them to play ball. We're still adversaries trying to mend bridges but we often never see eye to eye."

"We have an American citizen whose been kidnapped in Moscow and so we have a duty to her."

"I'll arrange a meeting with the Russian Ambassador and try and see what they know and how they could assist us. That's all I can do for now Jack. Diplomacy has to take its course first. That's the kind of world we live in today whether we like it or not. I'll get back to you when I have more."

CHAPTER 33

Vandenberg AFB, California 9.59 p.m. EST

After a flawless countdown, a modified Minuteman ICBM carrying a dummy warhead as a target was successfully launched from Vandenberg AFB. Its plume of white smoke as it ascended towards the darkness of space, was visible against the black canvass back drop. It was only the albedo from the sun which was being reflected from the moon surface which emitted a small amount of light that allowed the naked eye to follow its ascent.

* * *

The Dome, WSMR, same time

At the flick of a switch, Brad removed the dome cover which exposed the inside to the open sky and the billions of twinkling stars above. It was a warm evening with a slight breeze which made for perfect conditions. Both Ramirez and Diaz had already set up their work station and Diaz was filling in his authentication codes.

"Status?" asked Brad to Ramirez
"We're good and on-line."

"Okay, track and eliminate."

Twenty minutes after launch and nearly nine hundred and fifty miles away, Ramirez activated the kill switch and a beam of light was emitted from the dome and seconds later had made contact with the ICBM more than one hundred and forty miles above earth. The night sky lit up like a huge firework display which could easily be seen by the naked eye. This was the second successful intercept attempt initiated by the MIRACL but the first by its modified version. Brad's phone immediately rang,

"I was wondering how long it would take before you rang. Did you see it?" Brad asked with both delight and enthusiasm.

"Of course. Well done. I think we are now ready to move to the final stage."

"When?" asked Brad impatiently

"Tomorrow, once Diaz has the final coordinates."

* * *

Oval Office, Washington DC – 1000 a.m.
The Next Day

The US President was waiting impatiently in the Oval office for the Russian Ambassador. He was running ten minutes late to his annoyance. A knock on the door and the appearance of his secretary, was then followed by the Russian Ambassador.

"Mister Ambassador, you're late. You do not keep the occupant of this office waiting."

"My apologises mister President but you're traffic is bad."

"Well, lesson learnt. You should leave earlier. Now, please take a seat." The US President indicated to the sofa.

"Before we begin Mister President, I have to strongly voice Russia's concern at your missile firing yesterday. It threatens the nineteen seventy-two arms control agreement."

"Your concern is noted Mister Ambassador but we have a more important matter that we need to discuss. I'm hoping the Russian government can assist us."

"I will try. Please tell me."

"An American is being held in Moscow against her will. She is a CNN reporter and was kidnapped three days ago. Tell me that you knew this already?"

"I'm afraid I don't Mister President. This is news to me."

"Don't play the diplomat with me."

"But it is true. There may be other forces at work here to which we have no knowledge."

"You live in a secret world in Russia, nothing is done without someone somewhere monitoring what's going on. You sit there and tell me that you know nothing, well I find that hard to believe Mister Ambassador."

"Where is she being held?"

"That's the bit which is a little sketchy at the moment."

The US President knew a suspected location of where Elisabeth was being held, he also knew that the CIA were planning an assault but was reluctant at this stage to share any intelligence.

"If we do find out where she is, then I would expect the full cooperation of the Russian government and its special forces to initiate her release. Are we on the same page here Mister Ambassador?"

"Indeed, mister President."

"Make the call to your President. If he doesn't cooperate then I'm afraid he will have to deal with a greater mercy."

Both the President and the Ambassador stood up at the same time and shook each other's hand as a formal gesture.

"Is that a threat Mister President?" The Ambassador said calmly as he held onto the President's hand and looked into his eyes.

"Hopefully not. Let's just say, it's a shot across the bows."

* * *

CIA Briefing Room, US Embassy, Moscow
1800 hrs. same day

"Okay, what do have?" began the station chief to those in the room. "Bring it up on the big screen will you."

Moving the picture onto the screen, the analyst began, "Khodynka aerodrome has two runways, zero nine and twenty-seven that is constructed of concrete. Length is four thousand seven hundred and ninety feet. From any rescue point, it is long enough for any military aircraft and assault helicopters. As you can see from the satellite image, there are several aircraft by the terminal building. These look as though they are new ones waiting to be shipped out. In addition to the terminal building however, there are several hangers to store aircraft which our Russian analysts suggest would not be suitable to hold anyone and be able to defend themselves. Their option is this building." The analyst used a stick pointer to identify the main airport building."

"How old is the picture?"

"Timed an hour ago."

"Anything else?"

"There are two floors which extend either side of the building entrance. There are lots of rooms which will take time to go through but if we can see movement on the satellite image, then that could be our best chance of narrowing the location. It's our guess that if Elisabeth is here, then she is being held in this building. It offers everything to the captors. It's unlikely they'll be on the ground floor as taking the moral high ground would be their best form of defence."

"I agree. Come up with a plan and get back to me."

"Umm, who's the plan for, them or us?" Cummings knew that he meant either the CIA, FSB or Russian special forces.

"You work for the CIA, figure it out."

* * *

Khodynka, Moscow – Same Day

Being held captive was a way to reflect on life. You had no choice as there was far too much time to think about things both good and bad. Maybe not so much about what you've achieved but what you could've done better. She was pleased that she had met Jack for sure. He had changed her life completely and they were both hoping to build one together maybe in Italy but for now she knew she was in this position, indirectly because of him. She thought constantly of her family both close and distant and reminisced on her child hood with her brother and father. Tears began to roll down her cheeks through the memories which were still raw and would be until the end. The bond between father and daughter were personally treasured moments that no-one else could ever come close to understanding. There was a noise at the door as the key was inserted and then pulled open. She wiped the tears away and managed to console and compose herself when the guard came into the room with his dutiful tray and then routinely placed it on the chair. As he turned, she recognised the build and eyes as that of Neil.

"If anyone wants to be on a forced diet, this is a great place to be." She commented sarcastically

"You should be grateful you get anything at all."

"You need me to make sure that Jack does what you ask so I think feeding me is a given." Her tone was a scorning one which tipped Neil over the edge. Perhaps things weren't going according to plan or he was frustrated at the speed in which events were unfolding.

He came closer and slapped Elisabeth across her face on both sides causing her to whip her head to the right and then to the left. The second hit was more powerful than the first which caused her head to hit the wall breaking the skin on her left temple. She placed both her hands on her cheeks to soothe and comfort the pain. Then she felt the warm trickle of blood on her hands. Tears again ran down her cheeks as her eyes began to fill up and then grabbed by the sensation of pain to her head. She began to realise that all this could end badly. Once they had what they wanted, she wouldn't be needed anymore and... *That was something she didn't want to think about.*

"Stop, stop." She shouted.

"Just be quiet and you won't be harmed."

"When am getting out of here?"

"As soon as our mission has been accomplished and we'll let the embassy know where they can find you."

"So, I'll just be discarded."

"If you want to put it that way, yes."

"I saw a different person in you when we were meeting with Syromokov. What happened?"

"This was always going to happen. I'd be a fool to think that I'd get out of this alive though. The mission is complexed but they paid me well so how could I refuse. It served my purpose and hopefully I will make a change in the world."

"You'll be remembered for all the wrong reasons. Treason to your home country. Is that your legacy and contribution to the world? If you don't die here then you'll certainly have the death penalty back home. Is that what you want?"

"There's no extradition with Russia." He responded curtly.

"If you die here, you won't get your star on the wall of fame at Langley. Look back at your service with the agency. All those dedicated years and unblemished at the same time. You're a fool who was persuaded by the greed of money like most men. It's not too late to make a difference in a different way. You can make this right."

"Stop doing this. You're getting into my head." The guard put both his hands over his ears as if trying to block out anything else from Elisabeth and then kicked the chair with the swing of his right foot causing it to topple over and the tray of food to be spilled. "Yes, it is too late."
Elisabeth knew that she had hit a nerve with the guard and she could either exploit this or quit whilst she was still in one piece. If she wasn't get out of this situation herself, then she at least would want to know what is going on so she decided on the former.

"Neither of us is going anywhere anytime soon so tell me, what is going to happen that is so important to you that has convinced you it is worth giving everything up for?"

"You'll never understand."

"Try me." She tested

"The world is spending money like there is no tomorrow on projects which are futile. Space exploration is just one of those examples. It will be come to an end soon."

"How do you mean? In what way? Are you going to destroy the ISS? Is that what this is all about. Kidnap me to keep Jack out the way so he would think twice before he responds to the situation. Well, you don't know Jack as well as I do and I can assure you now, he doesn't give a damn about the fact that I'm here in this filthy squalor." She knew in her heart that it wasn't true but she hoped it would give the impression that it was, "He has a job to do and he'll be down on you like a ton of bricks."

The guard listened to what Elisabeth had to say but realised that he had said too much, again. He turned and headed back towards the door and then gave a single knock. Before the door was opened, he turned, "You'll be out soon." He said with a reassuring tone.

CHAPTER 34

CIA Briefing Room, US Embassy Moscow
Same Day

Cummings entered the room and noticed a scaled model of the terminal building at Khodynka aerodrome laid out on the table. There was also the profile of CIA agent Neil Johnson on the screen.

"Is this to scale?" Cummings began

"As much as it can be, yep." Responded one of the analysts.

"There can be no margins for error. Even down to the doors opening the right way"

"We've gone from the aerial shots to ground floor plans and we feel this is a workable model."

"Okay, go ahead. Sell it to me."

"Before I start, I looked into the name Orlov at the Kremlin. Guess what?"

"Put me out my misery, what is it?"

"It's only the name of the Defence Minister, Maksim Orlov."

"Well, well, well. I'll be damned. Keep hold of that for now. Carry on."

The analyst began to explain firstly the layout, number of rooms, stair wells & doors. He also pointed out that from a recent sat picture, there was a concentrated number of people in and around a room on the second floor. No more than three people. Plus, there was a heat signature of a single person who never came out the room. He explained that there was a strong probability that this was more likely to be where Elisabeth Young was being held captive.

"What would you give as a percentage that the reporter is in this room?"

"Ninety percent." He said confidently

"That good uh?"

"Yes sir."

"Okay. Give me a strike analysis. May have to feed this back to Jack Copeland."

"Tactics is not my forte. That'll be down to others like General Copeland."

"Okay, hold off there for now. Well done everyone."

Cummings left the room and headed back to his office. He picked up his desk phone and called a number. After a couple of clicks and switches he made a connection.

"Karl, it's Rob Cummings."

"Hey Rob. What's the latest?"

"We have the idea but not the plan. We can use our assets here but I think we'll need General Copeland to run point with this. Can we get him out here?"

"A serving military US general in Russia. Ouch, could you imagine the fallout from that. The airports are watched by domestic intelligence and it would be difficult to sneak him in at any point."

"What about local assets?"

"Not yet tapped into that. We'd need our President's support and mediation with the Russians though for that to happen. We don't know how long she has so we need to move fast."

"Leave it with me. I'll get back to you."

* * *

CIA Headquarters, Langley
Office of the Director

Karl preselected the number on his desk phone.

"Mister President." Karl began, "We have a strategic plan to assault the location where we believe that Elisabeth is being held, but we don't have the assets to initiate."

"So, what are you asking for?"

"Local military or civilian assets to work with us."

"I've already reached out to the Russian President through the Russian Ambassador here in DC. Had nothing back as yet. What's your numbers in terms of reliability that Elisabeth is where you say she is?"

"Given all the data that has been monitored and sat images that have been carefully looked through, I would say that there is a ninety percent chance we know where she is and in which room."

"Pretty good odds Karl. Okay, I can't authorise US troops from here to deploy to Russia as that would almost be seen by many as a preclude for an invasion. Let me reach out again to the Ambassador."

"Bit of a long shot mister President, but we could do with Jack Copeland out in Moscow to run quarter back on this. Any chance?"

"Hold that thought, I'll get back to you."

* * *

The White House, Oval Office

"Mister Ambassador. Thank you for coming back in again. A lot of things have happened and well, to be frank, I need your countries help."

"Is this to do with your missing reporter?"

"We know where she is being held captive but of course it's on foreign soil and we don't have the assets to be able to carry out the assault?"

"So, you would like us to help you?"

"Very smart Ambassador. I knew we'd get on."

"A joint operation is always good for training. I have the authority from my President to offer you any assistance as is necessary. We of course do not want any bad feelings between our two countries."

"The people of the US thank you for your understanding. I have one other request."

"And that is mister President?"

"I would like one of my senior military officers to run with this."

"Okay, I think that could work."

"Not from here but in Moscow."

The Ambassador sat back on the sofa as if he'd been given a body blow and was now winded.

"That is an unprecedented request mister President."

"Not really. These are unprecedented times. We both know that all our embassies around the world have military liaison officers which are intelligence led. Can we make it happen for the purposes of cooperation?" The President pointed towards his desk, "Use my phone and make the call." Having been put on the spot, the Ambassador moved awkwardly towards the President's desk and took the handset which the President had handed to him. The connection had already been requested and the Ambassador began to speak with the Russian President. After several minutes of conversation either way, the Ambassador handed the phone back to the President who placed it back on its cradle.

"Well, how did it go mister Ambassador?"

"The President has reluctantly agreed on this occasion. Your military man will be welcome in Moscow until the operation has been concluded. He will then be escorted out of our country."

"Agreed. I think that is very sensible. Thank you for your cooperation again mister Ambassador." The Ambassador accepted the acknowledgment with a simple nod of his head. As he headed back towards the door, he stopped and turned around, "Bye the way, what is the name of your military man?"

"Copeland, General Jack Copeland."

* * *

Whilst the ball was rolling, the US President had to keep things in motion now that he had the full approval at the highest level of the Russian government. Every minute wasted was a minute too long and those minutes could be translated into either failure or success. Stepping on the Russians toes was never a good idea and certainly doing anything through the back door was suicidal. Coming clean about your intentions was often good diplomacy.

"Karl, it's the President. We have a green light to use local assets in Moscow. Also, I'll be sending General Copeland as liaison officer to run quarter back on the op."

"That's great news sir. I'll pass it onto Station Chief Rob Cummings in Moscow. When will Jack be heading out?"

"First flight tomorrow. Arrange his reception, would you?"

"Consider it done mister President."

* * *

Sheremetyevo Airport, Moscow – 5.20 p.m. the same day

Copeland had caught the red eye flight out of JFK on Aeroflot SU 123 in the early hours of the morning. It was a direct flight to Moscow with a scheduled flight time of nine hours and fifteen minutes. This would give him chance to get some rest before his full attention would be needed. Copeland knew that he would have to go through at least six different time zones as he crossed over the Atlantic and anything more than three would likely affect his circadian rhythm. The flight was thirty minutes late in arriving and having cleared through international control and collected his baggage of one suitcase, he was met in arrivals by his welcoming committee of CIA station chief and local domestic intelligence staff. They didn't want to miss a beat on having a senior military figure on Russian soil and he expected to be followed everywhere he went. He also knew that he was being watched by the many cameras around the airport, but he didn't care, he was on official business after all and at the invitation of the Russian government in a roundabout way. Outside the terminal building, Copeland jumped into the official diplomatic vehicle whilst the local staff climbed into their follow vehicle. The journey time to the US embassy would be thirty-five minutes and not wanting to waste any time, Copeland jumped straight in.

"Okay, give it to me. Where are we at?"
Cummings left nothing out. He gave an overview of the Aerodrome, confirmed possible location of Elisabeth, number of hostiles, available local assets of personnel, vehicles and helicopters.

"Fantastic. Where are the assets?"

"We have the Spetsnaz second brigade on standby at Kubinka airbase. It's a hop of about twenty minutes once *'GO'* has been confirmed."

"As soon as we get to the situation room at the Embassy, let's formulate the action plan and get this executed."

"The Spetsnaz commander, Colonel Viktor Sokolov will be at the briefing."

"Good, I want Elisabeth out of there by midnight tonight."

* * *

CIA Briefing Room, US Embassy, Moscow
1930 hrs.

The room was packed with analysts, intel officers, and now Copeland and Colonel Sokolov joined in the mix giving an impression to anyone else that this gathering was a high-powered meeting. Copeland turned to Sokolov.

"Colonel, welcome. Good to have you on board."

"Thank you General. We are at your disposal."

"Okay let's get to it. What's the latest intel Rob?"

"We've been monitoring the area for a while now and we have only identified possibly three hostiles who always seem to be in these two areas." Cummings pointed to the aerial picture, "Here and here."

"Okay. What's the building used for?"

"Mainly offices. The building is due to close next year so has been winding down considerably. There's not a lot of activity going on there at the moment as you can see from these satellite images."

"What about blue prints and schematics?"

Cummings turned around to the table against the back wall, "Yep, they're over here." He said and at the same time, gathered them together and brought them back to the main table and spread them out.

"How many hostiles are we expecting to encounter?"

"We're almost sure there are three."

"Almost?" questioned Copeland

"Ninety percent sure."

"That's good enough for me. What about weapons?"

"It's a kidnap situation and it's often the case that there is limited hostiles and minimum weapon systems. It's likely they have side arms as well as barrelled weapons. No heavy stuff has been identified."

"Seems like they're not expecting visitors. Well, I have a surprise party waiting for them."
Copeland turned to his left side to where Sokolov was standing.

"Colonel, what assets do you have available?"

"Helicopters from the three hundred and seventy eighth aviation squadron and Spetsnaz personnel and ground assault troops from the twenty fourth Special Purpose Brigade should you need them. They are currently near Moscow on a tactical training exercise but can be redirected if need be."

"Do it Colonel. I need them all if I'm to contain this situation and box it off so no one has the chance to evade us. This will be a shoot to kill order. I want Elisabeth out of there alive. Understood?"
Everyone in the room either nodded or muttered acknowledgements.

Copeland went through the full mission briefing and the several phases needed to execute the action plan. The ground troops would go in first with armoured vehicles as a distraction and to be the catchers of any unknown heavy fire power that hadn't been identified. Three helicopters would be used for the Spetsnaz troops who would fast rope and enter the building through the many windows along the two sides which had been identified earlier in the briefing.

"Rob, can you make sure the analysts monitor the area in real time and send live up links to everyone. I don't want any surprises at our end. I want this to be clinical."

Cummings nodded and then looked at one of the analysts in the room as if to visually give her the responsibility. Copeland then scanned the room.

"Any questions?"

"Where will you be General?" it was Sokolov who chipped in.

"I'll be running solo but on the ground. Once I give the code word for a mission execute you guys will be on their own from launch to execute to extraction."

"When will we know we have a green light?" again it was the Colonel.

"If there are no changes to the plan and the hostiles make no changes themselves, then you'll get a green light whilst airborne. If it's a mission abort, you'll get the code issued earlier. Okay, if there are no further questions." Copeland turned towards the Colonel, "then I'd like wheels up for your helo's at twenty-three hundred hours. They need to be on station by twenty-three twenty. Your ground troops will need to be in position by twenty-three fifteen so that one event follows the next. If there's a gap then we 'll lose the edge. Once all clear and hostage is recovered, then send the code word that she's secure. I'll be in the building shortly after. Synchronise watches everyone. It's twenty forty-five" after a short pause, "Now."

Copeland had every confidence in the Russian Special Operations Forces Command [KSSO]. They'd been tried and tested and were battle-hardened forces of exceptional skill. He just hoped they weren't as ruthless as their reputation preceded them. They were often used as a clearing team which meant, no one walked out the building alive.

CHAPTER 35

The Dome, WSMR – 1055 a.m. UTC-3

Brad knew that he had hours left on the clock. He couldn't believe his luck that he hadn't been rumbled yet. It surely was a matter of time. He looked over to Diaz.

"When will the target be overhead?"

"Thirty-eight minutes."

He didn't reply. He hadn't realised it would be so soon. Whilst he had understood the reasoning for what he was about to do, he also had thoughts that it would set the developed countries back many years. Whilst Ramirez was busying himself setting up his laptop, Brad hit the button to slide the dome roof backwards. As the mechanics kicked in and the rumble of the metal on the runners began, Brad knew there was no way back. He had to go through with this, it was now or never and the more he thought about it, the more convinced he was that he was doing the right thing. As the roof locked into the fully open position, Ramirez traversed the MIRACL so that it was aligned correctly and tracking the target. With seven minutes to go, Brad heard something that made him freeze on the spot.

"Be quiet everyone. You hear that?"

"What you talking about. Can't hear...."

Suddenly there was the deep thunder noise of unmistakable helicopter rotors as they thundered through the air. It didn't sound like just one, it sounded like several.

"Get this thing fired up quickly." Brad demanded to Ramirez.

"Two minutes."

"We don't have two minutes. Fire now."

As Ramirez was about to hit the execute button, there was a whoosh sound followed by an explosion which blew a side away from the dome. Diaz had been hit by masonry and flying metal and was laid out in a strange position. He didn't look too good but that was the least of their problems. Ramirez had been knocked off his feet and to the ground. He hit his head on the side of his computer desk which dazed him momentarily. He picked himself up and held onto whatever he could to control his walk back to the computer.

"It's been knocked out of alignment." Shouted Ramirez uncontrollably as he looked at the computer screen and against the noise of the helicopters coming into view overhead.

"Fire it NOW." Screamed Brad, "This is our last chance, do it NOW."

Brad stood in the middle of the dome as Ramirez stretched over his mangled mess of what used to be his desk and pressed the execute button releasing a beam of light which shot into the sky. He knew what was coming next. He waited for what seemed like forever then he heard it; the whoosh of another released missile.

* * *

On-board the ISS

"Commander, we need a private word with you." Came the words of the flight director, Matt Roberts, "Can you switch to single comm?"
Anderson clicked the switch, "Go ahead Houston."

"We've received credible intelligence that there is a real threat to the ISS. We're not sure how or when as yet but this is being looked into."

"Looked into. That's kinda vague. What does that mean and how much time do we have?"

"There are Federal agents following on leads as we speak."

The only threats that Anderson could imagine whilst on board the ISS were those from deep space. "What we looking at here, a solar storm or are we expecting a meteor shower or something or an asteroid?"

There was a slight pause, "No. The threat is from earth and is real."

"Well that's a welcome relief." Responded Anderson sarcastically. "How can earth be a threat to us? You have to give me more than that Houston. Are we to expect a bumpy ride?"

"In some ways yes. We'll be making some correctional manoeuvres to the ISS to change your alignment so that your exposure is minimal."

"That's comforting to know but it doesn't answer my question. What's the threat? I'm responsible for the crew and this craft and I need to know if we're doomed or not."

"We'll do everything we can to make sure that it doesn't come to that. The threat is from a laser, similar to the one you have on board but is earth based. That's all we know at the moment but we need to act upon it so that we're prepared. Geo are inputting some numbers to change your profile so you will notice the ISS roll. This'll be completely normal."

"Is there anything we can do up here Houston?"

"Nothing, just buckle up and let's get through the storm."

* * *

On-board JTTF Pavelow Helicopter, New Mexico

Felix had managed to scramble together sufficient manpower to go along with Copeland's request. He had two Apache AH-64's and a Sikorsky MH-53 Pavelow helicopter loaded with ten 'Scorpion' troops and fifteen FBI JTTF personnel. He figured that'd be sufficient. They were seven minutes out.

"Target ahead." Came the words of the pilot of the Pavelow.

Looking out the side door, Felix could see that the two Apaches were flanking the Pavelow for defensive positions and to protect the Pavelow during its landing manoeuvre.

"Roof is off." Observed the pilot

Felix was gathering as much information as he could. If this was a threat then he needed to act upon it.

"Object is aligning." Pilot again commentated.

Fire Storm

"Fire a warning missile." Ordered Felix. He'd take the shit later on if this turned out to be nothing. He'd probably, no definitely would lose his job. No pension and no prospects. Not a pretty sight looking into the future.

"Missile away." Came the words from the Apache to the right of Felix.
The explosion was loud when it happened and almost buffeted his helicopter with the sound wave.

"There's still activity inside. Looks like they're about to do something. Instructions?" questioned the Apache pilot.

"Fire again."
Felix saw the plume of smoke behind the second missile as it headed towards its target. What he also saw as the missile hit was a beam of light emitted upwards from the dome. He wasn't sure what the light's intended target was but as far as Felix was concerned, he had eliminated what Copeland had sensed as a direct threat to national security. He wished that he had acted upon this sooner though. He reckoned he might just be able to hang on to his job a little longer before picking up his pension.

"Okay, take me down." Felix instructed his pilot over his head phones to land. He needed to secure the site for forensic and evidential reasons. Once on the ground, Felix went into the smouldering remains of the dome along with several of his JTTF and Scorpion staff. Sifting through the rubble, they came across three bodies. The medic in the team checked them over but gave the thumbs down indicator. Moments later there was a shout from what would've been the far side of the dome.

"Hey boss, you need to get over here."
Felix headed over to where the agent summoned him from and having climbed over rubble, furniture and twisted metal, the agent looked at the remains of the table in front of him."

"You need to see this." As he turned and pointed.

What Felix was looking at made his heart sink and the feeling of nausea begin to take hold as his stomach tightened. He was looking at a chard picture of the International Space Station along with its coordinates. Stepping to one side, Felix looked up towards the sky.

"Holly shit." Were the only words he could muster. Anything else would've been pointless and meaningless.

* * *

Khodynka Aerodrome, Moscow

It was twenty-two thirty and Copeland decided to head out to the airfield to get a feel of the area first hand. He also wanted to be there when Elisabeth had been finally rescued and that he would be the first friendly face that she would see. There were no if's or buts and Copeland was hell bent on making sure she wasn't harmed in any way. Cummings decided to join Copeland for the twenty-five-minute drive to the aerodrome. On the way, Copeland was able to get to know more about Cummings as he opened up about his life before and during his agency time. He was married with four kids, two girls and two boys. He was from a large family himself with four brothers and two sisters. He'd joined the agency by accident, one of those times of being in the right place at the right time. He'd studied Russian at the University of Illinois in Chicago. At the time, the agency was seeking linguists in Russian as part of the cold war era. Although he had never thought of a career at the agency, he was approached with an offer he couldn't refuse. Eighty thousand dollars a year, chance of travel and excellent promotional prospects. He didn't have much going for him back at home and he couldn't really explain to his family what he was intending. He went through the obligatory training in clandestine operations at Camp Peary, affectionately known as the 'Farm' near Williamsburg, Virginia. He'd headed up the Russian desk at Langley for six years and dealt with several key assets in Moscow who wanted to defect. Copeland exchanged his own bio with Cummings which certainly passed the time and before they knew it, they were two minutes from their end point.

Copeland switched off his headlights and drove cautiously through the unmanned and opened perimeter gate and stopped short at about one hundred and fifty yards from the front of the building. It was both far enough and close enough to get a good vantage point for himself and the assault later on. Having settled into position and watched the building through his single night scope for about ten minutes, he was satisfied that the rooms identified at the briefing were indeed the ones the assault teams would breech. He looked at his watch which was illuminated showing twenty-three ten hours. Knowing the helo's would be inbound, he gave the execute code word 'Moscow' over his radio. All he could do now was wait and watch as the attack was implemented in stages.

Right on cue, the assault vehicles rolled onto the ground in front of the terminal building and as was expected, shots were fired from the second-floor windows. A brilliant strategy which drew them to that side of the building and gave a confirmatory indicator as to where the hostiles were holding out. There was no heavy stuff, just 7.62 AK-47 rounds. Useless against the heavy machines of the Spetsnaz.

* * *

Inside the Terminal Building, Khodynka Aerodrome

Both widget and stretch were outside Elisabeth's room, "What's that noise?" began widget.

"Can't hear a thing. You're going crazy." Said stretch

"Be quiet, listen will you for once."
They both cocked their ears to one side and they both looked at each other when they heard the deep throaty noise of a heavy-duty vehicle.

"They're here." Added widget

"Who's they? Are we expecting someone?" questioned stretch

"It's the army you idiot." Widget offered. "I'm going to have a look. Stay here."
Widget moved past Elisabeth's room to another window almost above the entrance to the building.

Fire Storm

He crouched at first, then popped his head up to get a better look. It was a full moon which gave enough lighting for him to see four, what looked like heavy-duty military vehicles. Not tracked but wheeled, probably APC's he thought. Surely there must be more than this if they intended to assault the building. Where were the 'special forces' the Russians so readily depend on? He decided to open a window and test their response. He fired several shots at the lead vehicle which bounced off which confirmed to him that they were armoured. His weapon would have no effect on them so he decided to conserve his ammo. He waited several minutes, there was no return fire, the vehicles didn't move and nor did any contents of vehicles spill out. It then suddenly dawned on him, it was decoy. A way of dragging them all to one side of the building. He quickly rushed back to stretch leaving the window open as he went.

"It's a trap." Widget began, "They've got four vehicles out front as a distraction. They'll be coming through the back door soon, I guarantee that."

Stretch hadn't signed up for this and was starting to realise that it was about to get serious. "How we going to defend this place? There's only three of us."

"Have you not figured it out yet dummy. We're not walking out of here."

"You mean?" realism hit stretch between the eyes.

"Were you born with brains or are you naturally like this? How many mags do you have?"

"Three."

"Me too. Where's Neil?"

"He's gone to the bathroom."

"Go get him, quickly." Ordered widget.

Neil returned seconds later and was told about the vehicles that had been seen out front. He gave instructions to widget and stretch to keep an eye out the windows for anything else. Whilst they were occupied, he opened Elisabeth's door and having gone in, he closed it shut behind him. He knew they wouldn't take the risk and shoot him whilst he had their prized possession close by. He was relatively safe, for now at least.

* * *

The stillness of the night always magnified sound to a greater level than would be evident during the day and Copeland could hear the deep thud thud thud of the incoming helicopter rotors as they chopped through the late evening air. The sound always made the hairs on the back of his neck stand up. It wasn't because of the adrenaline rush, but he knew full well it was the thrill of being part of such a mighty fighting force. Copeland stepped out from his vehicle and looked beyond the building. He saw two MiL Mi-24 'Super Hind' gunships. Although he could only see their outline, he knew they'd be fully loaded as a precautionary measure. Both were flanking a MiL 17 combat transport helicopter which would have Russia's finest on board. As the MiL 17 quickly came to hover above the terminal, Copeland saw ropes being spilled out from both sides and falling onto the roof top and eight Spetsnaz troops fast roping to the roof, four from each side. The

Fire Storm

'Super Hinds' continued to fly past and began to circle the areas on the other sides. They weren't going to take any chances and they had the fire power to deal with anything thrown their way.

* * *

Widget and stretch were by the window hoping to hear at first hand any noise that would indicate trouble. Whilst peering out the window for a matter of seconds, one minute there was nothing there and the next was filled with three very large helicopters. Two had a menacing array of fire power attached to their pods slung under the wings. The third helicopter moved slowly over the building almost like a UFO mother ship crawling into position. The sound of several things dropping onto the roof made the stretch and widget uneasy. They lowered their window and began to fire their weapons towards the 'Gunships' only to find that their rounds bounced off the plating and at the same time was followed by a heavy thud on the roof as if something was about to come through.

With the window open and the deafening roar of the rotors, widget tapped the other on the shoulder and said, "Safe your rounds. Let's keep them for the soldiers on the roof when they crash through the windows. Move over there." widget pointed towards Elisabeth's room and then began to run. Stretch stayed by the window whilst widget ran in a low crouched position towards the back wall. Running low and fast caused widget to lose his balance and to stumble but he somehow managed to keep himself from falling and quickly regained his composure. Having reached the wall, he looked back towards the window and realised that stretch had stayed put.

"Get over here." Shouted widget

Stretch ignored him and he began to unclip the long box under the window and then lifted the lid. He stood looking at the contents in the box for what seemed like ages but probably was only seconds. He bent down below window height and picked up the metal cylinder together with a tube and began to assemble them. Widget ran back to the window.

"What the fuck you doing? What is this?" questioned widget although he knew the answer.

"Now who's being the dumb ass. I'm your best friend now then I take it? It's our insurance."

"You're full of surprises. Do you know which way to point this thing?"

"Very funny."

"How many do you have?"

"One." Stretch said reluctantly.

"How's that gonna work? There's three helicopters." Queried widget

"If we take one down we stand a better chance."

"Against what? I know it's dark outside but have you seen what's out there? You can hear the damn things, Gunships – hello. These things fire back with far more than you have here."

"They never said it would get to this point. That's why I volunteered. It was supposed to be an easy way of getting some money and that's why we only have one."

"Brilliant. We have AK's with three magazines each of thirty rounds and one RPG rocket to ward off Russia's finest. I'm no mathematician, but those odds don't look like anything favourable to me. Why is Neil in there in any case?" asked widget as he pointed to the hostage room, "We need all the help we can get out here. Hold everything until I get back."

Widget began to run towards where Neil was holding up when suddenly there was a blast of hot air which knocked him to the ground. He fell flat onto his front and quickly turned around to see a gunship falling to the ground with flames spouting from the engine block. *'Oh shit, what the fuck have you just done'* he said to himself. As quickly as that had happened, three grenades were thrown into the room and seconds later exploded.

CHAPTER 36

Russian Defence Ministry, Arbatskaya Square, Moscow

Maksim Orlov was the first uniformed civilian defence minister and previously the secretary of the security council of the Russian Federation. He was personally appointed to his current position in March two thousand and one by a vote of confidence from the President himself.

"What's happening? I've lost contact with Syromokov."

"We're under attack at the airfield. Is that all you can think about? It's all your fault. You delayed everything far too long and that's why we're in this shit hole right now."

"Who's attacking you?"

"No idea but we've got armoured vehicles at the front and I can hear helicopters overhead, at least two. You're the defence minister, call them off."

"That's easier said than done. I don't know who they are."

"It's got to be a military unit. Find out or it'll be too late by the time you do. This has been fucked up right from the start. You're in your plush office and you don't give a shit what happens here. We're all doomed anyway."

"Is the hostage still alive?"

"Yes, but of no use now the attack is under way."

"Can you get out with her?"

"Really, seriously, this place is surrounded. What planet are you on?" he said rhetorically, "Have you not been listening to what I've been saying?"

"It's dark and you could use the shadows to your advantage. That's your tradecraft after all."
Johnson suddenly thought that Orlov had a point. Whilst mulling it over, he heard the sound of an explosion in the next room followed by three further explosions which sounded different.

"It's like a frigging war zone here. There's no way I can get out now."

"Don't let yourself be captured. You know too much" Orlov said hesitantly and nervously.

"You're worried I'll spill, well I may just do that. I lost a career when you said this was water tight. Turns out you had nothing to offer me and this was leaking all the time. It was all about furthering your own career, sod anyone else. I'm done here. See you around." Neil looked at his phone for a split second before he cut the call and thinking had he done the right thing. He looked over towards Elisabeth who by now was cowering on her bed as if to protect herself the best she could from the sound of gunfire, explosions and masonry falling from the ceiling.

"I told you this would all end badly."

"Shut up. You're in no position to say anything."

"Looking from where I'm sat, I'd say neither are you."

Johnson looked defeated and vulnerable. He was outside of his comfort zone and hadn't a clue what to do next. He had no idea what was happening in the other room or whether or not the other two were still alive. As far as he was concerned, he was on his own.

* * *

On-Board the MiL 17 Transport Helicopter

Lieutenant Aleksandr Vasiliev had been hand-picked by Colonel Solokov to lead a team of six commandos aboard the transport helicopter. To meet the hardiest of hostiles, they were all dressed in standard black fatigues equipped with night vision goggles and an array of weapon systems. They had no real idea what they were heading into. The helicopter itself had no pods as this would've impeded the fast roping and they were escorted by two fully-loaded Hind gunships on each flank in any case. Each were equipped with a full array of rockets, missiles and a 12.7mm fixed chin turret mini-gun with one thousand four hundred and seventy rounds. It also had flares and heat diffusers for any hostile rockets or missiles. Five minutes out from the DZ, Vasiliev received radio chatter from Copeland, which simply said '*Moscow*'. He knew then that the green light had been given and the mission was a go. Vasiliev gave the thumbs up to everyone else in the chopper

Fire Storm

indicating clearance and then raised his open hand to signify five minutes out. Everyone was ready, they'd trained for occasions like this and they all had each other's back. It was a team bond that was synonymous to specialist military units. They were indeed a band of brothers.

As the helicopters approached the apron side of the terminal building, the right flank gunship, callsign Alpha one continued over the building and towards where Copeland was cited. The second one, callsign Alpha two hovered next to Vasiliev's helicopter to protect it whilst his hovered over the roof. On approach, the doors were slid open and a rope on either side was dropped quickly followed by three fast roping commandos on each side. Vasiliev would be the last pair out and as the commandos began to drop, there was automatic gun fire being fired from inside the building towards the gunship next to Vasiliev's. Rounds bounced off the armour and ricocheted deflecting them in all directions. Two stray rounds hit one of the commandos as he was half way down the rope causing him to lose his grip and fall directly onto the roof with a deep thud as he hit the building on his front. At the same time, the rounds caused the pilot to slip his stick to the right so the helicopter was slightly tilted so any further rounds would hit the bottom. Once stabilised, the pilot brought his aircraft back on point to let the last two troops drop. Before Vasiliev cleared from the aircraft, he looked down towards the commando, he wasn't moving and it didn't look good.

"One of the hostiles has gone to the back of the room," began the pilot of Alpha two. "The second one is next to the window and looks like he's up to no good. He's squatting down at the moment."

The fall of the commando distracted Alpha two pilot momentarily as he was conscious of the fact that he may fall onto the blades, "Oh shit, RPG." Came the exasperated words of the pilot as he lifted the gunship to try and evade the missile. It was already inbound and any effort was futile. The rocket hit the gearbox under the rotor causing a complete malfunction with audible tones sounding and red lights illuminating the console as system failure after failure were being reported. The engine coughed and spluttered and the pilot had no further control of the gunship or its direction. It simply fell backwards and hit the ground in a huge explosion and fire ball.

* * *

Outside the Khodynka Terminal Building

"What the fuck just happened?" came the words of Copeland to Cummings as he saw and heard the gunship go down. "Was it a missile or a malfunction?"

"No idea but in the heat of battle, anything can happen."

"That was no malfunction, it had to be an RPG. But where the fuck did they get that from?"

"Well, we are in Russia." Came the not so comforting words of Cummings. As he was saying them, Copeland, who wasn't listening to what he was saying, leapt out the vehicle and quickly jogged towards the terminal building entrance. Cummings decided to stay put. He wasn't a military man so he saw no reason to become involved in a fire fight. Even then, Copeland wasn't armed either.

On reaching the doors, he pushed them open and saw the staircase leading to the upper floors in front of him. He climbed them slowly as they came back on themselves until he reached the second level. On looking out the window, he realised it was the top floor. The smell of cordite and smoke was now intense. He was certainly on the right floor. He hoped that Elisabeth hadn't been caught in the middle of all this. He knew she was a tough cookie but there were somethings which even for the most hardened person, it can become just too much. There was a double swing door in front of him which clearly lead to the floor where the hostiles have put themselves.

The doors had round glass portals which Copeland peered through. Over to the left was a tall guy who had just thrown the tube down and picked up his AK and began to jog back to the back wall and to the right of Copeland. *'Where were the other two guys?'* he asked himself but then quickly saw a second guy over to the right where Copeland had been looking. He was shorter than the other one but armed with his own AK. As the taller guy began his run, Copeland heard three familiar thuds. He knew what they were and quickly moved away from the door and around the safety of a corner wall plugging his ears with his forefingers as he went. All three exploded at the same time. They weren't fragmentation grenades but flash grenades designed to disorientate hostiles senses with a blinding flash of light of around seven million candelas followed by an intense bang of greater than one hundred and seventy decibels. They were so effective that it was game over for those who had found themselves on the receiving end. Seconds later, Copeland heard the smashing of glass as the commandos breeched the building. He quickly peeked back through the porthole and saw the two hostiles firing at the troops who quickly neutralised them with several volleys which weren't exactly controlled shots as they splattered against the wall behind them but nevertheless, it did the trick.

* * *

After the explosions and for her own safety, Elisabeth was by now cowering under her metal bed frame. This was getting a little too heated and close for comfort. She needed to protect herself, no one else was able to. She knew that Johnson was still standing in the centre of the room but she didn't hold much hope for his survival if things became any worse. It was almost like he knew himself. Bullets began to penetrate the wall and at least two had hit Johnson. He slumped to the floor and dragged himself to the wall underneath the window and propped himself up so that he was looking back into the room and towards the door. He wanted to see if it would be his saviour or his tormentor. He also wanted to look him in the eye. Johnson knew that he'd been hit on his right leg above the knee and his left shoulder. He wasn't too concerned about those although painful, it was the sucking wound that was on his right side, which suggested a punctured lung. He was losing a lot of blood and he knew he didn't have much time left until he began to lose consciousness. He held his hand over the wound on his side to ease the discomfort and in an attempt to stem the flow. He glanced slowly towards Elisabeth in the hope that she would somehow see some empathy and come to his aid. Clearly, that was never going to happen. He'd held her captive after all and was disrespectful to her so he understood her lack of compassion. If he was honest with himself, then he hoped no one would save him as the options for his life from here, didn't seem too appealing.

* * *

After the gunfire died down, Copeland gave chatter on the radio to Vasiliev letting him know that he was in the building. Last thing he wanted was blue on blue. He slowly opened the double doors and moved into the room where he looked around to survey the carnage. The two hostiles were slummed against each other. Copeland hugged Vasiliev for a job well done.

"That's a little premature Jack. We need to locate the third one that's still out there. There's also the hostage."

Whilst he knew that it was the wrong thing to do, he was nevertheless pleased that Vasiliev and his troops had breached the building bringing them a step closer to ending this once and for all, "Lots of explosions tonight Alex, were there any casualties?"

"It was a heavy night. We lost one commando on the roof who was hit by stray bullets and the two crew of the gunship that was taken down by the RPG. They all know the dangers on each task. War has casualties whether on the good side or the bad one."

"Indeed. I'm indebted to you Alex. We now need to find Elisabeth and the third hostile."

Alex pointed to the room behind the two dead hostiles indicating this to be the room. A quick check of the door soon became apparent that it was locked. Copeland and Vasiliev decided not to use any charges as this would most likely cause injury to those in the room since it was a small room in any case. One of the commandoes checked the pocket of the dead hostiles and came up with a key ring with two keys on it. Having tested which one, they unlocked the door and then swung it open whilst at the same time two commandos stormed in with guns at the ready to neutralise any threat. With guns lowered, Copeland and Vasiliev walked into the room. He wasn't too fussed about Johnson, he wanted to make sure Elisabeth was safe and unhurt. He quickly walked to her as she came out from under the bed and they cuddled and kissed each other in a warm and loving embrace. It'd been a long time since they'd seen each other but he had something else that he needed to attend before they could have time together. He gave her another kiss then turned towards Johnson. He wasn't looking in good shape, he was wheezing and leaking. Copeland bent down to his level.

"Well, we finally meet agent Johnson. You're currently MIA and probably KIA soon but on the wrong side. Before that happens, we're going to have a little chat where I ask you some questions and you give me the answer that I need. Is that a fair game?"

Johnson nodded whether in agreement or not.

"Let's start from the very beginning which I often feel is the best place so that I can get a better understanding for my own peace of mind."

Elisabeth was now sat on the edge of her bed once again and Vasiliev gave her a blanket to wrap around her shoulders. Shock has a funny way of dealing with situations. It can happen straight away or can be delayed. It can also be a killer.

"You have nothing to lose by cooperating and equally you have nothing to gain either. Your demise is guaranteed but I'm sure you'd rather go out knowing that you have slightly redeemed yourself and done good in the end. Are we on the same page here?'

Again, Johnson nodded his acknowledgement of the question. Copeland hoped that he would get what he needed from Johnson before his lights went out.

"What was the end game?"

Johnson, coughed slightly and his voice was wheezing, "To destroy the space station."

"Why? For what purpose. It benefits the world over in its research capabilities."

"It had nothing to do with that. It was so that its own laser couldn't be used."

"Who would gain from this?"

"The Russian." He coughed again and blood splattered on his clothing, "government."

Copeland looked at Vasiliev and silently asked for the medic to temporarily patch him up. The medic stepped forward and cut away his clothing around the wound. He then ripped open a sachet of seal powder, which the medic sprinkled onto the wound with the intention that it would quickly form a scab and stop the bleeding. Moments later, the wheezing had stopped and Copeland knelt back down to begin again,

He looked glancingly across to Elisabeth and then back again before saying, "Why Elisabeth?"

"We knew that if we had her that you would think twice about becoming involved and stopping us."

"Who's we?"

"I only ever spoke to him on the phone. Never met him."

"Is he Russian or American?"

"Russian."

Copeland was thinking that this may well go to the top.

"Was he government himself?"

"I think so."

"Which department."

"I was told defence but I can't confirm."

"You're CIA. You must've had an idea. You don't leave lose ends."

"I was suspicious for sure, but I'm sure he was defence."

"What was Syromokov's involvement?"

"We needed him because of the space programme involving the two Cosmonauts."

"But they didn't do anything."

"In the end no."

"What were they supposed to do?"

"Use the laser on the ISS to hold earth to ransom."

"That's a bit far-fetched and science fiction stuff and a bit of a tall order. All we'd have to do is knock the station out."

"We'd neutralise the land-based lasers first. Then we'd have total control."

"Oh my god." Shouted Elisabeth as she stood up from her bed and put her hands up to her mouth. Everyone in the room looked towards her, "You're worse than I imagined. You're evil. You deserve to die yourself. What is wrong with you people. Why can't we all live in peace instead of trying to tear everyone apart. For what? No one gains very much in the end. Your scheme is proof of that." Elisabeth moved towards Johnson and bent down, "You failed in the end." She stood up and spat towards Johnson before walking back and sitting on her bed. Disgusted with herself, but she felt better for it. Copeland was surprised at Elisabeth's outburst but silently gave her his support considering what he would've done to him himself was far worse. The difference was that he needed answers to so many questions and whilst he despised the man, he was key to finishing this off.

"Just so that you know, your little stunt was a failure. The ISS wasn't destroyed and you went

through all this for nothing. You're a traitor, you're an embarrassment and you're a complete failure."
Johnson coughed again, "I'm flattered."

"We can make some of this good so that you don't come out of this so shameful but you have to meet me half way. You know how it works."

"How's that?"

"Well, give me a name for starters."

Johnson looked straight ahead. He wasn't focusing on anything in particular. His eyes were fixated on the door almost trance like.

"Orlov. Does that mean anything to you?"

His eyes flinched in recognition of the name but he remained silent.

"Was he the one orchestrating all this? Was he the power player?"

Johnson nodded. His silence was all that Copeland needed. He stood up and he knew what he had to do next. He stepped out the room and thumbed through his contacts on his cell before selecting one and making the call.

* * *

After being patched up by the medics and two days later, both Copeland and Elisabeth were given a police escort to Sheremetyevo Airport to ensure that they departed the country as requested. Any longer and they would've over stayed their invitation. Neither were disappointed, in fact they were both relieved. They said their farewells to everyone involved and gave their condolences to the families of those who'd been lost for the greater good. This was a series of events they both wanted to put behind them. Copeland looked towards Elisabeth in the back of the car.

"It's funny how some events bring people closer together especially when it involves those two very same people."

Elisabeth didn't say anything in response. Her actions spoke louder than words. She dropped her head onto his shoulder snuggling up in an embrace which said more than he needed to know.

CHAPTER 37

Pentagon Command Centre – Next Day

The recovery of the ISS will take far longer than imagined. Currently in low orbit, redundant and a shell of its original creation, it will need to be nurtured and brought back to earth within a controlled environment. Most of it would burn up as it entered the atmosphere. The most hazard part of a space flight has always been the return journey even when it is piloted, but one without a pilot just makes it ten times worse. The space station must hit the upper atmosphere at exactly the right angle, and it only gets one chance. The ISS will need to enter the atmosphere at four hundred thousand feet and at a speed of twenty-two times the speed of sound with a tilt of forty degrees. Parts of the ISS will break off the main structure during re-entry including the solar panels as it will be hit by a wind speed of around one thousand seven hundred miles per hour and a temperature near to one thousand five hundred degrees Celsius stripping electrons from the atoms in the surrounding atmosphere. Communication will be lost with the station at this point as there will be a zone of electromagnetic disturbance. This will last for approximately seventeen or more minutes as it loses three feet of height for every fifteen feet covered.

Looking like a lame duck, it no longer functions as it was originally intended. It was an icon of modern technology and innovation where the worlds brightest created a laboratory for the benefit of the world over. Recovery will be time consuming and expensive but it cannot remain in orbit as space junk indefinitely; there's enough out there already. Copeland was looking at the massive screens in the Pentagon Command Centre as pictures were being streamed back from the inspection vessel sent to capture the scale of the damage inflicted on the station. The ISS was a new chapter in scientific research with a life expectancy of twenty-five years but as a weaponised outpost, it became vulnerable to those who had a different agenda and who exploited its vulnerabilities and capabilities as a means to an end for political, personal or for financial gains. It didn't matter what their agenda really was, but they achieved a massive set back in scientific research in both cost and time. NASA would not make the same mistake twice and future research would be conducted on the surface of the moon and as a joint venture with other like-minded nations.

* * *

The White House, Pennsylvania Avenue – Washington

"Jack.", the President began having made the call to Copeland, "The country is indebted to you once again. Your knack at seeking out trouble has been both underestimated and invaluable. My own sense of doubt at the beginning was totally unfounded and if I had listened to your convictions, then I'm sure this matter would've been resolved sooner rather than later."

"Mister President, you don't have to apologise. I was doing my duty but if truth be known, I had doubts myself that something like this could've been pulled off. We always like to think the best in people but even the smartest cookies can turn the tables in the blink of an eye."

"You'll get the Congressional medal of honour for this Jack in recognition of your acts of valour, courage, gallantry and a selfless act which went above and beyond the call of duty. You're a hero; you saved this country, in fact you saved the whole world from an unthinkable obliteration and annihilation from a madman. Armageddon doesn't even come close. Enjoy the moment while you can. They don't come around that often."

"Thank you, Mister President. It was a team effort overall."

"Indeed, it was, but led by you at the helm. It's well deserved. Don't be too proud on yourself as I might change my mind although the country will never forgive me for it. So, what's next for you?"

"I'll be taking some time out and well-earned leave. It's been a while since I had a real break."

"Anywhere nice?"

"I'm taking Elisabeth to Italy. It's a place we both love very much. She had a raw deal during the time she was in the hands of her captors. She needs a rest too and time to heal. In fact, we need time together to reflect on things."

"When are you two getting hitched by the way? I could do with a good wedding to brighten things up around here. If there is one other thing which is overdue, it's got to be that."

"Is there ever a right time?" I believe in spontaneity though."

"Good luck with that one. Elisabeth will let you know when the time is right and you'll be able to sense it yourself too. You're good at sensing things Jack and I only wish I had your intuition, so don't fail on this mission son. There's no EVAC procedure for this; you're on your own."

"Roger that, Mister President."

* * *

Grand Hotel Convento di Amalfi, Italy
2 days later

Copeland and Elisabeth arrived at Naples International Airport after a ten-hour flight connected through London. The Pentagon had arranged with the US Consulate in Naples for an official vehicle to meet them and take them to their hotel. Liaison with the Italian government allowed for Copeland and Elisabeth to fast track immigration. They were met on the tarmac and sped away as quickly as possible for the one-and-a-half-hour journey to their hotel. The US Consulate had arranged with the Ministry of Interior for a police escort to ensure they were not impeded. Their baggage would follow on later; Copeland after all was a hero and he wanted for nothing. He could name his price. Whilst that was a great situation to be in, he knew that he had the most precious item with him and nothing else mattered at that moment. As the scenery passed by, Copeland's cell rang disturbing the calmness of the journey. He looked at the number which he didn't recognise.

"Copeland." He answered.
"He's been located." The caller simply said.
"Okay, do it."
"What's the script?"
"Complete deniability."
"Good enough for me. Consider it done. This'll be my last call."
Elisabeth looked towards Copeland, "Who was that?"

"Just some unfinished business." He took Elisabeth's hand and looked her in the eye, "Now let's enjoy our holiday."

EPILOGUE

President Reagan's remarks following the loss of the Space Shuttle Challenger and her crew.

Broadcast at 5 p.m. EST, Jan 28, 1986.

"Ladies and gentlemen, I'd planned to speak to you tonight to report on the state of the Union, but the events of earlier today have led me to change those plans. Today is a day for mourning and remembering.

Nancy and I are pained to the core by the tragedy of the shuttle Challenger. We know we share this pain with all of the people of our country. This is truly a national loss.

Nineteen years ago, almost to the day, we lost three astronauts in a terrible accident on the ground. But we've never lost an astronaut in flight; we've never had a tragedy like this. And perhaps we've forgotten the courage it took for the crew of the shuttle; but they, the Challenger Seven, were aware of the dangers, but overcame them and did their jobs brilliantly. We mourn seven heroes: Michael Smith, Dick Scobee, Judith Resnik, Ronald McNair, Ellison

Onizuka, Gregory Jarvis, and Christa McAuliffe. We mourn their loss as a nation together.

For the families of the seven, we cannot bear, as you do, the full impact of this tragedy. But we feel the loss, and we're thinking about you so very much. Your loved ones were daring and brave, and they had that special grace, that special spirit that says, "Give me a challenge and I'll meet it with joy." They had a hunger to explore the universe and discover its truths. They wished to serve, and they did. They served all of us.

We've grown used to wonders in this century. It's hard to dazzle us. But for 25 years the United States space program has been doing just that. We've grown used to the idea of space, and perhaps we forget that we've only just begun. We're still pioneers. They, the members of the Challenger crew, were pioneers.

And I want to say something to the schoolchildren of America who were watching the live coverage of the shuttle's take-off. I know it is hard to understand, but sometimes painful things like this happen. It's all part of the process of exploration and discovery. It's all part of taking a chance and expanding man's horizons. The future doesn't belong to the fainthearted; it belongs to the brave. The Challenger crew was pulling us into the future, and we'll continue to follow them.

I've always had great faith in and respect for our space program, and what happened today does

Fire Storm

nothing to diminish it. We don't hide our space program. We don't keep secrets and cover things up. We do it all up front and in public. That's the way freedom is, and we wouldn't change it for a minute. We'll continue our quest in space. There will be more shuttle flights and more shuttle crews and, yes, more volunteers, more civilians, more teachers in space. Nothing ends here; our hopes and our journeys continue.

I want to add that I wish I could talk to every man and woman who works for NASA or who worked on this mission and tell them: "Your dedication and professionalism have moved and impressed us for decades. And we know of your anguish. We share it."

There's a coincidence today. On this day 390 years ago, the great explorer Sir Francis Drake died aboard his ship off the coast of Panama. In his lifetime the great frontiers were the oceans, and an historian later said, "He lived by the sea, died on it, and was buried in it." Well, today we can say of the Challenger crew: Their dedication was, like Drake's, complete.

The crew of the space shuttle Challenger honoured us by the manner in which they lived their lives. We will never forget them, nor the last time we saw them, this morning, as they prepared for their journey and waved goodbye and "slipped the surly bonds of earth" to "touch the face of God."

The tragedy of the space shuttle, Columbia, destroyed on re-entry on 01 Feb 2003, highlighted the dangers faced by these intrepid explorers. This was the second loss of a space shuttle and its crew. The first being the space shuttle, Challenger during its launch on 28 Jan 1986 with the loss of its seven crew members who assumed great risk in the service of all humanity. It was left to the then President, George W Bush to address the nation. "

"My fellow Americans, this day has brought terrible news and great sadness to our country. At 9.00 a.m. this morning, Mission Control in Houston lost contact with our Space Shuttle Columbia. A short time later, debris was seen falling from the skies above Texas. The Columbia is lost; there are no survivors."

'LEST WE NEVER FORGET THEM AND ALL THE OTHER INTREPID EXPLORERS WHO SACRIFCE THEIR LIVES FOR THE BENEFIT OF OTHERS'

How To Become A Master Problem Solver

Develop Great problem solving and decision-making skills

JAY RUSH

CRITICAL INFORMATION

I am glad you are here. If what you are looking for is quick and effective knowledge that gives results, then you have the right book.

If what you are looking for is result oriented information without any beating around the bush, this book is for you.

I pride myself in delivering books that are simple and deliver results in the fastest possible time.

That is why my books are valuable, you will always get more than you pay for them. More often than not, you will get more than 100 times what you paid for my books and other materials if you put them into practice.

My name is Jay Rush.... I deliver fast effective results.

FREE COURSE:

3 DAY COURSE ON LEGACY

How to be remembered long after you leave the earth

Just to say Thank You for investing in my book, I'd like to give you this course for free.

Get this course if you want to be remembered in life because too many people die with no legacy.

Get the course for **FREE**

Other books by Jay Rush

Three Steps To Explosive Success

Contents

INTRODUCTION 8

CHAPTER ONE: THE VALUE OF PROBLEM SOLVING .. 14

CHAPTER TWO: ANYONE CAN SOLVE PROBLEMS 28

CHAPTER THREE: FIRST KEY OF MASTER PROBLEM SOLVERS 44

CHAPTER FOUR: SECOND KEY OF MASTER PROBLEM SOLVERS 59

CHAPTER FIVE: THIRD KEY OF MASTER PROBLEM SOLVERS 73

CHAPTER SIX: FOURTH KEY OF MASTER PROBLEM SOLVERS 85

CHAPTER SEVEN: PRACTICE MAKES PERFECT 98

INTRODUCTION

The world is full of problems. It is also full of people who have problems.

Think of anything at all, I can bet that it has problems associated with it.

For instance:

Marriage has marriage problems, businesses have business problems, countries have national problems.

There are childbirth problems, financial problems, relationship problems, parenting problems, communication problems and the list goes on and on.

If there is an abundance of anything in this world, then it is surely problems. They abound in every corner of the world we live in.

Recently, I saw a country that had a sanitation problem. There was filth all over the cities of the country to the extent that the government had now given up.

You could see the frustration on the faces of the officials. They had no clue as to how to make the problem disappear.

They had spent so much money on the problem, yet the problem prevailed. There is a lesson to be learned there: problem solving is not about throwing money to the problem. They had to pick up that lesson the hard way.

Even though they had spent millions of dollars on the sanitation problem, the situation remained the same.

It was not until they appointed a man who many felt was unqualified for the job, that their sanitation problem was solved.

Many of us would have rejected that man too. He had no knowledge on sanitation or experience in the sector. Actually, the only reason he got the job was that the man who recommended him to the president said he was a problem solver.

Within three months of his appointment, the sanitation problem that had plagued the country for decades was solved. Not only was it solved, it was solved permanently.

That man is part of a rare breed of master problem solvers. When the other problems he had solved became public news, the populace now gave him the resect he deserved.

Master problems solvers may not be your typical go to guy, but they have one skill that they have developed to its peak.

The skill of problem solving.

Problem solvers are valuable. The bring solutions wherever they go and are paid for their problem-solving skills.

Problem solving is a valuable skill. If you are a master problem solver, you will solve your personal problems, then progress to solving family, community, national and international problems.

You will begin to enjoy life because of the invaluable skill of problem solving you possess.

The skill which this book will impart to you.

Problem solvers are a rare breed. That is why there are so many problems and so little solutions.

It is because there are not many problem solvers in our current world. Majority of the people are just adding to the problems.

The aim of this book is to turn you into a problem solver. Not just an ordinary problem solver, but a master problem solver.

Your legacy as a master problem will transcend generations and you will be adored by many.

Problem solving can be studied and practised till one becomes very good at it.

Once the skill is perfected and the necessary tools developed to aid the process of problem solving, life will become better for you and every one you come into contact with.

Welcome to the making of a master problem solver.

CHAPTER ONE: THE VALUE OF PROBLEM SOLVING

Problem solving is valuable.

The value of problem solving comes in many ways.

There is the monetary value of solving problems, there is the social value of solving problems and there is the personal value of solving problems. There are many more intangible values that accrue to the problem solver.

When a person thus becomes a problem solver, and a master problem solver at that, he or she is sure to enjoy all these valuable things that problem-solving presents.

Let us go deeper into the value problem solving brings to the problem solver.

Monetary value of problem solving.

Problem solving has monetary gains. In the economic world, solving problems has money associated with it.

People are paid to solve problems. The bigger the problem you solve, the bigger the pay check you go home with.

That is why it is important you become a master problem solver regardless of where you are today on that ladder.

Take a look at all the major problem solvers in the world, they all had some monetary gain in one way or the other.

From Henry Ford to Jack Ma to Thomas Edison, they all made significant money solving problems.

The people in your community you are praising for having so much money are simply problem solvers.

They are rewarded for the problems they solve.

These people are not just existing, they are identifying problems and solving them, hence the monetary again you see in their lives.

You will join their ranks soon as you diligently finish this book.

Problem solving has huge value in terms of money, especially when you solve problems for the right people.

Solving problems for the wrong people may not give you any money at all, so take note of the people you solve problems for.

Look at Engineers and architects who solve structural problems for the building of huge stadiums and other edifices.

The money they are paid for such work is enormous. Some people may never be able to earn such amounts in five lifetimes.

Let me use a story to illustrate the point I am making about the monetary value of problem solving:

A rich man had a daughter who was very sick. His daughter meant the world to him. Despite the many medical interventions for his daughter, none seemed to work.

He had spent so money to no avail.

Finally, he announced that anyone who could heal his daughter would receive half of his estate.

He felt that was enough motivation to bring out the best medical problem solvers.

He was willing to put half of all he owned down for whoever could solve the problem of his daughter's health.

Sure enough, that motivated several people to attempt finding the solution until finally an elderly man found the cure to his daughters' ailment.

This man was rewarded so well that his financial fortunes changed.

His problem-solving ability had given him monetary gain.

There are problems in this world with monetary gain looking for problem solvers to tackle them.

Can we count on you to solve some of these problems and take away the gain associated with it?

Social Value of problem solving

Apart from the monetary gains of solving problems, there is also the aspect of social value.

Problem solvers tend to be recognised and rewarded in their communities for the problems they solve.

You would see schools named after them, statues erected in their honour or even streets in their name.

Their popularity tends to increase too, because whenever the solution is mentioned, the problems solvers are spoken about in the same breadth.

Sometimes, their names are known when even the faces of these individuals are not known. Talk of names preceding people.

This is akin to the famous story of David defeating Goliath. Goliath had become a huge problem. He was a problem that no man had attempted to solve in the whole of Israel. They thought themselves incapable of solving such a gigantic problem.

When David heard of the monetary gain as well as the other incentives associated with defeating Goliath, he stepped forward to the task of solving the "Goliath problem".

Indeed, he was able to defeat Goliath.

This feat gave him a lot of social benefits. Songs were composed about him, women sang his name across the country and men hailed him and wished they were him.

Children had not even come in.

The children adored him and recited his story every day. He was a hero, a hero who is still idolised in societies today because of the problem he solved.

May you solve such a problem to receive world acclaim. Nonetheless, if even the skills you learn only help you solve your personal problems, it would still be a great achievement.

Problem solving opens doors for the problem solver. Places they never thought they could go become easily accessible to them once they solve problems.

I remember clearly a young boy who met the president of Ghana just because he had solved the water problem of his community using a technique he had read in a book.

He became an instant hero in his community and the country. Scholarships were given to him from every corner, they overwhelmed him.

His name became a household name, and the only reason it had happened was because he had solved a community problem.

This emphasizes the fact that the bigger the problem you solve, the bigger the societal value you will get from solving them.

There is social value in solving problems and becoming a problem solver.

Some people live for it because, their names can transcend generations because of the problems they solve.

Though dead, there are many problem solvers who continue to live in the hearts and lips of many people.

Personal value of problem solving

Problem solving has personal value for the problem solver.

One thing about problem solving is that it gives you so much confidence that you begin to believe there is no problem you cannot solve.

Take it from me. Every problem solver of great acclaim didn't just get there.

They started by solving little problems and honing their skills. The confidence and self esteem they derived from early problem solving is what urged them on to tackle bigger problems.

The invaluable skills, insights and processes they acquired in problem-solving cannot be valued in monetary terms.

You could say that they are priceless. The experience of problem solving and the stories the problem solver gets to tell are also of great value.

Think of yourself and the things you reminisce, they fill your heart with such unspeakable joy.

Such is the feeling of problem solvers when they also begin to think about the problems they have solved, their impact on people, the challenges they went through, the bottlenecks, the opposition and the people who supported them.

These are great memories to have in hindsight.

Another great thing problem solvers gain in terms of value are the relationships they establish as a result of the problems they solve.

Some meet their lifetime partners as a result, others meet strategic people who are able to help them forge the futures they dream of.

There are countless people who have had strategic relationships because of the problems they solved.

Some of these relationships, the problem solvers are aware they would never have come into contact with had it not been for their problem-solving activities.

Such things are invaluable to the problem solver and every problem solver will have his or her fair share of personal benefits.

Much of it will be within him or her but such benefits are the toughest to come by. Afterall, you cannot buy joy in the market place.

Now that you know how valuable problem solving is, it is time to make yourself a problem solver, not only that, a master problem solver.

Let us venture into deeper waters and get closer to our goal of becoming master problem solvers.

CHAPTER TWO: ANYONE CAN SOLVE PROBLEMS

Anyone can solve problems once they understand the problem-solving process.

Many have not even bothered to find out the process of problem solving or even attempted solving problems properly.

They have kept doing what they feel like the best process for solving problems.

Knowledge they say is power and every knowledge required for every endeavour is present on this earth, unless you are not looking for it.

Now that you know you can solve problems by understanding the problem-solving process, let us go through that process so that you are well acquainted with it.

After that, you can practise problem solving with it for a while to assure yourself of basic problem-solving skills.

The next chapter will begin the training for master problem solving. For now, know that this chapter is just the basic problem-solving process everyone must know and understand.

Process of solving Problems

I will try to explain the problem-solving steps for you below so that you can easily embark on problem solving journeys. Let's go!

Step 1: Identify and Understand the Problem

It is often said that "Identifying the problem is half the problem solved".

This is so true in most situations.

Many people, organisations and countries agree that they have a problem but cannot accurately determine what exactly the problem is.

This then makes it difficult for them to even think of moving to the next step of finding solutions which is essentially what problem solving is.

To make the scenario clearer, imagine your car does not start in the morning. You have money to pay anyone who can solve the problem for your car to start so you call your electrician.

He tries all he can but cannot tell what the problem is, let alone solve it.

You call several others and they still cannot figure out where the problem is coming from.

This leaves you frustrated for weeks and months as you cannot drive the car, although you have money to pay for the solution to the problem.

The people you brought in begin to buy and change different parts of your car to no avail. Wasting your money and your time.

Finally, someone comes in that determines the problem, a very simple problem. Within 15 minutes he solves the problem.

This is remarkable, many people could not solve the problem after several weeks and months of trying, not because they didn't have the ability to solve the problem, but because they could not identify what the problem was in the first place.

These rendered all their other abilities useless.

Identifying what exactly the problem is when solving problems requires effort, knowledge and understanding.

Most of the time, people state problems in generalities. You, the problem solver is the one who must identify what the real issues are.

You must know and understand how the system you are working on operates, so that you can pinpoint exactly what the problem is.

For our example, you must know how a car starts and what it requires to start. Then you can test all the elements involved to determine the problem.

You must understand what can cause such problems as well as what cannot cause such problems. This knowledge will lead you to quickly move on from step one of identifying and understanding the problem.

Now that you have an idea of how to identify and understand problems, let us move on to the next step.

Step 2: Brainstorm Possible Solutions and Evaluate

After identifying and understanding the problem, you need to table possible solutions to it.

There is a saying that "there are many ways to kill a cat". For that reason, you need to look at different ways of solving the problem you have identified.

You can normally find solutions by brainstorming and asking yourself questions like "how can this problem be solved?" then you list a as many solutions that come to you as possible.

The list of possible solutions is to give you options to choose from and the opportunity to look at all the solutions and see which one is the best for the problem.

Choosing the best solution out of the many can only come after you have evaluated your possible solutions.

Evaluation of the solution requires several metrics to measure the solutions against.

One of the metrics you can look at when evaluating possible solutions is cost. Some solutions are very good but may cost too much.

Other solutions may also be very good but cost little. This helps to choose a great and affordable solution if that is what is needed.

Another metric is the time factor of implementing solutions. Some solutions may require too much time whiles other solutions can be implemented quickly. If speed is of the essence, then it makes choosing the faster project the obvious choice.

In the evaluation stage, you have to also consider the advantages and disadvantages of each solution as well as their strength and weaknesses.

This will ensure that the best solution possible is chosen out of the lot.

There are several reasons why many solutions must be tabled before one is selected.

One reason is that, sometimes one solution can cause other problems elsewhere when being implemented, thus it would not be suitable.

Another reason why many possible solutions are needed is that parties involved in the solution must be mostly happy with the solution to be implemented.

There will be the need for several solutions in case there is disagreement with one solution.

A country experienced a prolonged power crisis due to the inefficiency of their hydropower generation system.

They needed a solution to it, so they tabled many solutions to solve the crisis.

Some suggested the building of another dam, others suggested the building of thermal plants, another came up with the idea of a power barge.

They analysed the pros ad cons of all these solutions and finally chose the power barge as it was the quickest to implement though it was more expensive.

The good thing though is that they had many possible solutions to choose from.

What they chose was based on the metric of time, which was the most important to them and their citizenry at that moment.

Step 3: Choose and execute the best solution

Once the evaluation of the possible solutions is done, you have to choose the best solution and execute it.

The choice of the solution to execute can be based on several factors predetermined before starting the problem-solving process.

At the end of the day, the best solution is the one that takes into account the factors that are important to the one that needs the solution.

The best solution for one party may not necessarily be the best solution for another party.

That is why the considerations of the one you are solving the problem for are important. While some want speed of completion, others may prefer affordability of the solution with no regard to time of completion.

After the solution is chosen, the execution is as important as the other process.

If done well, all are able to smile. If done haphazardly, questions will be raised about the competence of the problem solver.

The solution might be good, but if not executed well, it may work against the problem solver.

That is why you, the problem solver must ensure that the best work is always done. This will protect your reputation and integrity.

Now that you understand the basic problem-solving process, it is time to learn the keys that will make you a master problem solver.

Before then, here is a problem and how the process was used to solve it.

Case study of a personal problem

Dennis cannot pay his rent. This has happened for over 3 years. He is always behind on his rent. That is his problem and he needs a solution.

Let us solve it using the steps.

1. Identify and understand the problems

Although Dennis thinks his problem is that he cannot pay his rent, his actual problem is that his income is not enough.

2. Brainstorm possible solutions and evaluate

He can do one of the following things:

1. Add a part-time job to his existing job to make additional income.

2. Start an online business

3. Initiate a passive income stream

4. Start a rental business

5.Upgrade his qualification to get a better job and income

Upon evaluation of the solutions and his needs, a passive income stream is what he needs based on his time limits.

3. Choose and execute the best solution

A passive income opportunity is identified and worked on three hours a day for 3 weeks.

Soon, he starts earning extra income.

After months of hard work, his passive income has exceeded his present income.

His rent is no longer a problem, he even pays in advance.

Problem solved.

By now, I believe you can implement the basic problem-solving steps.

Now, on to what master problem solvers do.

CHAPTER THREE: FIRST KEY OF MASTER PROBLEM SOLVERS

Master problem solvers do four things very well. In this chapter, we will talk about the first of such things.

By the time you are done understanding these four things in the rest of the chapters, you will become a master problem solver.

The four things master problem solvers do very well are:

1. They simplify problems

2. They build capacity

3. They execute solutions with speed and thorough precision

4. They do not know how to give up

Simplifying problems

The first key of master problem solvers that makes them unique is their ability to simplify problems.

If you want to become a master problem solver, you must learn how to simplify complex things all the time.

Some people are gifted with making simple things complex, but master problem solvers know how to do the reverse.

They make complex things simple.

This is what makes them so unique and enables them solve many problems that they encounter in their lifetime.

The truth is only one, master problem solvers solve many problems because they know how to simplify. They keep thigs simple.

Below are some of the ways master problem solvers simplify problems.

Learn them and add them to your arsenals so that you can also become a master problem solver.

They simplify difficult tasks

This is very important. Many people do not know how to simplify difficult tasks. They do not even think to do it.

Simplification is a basic mindset of master problem solvers. They always simplify difficult tasks. It is part of their nature to simplify.

When you talk to a master problem solver and inform him that your problem is that you cannot raise $10,000, just then he will seek to simplify the problem for you.

This is how a master problem solver will approach the simplification of raising $10,000:

$10, 000 is just a few units of $1,000. Only ten units I suppose. Is $1,000 dollars simple enough for you to raise?

If the first $1,000 can be raised, the rest can be raised.

If the $1,000 seems daunting to the one in need, he simply makes it 100 units of $100. If $100 seems fine with the one in need, the problem is solved using that as basis.

If the first $100 can be raised, the rest can be raised.

So, in case you want to solve your own money problems of perhaps raising an extra $1,000 for a project.

Do it like a master problem solver. Use simplification.

$1,000 is simply a few units of $10 or $100.

When you see things that way, you do not waste you $10 or your $100.

Many people can raise $10 or $100 but they feel $1,000 may be above reach.

They do not know that once you can raise $10 or $100, them you can raise a $1,000.

When you simplify, you are able to achieve. It is as simple as that.

One day I met a young man who had just completed his house. I asked him how he was able to do it.

He said something interesting.

"Someone gave me 50 pieces of blocks and asked me to start a building with it.

I started and figured I could build my house 50 blocks at a time."

You see, 10,000 blocks and 1000 bags of cement looked daunting, but 50 blocks was simple enough for him to start from.

He started because someone pushed him into the simplification agenda.

A house is just a matter of a few blocks. That was his simplification idea and it worked. Let us move on to other simplification techniques of master problem solvers.

They make the daunting look easy

Master problem solvers make daunting tasks look easy. There is nothing they consider beyond their reach.

They believe every problem can be solved given the right tools and personnel.

In their communication, they make daunting and complex things look very easy to accomplish.

They do this by their use of words and their actions.

Have you ever heard people narrating their problems before? They can talk for two hours just to let you know the problem they are facing.

At the end of the day, you can simply say their problem in one word.

Capital.

All they needed was capital to do their business.

If care is not taken, these people will cause you to even lose every sense of problem-solving ability in you because of how daunting they will make the problem seem.

One day a woman narrated her problems to me, I simplified the problem for her.

Guess what she did, she attacked me for not understanding what the problem was.

Till date, she is still facing that problem whiles I have helped countless others overcome that same problem.

To become a master problem solver, you need to make the daunting look easy. On to the next simplification approach.

They break processes down

Master problem solvers have a way of breaking processes down.

They can break a complex process into various components and identify which one must be dealt with and which one is okay.

When they are confronted with business growth challenges, they will breakdown the process of the business and simplify it for all to understand and know where the problem is coming from.

One day I was asked to help a business increase their revenue.

When I got there, I asked for their revenue making process. They manager spoke for hours without really pointing out any simple and straightforward process.

After hearing him out, I used 10 minutes to draw out a simple process for them and broke it down into components.

After the breaking down process, I realised their lead generation was the problem and instituted a simple lead generation system.

Within two months, their sales had doubled.

To become a master problem solver, learn to break down processes so that you can know where to work on and for the work t be easier to do.

The divide huge tasks into smaller bits

When confronted with a huge task, a master problem solver will break the task down into smaller chunks and accomplish them little by little.

This way, a sense of progress is achieved when the smaller chunks are completed.

This is a far better method than trying to do the whole task at once.

Take writing a book for instance, if broken down into chapters, every chapter written gives a sense of progress and accomplishment and the motivation to write the next chapter.

This is far better than trying to write the whole book as one unit.

They instil confidence

Master problem solvers know how to instil confidence, both in themselves and in others.

They are the kind of people that can speak to you for 5 minutes and thereafter you feel you can conquer the whole world.

An experience comes to mind:

I had an external exam to write one day. Three months to the exam, my brother sent me a card, and in the card, he wrote just one sentence.

"If there is anyone in this family that can make all A's, it is you"

Those words stirred up something in me. They spurred me on to develop a new learning regime.

And learning I did.

When I finally wrote the exam, I had all A's in ten subjects. The tutors of my school gathered together and lifted me as if I had won the world cup.

Someone had instilled confidence in me to solve a problem that many had failed woefully to solve.

I was the only one in my town to achieve that feat.

If you want to become a master problem solver, you need to instil confidence in yourself as well as those who are around you.

It is a very important trait of master problem solvers.

They make you bigger than the problem, thereby simplifying the problem for you to handle.

If you have the ability to make yourself or others bigger than you, then you are in good company.

Let us move on to the second key of master problem builders.

CHAPTER FOUR: SECOND KEY OF MASTER PROBLEM SOLVERS

The second thing master problems do very well is that, they build capacity.

Capacity building essentially makes you bigger than the problem you are solving in terms of knowledge and know-how.

In the beginning, the problem might be bigger than you because you do not yet have the capacity to solve it.

After you develop capacity, by learning, you become bigger than the problem and thus are able to solve it.

Here is a simple scenario:

When you were in primary school, addition was quite difficult for you. After acquiring more knowledge and getting to the university, primary school work has become so easy.

What happened for the problems that haunted you in primary school to become so easy? You built capacity.

You can imagine what will happen when you ask a university student to solve the following questions:

1+1=

2+2=

3+3=

2+1=

1+6=

Your guess is as good as mine. It would be so easy because of the capacity he has built.

It is the reason I am always surprised when many people do not have capacity building as part of their vocabulary.

They never think to build their capacities in certain areas.

I interacted with a young man the other day who wanted money from me to solve one of his numerous money problems.

For more than 5 years, that was his routine.

I was surprised when I realised that this young man who wanted his financial problems solved had never read a book on personal finances.

What?

Well, that is the story of many people who attempt to solve the personal problems they are confronted with.

They try to solve it all by themselves when they lack the capacity to do so.

Instead of building capacity, they keep attempting to solve problems bigger than them.

The sad reality is that, they lack capacity but keep on trying year after year to solve the same problem and guess what, they will never be able to solve it no matter the number of years they are given until they build capacity.

It is something many of them do not know until they die having not solved that same problem.

And for those who seek help, they seek the wrong kind of help. Instead of seeking help to build their capacity to solve personal problems, they just ask others to solve it for them.

The question is, how long can others tolerate your dumping of problems on them.

So then, what do master problem solvers do to build their capacity:

They acquire knowledge

One of the best ways to build capacity is to acquire knowledge. Master problem solvers do exactly that.

They can seclude themselves in their rooms for days to weeks or even months building capacity by acquiring knowledge.

Articles: They can read about 40 articles on how to solve one problem and then compose a proper solution from the capacity they have built by studying those articles.

Imagine reading 40 good articles on passive income, wont you have a good solution to your passive income problems?

Especially if you go further to narrow your reading to a particular passive income.

Books: Master problem solvers can read 5 to 20 good books on a single subject just to build their capacity in solving problems in that area.

Their focus is not disturbed, and they can camp themselves with books for months and when they come out of their camping or retreat, they would normally come out with incredible solutions.

One day I read 4 books on a certain problem that had plagued me for years.

In a matter of 3 days, I had solved the problem that had plagued me for years and it was just because I spent 3 days to build my capacity in the area of the problem I had.

Audios and videos: Master problem solvers can listen to so many audios on a subject that they virtually become one with the materials.

The same thing with videos.

These audios and videos give them valuable information that will build their capacity to solve problems.

When I wanted to double my business income, I got 60 different videos on the subject. For 9 days straight, I devoured the content of the videos.

I watched all the videos more than twice in that period.

After the 9 days, I was more than a PHD holder in marketing and increasing business revenue.

My business income tripled in six months. I had solved the business challenge that confronted me by building capacity in the area I needed. I built the capacity by watching videos continuously on the subject area till I understood the concepts and I could apply them.

One day a preacher recounted his story. He observed how another preacher healed the sick.

He went to his own room and watched several videos of this other preacher for 3 months. Three months later, he was healing the sick in much the same way.

This is what we call capacity building.

Whichever area you are confronted with a problem, you can build your capacity there.

And I will be fright in saying that after you build your capacity, the problem will cease to exist.

Master problem solvers build capacity, so should you.

They build teams

One of the major characteristics of master problem solvers is that, they recognize that they cannot solve all problems on their own, so they know how to assemble or build teams.

They are able to recognize the problem and also fish out people who have the ability to help them solve those problems.

They build strong teams and manage these people to solve the problems that have been presented to them.

To become a master problem solver, you must be able to recognize talented, efficient, capable and results oriented people.

After identifying them, you must be able to manage and coordinate their efforts to achieve the desired result.

Let me tell you another story to buttress this point;

Several years ago, I was given the opportunity to build a football team for a youth group.

I selected a very talented young man who had sterling leadership qualities to captain the team.

This gentleman recruited capable players from different areas and we built a team with these players.

Needless to say, we won the tournament. Mostly because I spotted a captain material who did all the recruitment, something I was incapable of at that moment.

I knew how to give strategies and instil confidence in the players but I lacked the recruitment ability or where to even begin recruiting from.

Master problem solvers know how to build teams. Incorporate this key in your arsenals so that you can become an excellent problem solver.

Master problem do more than building teams,

They consult experts

Master problem solvers have a humility that is unlike any other group of people.

They know their limitations and rely on experts when there is the need.

This makes them able to solve problems across several industries and across several continents.

They know how to consult people who have the precise knowledge they need.

From these people, they are able to formulate proper solutions for the problems they have been tasked to solve.

Not only do they consult experts, they know exactly which experts to consult for which situation. Some experts are experts by name, not by results. Master problem solvers seek experts by results not those who just carry the name "expert".

They always seek out the real deal.

You must be able to consult experts if you want o become a master problem solver and you must know how to differentiate between the two kinds of experts.

Now that you know the ways you can simplify problems, let us go to the next key of master problem solvers.

They ask relevant questions

Master problem solvers know how to ask the right questions to get the right answers.

The solutions you need are available. However, if you fail to ask the right question, you maty never get the solution you need.

A case in pint is that one day I wanted to learn how to sell 1,000 products a day.

I typed every question I could in google to get the information I needed to get those results.

From "how to sell 1,000 things a day, to what is the best strategy to sell 1,000 things a day," I asked every imaginable type of question.

Although I got and read 2 books and over 20 articles on the subject based on the options given by google for those questions I typed, I still couldn't get the answer I needed.

The content of the materials I read didn't seem right to me. It didn't seem like they could help me get the job done.

Then finally, it occurred to me to type this question:

How I sold 1,000 units daily?

This question led me to several books. In one of the books, I found the solution which I implemented to get similar results.

As a master problem solver, you must ask the right questions to get the right answers.

That is every essential.

Without the right questions, the answers will be available but you may never have access to them.

Now, let us move on to the next thing master problem solvers do very well.

CHAPTER FIVE: THIRD KEY OF MASTER PROBLEM SOLVERS

The third thing master problem solvers do very well is that, they execute with speed, understanding and thorough precision.

It is easy to separate master problem solvers from ordinary problem solvers.

Apart from the fact that you want your problems solved, you will agree with me that you would want it to be solved in time, solved efficiently and effectively.

That is what master problem solvers do, and that is why they are easily recognisable the world across.

SPEED

Master problem solvers work with considerations of the time factor of the projects or the problems they are required to solve.

If a problem is to be solved by a particular time and it is not, the consequences can be dire. This is the understanding with which master problem solvers incorporate the element of speed into their process of problem-solving.

They know that speed is different from hurry, and in their quest to solve problems on time, they do not cut corners. This is very important.

Hardly will you see a master problem solver delay in solving a problem.

They are mostly on time or ahead of schedule.

In your quest to become a master problem solver, you must understand that although delays are inevitable on some occasions, you must do your best to finish on time or ahead of schedule always.

That will only go a long way to enhance your reputation as a master problem solver.

There is no need solving a problem when the solution is no longer useful.

Imagine looking for an uber to go for a program which ends in two hours.

The uber arrives two hours later by which time the program is over. Even though the vehicle is a solution to your problem, the delay renders it a useless solution because you were not able to achieve the intended purpose of the solution because of the delay.

Keep that in mind when solving problems. Considerable speed is of the essence.

No excuses

Master problem solvers are absolute leaders who know how to take responsibility and deliver on their promises.

Giving excuses is not in their nature and for that reason it helps them deliver solutions when they are needed and how they are needed.

There are too many excuse givers out there.

They will blame the weather, the president, their grandmother and what have you.

What ever reason excuse givers can find, they will find and sometimes even conjure excuses from nowhere as to why they were not able to deliver a promised solution.

It is not so with master problems solvers. Master problem solvers are good at keeping their word.

This trait helps them to keep working when many of their colleagues are asleep or having a good time. They know there is a deadline to be met.

A master problem solver makes his problem solving a priority and doesn't take it for granted.

In your quest is to become a master problem solver, you must be one who hates excuses.

Let it be uncharacteristic of you to give excuses.

This will help create a certain sense of drive and urgency in your life for you to forge on and give birth to many brilliant and useful solutions in good time.

No procrastination

Procrastination is a thief of time.

You have heard that said many times.

People procrastinate for several reasons.

The task may be too daunting for them.

They may be feeling to lazy to get something going.

They may just be uninterested in what it is they have to work on.

At the end of the day, procrastination is something that attacks every problem solver. However, master problem solvers have learned to deal with it so that it does not affect their supply line of solutions.

Can you think of the person you are relying on for a solution relaxing somewhere and saying they do not feel like producing the solution?

Funny right.

It is not about how you feel, it is about getting the job done and that is exactly what master problem solvers do. They get the job done.

If a master problem solver cannot solve his own problem of procrastination, what sort of master problem solver is he?

If you have a procrastination problem, you can easily solve it because you have the problem-solving keys of master problems solvers.

Use them to your own advantage.

UNDERSTANDING

Problems are solved for a reason.

Understanding this reason helps problem solvers bring out the exact solution that is needed in a situation.

Do not be a problem solver who has no understanding of the problem and the kind of solution needed.

When you do that, you will only complicate things.

Many a time, understanding the problem and the kind of solution needed makes all the difference for a master problem solver.

Such an understanding more often than not leads to simple solutions that those who have no understanding of the problem nor the solution required can ever give.

They cannot give such simple solutions because of a lack of understanding.

It is that serious and can easily be a game changer in the problem-solving arena.

When you want to be a master problem solver, understand the problem, but most importantly understand why the solution is needed.

It will go a long way to help you in your journey as a master problem solver.

Don't forget it.

THOROUGH PRECISION

Master problem solvers are thorough and precise. That is what was lacking in a mechanic who nearly killed me.

After taking my car to him to work on. He was not thorough in making sure everything was done as expected.

On my way the car just fell apart. Had it not been for the fact that I was going very slow pace, my life would have been endangered.

It turns out that, certain bolts on the car were not tightened properly, others were not even put there at all.

Carelessness in the part of problem solvers can be costly, even deadly on some occasions.

Master problem solvers cannot do that. They must double cross and make sure that their solutions are thorough and precise.

You heard it right. Double cross to make sure all is right.

Without that, they risk putting everything they have gained in jeopardy as well as putting people in various risks including the risk of death.

Let me say this passionately.

As a master problem solver, the lives of people will depend on you.

Please and please again, be thorough and precise in what you do so that no harm comes to anybody because of you.

Quality over quantity

A hall mark of master problem solvers is the quality of their delivery.

It speaks for them several years after they have offered their solution.

Quality does that all the time.

Master problem solvers believe in quality.

There is nothing sweeter than your works of quality speaking for you over and over again.

It causes you to be recommended to solve problems for prominent people.

However, if you build your problem solving on shoddy solutions, soon no one will require your services.

You will be blacklisted in the market places.

Be advised.

Do it well the first time.

Redoing the same thing can be one of the most frustrating things in life.

That is why it is important to get it right the first time.

Put all your efforts and wits into doing the work of problem solving right the first time.

Imagine having to construct a 4-storey building and after getting to the third storey, you realise that the foundation was not done well.

All the effort you put into getting to the third storey level is wasted.

Not to talk of the money, time and what have you.

The stress and pain you will go through afterwards has not even come into question nor the damage to your reputation and other associated costs.

In plain terms, please do it right the first time.

No shoddy or lazy work.

Master problems solvers do it well and right the first time, so they do not have to do it again.

CHAPTER SIX: FOURTH KEY OF MASTER PROBLEM SOLVERS

The final thing master problem solvers do very well is that, they do not know how to give up.

Giving up is a common trait of many people. That cannot be said of master problem solvers.

It is one of the things they are masters in. They are masters at not giving up. They fight till they win.

That is the exact the description of what master problems solvers do very well.

There was a movie I watched that is similar to the mindset of a master problem solver. The title was "No retreat, no surrender".

That movie depicts that the only option is to win.

Believe you me, everybody loves winning and not giving up is one of the ways to get to the place of winning,

Quitters don't win

This saying is very popular amongst master problem solvers.

If quitters don't win, then winners don't quit.

It is a mantra that has made many people successful in the past, is making people successful in the present and will make many others successful in the future.

Stories abound of people who didn't quit and as a result had glorious testimonies in the end.

This morning, I met a good friend of mine who is now a chartered accountant.

Life is good for him now, but I vividly remember the time he was studying to become a chartered accountant.

On no occasion did he find it easy to pay his school or professional exam fees.

He used to work as a security guard at night and come to school during the day.

He would go days without food, yet he still did not quit when other people who had it better than him had already quit.

He is the embodiment of someone who understood that quitters don't win and winners don't quit.

His life is an example of not quitting till you win and win he certainly did.

We laughed over those days with so much joy. Joy he could not have expressed when he was going through those tough times.

He let me know that it was worth it not quitting although the circumstances were very tough to bear.

Not that the thought didn't come to quit. Not that the temptation didn't come.

They came, but he fought his way to winning.

To become a master problem solver, do not quit when a problem seems too difficult to solve.

Keep on till you solve it and crack the code.

Persistence and determination

When you are persistent and determined, there is no obstacle you cannot overcome.

Master problem solvers face a lot of obstacles. Without the traits of determination and persistence, they would not be able to surmount the obstacles that come their way.

Sometimes when you look at successful people who have solved problems, you would never know the obstacles they had to surmount before reaching where they are.

Your obstacles are nothing new, many people have faced similar or more difficult situations but have made it.

To become a master problem solver, you will have your fair share of obstacles you must overcome.

Persist in your efforts to overcome till you do.

That is where your victory lies.

That is where your story of inspiration lies.

A story is said of how Thomas Edison, the famous inventor, persisted more than 1000 times till he was able to make the light bulb work.

Let us travel to his laboratory way back in time. If he had not persisted after the first or tenth or six hundredth attempt, and decided to stop along the way, would he have invented the light bulb, the answer is a big No.

His determination to come out with the solution is what made him standout.

You have not tried one thousand times to solve a problem, so don't even think you have done all you can. And don't think of quitting.

You have not yet scratched the surface of effort. To become a master problem solver, you must be determined and persistent.

It is as simple as that.

Every problem has a solution

Understand this statement once and for all. Every problem has a solution.

The fact that you have not found the solution does not mean it does not exist.

The solution exists, it is your responsibility to find it.

That is what master problem solvers do. They know the solution exists and thus they do all they can to find it.

Without this mindset, it is difficult to keep going on. You may probably give up thinking that the solution doesn't exist.

Now you know differently. Solutions exist for every problem. You heard me right. There is more than one solution for every problem.

You are tasked with finding only one of such solutions. Don't blow that opportunity.

Think about it.

Cars now use petrol, diesel, electricity and gas to run.

Others use solar energy to move. These are countless solutions to just one problem. The fuel problem for cars.

You need to adopt this mindset to be a master problem solver.

It will take you places and help you to do a great deal of things.

Build a reputation of winning

Master problem solvers are so called because of their track record.

They have built a reputation of wining and solving problems on so many occasions.

To build such a track record, you cannot start by giving up on the problems you are confronted with.

Diligence and a lot of wisdom is required when you start out to become a master problem solver.

If master problem solvers are spending 10 hours a day working, you who aspires to be a master problem solver must spend at least 15 hours working and learning.

There is no other way you can also begin to build a reputation of solid success and problem solving without that extra effort.

It is very important.

Reputations are not built overnight, however people determine to build such reputations and put in the work required.

They pay the price for greatness and thus obtain greatness.

You should be ready to build a winning reputation, and the best way to do that is to put in the time and effort.

You already have the tools and the resources. You now have to put in the time and the effort to ensue that you are delivering quality solutions around the clock.

The good news is that if you work that way, you will be able to solve all your own personal problems first, then you can move on to solve the problems of others.

There is no joy greater than moving on to solve the problems of others because you have reduced your own problems.

The feeling is deep.

How I became the best mathematician in my class

Early in my academic career, I realised that I hated to quit when I couldn't solve a mathematics question.

I will work at it for days on end till I found the solution or what I was doing wrong.

This attitude soon made me a master of mathematics.

Other students I knew easily gave up when they could not solve a particular problem.

Because of that, they never totally mastered any topic.

On the other hand, I mastered every topic because more often than not, those questions I couldn't answer immediately had tricks in them that needed to be studied differently.

As you already know, those are the exact questions teachers and examiners delight in. Trick questions that are not like the normal questions.

Because I had cracked the code and knew the solution in most of such situations, I easily climbed to be the best mathematician in my class.

I vividly remember one examination where the examiner actually came out to say I had cheated because there was no way I could have scored the marks I scored.

It was a mock examination for an external exam, our final exams for that level. I destroyed the paper so bad that the examiner felt embarrassed.

Even more embarrassed were my fellow mates who were about 20 marks behind me. Hitherto were complaining that the exam was too difficult before they saw my results.

The attitude of not quitting is what brought me to that level.

I pray it takes you places too as a master problem solver.

Winning mentality

There are some people who hate to lose.

Their mantra is to win at all costs.

As a master problem solver, you must have that same mentality.

The winning mentality.

Every great person has that mentality.

They are never comfortable with losing. They hate to lose and for that reason, they hardly lose.

Because of their hatred for losing, they do all they can to make sure they win when the day of reckoning comes.

You have done so well reading to this point. Let us get into the last chapter of the book to make sure that you leave this book as a master problem solver with no shadow of doubt.

CHAPTER SEVEN: PRACTICE MAKES PERFECT

Practice makes perfect.

This statement is so true, nonetheless many of us hate to practice.

A lot of people do not know that matches are won, not on the playing field but on the training ground.

To excel as a master problem solver, you must practise often.

This will sharpen your skill and give you the needed experience fast.

The more you practise, the faster your development.

What may take others 3 years will take you only one year if you learn to practice often and practice well.

This will afford you the opportunity for growth.

Grow

No one becomes a master problem solver in a day.

It takes time for you to develop and hone your skills as well as perfect them.

This is all part of the growth process.

In this process of growth, you will learn what works and what doesn't work, you will also be exposed to different problems in different scenarios.

These will cause you to grow so much that you may not recognize who you are today from who you will become in an a few years of problem solving.

Like little kids learn to crawl, then walk, then run, it will be same with your problem-solving journey.

To grow you must practice or attempt solving a lot of real-life problems.

Some can be existing problems; others can be challenges you create for yourself to solve.

They way you create challenges for yourself to solve is, you can decide to achieve something and pursue the solution.

These are the best kind of practices. The challenges you set for yourself and not the problems you wait 3 years for that never come.

An example of a challenge is:

Earn an extra $1,000 in 3 months

Such challenges grow you as a person.

Since you can challenge yourself in several ways in several situations, you can easily develop your own growth and practice program.

When you solve one challenge, you move to the next till you keep growing your problem-solving skills as well as gathering valuable resources that can help you solve specific problems or making acquaintances with people, books and websites that have valuable problem-solving knowledge and know how.

I feel excited for you already because I know this is the path that will help you eliminate most of your personal problems so that you can move on to do more for others.

Mistakes

Mistakes are inevitable in every endeavour.

That is why you start by giving yourself personal challenges to solve as well as solving your personal problems.

In this way the consequences of your mistakes are minimal and you get to recover.

When you are now ready to take on bigger problems as well as the problems of others after several periods of practise, you would have already made and dealt with most of your mistakes and eliminated them from your journey.

Do not be too hard on yourself when you make mistakes.

Learn from them and move on.

I cannot begin to give you the list of mistakes all great men have made.

They are so much that, they will need all the paper of the whole world to write them in.

Be encouraged, in your journey to become a master problem solver, mistakes will come. Just learn from them and move on.

Practice Schedule

One thing that you surely have to work on immediately is your first challenge or problem to solve.

Thereafter, have a schedule to create and solve challenges either every week or very month.

Constant practise is what will make you a master.

Therefore, create your schedule now and make sure you follow it.

Such a thing cannot be left to chance or feelings.

Thank you very much for reading to this point. Do well to leave a great review of the book.

You are now ready to be a master problem solver.

Dreams do come to pass.

Make your dreams and that of others come to pass. Do well to talk to friends and loved ones about this book.

It is a way of helping solve problems of others.

Afterall, what is the purpose of a master problem solver if he or she doesn't raise other problem solvers.

Complimentary Key

Many problem solvers engage in fasting.

It has many benefits, chief among them is the clarity of thought and focus it gives the problem solver.

Do well to recommend the book.

Keep being great.

REVIEW

Because your review is important to help others benefit from these books, please leave a good review

Free Course:

3 DAY COURSE ON LEGACY

How to be remembered long after you leave the earth

Just to say Thank You for investing in my book, I'd like to give you this course for free.

Get this course if you want to be remembered in life because too many people die with no legacy.

Get the course for **FREE**

Printed in Poland
by Amazon Fulfillment
Poland Sp. z o.o., Wrocław

35624499R00061

Plot Twist:

Apparently, It's *Autism*

PUBLISHED BY: Sophie Barton

Plot Twist: Apparently, It's Autism
© 2025 Sophie Barton

All rights reserved. No part of this publication may be reproduced, stored in a retrieval system, or transmitted in any form or by any means, electronic, mechanical, photocopying, recording, or otherwise, without the prior written permission of the copyright holder, except in the case of brief quotations used in critical articles, reviews, or educational content with proper citation.

This book is a work of non-fiction based on personal experience. The author is not a medical professional, and this book is not intended to serve as medical advice, diagnosis, or treatment. Readers seeking medical guidance should consult a qualified healthcare provider.

The author has made every effort to ensure the accuracy of the information contained within this book at the time of publication. However, practices, diagnoses, and perspectives on autism are continuously evolving. The publisher and author disclaim any liability arising directly or indirectly from the use or application of any content within this book.

Names, characters, anecdotes, and dialogues drawn from real life have been rendered with care and respect. In some cases, names and identifying details have been changed to protect the privacy of individuals. Any resemblance to actual persons, living or deceased, is coincidental unless stated otherwise.

Cover design, interior illustrations, and character artwork © 2025 Sophie Barton. Illustrated character of "the brain" created by the author and used throughout this book as a recurring visual guide to support narrative themes. All character artwork is original and not to be reproduced without permission.

Contents of Plot Twist

The Mask Was Tight 7
   1.1: Social Chameleon Extraordinaire 8
   1.2: Performance of a Lifetime 12
   1.3: But You Seem So Normal 16

"You're Just a Bit Sensitive" 21
   2.1: The Diagnosis That Wasn't 22
   2.2: "You Always Overreact" 27
   2.3: Gaslit by Normalcy 32

Neurotypical, Apparently 36
   3.1: Why Is Everyone Else So Chill? 37
   3.2: Cracking the Social Code 42

Noticing the Glitches 47
   4.1: The Meltdown Files 48
   4.2: The One with the Earplugs 53
   4.3: Hyperfixation Nation 58

Dr. Google and the Rabbit Hole 63
   5.1: "Wait… This Is Me?" 64
   5.2: The Role of Social Media 68
   5.3: The Mirror Test 73

How Did They Miss It? 79
   6.1: Too Smart, Too Polite, Too Masked 80

6.2: The Diagnostic Checklist Wasn't Made for Me 84

Spectrum ≠ Straight Line 89

7.1: Not Mild, Not Wild—Just Me 90

7.2: The Infinite Spiderweb 95

7.3: Functioning Labels? Let's Not 99

Social Skills: Trial and Error Edition 104

8.1: Literal Girl in a Figurative World 105

8.3: Too Honest, Too Weird, Too Much 110

Disability, Identity, and Reclaiming Words 115

9.1: Am I Disabled? 116

9.2: Labels Aren't Always Bad 120

9.3: Pride Looks Good on Me 124

Relationships, Boundaries, and People Who Get It 128

10.1: Telling People 129

10.2: Boundary? I Barely Knew Her 133

The History They Don't Teach You 137

11.1: From Kanner to Controversy 138

11.2: Hans Asperger Wasn't a Hero 142

11.3: The Rise of Neurodiversity 146

I Was Always This Person 150

12.1: Nothing's Changed (Everything's Changed) 151

12.2: Autistic Adulthood, Reimagined 155

12.3: The Plot Twist Wasn't the End 159

An Introduction.

Plot twist: I was diagnosed with autism at 30. Not as a child prodigy, not after a dramatic meltdown in a supermarket, and not because a teacher noticed something. My diagnosis came after years wondering why things that seemed easy for everyone else made me feel like I was running on dial-up in a world of fibre Wi-Fi.

I wanted to write this book for the late bloomers. The quietly exhausted. The ones who always felt a little *different*, *too much*, but never quite "enough" to warrant a diagnosis. Maybe autism didn't even cross your mind until recently. Maybe you stumbled here after a suspiciously specific TikTok. Maybe a friend sent you this out of nowhere. Or maybe you're just tired of being the mystery in your own story.

Inside these pages, you'll find my personal journey to discovering I'm autistic, full of the awkward, funny, painful, and profound moments that led to that "aha!" moment. But this isn't just about me. It's about what it means to unlearn a lifetime of pretending. It's about masking, meltdowns, misdiagnoses, and memes that hit uncomfortably hard. It's about finally getting the language to describe yourself, and realizing you aren't purposely awkward, just a little misunderstood.

I'll also walk you through the big stuff: what autism really is (and isn't), why the "spectrum" isn't a straight line, and why representation still kinda sucks. There's space for joy here too, for reclaiming stims, special interests, and the weird, beautiful way our brains work.

This isn't a textbook. It's a field guide for the newly diagnosed, the maybe-autistic, and anyone who's ever felt like they missed the manual.

Spoiler: you didn't miss it. It was never written for you.

So, let's write our own.

Chapter One

The Mask Was Tight

1.1: Social Chameleon Extraordinaire

There should be an Olympic event for blending in. If there were, I'd have medalled every year since birth, probably while simultaneously overthinking how to accept the award without making it weird. You know that feeling when you walk into a room and instantly scan for the social weather report, who's loud, who's cool, who's safe, who's wearing sarcasm like a scent? Yeah. That's not just a feeling for me. That was my full-time job.

I didn't consciously apply for the role of "Social Chameleon Extraordinaire," but I got it anyway. No application, no interview, just a lifetime contract and a tight, tight mask. The dress code? Whatever made other people more comfortable. The hours? All of them. The pay? Crippling internal confusion and eventual burnout.

At school, I had a different personality per corridor. In science class, I was Quiet Girl Who Gets Good Grades But Isn't A Know-It-All (an important distinction). In the cafeteria, I was Just Funny Enough To Be Liked But Not So Funny That I'd Overshadow The Loud Kids. And in gym? In gym, I was a disappearing act. I once pretended to twist my ankle so I wouldn't have to play rounders. I limped with such conviction, I got out of it for a full term. Method acting, darling.

Friends? Oh, friends were a game of roulette. With the arty ones, I was deep, moody, and probably misunderstood. I wore scarves in summer and nodded a lot when people said things like "capitalism is a prison of the soul." With the sporty ones, I became strangely competitive, though I didn't know the rules to most games. Once, I shouted "foul!" during netball, and I don't think that's even a thing. But they cheered, so I rolled with it.

The irony was, I never felt lonelier than when I was surrounded by people I'd meticulously adapted myself for. You'd think all that effort would buy you a sense of belonging, but no. It just buys you a ticket to a performance where you're both the actor and the audience, and you're silently hoping no one notices you've got the script upside down.

And then we have the workplace. Where the stakes got higher and the costumes more corporate. I once sat through an entire Monday meeting nodding at jargon I did not understand. Someone said we needed to "pivot" our strategy and I thought we were about to spin in our chairs. I laughed. Nobody else did. They thought I was being ironic. I wasn't.

At work, I became Polished Professional With A Firm Handshake And Opinions About The Printer. I learned to say things like "Let's circle back" and "I'll touch base" even though both phrases made me feel like a malfunctioning robot. I once practiced small talk in the mirror before a team-building away day. Not speeches. Not presentations. Just small talk. My notes included "Ask about weather, then smile."

In meetings, I mirrored the energy of whoever spoke first. If Dave was enthusiastic, so was I. If Janet was sceptical, I was too. I once agreed with both sides of a debate in the same conversation and walked away feeling like a human ping-pong ball. But they all said I was "so adaptable," which felt like a compliment and a diagnosis.

Romantic relationships? Let's not. I became whoever I thought they needed. Outdoorsy? So was I. (Spoiler: I hate mud.) Vegan? Absolutely. (Until I ate a pepperoni stick in my car like a criminal.) I once tried to learn football stats to impress someone who hadn't asked me to do that, and when they did ask, I panicked and told them Wayne Rooney was still playing. In 2022.

It got exhausting. Like being in a long-running play that nobody else realised was theatre. Worse still, I didn't know I was acting. I thought everyone was doing it. I genuinely believed that socialising was meant to feel like a high-stakes escape room, where you win if no one realises you don't belong there.

I thought maybe I was just a "people pleaser," or "a bit quirky," or "a sponge for other people's moods," which sounds poetic but mostly feels like living in a house with too many thermostats. It wasn't until I started reading about masking in autism that I realised, oh. That's what I've been doing. Not just adapting. Masking. Constantly. Exhaustingly. Expertly.

So yes, I've been a social chameleon. I've had a thousand shades, a thousand shapes, and not a single sense of stability. And I'm brilliant at it. But being brilliant at something that erases you a little every time you do it? That's not a talent. That's survival.

I ignorantly had pictured autism as something that wasn't me, something loud or obvious or entirely other. I thought it looked a certain way, behaved a certain way, lived in someone else's world. I didn't see myself in the stereotypes, so I never thought to look closer.

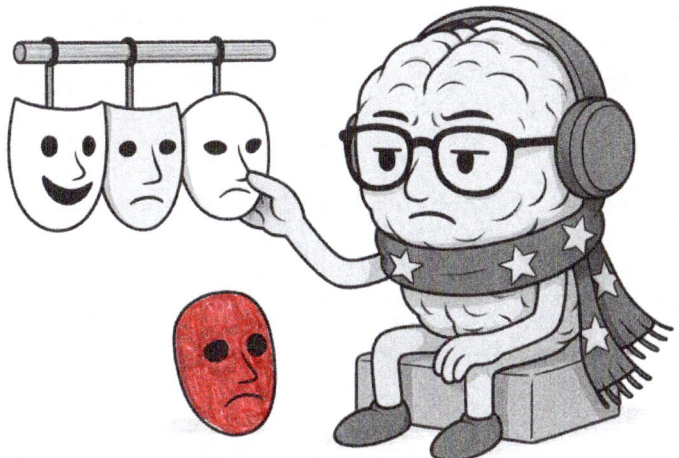

1.2: Performance of a Lifetime

The lights are low, the audience is silent, and I, the lead actress, am about to deliver the line I've rehearsed ten thousand times in the mirror while brushing my teeth, walking the dog, or blinking out of a social daydream.

The line is: "Oh I'm fine, thanks. How about you?"

Not exactly Shakespeare, but still, it has range. It's versatile. It can be cheerful, clipped, ironic, sincere, or breathlessly polite depending on the setting. I know because I've played every version of it.

What nobody tells you as a child, especially if you're autistic but don't know it yet, is that most people are improvising. Meanwhile, you're gripping your invisible script like it's the sacred scroll of human interaction, scribbled full of dos and don'ts and "try smiling here."

I've always had a script in my head. Not consciously, not like a playwright hunched over a desk, but it was there, humming in the background, running lines and cross-referencing what "normal" looks like. When someone laughed, I mentally bookmarked the sound so I could replicate it later. When a teacher told a joke, I paid more attention to how everyone reacted than to the joke itself. Not because I was humourless, but because I was studying. Constantly.

I'd watch people talk and rehearse how to say things the way they said them. I even noted the little pauses, the way they tilted their heads, when they leaned in, when they blinked. Like a method actor preparing for a role called "Acceptable Human."

Sometimes, I'd practice what to say days in advance. Entire conversations played out in my head like internal dress rehearsals. I'd try different openings, alternative punchlines, even exits, "if I say this, she might say that, so then I'll laugh, or maybe I'll nod, but not too fast." It was exhausting. I didn't realise most people don't do that.

I copied mannerisms. Borrowed facial expressions. I tried to look "interested" in conversations that were, frankly, about as riveting as lukewarm soup. But I furrowed my brows and nodded and said "oh yeah" and "no way!" on cue. If you'd watched closely, you might have seen the moment I broke character, when the eye contact lasted one second too long or I forgot which version of myself I was playing.

I was in a permanent state of adaptation. It wasn't just about fitting in, it was about survival. If I didn't mimic the right tone, I'd get called rude. If I didn't laugh when expected, I was cold. If I talked too much about something I actually cared about, I was intense. So, I tucked those parts away, carefully. The real me became the understudy.

I remember once spending two days practising how to tell a joke at work. Just one joke. I'd overheard it in the kitchen and thought,

"That one's safe. Not too edgy, not too weird." I tested it in my head, matched my tone to someone else's delivery, and slotted it into a conversation like a carefully placed prop. They laughed. Victory. But the high was short-lived, because now they expected me to be "funny." A new role. A new pressure.

It's not that I didn't know who I was, it's that I was never quite sure if who I was would be welcome. So, I wore versions. Polished ones. Polite ones. Smiling ones. I was like a shop window, but the stock was rearranged based on who was walking past.

And yet, somewhere behind the velvet curtain, the real me sat cross-legged with a sandwich and a script full of edits no one would ever read. She knew all the lines but wasn't sure when, or if, she'd ever get to deliver them.

The performance became second nature. Autopilot. I couldn't tell anymore which gestures were mine and which were borrowed. Which laughter was genuine, and which was a well-timed echo. It's not lying, it's layering. It's camouflage by charisma.

But it takes a toll. When the show ends, and the lights go down, you're left backstage peeling off a personality you wore too tightly all day. And some days, you forget where the costume ends and the skin begins.

I was never trying to deceive. I was trying to connect. To be liked. To be safe. To be something that felt like belonging. But I realise now, true connection can't exist where the script never stops.

And I've lived a thousand scenes with perfect blocking and flawless delivery. The only thing missing was… me.

1.3: But You Seem So Normal

Are you ready for the classic? The gold medallist in unhelpful feedback. The phrase that has been lovingly, and repeatedly, lobbed at me since the moment I started telling people I'm autistic.

"But you seem so normal."

Thank you? I think? Or, wait, is this the part where I melt into a curtsy and accept the compliment I never asked for? Should I add "Passes As Neurotypical When Standing Still" to my CV?

Let's take a moment to unpack this glittering gem of a sentence. First off, "normal" is not the neutral little word people think it is. It's loaded. It's coded. It's basically society's way of saying, "You don't make me uncomfortable, so I will now bestow upon you the title of Acceptable Human." Congratulations. You've unlocked a badge in the Neurotypical Olympics.

"Normal" isn't real. It's a costume. A mood board. A greatest hits playlist of what people have decided counts as "relatable." And another spoiler alert: I've spent most of my life studying that playlist like it was gospel.

When someone says I "seem normal," what they're really saying is, "You're good at pretending." And they're not wrong. I *am* good at pretending. I've spent decades curating my behaviour like a social media feed: filtered, edited, captioned for clarity.

But just because the lighting's good doesn't mean it's the whole picture.

Let's talk about what "normal" actually looks like in a neurotypical world:

Making eye contact, but not *too* much. (Creepy.)

Laughing at jokes you don't find funny. (Social bonding.)

Knowing how close to stand without violating the unspoken Personal Space Treaty.

Remembering names, faces, birthdays, and whatever emotional subtext was laced into the way someone said "fine."

"Normal" means not stimming in public. It means suppressing your need for quiet when the pub's blaring with bass and everyone's shouting over each other like seagulls in a chip shop. It means answering "How are you?" with "Good, thanks!" even if you're currently living through an internal existential collapse.

And for years, I did all of that. Flawlessly. So flawlessly, in fact, that when I said, "Actually, I'm autistic," people didn't believe me. Because I didn't "look autistic."

Which is a whole other punch to the gut. What *does* autism look like, exactly? Is it a trench coat and sunglasses? A neon sign flashing **SOCIAL MALFUNCTION IN PROGRESS**?

The truth is, autism has no single face. No one voice. No checklist you can tick off from across the room. And the reason I "seem normal" is not because I'm not autistic, it's because I've been *performing* what you think normal is for so long that I forgot how not to.

It's like being praised for hiding a limp. "You're walking great!" Sure, but only because I've spent years clenching my jaw and pretending it doesn't hurt.

And honestly? It *does* hurt. Not always in a sobbing-on-the-floor way. Sometimes it's a quiet ache, a dull headache after a loud lunch. Sometimes it's the feeling of being out of sync, like you're in a room full of radios, and everyone's tuned to the same station except yours. You're picking up static and everyone else is dancing.

But when I say, "I'm autistic," and someone replies with, "But you're so normal," what I hear is, "I liked the version of you that didn't ask to be understood."

So, here's my counteroffer: maybe it's time we retire the word "normal." Not just toss it aside, but launch it into space with a little parachute and a thank-you note for its years of confusing service.

Because normal is a moving target. It's subjective, it's slippery, and frankly, it's a bit boring. I'd rather be real. I'd rather stim in public, leave early when I need to, say "no" without a fake excuse, and make eye contact only when it actually feels okay.

And if someone says, "You don't *seem* autistic," I'll smile and say, "That's funny, you don't *seem* ignorant."

(Okay, I won't *actually* say that. I'll think it. But one day. One day I might.)

Chapter Two

"You're Just a Bit Sensitive"

2.1: The Diagnosis That Wasn't

At school, the teachers would always describe me as sensitive during parents' evenings. Lovely, intelligent, but sensitive. Even now, looking back, I can't quite pinpoint how I was more sensitive than the other kids. But that word has followed me into adulthood. It still shows up, even when I feel like I'm not being sensitive at all.

Before anyone ever mentioned the word "autism," I had amassed a tidy little alphabet soup of other explanations. Anxiety. Depression. OCD. Trauma response. Sensory processing issues. Perfectionism. Burnout. Maybe just weird. Depending on the year or the cultural trend of the time, I had one or more of these labels attached to me like post-it notes fluttering in a breeze, none of them sticking quite right.

In some ways, each of those diagnoses felt accurate at some stage. At least on paper. I *did* have anxiety (but doesn't everyone?), I was hyperaware of everything and everyone, always scanning for signs that I was too much or not enough. I *did* have depressive episodes, periods of complete shutdown, when the world felt like a wall I couldn't climb and all I wanted was silence and invisibility. I *did* exhibit compulsive behaviours, I lined things up, I avoided stepping on cracks, and I had an internal rulebook no one could see but me. I *did* struggle with sensory things, tags, sounds, lights, certain fabrics, the wrong fork.

Sounds were always a big trigger. I probably should have known. I can't stand how loud hand dryers are, honestly, they give me goosebumps. I'll never forget standing outside a hotel when a jet flew overhead. It was loud, yes, but my reaction was something else entirely. It made me shudder. Everyone else looked up, mesmerised. I was the only one shrinking from the noise.

So, when the health professionals handed me puzzle pieces, I tried to make them fit. I took the meds. I tried the CBT. I did the journaling, the mindfulness apps, the grounding exercises. I became a walking textbook of coping strategies. But somehow, I was still *me*. Still struggling. Still misunderstood.

What I didn't realise then, what none of them seemed to clock, is that they were all treating branches instead of looking at the tree. Every teacher, doctor, or well-meaning adult saw each struggle in isolation. The anxiety, the sensitivity, the shutdowns, the meltdowns, the social confusion, they picked each one like a separate leaf, analysing it, labelling it, trying to fix it. But no one ever stepped back to see the whole picture. No one asked what kind of tree all these branches belonged to. And so, for years, I was left with a growing sense that something was wrong, but no one could tell me what it was, because they weren't looking at the roots.

The thing about these near-miss diagnoses is that they made sense from a certain angle. Anxiety? Sure, I looked anxious. Always overthinking, always alert, always reading the room like my life depended on it (because, socially, it kind of did). Depression? I wasn't *sad*, exactly, but I was tired. So, so tired. Tired from masking, from not fitting in, from trying to be normal. OCD? Not quite, but yes, I had rituals and rules. They weren't about germs or symmetry, though, they were about survival. A routine meant control. Predictability. Safety.

Every diagnosis I received was like being handed a jigsaw puzzle piece from the wrong box. You hold it up, turn it around, and think, "Maybe?", but the edges don't align, and the picture it paints is missing far too much. There's a strange kind of heartbreak in being misdiagnosed. Not the obvious kind, but the quiet disappointment of being half-seen. It's a false relief. A name is offered, but it only explains a fraction of the noise in your head, the confusion in your social life, the exhaustion in your bones. You start to believe you're just uniquely broken. That you're failing at getting better.

And then, worse still, you doubt your own experience. When therapy doesn't work "as expected," you wonder if *you're* the problem. Maybe you're just not trying hard enough. Maybe you *are* difficult. Maybe you *are* too sensitive, too complicated, too much.

One therapist said I had "an anxious attachment style." Another said I had "low distress tolerance." A third told me I needed to "toughen up." Admittedly only one of those therapists was on a pay roll.

I nodded. I tried. I internalised every scrap of their clinical language like it was gospel, tweaking myself to fit a framework that never quite matched my shape. And still, the same themes returned: Why do noises hurt? Why do people drain me? Why do I need so much *recovery time* after a five-minute phone call? Why do I seem to miss the memo that everyone else got about how to human?

I remember talking to a close friend, years into this carousel of almost, describing how I needed to script conversations before phone calls, how I rehearsed social interactions in the shower, how I could cry from someone using the wrong tone. She tilted her head and said, "You're clearly intelligent. You've just got to stop being so dramatic."

And there it was again. *Too sensitive.*

If I'd had the language, I might have asked her: "Too sensitive for what?" For a world that blares instead of whispers? For a life that assumes everyone's brain runs the same operating system? For a society that celebrates the bold and filters out the quiet?

Looking back now, I realise none of those early diagnoses were *wrong*. They were incomplete. They were symptoms, not sources. Secondary effects of living in a world not built with me in mind.

Finding out I was autistic didn't erase the anxiety, the depression, the sensory overload. It reframed them. It was like finally seeing the blueprint after years of living in a house full of hidden doors. The anxiety? That's what happens when you've spent a lifetime translating every social interaction like it's a foreign language. The depression? That's what happens when you feel like a misfit and no one sees you clearly. The rituals? Coping mechanisms. The shutdowns? Neurological fatigue, not laziness. The "too muchness"? A mind processing the world at full volume without a mute button.

I wish someone had looked at the whole picture sooner. I wish I had known sooner. But I also know I'm not alone. So many late-diagnosed autistic adults carry a similar trail of not-quite-right labels. We were anxious. Depressed. Obsessive. Burned out. But we were also autistic underneath, throughout, all along.

And once you see it, you can't unsee it. The diagnosis that wasn't… becomes the clarity that is.

2.2: "You Always Overreact"

As you can likely tell from 2.1, there is a very specific sting that comes from being told you're overreacting, especially when you're not.

When something genuinely *feels* like an assault on your senses, or when your emotions are boiling over like a pot left on the hob, the last thing you want is someone looking at you with that baffled, vaguely amused expression and saying, "Alright, calm down. It's not that bad." Oh, but it *is* that bad. And honestly, sometimes it's worse.

Let me take you on a sensory journey. Imagine this: you're sitting in a café, trying to enjoy your hot chocolate (because coffee makes your heart feel like it's doing jazz hands), and then it happens. A child screeches, full blast, no warning. The chair leg behind you scrapes across the floor with a high-pitched *screeeeee*. Someone turns on the hand dryer in the bathroom, and it sounds like a jet engine taking off. There's a flickering light in the corner. The door hinge squeaks every time someone comes in. You're trying to keep your face composed, trying not to seem "weird," but inside? Inside your brain is doing a fire drill.

This is what it means to "overreact." Not because we're dramatic. Not because we want attention. But because our sensory processing is like a soundboard with all the sliders turned up to eleven. We're not overreacting, we're reacting *accurately* to stimuli that most people are conveniently able to ignore. Congratulations on your low-sensitivity nervous system, Sharon. Some of us are raw-nerved bundles of electric spaghetti.

Don't even get me started on clothes. I literally only wear white socks and white trainers. Always have. I'm so particular about it, and for the longest time I didn't even realise. The idea of wearing anything else on my feet? Nope. Absolutely not. The thought alone makes me uncomfortable. White or nothing, it's not a fashion choice, it just *feels right*.

Tags? Torture devices. Seams? Betrayals. Jeans? The enemy. I spent half my childhood thinking I was just being fussy, because I had to change my socks three times to find a pair that didn't feel like tiny prison shackles on my toes. And don't pretend you don't know the agony of a bra strap that's twisted, or a jumper with sleeves that are *almost* but not quite the right length. Sensory discomfort isn't mild. It's not "a bit annoying." It's like a pebble in your shoe that somehow migrates into your *soul*.

I also *despise* having wet clothes. Not dislike, despise. The feeling of damp fabric clinging to my skin makes my whole body tense. Wet socks? Instant misery. It's like walking on cold slugs with every step. Wet trousers? They stick in all the wrong places, heavy and suffocating, making my skin crawl. The thought of being stuck somewhere without a change of clothes, forced to endure that soaked, clingy discomfort, it's unbearable. I don't just feel damp, I feel *wrong*. Like my body wants to escape itself. I'll go miles out of my way just to avoid it. Dry clothes are not optional, they're survival.

There's the emotional side of it. The classic "too sensitive" accusation again, but now dressed up as "you're overreacting." Crying during an advert about butter? Been there. Feeling physically winded when someone raises their voice, even if it's not at you? Absolutely. Having to leave a room because a scene in a film was just a *bit too intense*? Yes, and I will not be taking questions.

It's not that we're trying to be melodramatic. It's that emotions hit us *hard*. They land without warning and don't always come with a volume dial. Joy? Ecstatic. Sadness? Devastating. Embarrassment? Cue the internal screaming and planning to move to a new country. There's no middle ground, just a very steep hill with "mild discomfort" at the top and "full-blown existential meltdown" at the bottom.

And yet, because it doesn't always look how people expect it to, because we might laugh inappropriately, or freeze, or shut down rather than yell, it gets misread. "You're being silly." "You need to lighten up." "You're taking this too personally." These comments usually come from people who *aren't* currently being impaled by a wool jumper or emotionally derailed by someone using a different tone of voice than usual.

There's a special kind of humiliation saved for being told you're overreacting when you've already worked *so hard* to *not* react. When you've already bitten your tongue, counted to ten, dug your nails into your palm, smiled through the discomfort. And then someone rolls their eyes because you flinched when a balloon popped or got snappy after being overwhelmed at the supermarket. If only they knew what it cost to hold it together for as long as you did.

Don't get me wrong, there *is* a sense of humour in it. Like the time I had to pretend I wasn't dying inside because the fire alarm at work went off and everyone else calmly filed out while I looked like I was being shot at. Or the time a pigeon flew at my face and I screamed loud enough to frighten a jogger, whilst trying to lose the goosebump pimples on my arms. These moments are funny in hindsight. But they're also a reminder that my nervous system is basically a raccoon in a thunderstorm, perpetually startled, always braced for chaos.

So no, we're not "making a fuss." We're managing a world that feels like it was designed without people like us in mind. We're regulating, recalibrating, recovering. And sometimes we're just doing our very best not to yell "WHY IS THAT LIGHT BUZZING" in the middle of a polite dinner party.

Being autistic clinically means having a brain that feels things, sensory, emotional, existential, with the intensity of a marching band playing next to your ear while you're trying to read. It's not overreacting. It's just reacting, honestly and openly, to a world that rarely understands the volume we're dealing with.

Being autistic, to me, means moving through the world with a brain that's tuned to a slightly different frequency. It means noticing details other people miss and missing things they seem to notice without trying. It's feeling everything, sounds, emotions, textures, louder, deeper, sharper. It's needing routine but also needing space. It's questioning things that others take for granted and rehearsing conversations in my head like a full-scale production. It's a thousand tabs open in my brain at all times. It's not always easy, but it's honest. It's me, unfiltered. And once I stopped trying to be someone else, I realised it's actually kind of brilliant.

2.3: Gaslit by Normalcy

Sometimes, it feels like everyone else got a manual on how to be a person, and mine got lost in the post. When you spend your whole life surrounded by people who seem to instinctively know how to be in the world, how to talk, move, react, joke, dress, flirt, disagree, fit in, and you… don't. You start to assume the problem is *you*. Not the room. Not the lighting. Not the script you were never given. Just… you.

It's a quiet kind of gaslighting, really. Not the dramatic, overt kind where someone twists your words until you question your grip on reality. No, this is the slow, invisible erosion of self-trust. The kind that whispers, *Everyone else finds this easy, why can't you?* The kind that makes you question your instincts, mask your discomfort, mimic behaviours you don't understand, and carry shame for not being "natural." It doesn't even need to be said aloud. It lives in the raised eyebrows, the confused stares, the advice that's just a little too patronising. "You think too much." "You're reading into it." "You're being awkward." "You'll grow out of it." "You just need more confidence."

At some point, I internalised a belief so deeply it became part of my operating system: *I am fundamentally wrong, and everyone else is right.*

And what's wild is, people meant well. They weren't trying to harm me. They just lived in a framework built for neurotypicals, one where eye contact is respectful, small talk is necessary, parties are fun, group dynamics are intuitive, noise is ignorable, and social rules are obvious. That's the baseline. That's "normal." And if you can't thrive within that framework, or even function without feeling like your skin is on backwards, you get labelled. Difficult. Shy. Rude. Dramatic. Intense. Off.

So, you start to contort. You become a master shapeshifter. You study. You watch. You build a catalogue of "acceptable" behaviours and try to replicate them with the precision of a mimic octopus. You rehearse jokes. You plan smiles. You force yourself to go to events, then beat yourself up for needing three days to recover. You learn to say "I'm fine" with a tone that sounds convincing enough to escape further questioning. All the while, the gap between who you are and who you're pretending to be grows wider. But that's the cost of fitting in, right?

And yet… something never feels quite settled. You follow the rules but still get it wrong. You say the thing you rehearsed, and it lands strangely. You laugh at the wrong moment. You feel too much. You notice everything. You can't relax. And when you dare to express that things feel overwhelming, confusing, exhausting, you're met with confusion. Or pity. Or worse: correction.

So, you try harder. And harder. Until trying becomes living. And you forget there's any other way.

The first time autism was suggested to me, I laughed. Not because I didn't believe autistic people existed of course, or that it was a valid experience, but because it felt so… unrelated to the version of autism I'd been shown growing up. I wasn't obsessed over trains. I didn't flap my hands. I had friends (ish). I made eye contact (when I remembered). I was a functioning adult, sort of. I was *sensitive*, sure, and quirky, and weirdly intense about certain things, but I wasn't *autistic*. Right?

That moment was like someone pointing at a locked door in a house I'd lived in my whole life and saying, "You've never opened this one?" And behind it was everything. Every misstep. Every "overreaction." Every shutdown. Every odd social dynamic I couldn't decode. Every night I lay in bed wondering why I seemed to need a manual for humaning. It wasn't me. It was the framework. The one I'd been told was the only way to be. The one I bent myself to fit until I barely recognised my original shape.

Realising you're autistic, especially later in life, is not just a diagnosis. It's a reclamation. It's the unravelling of a lifelong lie told by omission. The lie that there's one correct way to exist, and if you don't match it, you must be broken.

But you're not broken.

You're not defective.

You were just trying to navigate a neurotypical world without the privilege of knowing you had a different user manual.

It may sound odd to say, but the grief is real. The mourning for all those years spent blaming yourself, all the energy wasted on shame, all the pain of trying to belong in a room that didn't even have a chair for you. But the clarity that follows is incandescent. You finally get to see yourself clearly, not as a failed version of "normal," but as a fully-formed, valid version of *you*.

Gaslit by normalcy, yes. But no longer.

Now, I rewrite the script. I question the frameworks. I trust the voice inside me that always said, *something doesn't add up*. Because now I know, it wasn't me who was missing the mark. It was the measure itself that was skewed.

And that truth? That's freedom.

Chapter Three

Neurotypical, Apparently

3.1: Why Is Everyone Else So Chill?

There was a moment I recall in school, Year 5, maybe, when I sat in the lunch hall, surrounded by the clatter of trays, the low buzz of chatter, and the occasional scream of someone discovering a rogue raisin in their dessert, and I remember thinking, "Am I the only one who finds this whole thing absolutely unbearable?" I wasn't having a dramatic day. No tragic events. No embarrassing incidents. Just the sheer intensity of being *in it*. The lights were too bright. The noises were too sharp. Everyone else was happily chatting or ignoring each other in that normal, casual way, and I was there, clutching my fork like it might double as a weapon in case things escalated.

It wasn't just lunch. It was school assemblies, group projects, birthday parties, any gathering of more than three humans. I'd look around and wonder, with increasing alarm, *how* everyone else was managing to glide through life so casually. Why wasn't everyone else drowning in the overwhelming volume of *everything* all the time? Were they just better at hiding it? Or had I missed a briefing on How To Human?

The strangest part was no one seemed to notice I was struggling. Teachers said I was "a bit quiet," "sensitive," or "a deep thinker", which is basically polite adult code for *we have no idea what's going on with you, but you seem harmless enough.* I was never the kid with obvious needs or an obvious meltdown. I was the one who went quiet, clenched their jaw, and mimicked what looked like normal behaviour based on years of frantic observation. I was always trying to crack the code.

Group dynamics were the worst. Especially when they involved unspoken rules. Which, to be clear, is most group dynamics.

I've always much preferred one-on-one conversations. Big groups overwhelm me, too many voices, too many dynamics, too much to track all at once. But in a quiet one-on-one chat, I can actually *breathe*. I can focus, listen properly, connect. There's no pressure to perform or jump in at the perfect moment. It feels calmer, safer, more human. That's where I can actually be myself.

For some reason, humans love implying things rather than just saying them. (Don't laugh – it's difficult to decode). They love subtle shifts in tone and eyebrow raises and knowing glances. They love inside jokes and sarcasm and mild social bullying disguised as "banter." Meanwhile, I'm stood there like an eager exchange student from another planet, mentally replaying everything in slow motion, trying to figure out what I missed and whether I've somehow committed social treason by laughing one second too late.

I once spent a week agonising over whether someone saying "Nice one" in a group chat meant "Well done" or "That was idiotic, but

I'm being sarcastic." I ended up deleting the message and pretending I'd lost WiFi. It felt safer.

I didn't lack friends, exactly. I had people around me. But I often felt like I was watching the party from behind glass. They all seemed to know how to be, effortlessly relaxed, loosely engaged, unbothered by the constant chaos. I was overthinking my facial expressions, the volume of my voice, whether I'd misjudged the moment to laugh, whether my tone was too serious or too weird or too *me*.

When I first spoke to my mum about my suspicions that I might be autistic, she was genuinely confused. "But you always had friends round!" she said. And it's true, I did. Our house was often full of people. What she didn't realise was that I was clock-watching the whole time, counting down the minutes until I could finally have my space back. I liked my friends, I really did. I just liked them *better* once they'd gone home.

Eventually, I started to assume I was just a bit broken. Or dramatic. Maybe I had an overactive imagination. Maybe I was the kind of person who just took things a bit too personally. Maybe I was, as someone once whispered with a smirk, "a bit intense."

Soon came the ultimate insult: "You need to learn to relax."

Relaxing, to me, has never felt like a natural state. It's a full-time job. I have to *schedule* it. And even then, I end up worrying about whether I'm relaxing properly. Do other people just do it? Instinctively? That's wild.

There's a real feeling of loneliness in watching the world spin with such confidence, while you're internally scrambling to match the rhythm. It's like being the only one who didn't get the choreography memo but still having to join the dance. Everyone else is doing jazz hands and high kicks. I'm just trying not to fall over.

I once remember watching a friend of mine walk into a room, plonk herself down, and immediately start chatting to someone she barely knew like it was the most natural thing in the world. I stared at her in awe. Did she not fear the silence? The awkwardness? The risk of being weird? Apparently not. And when I asked her later how she did that, how she just *existed* without spiralling, she blinked at me and said, "What do you mean?"

Just to be confusing, on the other end of the social spectrum, sometimes I have *no* fear walking into conversations. Like a kid barging in on their mum's phone call with the neighbour, completely unaware they've just steamrolled through a heartfelt moment. That's me, charging in, full of enthusiasm, absolutely oblivious. The problem is, I'm terrible at reading the room. So, I might be walking straight into a conversation that needs metaphorical crime scene tape, and I'll just keep going. Cheerfully. Cluelessly. No idea I've just stepped in it.

Looking back, I realise how often I was masking without even knowing what masking was. It wasn't performative. It wasn't conscious. It was survival. I was trying to blend in with a species that felt familiar but alien all at once. And the thing is, it worked. For a while. Enough to pass. Enough to earn gold stars and good reports and invitations to birthday parties. But inside, I always felt like I was one sentence away from a glitch.

I wasn't chill because I was processing a thousand layers of sensory data, emotional temperature checks, conversational subtext, and performance anxiety all at once. And nobody saw it, because I wasn't falling apart in the obvious ways. I was doing what looked like coping, but it was really just *containing*.

So, when I hear people talk about autism as something obvious or dramatic or rare, I want to shake them gently and say, "Hi. I was autistic *in the room with you*, the whole time. Just quieter about it."

Despite all the awkwardness, confusion, and internal gymnastics, I still made it through. Still here. Still weird. And still asking —, mostly in jest, but a little bit sincerely, *Why is everyone else so chill?*

3.2: Cracking the Social Code

I used to think small talk was some kind of social prank. Everyone practises small talk, right? People would stand beside each other and say things like "Bit chilly today, isn't it" or "Can you believe the traffic," and I would just stand there, blinking, wondering when the real conversation was going to start. It took me a long time to understand that small talk is not actually about talking. It is a ritual. A code. A non-threatening exchange that says, "I acknowledge your presence, and I come in peace."

But nobody told me that. Nobody sat me down and explained the purpose of talking about the weather, or asking what someone had for lunch, or declaring that Friday felt like a Wednesday. I assumed people were just... bored. Or very easily amused. I could not understand how someone could say, "Well, that's British summer for you," and receive a warm chuckle in return. I would try to participate, but my attempts always seemed to go sideways. I would skip the small stuff and jump straight to the deep questions. "What do you think happens after we die" is not, apparently, a good icebreaker.

It was like everyone had a shared manual for interaction, and I had missed the download. The rules were invisible but clearly understood by everyone else. You are supposed to make eye contact, but not too much. Smile, but not constantly. Laugh at jokes, even if you do not understand them, but only if everyone else is laughing too. There are dozens of these rules, maybe hundreds, and they are not taught. They are absorbed, like osmosis. Unless you are autistic. In which case, you might as well be trying to learn fencing by watching a ballet.

Eye contact was always especially confusing. I was told repeatedly to look people in the eyes, but when I tried, I often stared too long, which apparently made people uncomfortable. If I avoided eye contact, I was seen as rude or evasive. So, I invented workarounds. I stared at people's eyebrows, the bridge of their nose, the rim of their glasses. Sometimes I wouldn't listen to the conversation but focus on making sure I blinked and looked them dead in the eyes at least twice every ten seconds. Sometimes I nodded and timed my glances like I was ticking boxes on a form. It was all conscious. All effort. Nothing about it was automatic.

Let's talk group laughter, which is perhaps the most cryptic code of all. Laughter in groups does not always mean something is funny. Sometimes it is agreement, sometimes it is reassurance, and sometimes it is just an awkward noise people make to keep the flow going. I have laughed in conversations just because everyone else did, not knowing what I was agreeing to. I have stayed silent during jokes because I could not tell whether they were ironic, sarcastic, offensive, or just... unfunny. But when you do not laugh, you feel it. That shift in energy. That slight confusion. The glance that says, "Why are you not reacting like us"

I learned to mirror. To study. I watched interactions like they were theatre performances. How people tilted their heads, how they raised their voices when greeting someone, how they used filler words and half-smiles. I was a social scientist without the lab coat. Everything became data. I picked up catchphrases from people and tried them out in my own sentences. I borrowed rhythms of speech, nodding patterns, even the way people said goodbye. None of it felt natural, but it worked well enough to blend in.

It is funny looking back. I thought I was just a bit awkward, or shy, or overly serious. What I was doing, though I did not have the words for it then, was masking. I was building a kind of translator in my brain, one that took in the baffling language of everyday interaction and spat out something passably human.

Social codes are not neutral. They favour a certain kind of mind. They reward ease, spontaneity, and a light touch. If you process information slowly, if you need time to interpret facial expressions or decipher tone, then you are always half a beat behind. You are playing the same game, just with a delay. And often, you are penalised for not keeping up.

There were so many moments when I felt like I had almost cracked the code, only for someone to change the rules again. I would finally feel like I understood how to navigate a group conversation, and then someone would bring in a new level of sarcasm or reference something I had never heard of, and I would be back to square one.

Working in an office, this is hands down one of the most common frustrations for me, constantly playing catch-up with social cues. By the time I've figured out the tone of the conversation, pieced together the subtext, and worked out whether that last comment was serious or sarcastic, the moment has already passed. Caught up! Oh wait, never mind, they've moved on. New joke. New topic. New facial expressions to decode.

But over time, I got better at recognising patterns. I still don't think it comes naturally, but it no longer feels like an impossible puzzle. I have learned when to laugh, when to nod, when to let silence hang, and when to fill it. I still miss things, and I still get exhausted by long social interactions, but now I understand *why*. And that makes all the difference.

Cracking the social code did not make me any less autistic. It just helped me see that I was not defective for needing a different kind of instruction manual. I was not weird for asking "why" when others just knew. The rules may be invisible, but that does not mean they are sacred. And once you understand that, you get to decide which ones are worth following, and which ones can be gently ignored.

Turns out, small talk is not entirely useless. It can be a bridge, a truce, a way to say "I see you," even if it is through a shared complaint about the rain.

I still rehearse small talk. And honestly? There's nothing wrong with that. Some people can wing it, but I prefer to go in with a game plan. If I know I'm going to bump into someone at work or at the shop, you can bet I've already played out three versions of the conversation in my head. It's not about being fake, it's about feeling prepared. It helps me feel more in control, like I have a map instead of just wandering through the jungle of awkward pauses and unpredictable responses. For me, it's not overthinking. It's just *thinking ahead.*

Chapter Four

Noticing the Glitches

4.1: The Meltdown Files

Right before a meltdown, there is often silence. It's not the peaceful kind. It's a clenched, static-laced hush, the moment before a dam cracks. For most of my life, I didn't have the language to explain what was happening to me. I only knew that, sometimes, everything would get too loud, too bright, too much. And I would break.

The first time I can clearly remember having an internal melting down in public, I was nineteen and stranded in a train station with delayed services, flickering lights, and announcements that kept cutting out mid-sentence. I had already had a long day, the kind that drains your social battery down to fumes. I had skipped lunch, I'd forgotten my headphones, and my routine had already been shattered by unexpected schedule changes. Then, a woman's perfume near me triggered a headache that started behind my eyes. The final straw was someone brushing against me in the crowd, just a shoulder bump, something casual. But it felt like I had been barged out of the way.

Next I remember leaning against concrete. Not sobbing exactly, more like frozen and shaking. My body had gone on strike. I was dimly aware that people were looking, but I couldn't speak, couldn't explain. Someone asked if I was okay. I remember wanting to scream, "No, I'm not," but I couldn't get my mouth to form the words. A train guard eventually crouched beside me and spoke in the slow, careful tone people use when they think you might be dangerous. He asked if I needed medical help. I nodded. It felt safer to say nothing than to try to explain how my brain had just stopped cooperating with reality.

Don't get me wrong, this hasn't happened too often in my glorious thirty years, but on the occasions it did, I always assumed it was something ordinary. Maybe I hadn't slept well. Maybe I was burnt out from stress or overwhelmed by life piling up. I never considered that there might be a deeper reason. I brushed off the shutdowns and sensory overloads as flukes. Temporary glitches. Just me being dramatic or too sensitive or needing a break. I never linked them to anything larger because, in my mind, autism looked like something else. Something louder. Something more visible. Something that couldn't possibly belong to me.

For years, I called these moments "panic attacks," though that didn't really cover it. They weren't just anxiety, they were full-body shutdowns. Sometimes they came with tears, sometimes with rage, sometimes with complete silence. They happened after holding in too much, for too long. Too many people, too many lights, too many micro-decisions, too many misunderstandings. And unlike what I thought were "normal" panic attacks, mine didn't always feel like fear. Sometimes they felt like fury. Sometimes they felt like failure. Mostly, they just felt like everything all at once, crashing in.

At work, they looked like sudden bathroom breaks that lasted too long. At home, they looked like snapping over a teaspoon in the wrong drawer. Once, at a wedding, I had to hide in a bathroom stall for nearly an hour because the small talk, the crowd, and the pressure to be "on" had drained me dry. I stared at my phone, not doing anything, just trying to anchor myself with a familiar object. I didn't want to ruin the evening for anyone. I just needed to not exist for a bit.

Before I understood what was happening, I was convinced that I was just "too sensitive." I had been told that often enough. Teachers, friends, even partners had used those words, and I swallowed them whole. I would rehearse things like, "I'm just tired," or "Sorry, I don't know why I'm crying," or worse, "I'm being dramatic, ignore me." I labelled myself as a mess. What I didn't know was that I was burning out under a thousand invisible cuts.

Meltdowns are not tantrums. They are not attention-seeking, and they are not optional. They are what happens when the pressure inside a person exceeds what they can safely hold. For autistic people, that threshold might look different. It might be closer to the surface, because we're spending so much energy just trying to *function* in a world that often feels like it's set to the wrong frequency.

I have learned, over time, to recognize the warning signs. The clenching jaw. The sudden detachment. The narrowed vision. The invisible sirens in my chest that start to wail. Now, if I feel those things, I try to pause. I try to leave the room. I run cold water over my wrists. I cancel plans. But there were many years before that knowledge. Years filled with what I can now only describe as glitches, moments when the system overloaded, and all I could do was reboot.

It's still hard to talk about meltdowns without shame. Even now, even knowing what I know. There's always a part of me that whispers, "You should be able to handle this." That voice echoes every time someone in the past rolled their eyes, or told me to "calm down," or worse, laughed. But I am learning that there is no shame in being overwhelmed. There is no shame in needing quiet. In needing space. In crying in a carpark because the fluorescent lights at the supermarket were too much and someone asked a question I couldn't answer fast enough.

This chapter, these memories, they are not here to be pitied. They are here because they are real. Because they happened. Because for a long time, I moved through the world with no explanation for why certain things felt so hard, so heavy, so utterly out of sync. These stories are not here to make you feel sorry for me. They are here to be seen. To be named. Because they matter. If you have had those moments too, the silent, trembling ones or the loud, spiralling ones, I want you to know: you are not too much. You are responding to a world that wasn't built with you in mind. And you deserve compassion, not correction.

Meltdowns don't define me. They are not the sum total of who I am. But understanding them, finally seeing them for what they were, helped me reclaim pieces of myself that I had spent years trying to hide or explain away. For so long, I saw those moments as failures. As emotional outbursts. As proof that I was too much, too fragile, too dramatic. I felt ashamed of them, tried to erase them, tried to forget the way my body would shut down while my brain screamed in silence.

But each meltdown left a clue. A tiny breadcrumb along the trail I didn't know I was following. Each one pointed toward something deeper. Not brokenness, but difference. Not weakness but overwhelm. Not drama, but a nervous system pushed past its limit. I didn't have the language for it then, so I filled in the gaps with blame. I thought I was just failing at being a person.

That truth has a name now. Autism. And somehow, knowing that changes everything. Not the past, not the memories or the pain, but the way I carry them. The way I understand myself. The way I forgive the things I once tried to force into silence. It gives context to the chaos. It gives shape to the struggle. And in that shape, I have found compassion. I have found peace. I have found myself.

4.2: The One with the Earplugs

Imagine walking into a room and immediately being hit by a sound you can't locate. It isn't even particularly loud, just wrong. Like the hum of a fluorescent light that no one else seems to notice but feels to you like an off-key violin someone is bowing directly into your skull. The lights above are white, clinical, and feel like staring at a searchlight. The chair has a scratchy polyester cover that makes your skin crawl just by looking at it. Your jumper label might as well be made of tiny knives. Someone's chewing gum nearby. You can hear every squish.

Welcome to my world. We touched on sounds earlier, but lets talk about the reality of sensory overload.

This is the sensory soup I live in, sometimes a gentle simmer, sometimes a full rolling boil. I only started to realise it wasn't this way for everyone when I noticed how casually people walked through shopping centres. How they managed to hold conversations inside echoey cafes with ten different soundtracks competing for attention, clattering cutlery, coffee machine screeches, children shrieking nearby. I couldn't even think straight, let alone talk. They weren't blinking at the harsh overhead lighting or fidgeting with their cuffs. They weren't shifting uncomfortably because their shoes were doing something sinister to their ankles. They weren't flinching when someone's perfume wafted by like a chemical fog. I was. And I always had.

You know what's a really odd one for me? I am ridiculously picky when it comes to eating. And I don't just mean "not a fan of olives" or "mildly fussy about textures", I mean the full sensory roulette of food aversions that make even the idea of trying something new feel like a gamble. But here's the thing people often don't understand, I *want* to eat those things. I *want* to enjoy the beautiful cakes in the bakery window, the ones with the glossy icing and the perfect little swirls on top. I *want* to try scrambled eggs, or pasta with sauce, or whatever it is that everyone else seems to eat without a second thought.

Chances of me actually eating it? Honestly, there's probably more chance of me spontaneously learning to tap dance on a tightrope while reciting the periodic table backwards.

It's not about being difficult. It's not about being ungrateful or snobby or childish. It's about how certain smells, textures, and even temperatures can make my whole body scream *nope* before my brain even has a chance to weigh in. Sometimes it's the way a food feels in my mouth. Sometimes it's the unpredictability, will it be mushy? Stringy? Lumpy? Wet? Will it taste the way it smells? And if it doesn't, how bad is that going to feel? How quickly could I get rid of the taste if I don't like it?

I can't count the number of times I've wanted to join in, to say yes to the birthday cake or the brunch or the casual lunch invite without planning an exit strategy. I've wished I could just *get over it* and eat what's in front of me. But the reality is, it's not that simple. It's not about willpower. It's about wiring. And once I understood that my sensory system is just built differently, the shame started to loosen its grip. I still can't eat the scrambled egg. But now I know it's not because I'm broken. It's because I'm autistic. And that changes how I treat myself when I say no.

I used to think I was just high maintenance. Sensitive. A bit dramatic. I cut labels out of clothes and pretended it was a quirk. I wore sunglasses in places that felt absurd, like libraries or the dentist's waiting room. I avoided certain shops entirely because the music gave me a migraine. For the longest time, I thought it was just me being a bit extra. Then, one day, I read a description of sensory processing differences in autistic people, and it was like someone had finally put words to the chaos in my head. I almost cried. Not because it was sad, but because it made sense.

There's a pair of earplugs I carry in my pocket almost everywhere now. They're discreet, slightly translucent, and a genuine lifeline. I bought them on a whim after a particularly awful experience in a restaurant where the music was just loud enough to erase all conversation but not loud enough to feel intentional. I remember leaving with my ears buzzing, my shoulders hunched up to my ears from tension. Since then, the earplugs have become a sort of security blanket. If I feel the storm coming on, I pop them in, and suddenly the world muffles, softens, quiets. I can still hear, but it's like someone turned everything down from scream to whisper. It's magic.

Don't get me started on smells. Scented candles? Hazardous. Air fresheners? Basically, chemical warfare. Someone once sprayed deodorant in a changing room and I had to leave because my eyes started watering and my throat closed up like I was inhaling battery acid. Even walking past a soap aisle in a supermarket can be a minefield. I once chose a bus seat based solely on which direction someone's shampoo scent was blowing. It wasn't personal. Again, it was survival.

All of this used to make me feel like I was fussy or picky or difficult. Now I understand that I am navigating a world that's often too loud, too bright, too sharp, and too fast for the way my brain filters information. It doesn't mean I'm broken. It means my settings are just different. I receive more input than most people. And sometimes, that input turns into overload. Sometimes I need to leave a room. Sometimes I need to shut my eyes. Sometimes I need earplugs.

There is beauty in this, too. I can hear music in layers most people miss. A whisper of wind through trees feels like a symphony. Textures that feel right are a joy, like wrapping myself in a cloud. A good smell, the right one, can make my entire day better. I once cried over a freshly baked cinnamon bun, not because I was emotional, but because the warmth and scent and texture were so utterly perfect it overwhelmed me in the best possible way.

Living with a sensory system that's set to high gain can be exhausting, yes, but it also means I experience the world vividly. When something is good, it's *really* good. I fall in love with soft blankets, quiet corners, just-right lighting, gentle voices. I collect comfort like treasures. A hoodie that fits just so. A lamp that gives off the exact right shade of warm yellow. Noise-cancelling headphones. A chair that doesn't squeak.

So yes, I am the one with the earplugs. And the sunglasses. And the "no thanks" to scratchy fabrics. I am the one who leaves parties early and who changes outfits twice before finding one that doesn't make me itch. But I am also the one who notices the velvet hush of a snowfall, the perfect brush of a dogs fur against my ankle, the way candlelight flickers just right against a stone wall. I live inside a sensory story, every day. Some days it reads like a horror novel. Some days it's poetry.

And now, I finally know I'm not weird for feeling it all. I'm wired to.

4.3: Hyperfixation Nation

When I fall in love with something, I don't just like it, I *live* it. I breathe it. I will reorganise my entire schedule to make space for it. I will read everything about it, talk to anyone who will listen, and then talk to people who won't. I will become a walking, talking encyclopaedia on the topic of the month, whether that's medieval bread ovens, obscure cartoon lore, the layout of Victorian greenhouses, or the migratory patterns of jellyfish. There is no such thing as a casual interest in Hyperfixation Nation. We're all in, and we're proud of it.

I used to think this was just quirky. A bit much, maybe. I thought everyone else did this too, just maybe a little quieter, or with more self-restraint. But it turns out, not everyone rewatches a TV show sixteen times in a row because they like the way the dialogue flows. Not everyone stays up until 3 a.m. making an extremely detailed spreadsheet comparing the features of fictional magic systems. Not everyone cries because a certain book character eats a sandwich the exact same way they do. This is more than fandom. This is a neurological joyride with no brakes and a hyper-focus engine.

Don't roll your eyes, but I *loved* Pokémon as a youngster. Like, truly and deeply. It wasn't just a phase. It was a whole world I could disappear into. A world with rules I could understand, creatures I could memorise, and a kind of logic that made sense when the real world felt far too unpredictable. I still get actual chills when I think about it now, not just from nostalgia, but from something deeper. A kind of joy that still lives in me, dormant but not gone.

I don't sit there for hours playing the games anymore. I don't collect the cards or obsessively hunt for rare editions. I don't even follow the new series. But here's the strange and beautiful thing: it still makes me incredibly, disproportionately happy when I see anything Pokémon-related. A Pikachu plushie on a shelf. A set of themed socks. A mug shaped like a Poké Ball. It sparks something in me that is hard to put into words. Something warm. Something rooted in comfort and recognition.

It's not really about the game anymore. It's about the feeling. The feeling of something familiar in a world that still often feels like too much. The feeling of being connected to a version of myself that found joy in the details. That felt a sense of mastery in learning all the names and types and evolutions. That created elaborate stories with my favourite characters and imagined a world where I could thrive.

There's a kind of sensory happiness in it too. The bright colours. The soft sounds. The neat designs. They're like a balm for a tired brain. So even now, when I'm scrolling online and see a Pokémon-themed gift or something random with a little Snorlax or Bulbasaur on it, it makes me super, super happy. Not in a childish way. In a human way. In a *me* way.

It's a reminder that joy doesn't need to be justified. That you don't have to outgrow the things that made you feel safe or excited or understood. You can carry them with you. You can let them light you up, even if it's just for a moment, because joy like that is rare. And when it shows up, even in the shape of a cartoon electric mouse, I welcome it. Every single time.

I love it. Truly. Being autistic means I get to love things deeply, fiercely, and without shame, at least, now that I understand where this comes from. Before my diagnosis, I often felt embarrassed by how intense I could get. I'd try to dial it down, pretend I was only sort of interested in something, when really I was obsessed. I'd wait for people to show interest before I shared, testing the waters like it was a confession. But now, I understand this is one of the brightest parts of my brain. When I'm immersed in a hyperfixation, the world feels clear and electric. It's like turning the volume of life up to "YES."

Some of my obsessions have lasted years. Others burn hot and fast. All of them leave fingerprints on my life. There was the six-month stint where I couldn't stop learning about whales. I mean *really* learning. Species classifications, migratory paths, communication sounds, threats to habitats. I knew which whale was nicknamed the "canary of the sea." I had a favourite whale. I had *opinions* on whale documentaries. My friends started tagging me in every whale-related post they came across. I was the Whale Person, and I wore that badge proudly.

The beautiful thing about these fixations is that they're never wasted. Even when the intensity fades, I'm still left with the joy they brought me and the odd little facts tucked into my mental library. I've made friends through niche interests. I've found confidence through mastery of subjects that others might find obscure. I've found solace in solo research, in hours spent deep in thought, connecting dots and drawing meaning from patterns. While the world outside often felt chaotic and difficult to navigate, my special interests made sense. They had rules. They had logic. They had depth.

One of the first signs I was different came through play. As a child, I didn't flit between games the way other kids did. I stayed inside one imaginary world for months. I created entire sagas for my toys. My stories had timelines, politics, trade routes. My dolls lived through dramatic betrayals and historical events. I used to write long, looping scripts in crayon, detailing the next episode of their lives. My parents called it "imaginative." I now call it autistic joy. That intense focus didn't stop in childhood, it just got more sophisticated.

Even now, I have a favourite pen. A specific brand of notebook. A preferred angle for reading under a lamp. I don't just "like" things. I adore them. I elevate them. And yes, I'll talk your ear off about them, but only because I want you to feel the sparkle too. Hyperfixations have given me purpose during some of my hardest moments. They've anchored me when the rest of life felt impossible. They've reminded me of what it feels like to be truly *alive*.

There is something sacred in passion, especially when the world tells you to tone it down. I have spent years being told I was intense, overwhelming, "too much." But I have never felt more myself than when I am deep inside a subject I love, finding hidden connections, collecting facts like treasures, creating from the energy of excitement.

So yes, I may be part of Hyperfixation Nation. I'm not just a tourist, I'm on the local council. And I wouldn't change it for anything. Let others dabble. I'll dive headfirst. Let others try to be cool and aloof. I'll be over here with my stack of annotated maps, crying over fictional plot twists and explaining obscure trivia with my hands flailing like fireworks.

This isn't just part of my autism.

This is one of the brightest stars in my constellation.

Chapter Five

Dr. Google and the Rabbit Hole

5.1: "Wait... This Is Me?"

It always starts with something innocent. Maybe you're up too late again because your brain refuses to shut down before 2 a.m., even though your body is begging for mercy. You type something random into the search bar. "Why do I get so overwhelmed by supermarket lights?" Or "Why do I rehearse conversations before they happen?" Or the classic, "Why am I like this?" You hit enter, expecting some vague self-help article or a BuzzFeed quiz, but instead you stumble across a list. A list of autistic traits in adults. You read the first few with a shrug. Interesting. Familiar, maybe. Then you scroll a bit more and suddenly you're blinking in disbelief because, hold on, this isn't just relatable. This is *uncannily* accurate. This list is reading you like a diary. And just like that, you're Alice. But instead of Wonderland, you've just fallen into the diagnostic rabbit hole of neurodivergence.

At first, it feels surreal. You're not new to introspection. You've tried on every label like a desperate shopper in a badly lit fitting room. Anxiety? Been there. Depression? Got the sweatshirt. ADHD? Flirted with it. But this, this feels different. This is not just about moods or focus. It's about *you*. The way you process the world. The way you've *always* processed it, even if you didn't have the words for it. It's not about one symptom or one trait. It's about a pattern. A constellation. A system. And you're sitting there at 1:47 a.m., laptop glowing like a portal to another universe, whispering to yourself, "Wait... this is me?"

You keep scrolling. The more you read, the more your stomach tightens in that weird twisty way it does when you realize something very important and slightly terrifying. You don't just relate to one or two things. You relate to *everything*. Eye contact is awkward and sometimes feels like staring directly into the sun. You rehearse conversations in your head like a playwright with a one-person cast. You thought everyone hated tags in clothes and needed noise-cancelling headphones in shopping centres. Doesn't *everyone* hear electricity humming? Doesn't *everyone* cry when their routine is unexpectedly disrupted? Apparently not. Apparently, that's... a thing. A *trait*.

You sit back, stunned, as memories start to unravel themselves from the past like a slow, glitchy montage. That time you had a meltdown at a birthday party because your sparkly tights felt "wrong." The way you always had to eat your food in a particular order. Your obsession with ancient Egypt that consumed your entire Year Six. The fact that you *still* hyperfixate, and once spent three months reading everything about mushrooms and mycelium networks like your life depended on it. You thought you were just quirky. Intense. Maybe a little dramatic. But now? You're starting to wonder if all of that was something else. Something with a name.

And the feelings that come with this realization? Oh, they're a mixed bag. Relief, first and foremost. Like you've finally found the instruction manual to your brain, buried under a pile of self-help books and misguided personality quizzes. But also grief, because if this is true, then why didn't anyone notice? Why did you spend so many years blaming yourself for being "too much" or "too sensitive" or "weird"? Why did you try so hard to be normal, when normal was never the goalpost that made sense for you in the first place?

There's a kind of awe, too. A marvelling at how something so big could have been hiding in plain sight for so long. You start to remember things people said to you, little comments, often meant kindly or offhand. "You're just a bit intense." "You overthink everything." "You're very particular." Like puzzle pieces you dismissed because you thought they belonged to a different picture. But now, the image is forming. And it looks suspiciously like... well, *you*.

Of course, the internet is both a gift and a chaotic mess. For every insightful blog post or article by a late-diagnosed autistic person, there's a sea of misinformation and stereotypes. You have to sift through the noise. No, you don't have to be a math genius or have a photographic memory to be autistic. No, you don't need to rock back and forth or count matchsticks in a rainstorm. But yes, you *can* be articulate, empathetic, and socially active and *still* be autistic. Because, plot twist, autism isn't a fixed costume, it's a spectrum, and you've been painting on that palette all along.

Eventually, the tabs on your browser start to multiply. You find yourself nodding along to videos, crying at personal essays, and taking self-assessments with the intensity of a scholar. And while you know that no internet checklist can diagnose you officially, you can't unsee what you now see. You can't unknow what you now know. Something has shifted. And for the first time, maybe in forever, it feels like you've stopped trying to shove yourself into a shape that doesn't fit.

You close your laptop, not with answers, but with a sense of clarity you didn't know you needed. You still don't know what comes next, but you know that tonight, under the blanket of glow from your screen and the quiet hum of your brain finally feeling seen, something clicked.

The questions are still there, but they feel softer now. Less like accusations and more like invitations. You're not fixed, because you were never broken. You're just beginning to understand the shape of yourself, and that knowing feels like a kind of peace. You don't have it all figured out, but for the first time, that feels okay.

5.2: The Role of Social Media

It's a peculiar moment when your phone knows something about you before you do. (Blame the algorithm. Blame the softly suspicious way it listens when you're not talking. Blame the digital cosmos that somehow clocked your lifelong confusion before you had the language for it). One minute, you're idly scrolling through your feed, thinking about snacks or whether your left shoe feels weird, and then, there it is. A video. A post. A tweet. It's titled something like, "You might be autistic if…" or "Things I thought were just personality quirks but turned out to be neurodivergence." You pause. You watch. And just like that, your own habits, tics, and lifelong ways of being are reflected back at you with startling precision. Welcome to the age of algorithmic self-discovery.

The role social media plays in late-diagnosed autism is both weirdly magical and completely absurd. It's also brilliant at making everyone think they have every condition under the sun after a five-minute scroll. A good meme is not a clinical tool. A relatable post is not a full assessment. And for all the genuine community and knowledge-sharing out there, there is also a flood of oversimplified content that can confuse as much as it clarifies. Autism is nuanced. It is diverse. It presents differently in every person. No carousel of infographics can hold the full depth of your lived experience.

It's hard to explain to someone who hasn't experienced it. It's not just that people are sharing their stories. It's that the internet has become a sort of accidental diagnostic tool, a sprawling network of content where other people's anecdotes and epiphanies act as a mirror. You're not Googling "Am I autistic?" at this point. You're just trying to watch a baking video or doomscroll your way to sleep, and the next thing you know you're sitting upright thinking, "Wait. Why does this random stranger's life feel like mine?"

It's easy to dismiss this as overidentification or online hype. But that underestimates what it feels like to see yourself clearly for the first time through the lens of someone else's messy, human, vulnerable account. Social media isn't giving you a textbook, it's giving you lived experience. And that hits different. Because the truth is, most of us didn't relate to the dusty diagnostic lists written decades ago by people who studied autism mostly in boys under twelve. We read those and thought, "Well, I like people, so I guess that's not me." But then we stumbled onto a post where someone says, "I hate being interrupted mid-task. I cry if I lose my routine. I don't understand the point of small talk." And we feel that jolt. That sting of familiarity. Not because we're impressionable, but because for the first time, someone's speaking our language.

Social media's magic lies in its specificity. In the hands of autistic creators, it becomes a place of joyful nuance. Memes about sensory hellscapes, reels about masking fatigue, threads about the euphoric bliss of hyperfocus. It's not medical. It's personal. And strangely enough, that makes it feel more valid. It's not trying to define you, it's simply describing itself, and in doing so, offering you an open door.

Of course as we mentioned before, there's also the algorithm. The all-knowing, slightly creepy, always-listening algorithm. Is it a coincidence that you saw five autism-related posts in a week, or did you linger just long enough on one for the platform to decide that this is your new personality? Who knows. But the result is the same. Suddenly your feed is a neurodivergent buffet. ADHD side of TikTok. Late-diagnosed-autism Tumblr. Instagram reels narrated by people who just got their diagnosis and can't stop talking about their past with brand-new eyes.

Some might call it a feedback loop. Others might say it's a confirmation bias generator. And yes, it's true that algorithms are not a substitute for proper diagnosis or careful self-reflection. But also… when you've spent your whole life thinking you're the weird one, seeing a constant stream of people saying, "Hey, me too," can be profoundly healing.

It's not just about consuming content. It's about community. You find people. People who get it. Not just your quirks or your meltdowns, but the *why* behind them. You learn new words. You hear someone talk about monotropism or auditory processing delay and your brain lights up like a Christmas tree. These aren't things that came up in your childhood, or even in your therapist's office. But here they are, in your pocket, delivered to you via captioned videos and story time-style monologues. It's like getting handed a secret decoder ring for your own life.

The best part is how casual it all feels. No one is speaking from a pedestal. It's people in their kitchens or on walks, ranting or laughing or just being themselves. They're not diagnosing you. They're sharing what it's like to *be* them. And in doing so, they're creating space for people like you to say, "Actually, I think that might be me too."

Of course, there are downsides. The internet is a messy place. Sometimes people gatekeep. Sometimes there's misinformation or unhelpful stereotypes. Sometimes a single viral post can make autism seem like a trend rather than a lifelong way of experiencing the world. But if you stick around, if you find the good corners, the honest voices, the thoughtful creators, then what you get is something no diagnostic checklist ever gave you, representation. Not the polished kind. The real, raw, funny, tired, overstimulated kind.

That's where the serendipity comes in. You didn't go looking for this, not really. You weren't trying to find a new identity. But it found you. Through comments, through creators, through posts that you saved and then reread three times because they made something click. It's oddly poetic that the same platforms that once fed us imposter syndrome and FOMO could also offer such clarity, such unexpected affirmation.

So yes, maybe it was the algorithm. Maybe it was a lucky stumble. Maybe it was someone else's offhand TikTok that planted the seed. But whatever it was, it matters. Because now you're here, and you're not alone. In a world that never quite made space for you, you've found a strange, glitchy little corner where people *do* make space. Where the comment section feels more validating than any classroom or office ever did.

And for once, you don't have to explain why you are the way you are. You just have to scroll.

5.3: The Mirror Test

There is something quietly seismic about seeing yourself in someone else's story. Not in a vague, "oh I've done that too" kind of way, but in a gut-deep, bone-anchored, world-tilting kind of way. It's the kind of recognition that stops you mid-scroll, mid-thought, mid-breath. A stranger is speaking, writing, filming, just being, and yet, somehow, they are reaching across time and space to tap you on the shoulder and say, "Hey, I think we've lived the same script."

At first, you try to rationalize it. Maybe it's just coincidence. Maybe you're being overly impressionable. Maybe everyone feels this way and you're just noticing it now because you're looking for patterns. But then the feeling comes again. And again. A post about masking resonates so strongly that your chest tightens. A thread about childhood meltdowns reads like an entry from your own forgotten journal. A video describes the exact way your body feels when someone interrupts your routine, or when the noise in a café starts to blur your ability to think. And you know, deep in the hush between thoughts, that this isn't about suggestion. This is about reflection.

It's like standing in front of a mirror for the first time in years and realizing you've been walking around smudged, out of focus, and half-seen. And now, slowly, your own image is coming into clarity. You are not imagining it. You are not too sensitive, too dramatic, too rigid, too much. You are not broken. You are not a puzzle missing pieces. You are a person with a whole new lens, one that explains why the world has always felt slightly off-kilter.

And yet the clarity comes with whiplash.

Because with every moment of recognition comes a flood of memory. Things you never thought to question before are suddenly highlighted and framed. You start rewatching the film of your life with director's commentary. Why did I feel so different at school? Why did I spend so much time copying the people around me just to seem normal? Why did no one notice how much I was struggling beneath the surface? That question echoed in my mind for weeks after I first started to seriously consider that I might be autistic. It crept in late at night, slid beneath old memories, and tangled itself into every moment where I had felt misunderstood, dismissed, or silently overwhelmed.

At first, I was angry. Not confused. Not sad. Angry. It came in waves, raw and unfiltered. How could the people closest to me, the people who claimed to know and love me best, have missed it? How did they not notice the meltdowns disguised as mood swings, the exhaustion after socialising, the panic over change, the desperate need for predictability, or the way I clung to routines like a lifeline? How did they not see me breaking and bending and contorting myself just to keep up? To appear fine?

Maybe I was *too* good at masking, too good at pretending, too determined to pass for someone who was coping when I was quietly falling apart. But still, part of me expected that someone should have seen through it. A teacher. A friend. A parent. A partner. Someone.

You remember moments that once felt random or small, but now gleam with new meaning. The panic you felt during group projects. The exhaustion after social events. The obsession with one topic that everyone else eventually grew bored of while you just... couldn't stop. The moments of inexplicable shutdown. The way you always kept a mental script for every conversation, and the heartbreak when someone didn't stick to it. The mirror shows you all of it. Not as flaws, but as symptoms of a misunderstood design.

As much as I've talked about the lesser pleasant sides of late realisation, it's not all bad. There's joy too, the kind that bubbles up when you realize you're not alone in your oddness. That other people flinch at the sound of fluorescent lights. That others find eye contact painful. That someone else also hums a specific tune on repeat in their head to block out overstimulation. There's power in that shared understanding. In finally having a name for what you are. And in seeing that name worn with pride by people you admire. Poets. Artists. Scientists. People who have not just survived, but thrived, because of, not in spite of, their brains.

But it's a lot to hold. A thousand tiny epiphanies arrive at once. You realize that you spent so much of your life trying to become someone you were never built to be. That the masks you wore became so convincing you even fooled yourself. And now, as the mirror offers you the truth, there's a trembling sort of liberation. You don't have to pretend anymore. You don't have to twist yourself to fit anymore.

Still, the rethinking is constant. It spills into everything. Your job. Your friendships. Your past relationships. The way people described you. The way you described yourself. Every piece gets pulled apart and re-examined. You grieve the version of you who didn't know. You ache for the child you were, who needed support and didn't have the words to ask for it. And at the same time, you marvel at the resilience it took to get here without a map.

Because that's what this is, really. A remapping. A process of redrawing the territory of your own identity. You are not starting from scratch, but you are starting anew. With a clearer picture. With softer eyes. With more compassion.

Eventually, the whiplash settles into momentum. You start to move forward, still holding the mirror, but not with the same wide-eyed shock. Now you carry it more like a guide, something that helps you check in with yourself. Am I being honest about my needs? Am I unmasking when it's safe? Am I giving myself the grace to be who I am, not who I was taught to be?

This chapter of recognition is both tender and powerful. It shakes you, then steadies you. And maybe, just maybe, it begins to transform you. Because once you've seen yourself clearly, it's impossible to go back to blurring your edges. You start telling the truth, first to yourself, then to others. And with each truth told, the mirror becomes less frightening and more freeing.

This is where the real story begins. Not the moment you found the word, but the moment the word helped you find yourself.

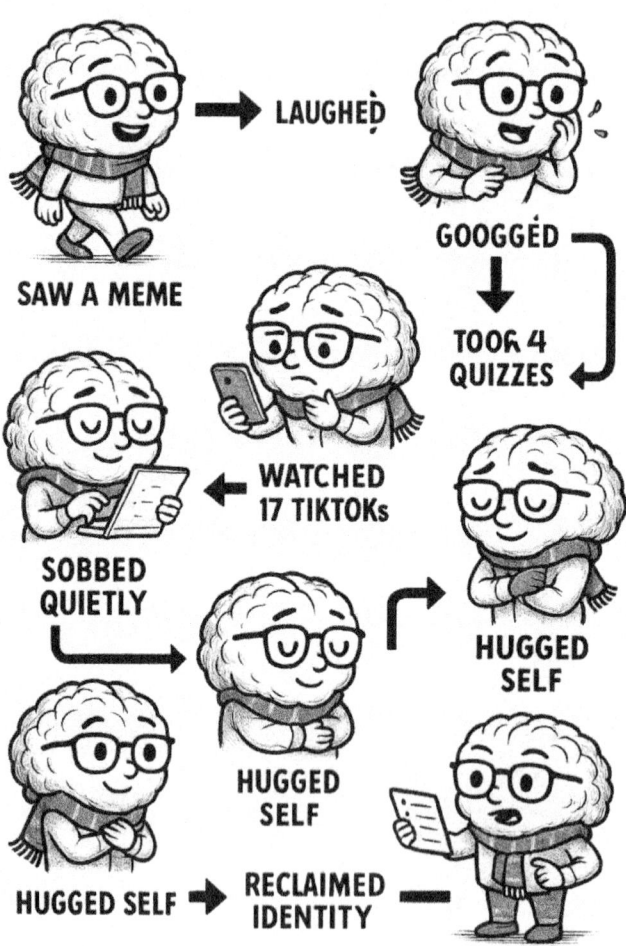

Chapter Six

How Did They Miss It?

6.1: Too Smart, Too Polite, Too Masked

Too clever. Too polite. Too good at eye contact when I focused hard enough to do it. Too verbal. Too put-together. That's the thing about masking. When you've trained yourself to perform normal so convincingly, no one thinks to look for what's underneath. You become a magic trick. A convincing illusion. But it costs you everything.

There's a kind of invisibility that comes with being "high-functioning," a label I now deeply resent. It's one of those terms that sounds like a compliment, but really it just means "you make *us* comfortable." It means your struggles are invisible enough that they can be ignored. You're not melting down in public, so what could be wrong? You have friends, you went to university, you have a job, so clearly you're not *really* autistic. As though autism only counts if you're visibly falling apart. As though surviving in a world not built for you is the same thing as thriving.

For a long time, I played along. I laughed when I was confused in conversations. I nodded when I didn't understand instructions. I mimicked the facial expressions of people around me like I was trying to pass a drama exam. I studied humans like they were a foreign species. And I was good at it. Really good. So good that even therapists (on and off payroll) missed it. So good that I missed it.

The masking started so early I can't even tell where the performance ends and I begin. It wasn't just social stuff either. I learned the scripts, yes, but I also learned how to intellectualize my emotions to avoid being "too much." I downplayed sensory overload. I blamed myself for exhaustion. I assumed I was just bad at being a person. That everyone else was out here loving parties, small talk, group projects, and I was the only one crawling out of my skin.

I wasn't unwell enough to be noticed. And when I did ask for help, the stereotypes got in the way. Doctors saw a girl who was doing fine on paper. I'd make jokes in appointments. I'd explain myself clearly. I didn't seem "weird." Not like their idea of weird. I wasn't obsessed with trains. I didn't flap my hands. I had feelings. I could smile.

The problem with stereotypes is they're just snapshots, not systems. They're shaped by who gets studied and who gets listened to. For decades, autism research focused on young boys. Boys who were struggling *externally*. Boys who weren't performing. Girls, and those assigned female at birth, were overlooked. Because we tend to internalize. We mimic. We manage. We make ourselves small to fit in. And we're praised for it. We're called "mature for our age." We're labelled "gifted" or "sensitive" or "shy" instead of supported.

Being articulate became a double-edged sword. It made people assume I was fine. But being able to *say* "I'm struggling" is not the same thing as not struggling. In fact, sometimes the ones who can explain their pain in detail are the ones who've had the most practice carrying it. No one thought to look beneath the language. They just heard my vocabulary and thought, "She's fine."

I now understand that being smart doesn't cancel out autism. Being polite doesn't erase it. Masking doesn't mean it's not there. It just means it's harder to see. And when something is harder to see, it's easier to ignore.

If anything, autistic people are clever. Exceptionally so. And I don't just mean academically, though that can certainly be true too. I mean clever in the way we observe, adapt, and decode a world that was not built with us in mind.

So, I fell through the cracks. Not because I wasn't autistic enough, but because I was *too* good at compensating. Too good at being palatable. I've since read the phrase "weaponized competence," and it hit hard. That was me. Always capable enough that I couldn't be struggling that badly. Always tidy enough to disqualify myself from help.

It took thirty years for anyone to even suggest the word autism. And even then, I hesitated. Because I had internalized all those messages too. I didn't look like the picture in the pamphlet. I didn't feel "autistic enough." But here's the truth I wish I had known sooner: autism doesn't look like one thing. It doesn't sound like one voice. It doesn't behave one way. And it certainly doesn't disappear because someone's good at hiding it.

I was too smart. Too polite. Too masked. And that's exactly why they missed it.

But I won't miss it anymore.

6.2: The Diagnostic Checklist Wasn't Made for Me

I remember once sitting in front of my laptop googling "Am I autistic?" and clicking through those diagnostic checklists that float around on mental health websites. The questions felt clinical, detached, and curiously... not me. "Do you have an unusual interest in train timetables?" "Do you struggle to understand jokes or sarcasm?" "Do you engage in repetitive movements?" "Can you do your twenty six times tables in French?" I squinted at the screen and wondered if I was just being dramatic. I like sarcasm. I don't count bus schedules for fun. I didn't flap my hands. Was I just looking for something to explain myself, or was the explanation just not shaped like me?

What I didn't realize then, and what so many people still don't, is that those checklists were never designed to catch someone like me. They weren't designed for articulate people who can fake a smile at a dinner party and then spend the next day curled up under a weighted blanket wondering why socializing feels like a hangover. They weren't designed for queer people who navigate a constant loop of code-switching. They weren't designed for people of colour who are already navigating stereotypes and biases that make it dangerous to express distress. And they definitely weren't designed for anyone who learned early on that if you want to be safe, you need to perform being fine.

Autism research, for most of its history, has centred around white, cisgender boys. Boys who showed "classic" signs. Boys who were visibly different. Boys whose behaviours disrupted classrooms or made parenting difficult. They were the ones studied, tested, documented. So, the diagnostic criteria were built around those boys. Their symptoms became *the* symptoms. Their behaviours became the checklist.

I've learnt that autism doesn't just present in one way. It doesn't follow a neat template. And yet the entire diagnostic process has been clinging to that outdated blueprint like it's gospel. What does that mean for the rest of us? It means misdiagnosis. It means being dismissed. It means being told we're just anxious, just shy, just hormonal, just difficult. It means decades of confusion. It means being left to figure it out ourselves.

It means I walked around thinking something was off with me but not being able to name it because my reality didn't match the script. I had intense sensory experiences but didn't realize they "counted" because I wasn't covering my ears in public. I struggled with transitions and unpredictability but was so well-behaved that no one noticed the internal panic. I was rigid in my thinking but called it "being principled." I hyper focused on niche interests and buried myself in them like oxygen tanks, but because they weren't dinosaurs or weather patterns, no one thought it was a "special interest." Just a quirky hobby. A passion. A personality trait.

This mismatch between real-life experience and clinical criteria is a structural failure. And the consequences are not small. They ripple outward, quietly but profoundly, affecting every part of a person's life. It's not just about delayed diagnosis. It's about a lifetime of not being understood. Of feeling broken without knowing why. Of being punished for traits you can't control. Of blaming yourself for not fitting into a world that was never built with your brain in mind.

And perhaps most cruelly, it's about being punished for the very traits that would be seen as symptoms *if* someone had known what to look for. Your shutdowns are mistaken for sulking. Your need for routine is labelled controlling. Your sensory distress is seen as drama. Your bluntness is considered rude. Your silence makes you cold. Your stimming is weird. Your overwhelm is inconvenient.

The diagnostic tools are evolving, slowly, but they're still rooted in outdated assumptions. Many clinicians still rely on the DSM criteria without considering context or nuance. Many don't recognize how autism might look when it's masked, or how it intersects with trauma, gender identity, or cultural background. There's also this bizarre idea that you have to tick every box to qualify, like neurodivergence is a club with strict entry requirements. But humans are not checklists. We're patterns. We're trends. We're clusters of experience that don't always line up neatly.

There's an unspoken message built into those forms. If you don't match the model, you're not really autistic. Which leads people like me to assume we must be something else. We end up bouncing through diagnoses like depression, anxiety, OCD, eating disorders, all of which can be comorbid, yes, but often they're just fragments of a larger picture no one's piecing together.

I can't count how many people I've spoken to who have said the same thing: "I never thought I could be autistic because I don't look like the stereotype." That sentence breaks my heart because it reveals the failure of the system so clearly. We don't just need more inclusive research. We need a cultural reframe. We need to redefine what autism looks like, sounds like, *feels* like. We need to listen to lived experiences and stop treating the outdated model as the gold standard.

When I finally found clinicians who understood neurodiversity beyond the boy-based mould, it was like someone turned on a light. They asked better questions. They looked at the subtleties. They listened. They saw the strain underneath the smile. And most importantly, they believed me. It shouldn't have taken this long.

So yes, I "passed" those checklists. I aced the test by being invisible. By adapting. By translating my experience into something digestible. But I was always autistic. The checklist just wasn't built for me.

It's time to rebuild it.

Chapter Seven

Spectrum ≠ Straight Line

7.1: Not Mild, Not Wild—Just Me

If I had a coin for every time someone said, "Oh, you must be very mild," I could afford a small island and scream into the void uninterrupted. The world seems oddly attached to categorizing autistic people as either "mild" or "severe," like we're hot sauces at a taco stand. Spoiler alert: that's not how it works. Not only is it wrong, it's also wildly unhelpful.

"Mild" makes it sound like I'm just a quirky sidekick in someone else's story. "Severe" makes it sound like someone needs saving. Neither option allows much space for nuance, context, or, you know, personhood. And yet those are the words people cling to. They feel safer, simpler, easier to manage. But easy for *who* exactly? Definitely not for the autistic person trying to be understood in a world obsessed with fitting everyone into tidy little boxes.

Here's the thing about the so-called "spectrum": people imagine it as a single horizontal line. On one end you've got the math genius who doesn't like eye contact. On the other end you've got the non-speaking person who needs full-time support. One line. Pick your spot. That's your diagnosis. Done. But the truth is the autism spectrum is more like a colour wheel, dynamic, multidimensional, and affected by everything from environment to energy levels to who you're interacting with on a Tuesday afternoon.

You might be articulate at work and completely non-verbal at home when the mask falls off. You might cook elaborate meals for friends but melt down at the sound of a hairdryer. You might love hugs from your partner but flinch when your sleeve brushes your arm the wrong way. None of this is mild or severe. It's autistic. Full stop.

When people label someone as "mild," what they usually mean is *palatable*. They mean you don't make them uncomfortable. You blend just enough. You laugh when you're supposed to. You don't rock the boat too hard. But being "mild" often just means your suffering is invisible. That your mask is tight enough to hide the cost. It means people see your smile but not the shutdown that follows. It means you don't get accommodations because they think you don't *need* them. As if functioning well on the outside erases the internal exhaustion it takes to do so.

"Mild" is often confused with "less autistic." But there's no such thing. You're either autistic or you're not. How that looks varies wildly, across people, across time, even across one person's day. But the diagnostic label isn't a volume knob. It's not like I'm playing life at a comfortable level three and someone else is blasting it at eleven. We're just wired differently and navigating a world that often wasn't built with us in mind.

At the same time, calling someone "severe" is its own kind of violence. It strips away their complexity. It assumes their experience is nothing but limitation. It defines them by perceived deficits, not lived strengths. I know autistic people who don't speak a single word, but who communicate through art, or typing, or sheer presence with a richness that knocks you sideways. I also know people who seem "high functioning" until they burn out so spectacularly that it takes weeks to recover. So, what are we even measuring?

The "functioning" labels, high or low, are more about how easy someone is for others to deal with than about how they actually experience their life. You might function "well" until you don't. And the moment you stop, people don't know what to do with you anymore. It's a system built to fail everyone.

Let's be clear: the spectrum is not linear. It's spiky. It's messy. It shifts depending on sleep, stress, support, sensory input, hormones, time of day, and whether Mercury is in retrograde. You might be brilliant at spreadsheets and terrible at phone calls. You might be great in a crisis but crumble in small talk. That doesn't make you mildly autistic. It makes you *you*.

People who meet me often say, "But you're not *that* autistic," as if it's a compliment. What they mean is, "You make eye contact and wear mascara, so I'm comfortable enough to ignore what you're telling me." When I mention burnout, or how hard I work to keep things together, they act surprised. Because their idea of autism was based on a movie character from the 90s or a documentary with sad piano music.

So, let's burn the spectrum line. Let's shatter the mild-to-severe continuum and toss it in the recycling bin of outdated metaphors. Instead, imagine a control panel with a hundred different dials. Social intuition, sensory processing, executive function, empathy, emotional regulation, speech, motor coordination, pattern recognition, the settings aren't fixed. They fluctuate. They peak in some areas and crash in others. That's what real autistic life looks like. That's what real neurodiversity means.

We are not a scale to be ranked. We are not puzzle pieces to be solved. And we are definitely not here to make you feel better about what you think autism is.

The next time someone says I must be "mild," I'll smile politely. Then I'll go home and stim like hell, blast the fan for sensory regulation, rewrite this chapter three times, and need three hours to emotionally recover from a casual conversation. Not because I'm broken. Because I'm me. Not mild, not wild, just gloriously, chaotically, wonderfully autistic me.

7.2: The Infinite Spiderweb

Imagine holding a spiderweb in your hands. Not a real one, of course, no need for panic or arachnid evictions, just a glowing, metaphorical web. Now imagine that every point on this web represents a different area of life. There's one for social interaction, one for sensory sensitivity, one for language, another for memory, another for motor skills. Some points are close together. Some are stretched far apart. When you map a person's autistic profile onto that web, it doesn't form a neat circle. It twists and spikes and swoops and warps in unexpected ways. That, right there, is what autism really looks like.

This is the "spiky profile" idea. It's one of the most helpful ways to reimagine the outdated spectrum model. Not a line. Not a scale. Not a binary of "more autistic" or "less autistic." A web. A radar chart. A living, breathing constellation of strengths and challenges, fluctuating all the time, unique to every individual.

I used to think being autistic meant I had to act a certain way all the time. That I needed to match some fictional benchmark of "autistic enough" to count. But then I looked at my own spiderweb, and it made sense for the first time. I am incredibly verbal and articulate, which makes people assume I must be socially fluent. But that same spiderweb shows a sharp dip when it comes to reading facial expressions or knowing when it's my turn to speak. I can solve complex problems in my head, but I regularly forget how to work a microwave. I have empathy like a flood, yet I shut down when I see someone crying because I don't know what to *do* with it.

The spiderweb doesn't flatten you. It shows the contours. The shape. The individuality. It invites you to move beyond the lazy stereotypes and instead ask, "How does this person *work*? Where do they shine? Where do they struggle? And how does that shift over time?"

In school, I was labelled smart but stubborn. I could ace tests but would cry over group projects. Teachers saw one node on the web—academic ability—and assumed the rest of the web must look the same. But no one saw the sensory chaos of sitting under a flickering light or the physical pain of seams on my socks. They thought I was rude or fussy or dramatic, when really, I was just experiencing the world at full volume. It wasn't until I met the spiderweb that I realized I wasn't failing. I was just shaped differently.

Some people have profiles with dramatic peaks. They might be exceptional in visual memory or musical ability but deeply struggle with verbal communication. Others might have a more even spread, but still live with intense sensory experiences or chronic executive dysfunction. There is no single autistic shape. No fixed position. That's the beauty of it—and the challenge. Because systems built for "standard humans" often can't accommodate people who don't follow the standard rulebook.

The web also shifts. It breathes. You might be able to handle bright lights on a good day, but collapse under them on a day when you're already drained. You might speak fluidly in a familiar environment but lose your words under stress. That's not inconsistency. That's life filtered through a neurodivergent lens. If we want to support autistic people, we have to stop asking, "How autistic are you?" and start asking, "What does your spiderweb look like today?"

This model also offers space for growth. You're not trapped at the "low" end of a linear spectrum. You can strengthen areas with support, rest, and understanding. And in some cases, you'll find peace not by changing the web, but by changing how you live within it. Avoiding fluorescent lights, using noise-cancelling headphones, ditching forced eye contact—all of that isn't weakness. It's wisdom. It's choosing to live in harmony with your spiderweb instead of fighting it.

Here's something most people forget: neurotypical people have spiderwebs too. Everyone has spiky profiles. The difference is that society is designed to accommodate the spikes of the majority. If you struggle with organization but can make small talk and tolerate shopping malls, your web is socially compatible. If you're hyperlexic but meltdown at the sound of a vacuum, your web is "weird." But weird only means unfamiliar. Once you understand the web, it stops being scary. It becomes a map.

So, when people ask me what autism looks like, I tell them: it looks like a spiderweb. Infinite combinations. Infinite presentations. No two are alike. And no one is better or worse. Just different threads in a vast, shining net of human variation.

The next time you catch yourself wondering whether someone is "really" autistic, or whether they "seem too high functioning," pause. That's a line-based question. Try asking a web-based one instead. What does their day look like? What helps them thrive? Where do they need support? What lights them up?

And most importantly, where does your web intersect with theirs? Because that's where understanding begins—not with a diagnosis or a label, but with connection, curiosity, and the willingness to step off the line and into the web.

7.3: Functioning Labels? Let's Not

We talked a little about different types of 'functioning' before. Let's go there again but delve a little deeper. There's something deeply disingenuous about the way society tries to sort autistic people into neat categories. High-functioning. Low-functioning. A binary made up to make the rest of the world feel more in control of what it doesn't understand. It sounds clinical, even helpful. But underneath that tidy label is a blunt instrument that hurts real people.

Let's talk about "high-functioning." When someone says that to me, it's usually meant as a compliment. "You don't seem autistic." "You're so high-functioning." "You're one of the good ones." They don't realize that what they're really saying is, "You make me comfortable." They see fluency in language, some social camouflage, maybe a job or a diploma, and assume that's the whole picture. They assume ease because they see performance. But functioning labels don't measure effort. They don't account for the migraines from fluorescent lights, the sensory shutdowns after supermarket trips, the absolute paralysis that hits when plans change suddenly.

Being called "high-functioning" often means your support needs are ignored because you *appear* to be coping. You don't get accommodations because you look fine. You don't get believed when you say you're overwhelmed. You get penalized for not falling apart in ways that others can see.

Then there's "low-functioning." A label slapped on people who don't fit into the expected mold of independence. Non-speaking. Assisted living. Unusual movement. The world calls them "low-functioning" and immediately lowers the bar on what they think that person can feel, think, or dream. It becomes a cage. A limit on opportunity. A subtle excuse not to try harder to understand or include. These people are often infantilized, spoken about as if they aren't in the room, or pitied like their lives must be nothing but suffering.

And the cruellest twist? Many autistic people move between both sides of this invented scale depending on context. You can appear high-functioning in a calm, quiet space with people you trust and completely shut down in a chaotic, unfamiliar one. You can be articulate about your needs and then lose speech when you're overstimulated or exhausted. You can write a book and still need help managing basic life admin. Which part of that profile should define how you're treated?

Functioning labels erase complexity. They don't reflect the nuanced ways in which autistic people navigate the world. They don't reflect the internal effort it takes to "pass," or the barriers people face when they can't. They are shorthand for convenience, not understanding. And more often than not, they're used to determine who deserves empathy and who doesn't. Who gets support and who's "too far gone." Who should be admired and who should be pitied.

This is not just a language problem. It has real-world consequences. A child labelled "low-functioning" may be denied access to age-appropriate education or written off as incapable of learning. An adult labelled "high-functioning" may go undiagnosed for decades and burn out in silence. These terms are used to gatekeep everything from healthcare to housing to dignity. They can isolate. They can diminish. And they can destroy a person's sense of self-worth.

Some people will argue that we need *some* kind of label to describe support needs. And yes, support needs matter. But we already have language for that. We can talk about someone who has high support needs for communication or low support needs for daily living skills. That's specific. That's respectful. That gives people space to grow and change without defining their identity by one observable trait. Support needs are not a hierarchy of value. They're just information. And we can hold that information without flattening the person it belongs to.

Functioning labels are not about the autistic person. They're about the people around them. They tell the world how *inconvenient* someone is expected to be. They tell parents what future to dread or hope for. They tell teachers whether to make room or expect compliance. They tell employers whether to bother adapting anything. They don't tell you anything about what it's like to be autistic. They only tell you what it's like to be judged by people who haven't taken the time to look deeper.

So, let's not. Let's not sort people into tidy piles. Let's not build ladders where no one is actually climbing. Let's not decide someone's worth based on whether their brain makes other people uncomfortable.

Instead, let's ask better questions. What does this person need to thrive? How can we help them feel safe and included? What do they love? What makes them anxious? What are their strengths, their triggers, their passions, their ways of connecting with the world?

If someone says I seem high-functioning, I know they're only seeing the surface. They don't see the years of unspoken meltdowns. The scripts I rehearse for phone calls. The hours of recovery after socialising. I am not high-functioning. I am a person. And every autistic person deserves to be seen as whole, not split in two by lazy language.

Throw the labels out. Start with the person. Always.

Chapter Eight

Social Skills: Trial and Error Edition

8.1: Literal Girl in a Figurative World

I was far too old in the tooth when I realised people do not, in fact, *literally* die of embarrassment. It may sound silly, but this was not always obvious to me. As a kid, I would hear people say things like "I nearly died when she said that" or "I wanted the ground to swallow me whole" and I would freeze. Wait, what? Is this a medical emergency? Should we be alerting someone? Why is everyone so calm?

It turns out the world is stuffed to the brim with expressions that are not meant to be taken at face value. And for someone like me, someone who leans towards literal interpretations, this can lead to a lot of unnecessary panic, confusion, and deeply awkward moments. I have made peace with being the person who takes things seriously that were never meant seriously in the first place. But oh, what a journey it's been.

It's a double-edged sword, really. On one side, I often miss sarcasm entirely. It just sails past while I stand there blinking, trying to decode whether someone's being serious or not. But on the other side, plot twist, I'm actually very sarcastic myself. Razor-sharp even. I've been told my dry humour is funny once people realise I'm joking... but that's the catch. Apparently, the only sarcasm I truly understand is my own. It's like I've got the deluxe premium sarcasm package installed, but it only plays in one direction. So, while I might dish it out with perfect timing and a poker face, I can't for the life of me tell when someone else is serving it back. Social ping-pong, but I brought a spoon.

The thing is, I love language. I love words. I collect unusual ones and obsess over etymology. But I also like my language to make sense. If you say one thing but mean another, I will need a minute to process that. Or five. And even then, I may come back to you hours later once processed.

Sarcasm is a realm of mystery. I remember being at a family dinner and someone said to me, "Oh yeah, Sophie, because *that's* a great idea," and I beamed and said thank you. I had no idea I was being mocked. Or at the very least, gently teased. The tone of voice was lost on me. The eye roll didn't register. I thought they were genuinely praising my suggestion to bring glow sticks to my cousin's wedding.

Eventually, I did learn to recognise sarcasm. Sort of. But it never became natural. It's like trying to read a language that uses the same alphabet as yours but arranges it in a completely different way. Every time someone says something sarcastic, I pause, scan their face, run it through my internal sarcasm translator, and then respond, usually half a beat too late. By then the moment has passed and I've either laughed at something that wasn't a joke or gotten defensive about something that was. It's a minefield.

Idioms are just as tricky. "Hold your horses," someone once snapped at me in Year Five, and I remember glancing around, panicked, wondering where the horses had come from and how one was meant to hold them. "It's raining cats and dogs" made me look up, slightly worried about animal welfare. And "kick the bucket"? I mean, what did the bucket do?

You have no idea how many hours I've spent spiralling over the origins of sayings like "nothing but an old fur coat and no knickers." What does that even mean? I mean, really think about it. Who said that first? And why? Were they describing someone fancy on the outside but scandalous underneath? Or was it meant literally? Was there a scandalous incident involving actual fur and a breezy undercarriage that we've all just decided to turn into metaphor?

I can't help it, my brain latches onto these things like a dog with a sock. I'll be brushing my teeth or walking to the shop and suddenly I'm deep in an imaginary 1920s London back alley trying to figure out if someone shouted it as an insult or a compliment. Was it a judgmental aunt? A cheeky bartender? Who coined it? And why has it stood the test of time?

While other people just laugh and move on, I'm three Google searches deep and seriously considering emailing a linguist. I think this is what happens when your brain is wired for patterns and puzzles and can't rest until something makes sense. Even if that something is, apparently, vintage undergarment idioms.

For a long time, I thought the issue was me. That I was just a bit slow or not quite clever enough to keep up. It didn't help that other people treated my confusion as endearing at best and irritating at worst. Teachers would tell me to "use common sense" and classmates would laugh and say "you're so literal" like it was a flaw.

But then I realised something: being literal isn't wrong. It's just different. My brain likes clarity. It doesn't enjoy guesswork or implication. It wants people to mean what they say and say what they mean. That isn't a failure of comprehension. It's a different kind of comprehension. And once I reframed it that way, everything felt a little less like a social disaster and a little more like a quirk of wiring.

There's actually something beautiful about seeing things as they are. If someone tells me they're carrying the weight of the world, I will probably picture them hunched over like Atlas. But I'll also understand that they are overwhelmed, just in my own visual, metaphor-turned-real kind of way. My brain makes things concrete. That can be useful. It makes me a good explainer. A good visual thinker. Someone who can spot when other people are accidentally saying the opposite of what they mean.

I have learned to ask clarifying questions. To pause when something sounds odd and say "Do you mean that literally?" or "Is that a figure of speech?" And more often than not, people are happy to explain. And sometimes we end up laughing. Because yes, I did think you wanted me to actually break a leg before my performance. No, I didn't realise "spill the tea" meant gossip. And I'm still slightly disappointed that when you say "I'm starving," you're just mildly peckish.

There is a certain charm in miscommunication. In the moments where the literal and the figurative collide, there is a kind of gentle comedy that keeps life interesting. I may never master the art of sarcasm, and metaphors will probably always be a bit suspicious to me, but I've learned to embrace my literal lens. It makes the world weird. And wonderful.

So, if you say you're going to hit the road, I'll try not to picture you smacking the pavement. But don't be surprised if I still ask whether you'll need a cushion. Just in case.

8.3: Too Honest, Too Weird, Too Much

I have always been a bit much. Too curious. Too enthusiastic. Too blunt. Too intense. Too everything. At least, that's how it seemed when I was younger. I would open my mouth and speak my truth and watch it land like a piano in the middle of a quiet room. Conversations would halt. Eyebrows would rise. People would exchange glances that said, "Did she really just say that?"

Yes. Yes, she did. Eventually, you learn that most people are so wrapped up in themselves that their momentary judgment passes quicker than you think.

And what I said probably wasn't wrong. It might have even been insightful or heartfelt or funny. But it wasn't *correct* in the social sense. It didn't match the volume or tone or emotional distance the moment required. It didn't sit in the neat little boundary of what people call "appropriate." Because I hadn't learned those rules. I hadn't internalised the social script that tells you when to speak and when to hold back and which parts of yourself are considered too much for daylight.

I used to get told off for interrupting grown-up conversations because I had something "important" to add. I'd blurt out facts about jellyfish while people were discussing the weather. I would tell the truth when people were clearly expecting a lie, like admitting I didn't like the birthday cake or that I already had that toy and didn't want another. Not out of rudeness, but out of honesty. I assumed we were all here to be real with each other. Apparently not.

Somewhere along the way, I got the memo. Not the full instruction manual, but enough to know I was meant to soften myself. To edit. To hide the obsessive excitement that made me gush about a niche interest for twenty solid minutes. To stop asking so many questions. To pretend I didn't notice when someone said one thing and meant another. To *not* launch into a passionate monologue about volcanoes when someone casually mentioned lava lamps.

I started to shrink. I rehearsed small talk in the mirror. I taught myself to ask about other people's weekends even when I didn't care because that's what polite people do. I nodded and smiled through conversations I didn't understand. I learned to apologise for being "too much" before anyone had the chance to say it out loud. It was exhausting. And confusing. Because what people said they wanted, authenticity, depth, honesty, was rarely what they actually responded well to.

And so as we talked about in the opening chapter, I became very good at pretending to be fine. Very good at masking. At being the slightly quieter version of myself that didn't make people uncomfortable. But every now and then the real me would slip out.

The one who gets unreasonably excited about an oddly shaped cloud. The one who notices patterns in conversations and names the tension in the room before anyone is ready to admit it's there. The one who asks "Why are we doing this?" not to be difficult but because she genuinely wants to know.

Sometimes that real me is met with love. With laughter. With relief. Other times she's met with confusion. Or silence. Or a quick change of topic. The inconsistency can make you feel like your very existence is something to be carefully rationed. Like you have to spoon-feed the world tiny, acceptable doses of yourself in order to be tolerated.

Being "too much" is just another way of saying *more than people expected*. And honestly, I've grown tired of editing myself to fit other people's expectations. I've learned that intensity is not a flaw. It's just depth. And honesty is not rudeness. It's clarity. And weirdness is not a defect. It's originality.

I know now that my way of communicating is not wrong. It's just different. I may not always know when to stop talking, but I talk because I care. I may dive deep instead of skimming the surface, but that's because I crave real connection. I may say things others wouldn't dare say out loud, but that's because I don't see the point in pretending.

There is a certain power in being too much. It means you can't be easily ignored. It means you feel things fully and express them without apology. It means you are real in a world that often rewards performance over presence.

Of course, I still sometimes get it wrong. I still overshare. I still misjudge the vibe. I still get that awkward pause after I say something too honest too quickly. But I'm no longer trying to erase those moments. I'm trying to own them. Laugh at them. Learn from them when I want to, and ignore them when I don't.

Because I would rather be too honest than fake. Too weird than boring. Too much than not enough.

So here I am. Not asking for permission to be myself. Not diluting who I am to keep everyone else comfortable. Just showing up. Intense. Honest. Passionate. Sometimes awkward. Always real. And if that's too much, then maybe it's time we start expanding what "enough" looks like.

Chapter Nine

Disability, Identity, and Reclaiming Words

9.1: Am I Disabled?

It took me an embarrassingly long time to say the word out loud. Not whisper it or cautiously mumble it behind closed doors, but *say it*, as in, declare it with my full chest. Disabled. Even typing it now feels like stepping into a cold pool. It's not shame, exactly. It's something heavier and more tangled than that. It's the weight of everything I thought that word meant. The way the world taught me to see it. The way I was taught not to see myself.

For most of my life, "disabled" lived in a different zip code. At the risk of sounding super ignorant, it was a word I associated with ramps, wheelchairs, canes, and blue parking signs. A word that didn't apply to me because I could walk, talk, write, drive, work, at least on paper. I wasn't disabled. I was "just quirky." "Just anxious." "Just sensitive." I passed. I masked. I fell apart in private and showed up in public with a smile so forced it ought to have been medically billed.

So, when I was finally diagnosed as autistic in adulthood, I had to face an uncomfortable truth: this wasn't something I could wellness-journal my way out of. It wasn't a phase or a set of "issues to work on." It was who I was. And that meant revisiting everything I thought I knew about the word "disabled."

It's hard to describe the internal resistance I felt at first. There was a voice in my head, not mine exactly, but inherited from years of subtle conditioning, that whispered, "But you're not *really* disabled." It compared me to others. It pointed to the fact that I didn't need a wheelchair, that I could hold down a conversation (for a while at least), that I looked "fine." The voice was sneaky. It disguised itself as humility, as not wanting to take up space, as being "realistic." But let's call it what it was: internalized ableism.

Ableism is not just big, loud discrimination. It's also the quiet cultural script that defines worthiness by productivity. That assigns value to independence. That treats support as something shameful or indulgent rather than necessary. And once I saw that script, I couldn't unsee it. It was in every time I had pushed myself to exhaustion to meet neurotypical standards. Every time I denied how hard something was because I didn't want to be dramatic. Every time I over-explained or over-apologized or over-functioned to make others comfortable.

Autism is a disability. For me, that doesn't mean broken or less than. It means my brain and body function differently enough from the norm that I face real barriers in the world. Sometimes those barriers are physical, like fluorescent lights or overwhelming crowds. Sometimes they are invisible, like the unspoken rules of social interaction that seem obvious to others but require me to mentally rehearse like I'm studying for an exam. Sometimes the barrier is time itself, how much longer it takes me to recover from overstimulation, to make decisions, to trust that I'm not missing something obvious.

Being disabled also means I need support. That used to feel like a big word. Support sounded like failure. Like giving up. But now I understand support as adaptation, as design, as a way to actually live instead of just survive. It's scripting social exits, it's flexible deadlines, it's saying no without guilt. It's asking for what I need without shrinking myself to do it.

There's something powerful in claiming the word "disabled," not as a badge of shame but as a declaration of truth. Not everyone will feel the need to do that. Some autistic people don't identify with it. Some do, some don't, some waffle back and forth depending on the day. And that's okay. Disability is not a fixed state or a one-size-fits-all label. It's contextual. It's shaped by environment and society and how well your needs are met, or ignored.

For me, embracing the word allowed me to step off the hamster wheel of pretending. It gave me access to a community that didn't just understand me but validated my experiences without a side of pity or performance. It allowed me to explore interdependence instead of independence. And perhaps most importantly, it gave me language. Language to explain why things are hard. Language to set boundaries. Language to stop feeling like I had to earn rest, or prove pain, or justify struggle.

I'm not saying it's easy. There are still days I hesitate to use the word. Days I downplay things out of fear of judgment or because I don't want to explain myself yet again. But there's a difference between not saying something because you're hiding and not saying it because you're choosing peace. I'm still learning where that line is.

What I do know is this: I'm not less for needing support. I'm not lazy for struggling. I'm not wrong for being different. I am disabled, and I am allowed to take up space. That might not be the final answer to the question, "Am I disabled?" but it's the most honest one I have right now.

9.2: Labels Aren't Always Bad

Some people flinch at the word "label." It conjures images of boxes, categories, neat little compartments with no room to stretch or breathe. Labels can feel limiting. They can be used to reduce a person to one trait or to impose assumptions. And yes, that's all true. But it's not the whole story.

Labels can also be lifelines.

Before I knew I was autistic, I just thought I was wrong. Not different, not unique, *wrong*. Like I was a glitchy human downloaded from a corrupted file. Every social struggle, every sensory meltdown, every moment I stared blankly while others laughed at an inside joke, just seemed like evidence that I was somehow behind on the secret syllabus of being a person. I didn't have a label. I just had a vague sense that I was too much and never enough, all at once.

Getting the label "autistic" didn't put me in a box. It let me *out* of one.

It gave me a framework to understand why I process the world the way I do. It didn't change who I was. It gave me a vocabulary to describe it. It gave me access to other people who speak the same internal language. And perhaps most importantly, it gave me a sense of legitimacy. I wasn't imagining things. I wasn't failing at "normal." I was wired differently. There's so much power in those three words.

The word "autistic" was my starting point. But it wasn't the only word I came across. There were others, neurodivergent, Aspie, AuDHD, that floated into view like new entries in a growing dictionary of self-understanding. Some of them fit. Some of them didn't. Some I've tried on and outgrown. Some I still use. And some I'm still deciding on. That's the thing about labels. When you get to choose them, they can be incredibly freeing.

"Neurodivergent" is one of the more flexible ones. It encompasses a wide range of brain types that diverge from the dominant "neurotypical" standard. ADHD, autism, dyslexia, Tourette's, OCD, and other cognitive variations all fall under its umbrella. For me, neurodivergent is a helpful social signal. It says, "Hey, my brain works a little differently, and that might affect how I show up in the world." It's broad, but that's part of the appeal. It links me to a bigger community while still allowing space for my individual experience.

Then there's "AuDHD", a mash-up of autism and ADHD, often co-occurring, often confusing, and often mistaken for one another. I only discovered the term after I had been diagnosed autistic, and suddenly so much made sense. The fidgeting. The impulsive purchases. The constant low-key chaos layered on top of the sensory overwhelm. AuDHD gave me a name for the beautiful mess that is my brain. And while it's a bit of a tongue-twister, it felt oddly specific in the best way.

Now, the word "Aspie" is more complicated. It's a term that some autistic people use to describe themselves, especially those previously diagnosed with Asperger's Syndrome before it was folded into the broader autism spectrum. Some find it helpful. Others avoid it, often because of its association with Hans Asperger, whose history includes ethically troubling connections. Personally, I've chosen not to use it, but I understand why some people do. For many, it was the first word that ever made them feel seen.

That's the key difference. *Who* is using the label, and *how* they're using it.

When a label is forced on you, it can feel like confinement. When you claim it for yourself, it can feel like liberation. The same word can wound or heal depending on the speaker and the intent. Calling someone "autistic" with sneer or pity is not the same as someone proudly saying it about themselves. Words have tone. Words have weight. Words have history. But they also have potential.

Labels become a problem when they stop being descriptive and start being prescriptive. When they start to dictate what you *should* be instead of explaining who you *are*. That's when it becomes a trap. But used with care, they can be guides. Signposts. Connection points.

I've learned to treat labels like tools, not tattoos. They don't define my entire identity, but they help me navigate it. They aren't static. I can put them down. I can pick up new ones. I can say "this fits right now" and change my mind later. It's not a betrayal of authenticity. It's the opposite. It's growth.

Some people don't want any labels at all, and that's valid. They prefer to be seen just as themselves, no prefixes or categories. But for me, the right label doesn't erase who I am. It adds dimension. It lets me find others who've walked a similar path. It makes me easier to find in a world that sometimes feels designed to overlook people like me.

Labels aren't always bad. In fact, they're sometimes the very thing that lets us breathe easier, ask for help, or find belonging. What matters most is that we get to choose which ones to carry—and which ones to leave behind.

9.3: Pride Looks Good on Me

I used to think pride was something loud people had. Bold people. Confident people. People who seemed so sure of themselves that nothing could shake them. I was not one of those people. I was cautious and self-questioning. I edited myself mid-sentence. I apologized before asking questions. I smiled too much in situations where I wanted to scream. I was not the kind of person who wore pride like a crown. Until I was.

It didn't happen all at once. There was no single moment of transformation where I stood in front of a mirror, declared I was autistic, and suddenly glowed with self-love. It was quieter than that. Pride crept in through the cracks that opened when I stopped trying to be someone else. It grew in the space I carved for my true self, little by little, like moss taking root on stone. Soft but persistent.

Autism pride doesn't mean I think I'm flawless. It doesn't mean I've never wished things were easier or that I'm immune to doubt. Pride, for me, is not about perfection. It's about recognition. It's about saying, this is who I am, and that's not something I need to hide, fix, or explain away. I spent so long contorting myself to fit into a world that didn't make space for me. Pride is what happens when I stop doing that.

I've learned to love things about myself I once thought were weaknesses. My intensity. My curiosity. My way of noticing patterns in people and language and light. The way I feel things so deeply that sometimes I cry over songs I've heard a thousand times. The way I lose track of time because I've followed a thought all the way down to its roots. These aren't glitches. These are features.

There's something undeniably powerful about reclaiming your difference as a strength. Not in a toxic positivity way. Not pretending everything is sunshine and sparkles when it isn't. But in a way that says, I am valid exactly as I am. My brain might not follow the standard route, but that doesn't mean it's taking the wrong one. It's just going a different way. And sometimes, that way leads to incredible places.

Autism pride is laughing at the fact that I need subtitles for conversations but not for ancient Norse runes in a video game. It's building a spreadsheet to plan my weekend and genuinely enjoying the process. It's finding a community that gets me, and realising that all the things that made me feel like an outsider were actually invitations to connection. I didn't have the wrong shape. I just hadn't found the right puzzle yet.

It took time to unlearn the idea that being different meant being deficient. That needing support made me lesser. That having meltdowns made me childish. That being too blunt or too quiet or too intense made me unlikable. All those beliefs were soaked into me by a world that only rewards sameness. Pride was the antidote. Not immediate. Not easy. But transformative.

I don't need to be neurotypical to be worthy. I don't need to soften my edges to be accepted. I don't need to shrink myself into an easier version of me to make other people comfortable. There is room in this world for how I exist, exactly as I am. And if there isn't, I'll help make more room. Pride says, not only do I belong, but I *have* always belonged. Even when I didn't know it yet.

There's joy in knowing that I am not alone. That autism isn't just a diagnosis, it's a shared language, a lived experience, a community with rhythm and richness and brilliance. Pride is the laughter in late-night conversations with fellow autistic people, the kind where you don't have to explain your pauses or your eye contact or your need to stim with a pen cap for forty minutes straight. It's the relief of being understood before you even speak.

Pride looks good on me because it comes from truth. It's not a costume or a cover. It's a glow that comes from shedding all the layers of should and shame. It's what happens when you step out from the shadows of self-doubt and finally stand in your own light. Not flawless. Not fixed. Just *whole*.

I still have hard days. I still get overwhelmed. I still have moments where I feel like a walking contradiction. But those moments don't define me. They don't erase the pride I've earned. Because I've lived through misunderstanding and misdiagnosis and mistaken identity. And I'm still here. Still autistic. Still brilliant in my own chaotic way.

So yeah. Pride looks good on me. And it looks good on you, too.

Chapter Ten

Relationships, Boundaries, and People Who Get It

10.1: Telling People

Lets circle back to 'telling people'. There is a particular kind of silence that follows the words, "I'm autistic." Sometimes it is a thoughtful pause. Sometimes it is confusion. Occasionally, it is relief. And sometimes, it is the sort of silence that makes you want to fill the space with nervous laughter or a hurried, "But it's not a big deal," even though, actually, it is.

Telling people about your autism diagnosis can feel like peeling back a layer of skin to show something raw underneath. Not because it's shameful. Not because you're unsure. But because so much of the world still doesn't know what to do with that information. People think they do. They think of stereotypes, TV characters, tragic news stories, or that one person they knew once who was "really good at maths." When you tell someone you're autistic, you're not just giving them a word. You're giving them an invitation. To know you differently. To see things they might have missed. To understand why you sometimes need to leave the room when the lights are too bright or why small talk makes you sweat behind your eyes.

The first person I told was someone I trusted. Even so, I rehearsed the sentence in my head a hundred times before I said it. "So I got diagnosed," I started. "With autism. Or, well, autism spectrum disorder, technically, but yeah." I said it like I was trying not to spook a horse. They blinked. Tilted their head. "Really?" they asked, and I braced for whatever might come next. But then they smiled. "That makes so much sense." And just like that, the weight I had been dragging behind me all day cracked a little, loosened, let in some air.

But not every reaction is like that. Sometimes people meet your truth with a frown. "You don't seem autistic," they say, like you've just told them you're part-dragon and they're not convinced. Sometimes they get defensive, like you've accused them of missing something obvious. Sometimes they turn the whole thing into a compliment. "Well you must be really high-functioning." Sometimes they joke. Sometimes they go quiet and never ask again.

I've learned that telling people is less about them and more about me. It's not about managing their comfort. It's about allowing myself to be seen. It's about making space for honesty. And that comes with risk. Because people don't always react how you hope they will. And yet, the power of telling the truth, even awkwardly, even in fragments, is worth it.

There are categories of telling. Telling friends is different from telling family. Family often think they know you best, which means your diagnosis can challenge their own narratives. "But you were always so chatty." "You just need to be more confident." "Are you sure this isn't just anxiety?" Sometimes they try to help by pulling out old childhood stories that feel irrelevant or misremembered. But occasionally, someone in your family will stop, consider everything anew, and say, "That explains so much," with a kind of softness that rewrites your history in real time.

Telling friends can be a mixed bag. Some people you expect to get it do not. Others surprise you with their grace. There is something beautiful about a friend who listens without trying to fix you. Who doesn't turn your diagnosis into a problem but into a prism. Who asks real questions. Who lets you say, "I need to cancel today" without guilt or performance. If you are lucky, you start to gather these people. People who get it. People who try. People who ask you what you need instead of assuming.

Work is trickier. There is the issue of disclosure and protection and culture. Do you tell your boss? Your colleagues? Will it help or harm? These are questions without universal answers. For me, I have chosen to tell selectively. When I feel it will bring understanding rather than scrutiny. When I need accommodations and honesty is the most direct path. But I always feel the catch in my chest. The moment where I brace. The possible consequences. It's not fair that being honest about who you are might cost you safety or credibility, but for many, it can.

Telling partners is its own tender thing. Romantic relationships are built on vulnerability, and there's something especially exposing about saying, "This is my brain. It works a bit differently. Here's how." You worry they will think you're too much or not enough. That they'll mistake your sensory needs for rejection. That your need for routine will feel like rigidity. But the right person listens. The right person doesn't flinch. The right person says, "Thanks for telling me," and actually means it.

Over time, telling people gets easier. You stop apologising in your tone. You stop dressing it up in disclaimers. You learn how to say it in ways that suit you: "I'm autistic." "I got diagnosed recently." "Turns out my brain is wired differently." You learn that telling is part of claiming. Not for them, but for you. To live more openly. To be understood, even if imperfectly.

And then, sometimes, someone tells you they are too. Or that they think they might be. Or that your story helped them rethink their own. Those are the moments that shimmer. The moments where disclosure turns into connection.

You don't owe your diagnosis to everyone. But you are allowed to share it. To say it with pride. To say it with hesitation. To say it with a laugh or a sigh or a carefully timed pause. However you tell it, it's still true. And that truth is a doorway. Sometimes it opens into awkwardness. Sometimes it opens into love. Often, it opens into something entirely new.

10.2: Boundary? I Barely Knew Her

I used to think boundaries were something other people had. Assertive people. Grown-ups with filing systems. People who said things like "Actually I'm not comfortable with that" without crying or making it weird. I, on the other hand, was the person who said "Sure, no problem" while blinking back sensory overload and quietly preparing to implode later. I wanted to be easygoing. Chill. Helpful. A team player. I wanted people to like me. I didn't know that what I was doing wasn't kindness. It was self-abandonment.

For a long time, I didn't even know what a boundary was. I thought they were walls, but they're actually doors. They're not there to shut people out, but to teach them how to come in respectfully. That lesson arrived late in my life, like most things about understanding myself post-diagnosis. Suddenly, everything that used to feel like a personal failure started to look suspiciously like a lack of boundaries. Saying yes when I meant no. Agreeing to plans that made me anxious. Sitting in noisy restaurants while my brain quietly screamed. Laughing off insults as jokes. Overexplaining every decision. That wasn't just being "nice." That was a boundary problem.

When you're autistic, boundaries can be particularly complicated. Sometimes it's because we struggle to identify our limits until they've already been crossed. Sometimes it's because we've spent years being told our needs were too much or too strange. We learn to ignore discomfort until it becomes distress. We get used to pretending things are fine when they are absolutely not. And because masking becomes second nature, so does people-pleasing. We don't always have the internal alarms that go off early enough to say, "Actually, this is too loud," or "I can't keep doing this without burning out." Often, we only notice we needed a boundary after we've melted down or shut down or ghosted the entire group chat for a month.

Here's the plot twist: boundaries are not rude. They are not selfish. They are not mean. They are survival tools. They are love notes to yourself written in the language of limits. Saying no is not a failure. It's a sentence full of power. And learning to say it, calmly, confidently, and sometimes repeatedly, is one of the most liberating things I've ever done.

Let's talk about saying no. Not the half-hearted "Um maybe not?" or the "I'll see how I feel" that everyone knows means "I don't want to but I don't know how to tell you." I mean a full-bodied, unapologetic no. No, I can't come out tonight. No, I don't want to be touched right now. No, I'm not available to talk about that. It felt impossible at first. Like I was being a terrible person. But with every no I said, I made a little more room for my yeses to actually mean something.

And it's not just about saying no. It's about explaining why I need the things I need. Communicating my sensory boundaries. Protecting my social energy. Being honest about what overstimulates me and what restores me. I used to think asking for accommodations made me difficult. Now I understand it makes me honest. "I'd love to come but I need to leave by nine." "I'm happy to meet up if it's somewhere quiet." "I need a little time before I respond to that." These are not unreasonable requests. They are survival instructions. They are my way of saying, "Here's how I can be present with you and not regret it for three days."

Sometimes people don't take it well. They think you've changed. They call you inflexible. They get defensive. That's okay. Let them. You are not responsible for how others respond to your limits. You are responsible for enforcing them. Boundaries are not about controlling other people's behavior. They are about clarifying what you will and will not tolerate. And once you've drawn that line, the only job you have is to hold it.

There is an odd sort of peace that comes with firm boundaries. You no longer carry the weight of everyone else's expectations. You no longer shape-shift to keep the peace. You no longer second-guess your every instinct. There is peace in knowing that you can say, "This is too much," and the world won't end. You might lose people. But you will never lose yourself again.

It's also worth mentioning that not all boundaries need to be verbal declarations. Sometimes the boundary is leaving the party early without explanation. Sometimes it's muting the group chat. Sometimes it's declining the call and texting back instead. Sometimes it's letting the email sit unopened until your brain is ready. These are quiet boundaries, but they are just as powerful. You don't need to justify your limits to earn them.

I used to feel guilty for needing so much space. Now I feel proud. Proud that I listen to myself. Proud that I protect my peace. Proud that I no longer make myself small so others can feel comfortable. Setting boundaries is still hard. Sometimes I still wobble. But I am learning to trust that I deserve relationships where my needs aren't a burden. Where I don't have to explain my brain every time I say no. Where my silence isn't mistaken for rudeness and my honesty isn't mistaken for hostility.

The truth is, boundaries are how we make relationships sustainable. For ourselves. For others. For the long haul. They are how we stay connected without burning out. How we show up without falling apart. How we honour who we are while allowing others to do the same. So now when someone crosses a line, I don't just freeze. I speak. I redirect. I hold the door open, but only if they've read the welcome sign.

I barely knew boundaries before. Now I greet them like old friends. I recommend you do too.

Chapter Eleven

The History They Don't Teach You

11.1: From Kanner to Controversy

Autism did not begin when you heard the word for the first time. It did not begin in a doctor's office or an online checklist or a moment of self-recognition. Long before it became part of your story, it was already buried in dusty psychiatric manuals, surrounded by academic infighting, misinterpretation, and a cocktail of bias and ignorance. To understand what autism *means* today, you have to dig into its murky beginnings. And like most origin stories built by outsiders looking in, this one has some serious issues.

In 1943, Leo Kanner, a psychiatrist working at Johns Hopkins, published a paper titled *Autistic Disturbances of Affective Contact*. He had observed a group of eleven children who shared a cluster of traits. They struggled with social connection, used language in unusual ways, showed intense focus on specific topics, and had what he called an "insistence on sameness." Kanner is widely credited with identifying autism as a distinct condition. But the way he framed it would cast a long and harmful shadow.

Kanner's model placed parents—particularly mothers—under the microscope. He described the families of these children as cold, intellectual, and emotionally distant. He did not blame genetics or neurology. He blamed "refrigerator mothers." The theory went like this: if a child did not develop typical emotional connections, it must be because the parent failed to provide warmth. This idea stuck. For decades. Despite lacking evidence. Despite contradicting observable facts. Despite the trauma it inflicted on families who were already desperate for understanding. Mothers were told they had emotionally damaged their children simply by being themselves. This theory devastated families and diverted attention away from the real nature of autism, something intrinsic, not caused.

Meanwhile, across the ocean, another figure was charting a parallel path. In 1944, Hans Asperger, an Austrian paediatrician, published his own paper describing a group of boys with similar patterns of behaviour, high verbal skills, intense interests, clumsy motor coordination, and profound social differences. He referred to them as having "autistic psychopathy," a term that sounds horrific now but was a clinical term at the time. Asperger's work remained relatively obscure for decades, partially due to the language barrier and partially because World War II was raging across Europe. It wasn't until the 1980s that the term "Asperger's Syndrome" started gaining traction, largely thanks to British psychiatrist Lorna Wing, who sought to expand the understanding of autism beyond Kanner's narrow definitions.

But Hans Asperger's legacy is not as innocent as it might seem. In recent years, researchers have uncovered deeply troubling ties between Asperger and Nazi-era eugenics policies. Evidence suggests that he cooperated with programs that targeted disabled children for extermination, referring some of his patients to the Spiegelgrund clinic, where many were killed. His work, while academically significant, cannot be separated from the political and ethical climate in which it was conducted. That uncomfortable truth has led many within the autistic community to reject the use of the term "Asperger's" altogether.

What both Kanner and Asperger had in common, besides their eerily similar names and overlapping timelines, was that they framed autism through a lens of pathology. Autism was defined by what it *lacked*, by what it *failed* to be. There was little room for understanding or celebrating difference. Autism, in their eyes, was a problem to solve, not a variation to understand. This model, the deficit model, became baked into diagnostic frameworks. It influenced education systems, therapy approaches, and how autistic people were treated by society. And while both men helped carve out a space for autism in clinical thought, that space was narrow and misaligned from the start.

It wasn't until the late twentieth century that the understanding of autism began to shift. Autistic adults started speaking up and pushing back against the narrative that framed them as broken or incomplete. They began reframing autism not as a disease but as a difference—a neurotype, not a malfunction. The term "neurodiversity," coined by sociologist Judy Singer in the 1990s, emerged as a way to conceptualize brain differences as natural and valuable. This idea gained momentum. Slowly. But it stood in stark contrast to the clinical foundations laid by Kanner and Asperger, where autistic people were studied but rarely heard.

Today, many diagnostic tools still echo those early perspectives. They assess autism in terms of impairments and compare behaviour to a neurotypical standard. The echoes of the refrigerator mother myth and the deficit-first model linger. But the conversation is changing. Thanks to autistic advocates, researchers, and thinkers, the narrative is being rewritten, not erased, but reinterpreted with lived experience at the centre.

It matters that we know this history, even when it is uncomfortable. It matters that we acknowledge how much of autism's early story was told by people who didn't live it and whose lenses were warped by the biases of their time. It matters that we grieve the harm caused by pathologizing difference and blaming parents. And it matters that we move forward informed, outraged, and determined to tell a better version of the story, one where autistic people write their own chapters.

So yes, the history of autism is complicated. It is not tidy. It is not heroic. But it is real. And like all stories built on misunderstanding, the best thing we can do is tell it again, more clearly, more honestly, and with autistic voices leading the way.

11.2: Hans Asperger Wasn't a Hero

For many years the name "Asperger's Syndrome" carried a certain aura. It was often used to describe those seen as intellectually gifted yet socially awkward. It became a shorthand for quirky geniuses and misunderstood thinkers. Popular media helped shape this image too, portraying characters with sharp minds and flat affect who seemed to fit the so-called Asperger's profile. For some people the label brought relief and clarity. It offered an explanation when the world didn't make sense and seemed to place them on the map of neurodiversity. But there is a story behind that name. And it is not one that can be separated from the atrocities of the time in which it emerged.

Hans Asperger was an Austrian paediatrician working in Vienna during the 1930s and 40s. He published a paper in 1944 that described children with what he termed "autistic psychopathy" a phrase that sounds jarring now but was common clinical language at the time. He noted children who were verbal and intelligent but who struggled with social reciprocity and exhibited intense focused interests. His descriptions were strikingly similar to Leo Kanner's earlier observations of autism although Asperger emphasized strengths like verbal ability and analytical thinking.

For a long time Hans Asperger was presented as a quiet hero. He was seen as someone who protected neurodivergent children in the face of rising fascism. Stories circulated that he had resisted the Nazi regime shielded his patients and championed their potential. His name was attached to a diagnosis officially added to the DSM-IV in 1994. Many people diagnosed with Asperger's Syndrome felt pride in the identity it gave them especially in contrast to the stigma that surrounded the broader autism label.

But in 2018 that image began to crumble.

Historian Herwig Czech published a groundbreaking paper that drew from previously untranslated documents and long-overlooked archives. What he found was deeply unsettling. Asperger was not the quiet resistor many believed him to be. He was a participant in a medical system that collaborated with Nazi ideology. He publicly praised the regime's views on race and purity and he referred children to the Am Spiegelgrund clinic, a facility known for its role in the child euthanasia program. At Spiegelgrund hundreds of children were murdered under the guise of medical care. Some of those children had disabilities. Some were simply different. Some were the very children Asperger had evaluated and deemed unfit.

The truth was hard to face. This was not just a case of someone surviving a brutal regime. This was someone actively involved in a system of eugenics. Asperger made judgments that directly influenced life and death decisions for disabled children. His clinical assessments were not always neutral. They were sometimes lethal. The weight of that cannot be ignored. Nor can it be softened.

In the wake of these revelations the autistic community faced a reckoning. Many people who had identified for years as having Asperger's Syndrome were forced to confront the legacy of the man behind the name. It felt like betrayal. For some it felt like grief. A label that had once offered belonging was now laced with horror. Communities began discussing alternatives. The DSM-5 had already retired the term in 2013 folding Asperger's Syndrome into the broader Autism Spectrum Disorder. But culturally the term lingered. Online groups books school programs and self-descriptions still clung to the word. That began to shift.

The decision to stop using the name Asperger is not about erasing history. It is about refusing to glorify a figure who made morally indefensible choices. It is about centring the voices of disabled people past and present. It is about honouring the memory of children whose lives were deemed unworthy by a system that saw them as expendable. Some people worry that letting go of the word means losing a part of their identity. But the traits, the differences, the experiences that define someone's neurodivergence do not disappear with a name. Identity is bigger than a diagnostic label. And it should never be built on the backs of the harmed.

There is a quiet strength in re-evaluation. In saying maybe we were wrong to admire him. Maybe we clung to a story that felt safe but was not true. It takes courage to step away from that. But it is necessary. Especially in a community that values truth justice and understanding.

Not everyone will feel ready to drop the name. For some it may remain part of their personal story. But more and more spaces, particularly autistic-led ones, are choosing not to use it. They talk instead about being autistic. About being neurodivergent. About being part of a spectrum that is neither linear nor fixed. They are reshaping the language to reflect not the opinions of past clinicians but the lived reality of present people.

Hans Asperger contributed to the early clinical framing of autism but that does not make him a hero. And it certainly does not mean his name should be a badge of identity. Knowing this history matters. It allows us to make informed choices about the language we use and the people we choose to uplift. It reminds us that science is never neutral. That diagnoses do not emerge from a vacuum. They are shaped by culture and politics and prejudice. And when those forces cause harm we have a responsibility to name it.

So, we tell the truth. Even when it is hard. Even when it hurts. Especially then.

11.3: The Rise of Neurodiversity

There was a time not long ago when autism lived mostly in whispers. It was spoken of in clinical tones behind closed doors or padded with euphemisms in education plans. It was framed as something unfortunate something tragic something to fix. The conversation centred around what was missing what was wrong and what needed to be corrected. For decades autistic people were either invisible or hyper-visible but almost never heard. And then something began to shift. Not from institutions or textbooks but from autistic people themselves.

The neurodiversity movement is not just a change in vocabulary. It is a revolution in perspective. It reframes autism and other neurodevelopmental differences not as disorders but as part of the natural variation of human minds. Instead of seeing divergence from the norm as a deficit it proposes that diversity in cognition is as essential as biodiversity in nature. And that seemingly radical idea has redefined everything.

The word "neurodiversity" first emerged in the late 1990s through the writing of Judy Singer an Australian sociologist and herself a member of the neurodivergent community. She introduced the term to name what so many already knew intuitively, that our brains are not all built the same way and that this difference is not automatically negative. Like the concept of biodiversity neurodiversity emphasizes value through variation. It moves away from the assumption that there is one correct way to think learn feel or process the world.

In the early days this idea was met with scepticism and sometimes outright hostility. Mainstream narratives around autism were still dominated by deficit models and grim portrayals. Media coverage leaned heavily on tragedy or cure-based rhetoric. Autism organizations spoke *about* autistic people but rarely *with* them. Resources were poured into behavioural compliance and masking rather than into communication and support. But neurodivergent voices refused to be quiet.

Online spaces became fertile ground for the neurodiversity movement. Autistic adults found one another in forums in comment sections in blogs and later across social media platforms. For the first time people who had been made to feel alone and broken discovered they were not. They began to share stories challenge stereotypes and assert their right to exist as they are. They were no longer cases to study or problems to manage. They were people. And they were building a community.

The language began to evolve. Instead of "person with autism" many began to prefer "autistic person" seeing it not as a burden carried but as an intrinsic part of who they are. The narrative stopped asking how to erase autism and started asking how to support autistic people in a world not built for them. Self-advocacy groups emerged led by autistic voices rather than professionals. They pushed back on harmful practices highlighted issues like sensory accessibility and demanded a seat at the table in discussions that affected their lives.

What had once been a pathologized diagnosis began to take on the shape of identity. Neurodivergence became a word of power. It created space not just for autistic people but for those with ADHD dyslexia Tourette's dyspraxia and more. It recognized that our minds are not faulty but uniquely wired. That difference does not equal danger. That support does not mean cure. That pride and disability are not mutually exclusive.

In schools and workplaces conversations about neurodiversity have started to ripple outward. The idea that there is not one right way to learn or work is slowly gaining ground. Companies have launched neurodiversity hiring initiatives. Classrooms have begun to incorporate more sensory-inclusive practices and flexible learning methods. These shifts are far from universal and the work is far from over but the roots have taken hold.

There is a quiet beauty in the way the neurodiversity movement has reclaimed space. It does not ask for pity. It does not beg for acceptance. It demands equity and respect. It says that difference is not a tragedy and that inclusion should not be conditional. It honours the past while refusing to be defined by it.

This movement has also illuminated the cost of erasure. It reminds us of the many people who were institutionalized misunderstood or lost before there were words to describe them. It honours those whose potential was ignored because they could not speak or sit still or meet someone's idea of "normal." It challenges us to imagine a future where no child is made to feel defective for the way their brain works.

Neurodiversity is not a trend. It is not a branding exercise. It is a paradigm shift. It tells autistic people that they belong. It reframes diagnosis as a tool for understanding not as a life sentence. It transforms a narrative of isolation into one of community. It plants the radical idea that you do not need to be fixed because you were never broken.

The rise of neurodiversity is not the end of the struggle, but it is a bright horizon. It shows what can happen when people tell their own stories when identity is claimed not given and when difference is finally seen as something worth celebrating. And in that light every late diagnosis every reframed childhood every aha moment becomes part of a larger legacy—one that says clearly and loudly you are not alone and you never were.

Chapter Twelve

I Was Always This Person

12.1: Nothing's Changed (Everything's Changed)

It is a strange kind of peace that settles in when you finally find the words for something you have always known but never understood. Like opening a book you have read a thousand times and suddenly discovering a new chapter that was there all along. That is what receiving an autism diagnosis in adulthood can feel like. Everything is the same. You still have the same memories, the same quirks, the same coping mechanisms and fears and fascinations. But now you also have a name. And with that name comes a lens. And with that lens comes clarity.

For a long time, I thought change would be louder. That revelation would come with a bang, that understanding myself would mean becoming someone new. But instead, it feels like returning home to a place I had forgotten was mine. Like slipping into a coat I thought I had outgrown and finding it still fits, still smells like me. The world hasn't changed. My past hasn't rewritten itself. But I have stopped fighting with it.

I used to look back and wince. Cringe at every odd thing I said, every social misfire, every meltdown I couldn't explain. I spent years trying to be easier, quieter, more likeable, more predictable. I thought I was just doing life wrong. Now I look back with softer eyes. The child who needed silence. The teenager who withdrew in noisy rooms. The adult who rehearsed phone calls like opening night monologues. They were all doing their best. And they were all autistic. I just didn't know it yet.

Now I do. And the knowledge has changed everything. Not in a dramatic way. Not in a Hollywood character arc kind of way. But in the way the morning light slowly shifts across the floor. Subtle. Warm. Steady. I still jump at sudden noises. I still get exhausted by casual conversations. I still struggle to explain emotions that feel like tangled cables inside my chest. But now I understand why. And that has made all the difference.

There is a calm that comes with naming things. With saying out loud, this is me. This is my brain. This is how I experience the world. Before, I thought my differences were mistakes. Errors to be fixed. Now I see them as patterns. Intricate, specific, meaningful. My brain isn't broken. It just operates with a different logic. A different rhythm. One I've always danced to, even if I never had a name for the music.

That doesn't mean life suddenly got easier. The world is still not built for people like me. The noise, the pace, the expectations of seamless small talk and eye contact and flexibility. It's still overwhelming. But I am no longer overwhelmed *alone*. I no longer gaslight myself into thinking I'm overreacting. I no longer pretend my exhaustion is laziness. I no longer feel like I need to earn rest. The diagnosis didn't fix things. But it gave me permission. Permission to ask for support.

To build boundaries. To rest without guilt. To speak honestly about what I need and why I need it.

It is hard to explain to others how nothing has changed but everything has. From the outside, I am still me. Same job. Same friends. Same routines. But internally, the landscape has shifted. Where there was fog, there is now a map. Where there was shame, there is now understanding. And where there was silence, there is now language. I can say I am autistic. And in saying it, I am saying I was never broken. I was always this person.

It has also reshaped my future. Not in the sense of rewriting all my plans. But in how I hold those plans. I no longer shape them around what I think I *should* want. I no longer push myself to tolerate things that drain me. I allow my joy to lead more often. I trust my instincts. I protect my energy. I know now that it is not weakness to design a life that fits your brain. It is wisdom.

There are still hard days. There always will be. But now when I have them, I don't spiral into self-loathing. I don't wonder what is wrong with me. I know. And I know it isn't wrong. It's just different. And different can be managed. Different can be celebrated. Different can be powerful.

In the end, it is not about becoming someone new. It is about meeting yourself fully for the first time. About gathering all the pieces you scattered trying to fit in and welcoming them home. The mask comes off. The curtain lifts. The script is yours to write now. And maybe for the first time in your life, you believe it could actually be a good story.

So yes. Nothing's changed. But also, everything has.

12.2: Autistic Adulthood, Reimagined

There was a time I thought adulthood meant settling. That it was a slow, inevitable narrowing of choices. That the things which once made me different were supposed to be smoothed out or suppressed in order to become functional. Normal. Acceptable. I believed the goal was to blend in well enough to earn a place at the table, even if it meant pretending to be someone I wasn't.

Then came the diagnosis. And with it, the invitation to imagine a very different kind of adulthood. Not one shaped by compromise and camouflage, but one built around truth. Around clarity. Around possibility.

Autistic adulthood is not the story we are often told. It is rarely portrayed as something to aspire to. Most of the narratives about autism stop in childhood. We hear about support needs in school, early intervention, tantrums, therapies. But what happens when the autistic child becomes an autistic adult? What happens when you are the one paying bills, scheduling appointments, setting boundaries, and trying to build a life that works for your brain?

That question used to scare me. Now it feels like a challenge I'm finally ready to answer on my own terms.

For the first time, I am not trying to live up to someone else's blueprint. I am asking what kind of life makes sense for me. What kind of work allows me to thrive without burning out. What kind of relationships leave me feeling seen and safe. What kind of routines soothe rather than restrict. These are not selfish questions. They are foundational. They are how I build a life that is sustainable and meaningful.

I am learning that it is okay to want different things. Maybe I do not want a fast-paced career ladder. Maybe I want structure, purpose, and quiet. Maybe I don't want a packed social calendar. Maybe I want a small circle of deep connections and lots of time to myself. Maybe I don't want to be spontaneous. Maybe I want to plan things out and know what's coming. These are not failures of adulthood. They are adaptations. They are how I move through the world with care.

There is power in building a life that supports your needs instead of constantly trying to overcome them. I no longer chase a version of success that requires me to betray myself to achieve it. I redefine success every time I choose rest over guilt. Every time I say no without apology. Every time I leave a gathering when I've had enough. Every time I stop masking even if it makes others uncomfortable.

The future is not a blank slate, but it feels more open now than it ever has. I am not trapped in a narrative of deficiency. I am not doomed to a life of struggle. I am allowed to imagine joy. Creativity.

Peace. Belonging. I am allowed to shape a world that fits me instead of forcing myself to fit into a world that never accounted for me in the first place.

Some days I still grieve the time I lost. The years I spent confused, exhausted, and ashamed. The relationships that faltered because I could not explain myself. The burnout that could have been avoided. But grief and hope can sit side by side. One does not cancel out the other. I carry both. And both are part of what propels me forward.

Autistic adulthood, reimagined, is not about perfection. It is about possibility. It is about unlearning the lie that difference is a deficit. It is about noticing your needs and meeting them without shame. It is about building habits that honour your brain and relationships that respect your boundaries. It is about finding your pace and choosing not to rush. It is about learning to trust your instincts and not constantly second-guess your own perceptions.

It is not always easy. But it is honest. And in that honesty, there is peace. There is agency. There is the kind of quiet confidence that comes not from finally fitting in, but from knowing you no longer have to.

I want a future where my needs are not minimized but understood. Where my enthusiasm is not too much but welcomed. Where my silences are not misread but respected. I want to keep growing in ways that make sense for me. Not bigger or louder, but deeper. Truer. More rooted in who I actually am.

Maybe autistic adulthood is not what I thought it would be. Maybe that is the best possible news. Maybe it is not about becoming someone new, but becoming more fully myself. With every accommodation I allow, with every mask I shed, with every person I meet who sees me clearly, I feel it becoming more real. This is my adulthood. And I get to choose how it looks.

It might not follow the usual script. But it is mine. And that makes all the difference.

12.3: The Plot Twist Wasn't the End

If you have made it this far through the book, thank you. Whether you read every chapter in a straight line or skipped around to the bits that made your chest ache or your eyebrows raise, I am glad you are here. And I hope you know that this story, mine, yours, ours, is not over. The plot twist wasn't the end. It was a beginning disguised as a revelation.

Maybe you are newly diagnosed, and everything feels raw and electric and confusing. Maybe you are wondering if autism could explain the parts of you that have never quite fit. Maybe you were diagnosed long ago but never saw your experience reflected in words that felt like your own. Or maybe you are reading because someone you love is autistic and you are trying to understand what that really means. However you found yourself here, I want you to know this: it is never too late to know yourself.

There is something tender and powerful about naming your truth. It changes the way you look at your past, certainly. But more than that, it shifts the way you hold your future. The diagnosis, or the realisation, or the quiet click of self-recognition, it does not fix everything. It does not erase struggle or pain. But it gives you context. It gives you language. It gives you permission to stop performing and start living.

For most of my life I thought I was too much or not enough. Too sensitive, too rigid, too quiet, too intense. Not outgoing enough, not adaptable enough, not effortless enough. I tried to adjust. To contort myself into whatever version of normal the moment demanded. It was exhausting. It was lonely. And I thought that was just how life was supposed to feel.

Learning I was autistic did not instantly make that go away. But it did allow me to stop trying to fix something that was never broken. I began to meet myself with curiosity instead of criticism. I stopped asking why I couldn't be more like everyone else and started asking what I actually needed. It was the first time in my life that I allowed myself to take up space without apology. To say no. To rest. To stim. To show up exactly as I am without padding the edges.

Autism did not appear out of nowhere the day I got a diagnosis. It had been with me all along. Woven into the way I think, feel, connect, move, and dream. The diagnosis didn't change who I was. It just gave me the clearest mirror I had ever seen. And for once, I did not flinch when I looked at my reflection. I nodded. I recognised her. I said, yes. That makes sense. That is me.

If you are standing at the edge of your own plot twist, uncertain of what it means or where it leads, let me offer this: let it lead you home. Let it be a way back to yourself. To the moments you buried, the feelings you suppressed, the truths you softened so others would stay comfortable. Let this be the part of your story where you reclaim those things. Let this be where you begin again.

You do not have to become someone new. You do not have to transform to be worthy of understanding or support or love. You are already someone. And that someone has always deserved gentleness. Has always deserved grace. Has always deserved space to be exactly who they are.

There is a particular kind of strength in late self-discovery. In choosing to meet yourself honestly when the world gave you a different script. In choosing to turn toward that knowledge instead of away from it. It takes courage. It takes patience. It takes unlearning and relearning and doing things a little differently than you used to. But you can. You already are.

This book was never meant to be a how-to guide. It was never a manual or a checklist. It was a conversation. A companion. A voice saying, me too. A reminder that you are not imagining things. That your experience is valid. That your questions are welcome. That your difference is not a burden. It is a story worth telling.

The plot twist is not the last page. It is the chapter break. It is the shift in tone. The change in perspective. It is the part of the story where you stop trying to survive and start learning how to live.

So, carry on. Build the life that fits you. Laugh too loudly. Wear the soft clothes. Leave the party early. Hyperfocus with abandon. Ask for clarity. Flap your hands. Cancel the plans. Follow the joy. Keep learning. Keep unmasking. Keep going.

You were always this person. You just didn't always have the words. Now you do.

And that is not the end. That is the beginning.

Printed in Dunstable, United Kingdom